Praise for *Living and Leaving M*

"Saferstein's journals read like fiction. Insightful and relatable, from marriage to career to following one's dreams, she keeps you turning pages with a rare honesty and authenticity. Readers will be forced to look inward while discovering the true magic of journaling."

— **Rochelle Weinstein, Bestselling author of** *When We Let Go*

"This book reads as a true labor of love and devotion to both the power of journaling and the gift of legacy writing. Merle Saferstein says in the opening of this book that she hopes readers will think about their own lives and legacy while reading about her life. While reading this legacy journal, I felt like I was getting to know the author in an intimate and meaningful way, while also reflecting on my own life and experiences in an important way too. I love how Merle kept her journals in a safety deposit box at a bank! This shows how truly special her journals were and are to her, and how precious such life documents are to all of us who are journal keepers. Merle made meaning out of her journals, beyond the experience of writing them in the first place, through mining them for all that has eventually been shared here within her *Living and Leaving My Legacy, Vol. 1*. Merle's love of teaching, living, and loving shine through in this legacy journal. Her devotion to living a self-aware life is captured word-by-word, journal entry after journal entry. Her willingness to inspire others to do the same is the silent invitation I heard flowing within the pages of this heartfelt collection."

— **Lynda Monk, Director, The International Association for Journal Writing**

"In Merle Saferstein's riveting and courageous memoir, she shows that one can live into every day, and not simply live through the day. In her daily exercise, or compulsion, to sit and record her joys, sorrows, hopes, fantasies and passing thoughts, she demonstrates that wisdom and insight is acquired not only through the reading of worldly wisdom, but every one of our lives is like a text, ready to reveal its hidden truths if we only take the time to consider them. In the very act of sharing what is at root very personal, she demonstrates an incredible generosity of spirit, in the hopes that others will be inspired to do the same. The book is not simply about her, but each of us, and I assure the reader that they will find themselves in her words as well."

— **Rabbi Frederick L. Klein, Director of Spiritual Care at the Greater Miami Jewish Federation**

"Life-changing! Genuine! Filled with universal truths! This book is about the everyday challenges and celebrations we live through at different stages of life. Saferstein's conversational narrative draws you in while at the same time inspiring you to deeply reflect on your own life. This is Saferstein's genius! Since reading this book, I am now living a more present life."

— **Reizel Larrea-Alvarez, Emmy Award-Winning Journalist**

"In this unique collection of journal excerpts, the reader opens a window into Merle Saferstein's soulfulness, and through her experiences that she shares so openly with us, we awaken to our own wisdom and gain knowledge through her lessons learnt. After each chapter, thought-provoking journal prompts provide a pathway to explore one's life questions and bring deeper meaning. I trust that the wisdoms from *Living and Leaving My Legacy* will spread and touch everyone's life who reads it and many lives for generations to come."

— **Agapi Stassinopoulos, Author of** *Speaking With Spirit* **and** *52 Prayers to Guide, Inspire and Uplift You*

"*Living and Leaving My Legacy* is an authentic journey of life. Filled with the trials we all face, the highs of great moments, and the lows of sometimes feeling despair, you will find yourself within the pages of Merle's life and the situations she faces. I've spent years researching what is needed for humans to thrive in life, leading to the creation of a blueprint for optimizing human capacity and energy. From boundaries to purpose, from control to personal values, you will see the proven behaviors that keep someone positively energized come to life on the pages. No matter your stage in life, or life circumstances, you will go on a journey of inspiration and self-discovery, with relatable advice that you can apply to the situations you face, for the learnings of a lifetime are within these pages."

— Sarah Deane, Founder of MEvolution

"Merle Saferstein's lifelong passion of capturing precious and unforgettable moments as they have unfolded over decades is indicative of the total embrace of her life and her determination not to let one moment pass her by. This will remain an important work for generations to come. It is a journey that never ends and you don't want it to. Five stars."

— W. Thomas Osborne, Journalist, founder, and anchor of *US-UN Report* and author of *The War of Politics: My Ten-Year Journey with Peter Jennings* and *Genocide for Beginners*

"In crystallizing the moments — good and bad, pronounced and more subtle — that comprise her life, Merle Saferstein offers us a profound and rare lens in which to better examine our own. If our life course is indeed a journey, this book is the very best roadmap for how best to navigate it. I will be returning to it regularly as I consider how to live, and leave, my own legacy."

— Mike Lewis, Author of *When to Jump: If the Job You Have Isn't the Life You Want*

"This is a unique presentation of the journal as art. Merle lets us into her life and heart. Her writing is hilarious, heart-wrenching, beautifully detailed. What we see here is a teacher not just of knowledge but of the process of being open and generous in life. She leaves room for encouraging and interacting with the reader too in this original sharing of the power of journaling. This book is filled with nuggets of feeling and wisdom, illumination and connection."

— Beth Jacobs, Ph.D. Psychologist and author of *Writing for Emotional Balance, A Buddhist Journal,* and *Long Shadows of Practice: poems*

"In this book, Merle Saferstein's honesty and introspection as she moves through various stages of life — marriage, motherhood, career, self-exploration and more — draw the reader in to not only a fascinating conversation about Merle's specific experiences, but to our own inner conversations about who we are, what we want, and what we believe. This book is a resource for anyone who wants more out of life and is daring to go for it."

— Lynne Golodner, Author, writing coach, creator of the *Finding Your Voice at Midlife* writers workshop, and *Make Meaning* podcast host

LIVING AND LEAVING
MY LEGACY

VOL. I

LIVING AND LEAVING MY LEGACY

VOL. I

A LEGACY JOURNAL

Merle R. Saferstein

GREAT
MOTHER
PRESS

Orlando, Florida

FIRST EDITION

ISBN number 978-0-9996960-9-5 (paperback)
ISBN number 978-0-9996960-5-7 (eBook)

Library of Congress LCCN 2022936337

Living and Leaving My Legacy, Vol. 1

Great Mother Press
Great Mother Press, LLC, Orlando Florida **www.greatmotherpress.com**

Name: Merle R. Saferstein

Illustration and format by Jenny Menzel **www.jennymenzel.com**

Author photograph by Pipe Yanguas

Printed in the United States of America

This is a work of nonfiction taken from the journals of Merle R. Saferstein. All individuals mentioned are actual people. The names and/or gender of some have been changed to protect their privacy.

For my family and friends in the next and future generations and especially to my children Rebecca and Michael, Sara and Dave, my granddaughters Sophia and Bella, and my nieces and nephews.

May this be a reminder that how you live your life becomes your legacy.

Table of Contents

Foreword

I met Merle R. Saferstein at a poetry therapy conference a decade or so ago. I remember being a little starstruck to fall into conversation somewhat by accident with the Miami chair of the traveling *Anne Frank in the World: 1929–1945* exhibit, an 800-photo installation from the Anne Frank Center in Amsterdam.

As that first conversation deepened, I felt echoes of another of my diary "grandmothers," Anais Nin. In particular, I marveled at Merle's light-hearted story about the safe she had hauled home to guard her journals, and how she was in the process of sorting excerpts from those journals into topic areas. (This very volume, in fact, is comprised of those made-by-hand snippets, stashed and locked up in her daughter's bedroom closet.)

Merle is a story gatherer, a midwife of secrets and stories untold, a skilled observer of life and its mysteries, and a passionate journal writer. She has chronicled with meticulous steadfastness her own life trajectory across over 40 years and 359 volumes, which she has catalogued and curated into 22 interweaving thematic timelines, half of which are presented in this first of two volumes.

As the director of educational outreach at the Holocaust Documentation and Education Center, Merle helped the Holocaust survivors, whom she worked with, share their stories with students. They knew the Holocaust only as vague history until they participated in Merle-organized student symposia.

About the inaugural Student Awareness Day she wrote:

> **May 7, 1986.** From now on, I'll be looking for every opportunity to speak with students, as I did with the many groups of school children at the exhibition. I have identified what it is I want to teach. I understand how important it is to make today's youth aware of the dangers of prejudice, bigotry, and indifference.

But her work as storyteller is only part of this legacy journal. Merle also offers unblinking, decades-spanning views of marriage, parenting, her spiritual quest, journaling, her early career, and her exploration of being a woman. The courage to unabashedly reveal roller-coaster highs and lows is outstanding modeling.

The timelines vary according to chapter — the marriage chapter starts in early 1975 and ends in mid-2017, while the Anne Frank chapter spans nine months in 1985–86. It is thus possible, if one is so inclined, to track parallel paths in Merle's life — what was happening with her and husband Daryl on the marital scene? How might that have been influenced by the feminism track? In the two-year interim period between career fields? On the parenting front? In this way, we get what is perhaps an entirely new form: A memoir that echoes Anais Nin's observation that "as always, my life continues as a musical score, on many lines at once."

Consider these parallel entries from early 1989:

January 15, 1989. From the chapter *On Being a Woman*. I woke up with a backache and menstrual cramps. I decided to go out and jog, hoping it would get my mind off how I felt. It is not always easy to be a woman.

The upside of this is that most women innately have a nurturing instinct that fewer men possess. So, as with almost everything in life, no one has it all.

February 10, 1989. From the chapter *Journey of Journaling*. If I were to allow myself a fantasy of what I'd like to happen to my journals, here it is. I would love someday to hold in my hands a great-grandchild, knowing this little person would be my kindred spirit — someone who would embrace my journals in a way few ever would. This is probably far-fetched, but I might as well enjoy my fantasies for whatever they're worth.

February 16, 1989. From the chapter *Holocaust Documentation and Education Center, Part One*. When I met with John Davies last week, he told me he feels that coming to a Student Awareness Day is by far the single best educational experience a student can have. That says a lot.

Because I was curious, I also checked out my own milestone date, November 5, 1985, against Merle's entries. That is the date I taught my first journal workshop and knew immediately that the intersection between journal writing and emotional healing was my work in the world. I still remember, with visceral clarity, the sense of hurtling toward my destiny with everything in my being. I found this, in the Anne Frank chapter:

November 5, 1985. I now have a star in the sky to reach for and a dream to make come true. Every morning when I awake, my first thoughts are of Anne Frank and the exhibition. The project is always on my mind.

Lastly, a word about legacy writing in general. Among the many reasons why people write journals is a desire to leave evidence of their unique life path, however noted or humble, to a known or unknown generation.

Yet, in my nearly 40 years of experience as a journal therapist, I've seen few writers actualize that desire prior to infirmity or death. Thus, sadly, many life legacies are discarded or shredded sight unseen. And when these volumes do end up in the hands of children or grandchildren, there is often inadequate preparation for what may feel like a Pandora's box of raw emotion or unfiltered process from a parent or grandparent who may not have shared this private side.

Informed legacy writing strategies could reduce or eliminate some of this heartache, and none is better equipped to model legacy writing at its most effective than my friend and colleague Merle R. Saferstein. She embodies what the late Dr. Ira Progoff said: The journal is a conduit to "savor the beauty and stare straight into the pain."

Most of us could not take on the monastic process of curating tens of thousands of pages and millions of words. But all of us can learn from this extraordinary work that models both the art and the craft of effective editing for cohesive legacy storytelling. Merle's commitment and devotion is a gift to all who aspire to leave a legacy story to a future generation.

Kathleen Adams LPC, PTJR
Registered Poetry/Journal Therapist
Founder/Director, Center for Journal Therapy, Inc.

Introduction

As a young girl, I wrote letters to my relatives who lived all over the United States. Around age nine, I vividly remember telling myself I needed to lead an interesting life to always have something to write about and share. Even back then, I was feeling the stirrings to be a writer.

At age thirty, I began to journal. At first, I wrote sporadically. However, by 1982, I was writing daily and sometimes multiple times a day. I felt compelled, as if I had no choice but to write. My journals became my most cherished possessions. To date, I have completed 380 volumes.

At some point, I grappled with what would happen to my journals after I died. As you will read in the first chapter on journaling, this has been a tremendous challenge.

Once I decided not to bequeath my journals to anyone, I came up with an alternative plan — the legacy journal project. At first, I intended to sort through the pages and find meaningful excerpts to share with my loved ones. When I realized this would become my written legacy, I decided to include a broader audience. Somewhere along the way, this morphed into what you are now reading.

Hopefully, you will think about your life while reading about mine. Perhaps my excerpts will open a window for you to look inward. My hope is that while reading this book, you will be inspired to think about your own experiences as well as your legacy.

When I began this project of creating a written legacy from my journals, I chose seventy topics, eventually narrowing them down to twenty-two. Initially, each subject was roughly 75 – 450 pages, all taken from journals dated between 1974 – 2016. After careful editing, I chose to include the excerpts that best captured my thoughts, feelings, conversations, encounters, memories, dreams, travel adventures, and more. Hopefully, sharing some of my life lessons, values and beliefs, and my hopes and dreams will prove valuable to you, the reader.

In compiling the two volumes of *Living and Leaving My Legacy*, I worked carefully to protect the confidentiality of those I wrote about whenever it felt necessary. Thus, there were instances when I used fictitious names or even switched genders. What mattered most was the point I wanted to share without exposing or hurting anyone.

Because *Living and Leaving My Legacy* is my story, I have included a sampling of my life — the good and bad, the easy and difficult, the ups and downs. Always, I gave much thought to what to include in this book and what would never see the light of day. It was of utmost importance that I remained authentic. Telling my truth in these excerpts has been my number one priority. I have often felt vulnerable but have stayed true to my promise to be completely honest.

In the journaling circles I facilitate, I ask participants to read what they wrote and reflect on it. What do they notice? How do they feel about what they have put down on paper? What have they learned about themselves? At the end of each chapter, I wrote a reflection on the excerpts I had included. Sometimes I added something that had taken place between 2016 and my final editing.

Following my reflections, I have included journal prompts on each subject. Then I've left blank pages on which you may write, should you be inspired by the prompts or by something you've read in the chapter. Just know there are no rules for journaling except dating each entry. What's important is that we write for ourselves.

I now invite you to join me in my journey through time and experience.

Merle R. Saferstein

Journey of Journaling

I write for myself and never with the idea that anyone will read my journals.
This frees my deepest secrets, heartfelt emotions,
and random thoughts to spill out onto the page.

— From the journals of Merle R. Saferstein

July 23, 1987

I deposited yet another journal in my safe deposit box today. I feel a sense of security and safety keeping all eighty-eight of them locked up at the Home Savings Bank on Hollywood Beach, where I can easily walk in and drop them off.

Generally, no one there ever says a word to me about them. However, today, as one of the bank employees walked with me upstairs to the safety deposit boxes, she asked what these books were and why I was putting them in safekeeping. I wonder if there are rules regarding the bank's "vault keepers" talking to customers about what they're depositing. However, I'm sure curiosity got the best of her. After all, they've been watching me come in for years, each time carrying a journal, which I place in one of my two safety deposit boxes. Most people secure their jewelry, money, and important documents, but journals??

July 25, 1987

Some woman just walked by me sitting on the bench and saw me writing in my journal. She called out, "I'd love to get a glimpse of that," and kept moving along. Yesterday I learned that my mom's friend Fran has kept journals for years and has written in them daily. When I spoke with her, Fran told me she doesn't want her daughters-in-law ever to read them. I didn't ask her if she wanted her sons to read them, but I should have. Fran has suffered from depression most of her life. I wonder if journaling has helped her cope with some of her feelings. It certainly has been an excellent tool for me to sort out mine.

November 22, 1987

I went to Jaffe's to buy a few journals. The last time I was there, they had beautiful ones, but today they had none. The journal I've just started writing in is my last blank one, so I'm desperate to find new ones. Just like always having books piled up waiting to read, I'm much the same when it comes to journals. I'm slightly panicked when I don't have a stack in reserve.

December 2, 1987

Today when I was making Rebecca's bed, I came across her diary peeking out from under the mattress. I didn't touch it but was tempted. If I want my family to respect my privacy, I have to allow them theirs. Not every family is as respectful of one another, so I consider myself fortunate that we have this unspoken agreement in our home.

December 31, 1987

Max mentioned how great that I'm "incredibly disciplined" to write in my journals daily. I let him know that it's not a matter of discipline but something I'm compelled to do. His response was, "Sounds like you're driven." What a perfect way to describe me. I sometimes wonder why I need to record so much of my life. My journaling is fundamental to my being—something I must do. It cleanses my soul. On those days when I haven't had the chance to write and need to wait until evening to do so, I feel unsettled.

February 15, 1988

I have a feeling this journal is going to be more exciting than most. Whenever I travel, I have a new perspective—a different backdrop to experience life.

March 4, 1988

Bernadette asked whether I'd come to speak to the writing class she's teaching and talk about my journaling process. She explained how she had journaled for years, but once her husband invaded her privacy and read one of her journals, that did her in. Since then, she's never written. How sad!

April 22, 1988

Today I completed my one-hundredth journal. Considering I began writing in 1974, this feels significant. I've come a long way from that first volume, which was a flimsy stenographer's pad. I remember buying it to record my dreams for the Gestalt class at Miami Dade Community College. Once the course ended, I started writing down my thoughts and feelings in addition to my dreams. That began my journey of journaling. By the time 1982 rolled around, I had finished four journals, and from then on, I became a serious journal writer.

May 2, 1988

Daryl asked me last night if I had talked with anyone about the argument we had. I told him I hadn't, which surprised him. He then asked if I had written about it. Now that's a different story!

Without question, journaling always helps me to process whatever is going on in my life. I'm grateful that I can express my emotions, come to terms with problems, figure out how to handle a situation, and eventually work through my concerns by journaling.

June 19, 1988

I wonder if I'll ever read this or any of my journals. I'm beginning to feel there is a greater reason for writing them than what seems apparent to me now. Only time will answer that. In the meantime, I don't miss a day without putting down what I'm thinking, feeling, dreaming, wishing for, and experiencing.

June 24, 1988

I asked my friend Joe the legal ramifications of having a safe deposit box and what would happen if I died. The bottom line is my executor will have access to the contents of my box. Knowing that, I must stipulate in my will what I want to be done with my journals.

I fear making that commitment because if I even thought for a second someone might be reading them, I might hesitate to write down everything that flows from my pen. I know Tom, my one friend who keeps journals faithfully, would like me to leave my journals to him. From the first day we met at Hollywood Beach in December of '82, we identified our mutual passion for writing. In all these years since he's lived elsewhere, our letters back and forth to each other have led to a friendship unlike any other I've ever had. He's become part of my family. In his will, Tom indicated that I am to inherit all of his writings, including his journals. If anyone were to appreciate mine, it would probably be him. Yet, at this point, I can't even consider leaving them to him or anyone else.

I finished reading *The Orton Diaries*, the diary of the thirty-four-year-old British playwright Joe Orton, killed by his lover Kenneth. The book contains diary entries written from December through August before he died. Toward the end, he mentioned that Kenneth had been acting odd, but he never indicated there were significant problems that might lead to something as serious as a murder-suicide. I wonder if he knew there was an issue but wasn't honest or was afraid to write about it in his journals.

August 6, 1988

I've been reading *Hot Flashes*, which is about friendship. It's partially written in journal form, where friends read the journals of their girlfriend who had died. The entries encompass one month and are filled with reflection. Reading it has led me to think about my journaling. While I write about my present thoughts, I also reflect on the past. Do others who journal do that?

August 16, 1988

Some guy just came up to me and peered over my shoulder. He asked if I was writing a book or a diary. He then said, "If I had kept a diary, I could have made a fortune after all I've been through in my life." He was hovering over me, which was unnerving, so I covered up what I was writing.

That upset him. "Not to worry," he said, "I won't read what you're writing." Damn right, he won't. No one reads this stuff.

November 9, 1988

I had a dream about my journals last night. I dreamt they were out on shelves and weren't safe from others' eyes. I woke up and reassured myself that they were protected and secure in the safe deposit box.

January 1, 1989

A woman asked me about her mother's journal, which she had written in 1938 and had given to her fifteen years ago. She didn't read it until after her mother's death and now wants to know whether, legally and ethically, it's okay to give it to her child. My answer was since her mother gave it to her without any stipulations, I believe she can do as she pleases with the journal. However, I suggested if what her mother wrote is sensitive, she might reconsider sharing it.

February 10, 1989

I'm at a journal workshop at FIU. The facilitator is using Ira Progroff's book *At a Journal Workshop* and *The New Diary* as guides. Some of my notes so far:

- Journaling is private writing.
- What to do with them down the road is something to consider for each person who keeps a journal.
- When we write in our journals, we establish a relationship. There's a honeymoon period and then routine period, which reflects a degree of intimacy and friendship.

During the break, I talked to Rosi Flam, an attorney, about the legal aspects of leaving one's journals to others. I've been thinking about what I want done with mine when I die. While I've always known I write for myself, I realize they could be my legacy if I step away from my attachment to them. If they live on, maybe in some way, I will too. I'm sure I'll be writing about this for a long time to come.

If I were to allow myself a fantasy of what I'd like to happen to my journals, here it is. I would love someday to hold in my hands a great-grandchild, knowing this little person would be my kindred spirit—someone who would embrace my journals in a way few ever would. This is probably far-fetched, but I might as well enjoy my fantasies for whatever they're worth.

During the session, Rosi described journal writing in this way: Movies and books are our escape, and journal writing is our "inscape."

February 17, 1989

Some man at the beach, who saw me writing, stopped and asked if I was familiar with Archibald

MacLeish, the American poet. He claimed by the year 2000, almost no one would be writing letters or keeping journals. So, this guy told me I should make sure to keep it up—as if I could stop doing either. I intend to prove Mr. MacLeish wrong.

February 20, 1989

From the Elder's Institute at Florida International University, Doris asked me to facilitate a follow-up session to the journal workshop I had attended. I love the idea, especially since I felt more qualified than the instructor at the one I participated in.

February 28, 1989

On the way to the airport last night, I told Daryl I was unsure about what to do with my journals after I died. He said he didn't understand why I wouldn't just leave them to him and the kids. When I asked him what he'd do with them, he said he didn't know. After a bit, he told me he'd read my journals and look for someone to help get them published. It got me thinking that maybe I will ask different people in my life that same question.

March 10, 1989

In my therapy session with Dorthea today, I talked about my journals. While I wasn't expecting answers, I felt exploring my feelings might help me decide what I want to do with them in the future. I told her what had been explained to me—including how I could have them sealed upon my death and left to my future descendants. At this point, that seems to be the best alternative.

Dorthea understands my journals are my most treasured possession. She admitted how intrigued she was with my extensive journaling. Dorthea disclosed that she had never had a client who knew herself better than I do and attributed it strictly to my writing.

I mentioned that I had asked a few people what they would do if I left them my journals. I told her Adele said she would not read them because she feels they are private and not for her. She said that in the event she died, she would leave them to Sheryl but with the idea of finding the right person, preferably a writer, to do something with them. Marsha said she would treasure them and read a little bit each day.

Lois said if I willed my journal collection to her, she'd put them away, and whenever she felt lonely and wanted to be with me, she would read one. As she talked about it, she began to cry, and so did I—a touching exchange. Her response makes me feel that maybe I will leave her a few of my journals from our trips together. It's too soon to make that decision, but it is something to think about.

Dorthea thought it was a good idea to continue asking people that question. She wondered if any of those I had spoken to asked me what I'd like them to do with my journals. Good point.

She listened as I told her how I had gone to my safe deposit box and randomly read pages from various volumes. I talked about how my whole being is within the pages of my journals—how everyone I know and relate to only knows pieces of the different facets of who I am. She explained how I'm in the process of integration of self, something Carl Jung calls individuation. Dorthea pointed out that she sees this journey as significant—incorporating my thoughts on death and dying, my journals, no longer smoking pot, and more.

Dorthea asked if I thought I would always write in my journals. I told her I couldn't imagine my life without doing so and admitted I needed to record daily.

I described the sad feelings I had leaving my journals at the bank last week, something I hadn't been consciously aware of until that moment. I suddenly realized how much I wish I could have my journals at home. She asked me what that would look like, and I began to visualize shelves over my bed where I could line up my journals and have them accessible to me at any given moment.

Dorthea asked if she could share what she was thinking, albeit unconventional for a therapist to do. Of course, I was anxious to hear. She said her image, which she admitted may be total projection because she's always wanted this for herself, was to have a beautiful teak piece of furniture with shelves, clear glass windows, and a key. Dorthea went one step further and said she saw it filled with my journals with only me having the key. She described how people would see them, be fascinated with the idea that the volumes contained my innermost secrets, and respect me enough to know it's a hands-off situation.

I told Dorthea I hoped to read all of my journals someday. It's one of my retirement goals.

Dorthea prefaced this next part by saying it may be totally off the wall and maybe only half real, the other half of her fantasy. She knows I don't want to part with my journals and realizes how hard it is to assign them to someone. Well, her dream was that I'd be reincarnated three generations from now and my journals would come back into my possession. Of course, I loved that one.

Meanwhile, talking to her about my journals was incredibly helpful for me. While I still don't have answers, this leaves me with much food for thought.

March 12, 1989

Is journaling self-indulgent? All I know is I would have much less understanding of who I am without writing.

March 16, 1989

I wrote a codicil to my will, which stipulates that my executor is to safely secure and seal my journals to save for my descendants fifty years from my death. That feels freeing, assuring me no one in my current life will ever read them.

March 17, 1989

This morning was the follow-up journal workshop at FIU. Before the session began, Rosi asked if I had written about her in my journal. As it happens, I had, and that delighted her.

I enjoyed the opportunity to be teaching again and felt good about helping the participants understand the value of journaling. I shared the following with them.

Journaling helps us to:

- Record our lives.
- Express ourselves.
- Work out issues and find solutions.
- Cope with difficult times.
- Reflect on our experiences.
- Ask questions, find answers, and awaken to new ways of thinking.
- Make sense of the world around us.
- Log events
- Observe and record the peaks and valleys in our life.
- Take notes on what we learn.
- Recall, digest, and record conversations, encounters, feelings, memories, dreams, travel adventures, and ideas.
- Explore thoughts and responses to what we see and hear.
- Center ourselves when we feel confused, unbalanced, or out of sorts.
- Watch the seeds we plant grow.
- Understand and be in touch with the meaning of our life.
- Embrace our past, discover joy in our present, and create our future.
- Clarify our goals.
- Say what's so without being judged.

March 25, 1989

Since last week when I finally decided what I want to do with my journals, I've noticed an occasional hesitation as I am about to write something that might be sensitive. I realize someone could be reading my journals decades from now. As a result, I have promised myself that I will not censor whatever comes to mind. I know it's the only way I can journal authentically. I told myself I would stop journaling if I did not write something down because I wouldn't want anyone to see it. That's drastic, but it's the only way to confirm how committed I am to be 100% honest and say everything I'm thinking and feeling in my journals.

April 15, 1989

I know the majority of this journal is going to be different from my usual ones. I'm off to Nashville to sit with Bonnie at Vanderbilt's hospital for the next four days. I imagine I'll have a lot of alone or quiet time, since she'll probably be resting because of the bone marrow transplant she recently had.

April 19, 1989

When we talked tonight, Daryl mentioned he told the guys at cards last night he's sure this journal I'm writing in now is filled with gut-wrenching thoughts and painful emotions. He's right about that. Everything I've been feeling has found its way onto the page because I have been in a cocoon here with Bonnie. I've talked only to her and Daryl. During these past few days, while Bonnie has slept, I have been writing non-stop. I am closing in on the completion of this volume, which I have filled in record time. Being in Nashville has been an intense experience, and I've recorded it in the best way I know.

April 27, 1989

One of the Jehovah's Witnesses, handing out her literature at the corner of Garfield Street near Angelo's, just asked me if I was writing a book or a journal. When I told her it was a journal, her comment to me was, "Oh, I thought you were a writer." Really? What am I, if not that?

July 15, 1989

Tom wondered if I would let him read the journal I'm writing in now. I said no. However, I did ask him what he'd do with my journals if I left them to him. His reply was, "The only reason I would want them, other than to read, would be to make sure they were given to the people who should have them." Tom sees them ultimately belonging not to my kids but my grandchildren.

July 16, 1989

This journal I'm writing in is my 125th. I had thought I might reach #125 by December. I guess I sold myself short.

July 19, 1989

My latest goal is that when I turn sixty, I'd like to retire from whatever I'm doing and get a place on the ocean—whether it be a home, an apartment, or even a studio. Then I want to review my journals one by one hoping to understand what has compelled me to record my life as I've lived it. For now, it's my dream, but almost always, when I set goals, I accomplish them.

September 12, 1989

In a conversation with Aemi yesterday, I asked her what she would do with my journals. She said she probably wouldn't read them because she's too close to me but might give them to the next generation.

Last night, Gerry and I had dinner at the Unicorn. We talked about my journals, and I also asked her the same question. She said she would probably lock herself in a room and read them non-stop. She admitted she wouldn't read them for the gossip, but she'd want to see how I think and feel about my life.

November 5, 1989

Daryl and I were talking about my journals and whether I've filled them with my fantasies. He felt sure I hadn't. I jokingly then asked him why he thought I kept them in the safe deposit box. The truth is I don't record most of my fantasies, but I do on occasion.

February 1, 1990

I'm facilitating another journal writing workshop at FIU now and will make at least $120. Seven people are attending, which is a perfect number. The prompt I've given is to write about someone who has inspired them. I always write along with them (but not necessarily using the prompt) because it's important to model behavior—although this group is eager to write and needs no prodding.

February 22, 1990

While I was waiting for my mammogram, some woman saw me journaling and asked about my writing. She also wanted to know if the courts could obtain and use someone's journal as evidence in a murder trial. I didn't know the answer to that but couldn't help but wonder why she asked.

April 16, 1990

In a conversation with Sandy, he told me how he's holding onto every word in the one diary he found of Bonnie's. She wrote it in high school when she was dating other guys. Yet to Sandy, it is precious. All the diaries I kept as a teenager are gone. I never did understand how my mom said I didn't come to get them when they moved. That just is so unlike me!

In any case, the more Sandy talked about Bonnie's diary, the more I started thinking about my journals. Hearing how he wants his boys to know about their mother makes me realize leaving my journals to my family may be an important legacy.

If something should happen to me now that I'm about to embark on my trip to Poland and Israel, I wonder if I should make provisions for Rebecca and Michael to have my journals someday. Do I owe them that? Would my journals be meaningful to them? Maybe I'll rethink this today and leave a letter before I go.

April 17, 1990

I am sitting on the patio of the Hollywood Café and just wrote a letter to Daryl which I'll leave at home "in the event of." I am doing something I never expected I would do. I wrote that I want him to have my journals to pass on to our children eventually.

I can hardly believe I have decided this, but suddenly, it feels like the right thing to do with this big trip ahead of me. I asked him to guard them closely and made it clear that I wrote these journals for myself and would never want anyone hurt by them. So, I am conflicted but am following my gut on this one for now.

November 8, 1990

I like the idea of writing in my 146th journal as I approach my 46th birthday. I have written a hundred journals in six years.

November 16, 1990

This journal feels like several chapters rolled into one — the deadline on the Holocaust resource manual and horrendous pressure at work, my time away with Lois, my visit with Tom, and, of course, the highs and lows that are part of daily living.

November 17, 1990

Sandy asked over one hundred people to send stories, photos, and memories of Bonnie for an album he's creating for his boys. In the hopes of finding some journal excerpts to share with them, I just reread the journal I had filled while visiting Bonnie in April of last year. On one page, I wrote, "For me, fear is the pit I feel in the bottom of my stomach, and my heart palpitations remind me that I have a heart."

Since I've hardly ever gone back and read any of my journals, reading this one gave me an overview of what I include when I write. For sure, I can go back in my adult life and find out where I was at almost any given moment. I'm starting to understand the merits of leaving my journals to my children and their children. They will undoubtedly see parts of me they might not have known — much like Sandy said he felt about Bonnie when reading her diary.

There's probably a good deal of useless information within the thousands of pages of my journals, but hopefully, there are also valuable jewels. For the most part, my writing is not particularly profound or intellectual, but it is a composite of who I am and what I'm all about.

Knowing that Rebecca and Michael will someday read my journals has not changed my writing. I cannot let that hold me back on anything I put down on the page. To vent, dream, record, fantasize, and more is too important to me.

January 1, 1991

On the first day of the year, I feel the way I do when I begin a new journal. There's a clean slate. I have no idea what's in store, what will fill my pages. It reminds me of the unpredictability of our days over which we often have little control. It's one of life's great mysteries.

February 10, 1991

When I talked to the guys at the bandshell earlier, one pointed to the journal I was writing in and asked if it's been a good chapter. Unfortunately, between Pop's death and the Gulf War, it's a volume filled with sadness.

Then another guy, whom I often see here at the beach, told me I'm one of the ten things about the beach he relies on for consistency. He described me as intense and focused when I write. He said he can always count on me sitting under the palm tree at Nevada Street across from Seawind Apartments and writing. He also told me he only recently realized that instead of being called the Boardwalk, the official name is the Hollywood Beach Broadwalk.

February 15, 1991

I just deposited a journal in my safe deposit box, which is so full I might not fit another one in. It looks like I'll need to rent a third box, but it will cost a lot of money. Yet, having my journals at the bank gives me peace of mind. Trade-offs!

April 26, 1991

When we went to Judy's to pay a *shiva* call, I brought her a journal. I wrote her a note saying, "Because I care and because we both know the value of the written word, I hope writing in this journal will bring some comfort to you." Hopefully, she'll find journaling helpful as she goes through the grief process.

July 18, 1991

Diane asked me if I write daily. When I told her I did, she then said, "It makes me think of those people who run five miles a day." I told her I do that too. So, she then asked me the next logical question. "Are you an alcoholic?" I said I wasn't but probably would be if I drank. Anaïs Nin talked about how her diary writing was much like an opium addiction. I guess in some ways it is, especially for me, who has an addictive personality.

September 24, 1991

Somehow, I made room for my recent journal in the safety deposit box and learned the bank was raising the rates. The size I have now is going up from $150 to $250 per year, and the bigger one I would need is $350. I have to decide what I'm going to do.

November 22, 1991

While at the bank today, I mentioned I would soon be taking my journals out and asked the woman if she had any ideas for safekeeping. She didn't suggest anything more than I already knew, but she told me they would miss me. I need to find another alternative. This is just too expensive.

January 16, 1992

I went to check out fireproof cabinets at the used office furniture warehouse Mike Swatt had suggested. I chose a five-drawer cabinet that weighs seven hundred pounds, is 3' x 2' x 4', and will resist direct fire for more than an hour. It'll cost me $300 plus $130 to move it into my house.

February 14, 1992

It took three men to bring the safe here. It's so large that it fills half of Rebecca's closet. I plan to put my journals in it today. I hid one key and will give Daryl the extra one to keep at his office.

Later. I'm stuck at the drawbridge. I just went to the bank and emptied my safe deposit boxes. I filled two big banker boxes and two large garbage bags with my journals, all of which were super heavy to carry. Hopefully, they won't fill the entire safe. I underestimated how bulky the journals are.

At home. My journals fill two drawers with one row in the third drawer. What an incredible feeling to have them all in my possession. At any given time, I can go right to my journals and read whatever I want. Plus, I have lots of room left, which makes me happy. Above all else, they will remain safe from fire.

February 19, 1992

In the past week, two friends asked if I had included what they had shared with me in my journals. One had told me not to put it in, to begin with, so I didn't. The other just realized that someday someone might read my journals, and she never wants her secret known.

She asked me to white out her name, and, of course, I will when I get home. I can live with that because the names aren't what's important. For me, writing about whatever the individual has shared is my way of processing what is told to me and absorbing it all. From now on, I won't name the person if something was said to me in confidence.

I don't like that I have to censor what I say about anyone in my journals. The trade-off would be they not confide in me, and that wouldn't feel right. So, I need to respect what people ask of me if I want to be trusted.

I do have other people's secrets in my journals. It is one reason why I am now beginning to rethink leaving them to Rebecca and Michael.

March 19, 1992

Yesterday after work, I stopped at Party Fashions. While there, I realized I didn't have my journal in my purse. That did not feel good. I feared that I left it at the Holocaust Center. When I got home, it was on my bed—what a relief. I would NOT want to leave my journal at the office or anywhere else, for that matter.

July 10, 1992

Last night when I was reading *The Diarists' Journal*, a magazine on journal writing, I came across an article about going from journal writing as a habit to an obsession. Some call it a compulsion. While I have no idea what to call my journaling, what I do know is that I write because it's as essential to me as eating, walking, or just plain living. It's my passion.

The article's author wrote, "I deserve no credit for keeping my diary regularly. Discipline has nothing to do with it. I am a compulsive diarist, a journal junkie.

"If I don't write down even these mundane things, will I really have done them? Or will the hours of my day be blank spaces, a vacuum that was not lived? Would my whole life disappear? Would I have to begin again, a newborn baby with gray hair?" I can certainly relate!

October 22, 1992

I asked Daryl to tell me honestly if he thinks he would someday read my journals if I left them to him. He admitted that he probably wouldn't. He is the least curious of anyone about my journals. He always claims he, above everyone else, knows the real me. I guess that's enough for him.

December 16, 1992

In book club last night, we talked about my journals. We were laughing about how some people would be in such trouble if my journals were ever published, which I have zero intention of doing. After joking about a few individuals, I explained how I hope someday the messages and pearls will be published but not the details that will expose other people.

February 6, 1993

When I went to call Tom, I put my journal with my good Cross fountain pen down by the phone booth in front of Howard Johnson's. I realized that both phones were out of order, so I quickly left to find another on the Broadwalk and unknowingly left my journal and pen by the phone.

After I hung up with Tom, I went back to my seat to write. I panicked when I realized what I had done and ran to look for my journal. I searched all over, but it wasn't anywhere—not by the phone booth, at the front desk of Howard Johnson's hotel, at the restaurant, in any garbage cans nearby, or in any bushes. I even walked along the sand to see if anyone was reading it but no such luck. I would have easily recognized the colorful, psychedelic tie-dyed cover from a distance.

I was on the verge of tears. I was sorry to lose my good fountain pen, which I don't have the money to replace, but I was even more devastated about my journal. I still am.

I keep thinking about who might have it. I pray it isn't anyone I know because that would be horrible. Much has gone on this week, and I have been putting it all down—some issues at work, a sexual fantasy, and other stuff I wouldn't want anyone to read.

Later. I am getting used to the idea of having lost my journal but thinking about who found it makes me nervous. I only hope it's a French Canadian who doesn't read English and threw it away.

July 28, 1993

After I hung up with Daryl, I looked out the window and saw a big fire truck outside Ocean Drive. I went into the hall and saw a fireman who said all was fine. For that split second, I became concerned about a real fire and quickly thought of what I would grab if I had to run out—my purse, the cash I had put in the freezer, the journals I brought with me to read, and this one I'm writing in.

I feel secure knowing aside from these few I have with me here at the Starlight Hotel on South Beach, my journals are locked away in my fireproof safe. It was indeed the best investment I've made.

August 20, 1993

I just finished reading an article about Anaïs Nin. She had 35,000 handwritten pages in her journals. I've never given much thought to the number of pages I've written; however, I do keep track of the number of volumes I've filled. Most journals probably have an average of two hundred pages, so in doing the math, I already have an estimated 35,200 completely-filled pages. I'm guessing that someday I will end up with a lot more than that.

November 9, 1993

In today's paper, there was an article about diaries, Senator Packwood, and the trouble he had with his. It claimed that everyone writes in a diary to be read. That isn't true in my case. It also divided writers into categories: chroniclers, travelers, pilgrims, creators, apologists, confessors, and prisoners. Aside from being a prisoner, I'm probably a little of each in some way.

May 14, 1994

One of the things I love about journaling is being able to recapture a moment. While I rarely look at old journals, it's all there for me—the raw emotions I had at the time, the experiences, one scene after another. On occasion, someone in my life will want to remember something that happened and will ask me to find details, a date, or whatever else they might want to know. In some ways, by default, it makes me the historian for family and friends.

May 26, 1994

I choose a journal to write in based on the selection I have on hand and, of course, the mood I'm in. This past week, I bought a new journal because none had appealed to me for my California trip. Each of my journals is a chapter interwoven with those which come before and after it. They're limited by the number of pages in the journal and not by what is going on in my life.

June 8, 1994

Tonight Daryl asked if I'd be angry with him all over again when I reread some of the journals with tough stuff in them. I told him I'd do my best to keep my emotions from the past back there and stay in the present. It may stir feelings, but I hope to keep it all in its proper place. How I'll do it is yet to be determined.

July 1, 1994

I sat with a twenty-six-year-old English teacher and avid journal writer at lunch today. She told me that before taking a trip to Europe, she had decided to leave her journals with her best friend. She made her promise not to read them, but at the last minute, she became concerned and decided to bury them in the ground. She uncovered them when she came home six months later.

It reminds me of Emanuel Ringelbaum's collection of diaries, important documents, and notes he wrote and collected while in the Warsaw Ghetto. He hid them in tin boxes and milk cans. Later, they were discovered and told the story of the secret operation, code-named *Oyneg Shabes*, which was part of the resistance during the Holocaust.

August 15, 1994

Going back to read my journals is proving to be fascinating in many ways. Sometimes, I get intimately personal in them and write about our sex life. At times, I laugh out loud when I read some of it. Do I want our kids to see this? Not at all! So far, in reading the journals this summer, I notice once I began to put them in the safe deposit box, I became much more sexually explicit. Unconsciously, I must have felt a greater sense of security, knowing no one would be reading them.

August 20, 1994

I wish there were someone to talk to about what I'm feeling right now. Maybe that's one of the reasons why I journal. When no one is on the other end, I always turn inward to these pages. What would I do without my journaling? What do others do?

August 24, 1994

Watching my life from this viewpoint is enlightening. Here I sit at the water's edge, reliving my experiences, thoughts, feelings, and so much more from my past. I had no idea how much I'd committed to paper.

Journal #30 smells like chocolate. It has a picture of my favorite candy, a Milky Way, on the cover. Somehow, the manufacturer had infused it with the smell of the candy bar. It's hard to believe the scent remains ten years later. It isn't helping my craving for chocolate.

August 25, 1994

I am a slave to my journals. The process captivates and lures me. It holds me tenaciously. Freedom escapes me as I sit bound to the next word, the next page, the next volume.

April 1, 1995

I read an article in the paper about Anne Frank's diary today. The writer said she was flighty and self-absorbed, which upset me. I immediately started to think about *A Necklace of Pearls* and wondered if others would say that about me when they read it. Sometimes when I get a compliment or someone writes something special to me, my journals are the place where I can pat myself on the back without feeling like I'm bragging. Where else but in my journals can I express the excitement I'm feeling about who I am or where I'm heading?

My journals are also a place where I can cry and moan when I am hurting, vent when I am angry, and celebrate when I am happy. They are the one place where I can say whatever I want and feel safe, relieved, in touch, accepted, and honest.

June 15, 1995

I loved the book *The Bridges of Madison County* and felt the same way about the movie, which we saw tonight. What touched me most was when Francesca's daughter and son found three of their mother's notebooks in which she had written about her four-day love affair. It all felt personal to me—knowing they had read about her secret romance. While I have nothing like that to hide from my family, I'm again questioning my decision to leave my journals to Rebecca and Michael.

July 15, 1995

Julia Cameron, the author of *The Artist's Way*, suggests writing three "morning pages" each day upon awakening. She explains how they open one up, which allows for creative and spiritual channeling. While I write most mornings, I don't do it exactly as she suggests; however, I will follow her instructions and see how it goes.

July 20, 1996

My latest decision is not to leave Rebecca and Michael any journals from 1995 going forward. They're filled with too much hardship and harsh feelings, which they don't need to read. Besides, I must have complete freedom to express all my feelings and not have to think twice about doing so. I told Daryl what I decided, and he felt it made a lot of sense.

February 20, 1997

I find refuge in my journaling. What would I do if I couldn't write? How would I ever express my feelings without exploring them on paper? I have a constant conversation with myself. Journaling serves as a key to my heart and soul.

Marsha talked about psychoanalysis last night in Group, and I shared how the two of us had decided my journal writing is much the same thing. While one talks non-stop to an analyst, I write down whatever is on my mind—saying it all on the page. It's the way I survive.

February 21, 1997

This has been one of the toughest journals I've filled, although I feel better having written in it. I wonder if I could have come to that place without my form of tranquilizer—my journaling.

After hours with pen in hand, I am regaining my equilibrium. I was drowning yesterday.

Once again, I wonder where I will be in my life when I reread this chapter for the first time. Will the pain feel as severe as it does now? How could it? Thank goodness, I have my journal as a record. Seeing it in black and white will someday provide me with the concrete reality of what was.

March 12, 1997

This chapter I had hoped would be peaceful and calm. I was ready for the harvest and festival of fruit on the cover, but I was a bit too premature. Once again, I have written myself out of a frenzy. I have had time to decipher the last personal hurricane that blew through this week. I am picking up the pieces and examining them to determine the extent of the damage.

May 5, 1997

I cannot believe I lost another journal. I have not stopped thinking about it. The best-case scenario is that it's at my mother's apartment. The worst is that someone who knows me found it. My hope is that if I did leave it on a bench at the beach and someone found it, that person immediately tossed it in a dumpster. Then, I like to think that Public Works emptied the trash today, and now, it's in a paper shredder of a recycling plant. First, though, I hope it got drenched in the torrential downpour last night.

May 6, 1997

I can't stop thinking about what's in the journal I lost. For me, the darkest secret in it was getting high before sunrise, along with the wild sexual fantasy I had. Now, I'm looking at what it means to bare one's soul. That journal could destroy me. I keep imagining all kinds of scenarios of who found it. My mind wanders.

May 9, 1997

Losing my journal was a biggie. The last time I wrote in it was right here last Sunday. A dream come true would be if big, loud Dennis handed it to me. I would be indebted to him forever. Of course, he could also use it to blackmail me, which is a scary thought—a chapter I hope never to write.

I went around asking people if they found my journal: the servers at Angelo's, some of the regulars on the Broadwalk, and Henry, the Public Works guy who cleans the beach picnic area. He told me he was upset that I had lost my journal.

May 30, 1997

Someone from Danny's apartment called me over and asked if, by any chance, I had lost a book I was writing in. He said some older man found it and asked Mike from the Riptide if he knew who it belonged to. Mike thought it might be mine and said he'd take it for me, but the guy wouldn't give it to him. I don't know if he still has it. This man who told me said he thought the guy may have left his number somewhere.

May 31, 1997

I went in search of my journal. Mike told me the man turned it in to a lifeguard, and so I went there first. After that, I walked over to the lifeguard headquarters, and they didn't have it. They took my number in case my journal turns up. I had imagined and visualized it to be there and was deeply disappointed to discover it wasn't. They called the lifeguard shack nearby, and it wasn't there either.

Later. The journal saga continues. The man who found it gave the lifeguard his number but not my journal. So, he may still have it. All hope is not lost. We'll see what happens, but I am greatly encouraged and will not give up on the idea.

June 6, 1997

I stopped at the lifeguard headquarters again today to see if anyone knew more about my journal or had the number of the man who found it. I was glad that Bob, the chief of the lifeguards, was there to get the whole story. He was kind and said he'd do whatever he could to get it back. After all my years here at Hollywood Beach, the lifeguards all know me as the woman who jogs and walks along the beach and then sits and writes.

June 15, 1997

No luck. My journal is gone forever, and with it, so is a chapter in my life. I'm devastated, but it's time for me to face the reality. I have no choice. I can only hope that no one I know found it, but by now, I think I'd know if they did.

June 16, 1997

As always, on the first Monday of our teacher institute, I introduced journaling. We want teachers to understand how helpful journal writing will be for them and their students when studying the Holocaust. It's a way for them to process their emotions and the difficult information they'll be exposed to.

September 21, 1997

The completion of my 250th journal passed with no fanfare or even mention to anyone. In two years and nine months, I finished fifty journals. That says something about how prolific I've been. And so, my story continues. It all goes down on paper and is locked away. The lives I touch and those that touch me remain forever as I record it all.

October 7, 1997

I've been waking myself up each day to get three morning pages written before I go out to run. This writing comes right from my sleep, so I am more in touch with my unconscious. Already, I am much more inclined to pluck out a dream from my memory banks. Melody Beattie says that's when we get to the edge of our super conscious — when the veil is thin.

October 19, 1997

I have moments when I wonder about my journals. Will they get me in trouble? Will they be subject to scrutiny? Julia Cameron says to show up on the page. She claims the best will come. What great insight might pour out of me? Or not? Where will the next moment take me, and what is my future? How can I make my life meaningful? It is what I strive to do. Fortunately, I find meaning in my work and my relationships. That seems to be the key. I need to translate that onto paper.

February 6, 1998

Someone from Donna Klein Academy asked me to do a kick-off journal writing session for the Holocaust unit they'll be studying. Unfortunately, with this being my busy time at the Holocaust Center, there's no way I can do it for them. It was flattering, though, to hear they consider me the journal expert and the one who could best introduce journaling to their students.

February 18, 1998

I still get excited when I begin a new journal. One would think that after all these years and volumes, it would become mundane. But instead, I look at the blank pages ahead with a sense of wonder. What will I end up writing across its pages? I wonder how I will live my life. What challenges will come my way? What surprises? What issues will I need to face and deal with? What will bring me happiness and sadness, frustration and peace?

May 4, 1998

I hope to choose excerpts from my experiences in Poland and Israel to include in a letter for others to read. I only filled one journal on this trip as opposed to two on the last one, but I'm sure I wrote more than anyone else.

Lots of people commented on my constant writing no matter where we were. At the airport yesterday, Risa's father said, "Since I didn't keep up with my journal, maybe I can get a photocopy of yours." I responded, "I don't think so!"

July 7, 1998

Journals that have pictures and words pre-printed on the pages are my least favorite. They get in the way—like the grasshopper at the bottom of this page. My favorite journals are still the ones that are thin-lined. Occasionally, I like to write in journals with no lines at all, but my writing is much smaller in those. As a result, I have noticed that some of my unlined journals have as much content as two lined journals.

August 29, 1998

I had no idea I was using a blue pen when I wrote last night's entry. We were in a restaurant, and while Daryl went out for a cigarette, I took advantage of the few minutes alone to get some thoughts down. It was dark, so I grabbed the first pen I dug out from my purse.

Seeing a different color now reminds me of when I wrote with peacock blue ink for years, but I've been on a black ink kick for a long time now. So, when I opened my journal this morning and saw blue ink, it looked strange to me.

October 2, 1998

I saw *A Soldier's Daughter Never Cries* today. It's about a boy who was adopted. His biological mother, who was fifteen when she was pregnant, kept a journal and gave it to his adoptive parents when she signed the official papers. In the end, he was given the journal to read—a meaningful gift, for sure.

March 7, 1999

This journal has taken me longer to fill than any in years. When I bought it for my birthday and began it at the end of December, I had no idea it would contain all it had. There has been a lot of shit in here—besides Daryl's stressful office move, even more difficult was his unexpected quadruple bypass. The good news is that he is alive and well. Thus, this journal is ending on a happy, positive note.

April 10, 1999

I still have more to say, so as I conclude this journal, I realize it will be continued—as it always is with each new journal I begin. Few ever have a neatly-tied bow on the package because my days flow from one to the next. Something is almost always carried over to the subsequent volume. At present, I am in limbo—a place I do not like to be—so the threads are dangling in every direction.

July 2, 1999

Gerry said she was telling someone what a prolific journal writer I am but then realized that prolific isn't a strong enough word to describe my writing. She also told me she's sure that because of my journal writing, I must know myself better than 99% of the people in the world. I would guess that's true of anyone who consistently keeps journals.

August 20, 1999

Josse and I spent time last night talking about journaling. She has been keeping journals for a while and is currently writing in one. I took her into Rebecca's room and opened the drawers of my safe so she could see my journals. I can't even imagine what they look like to someone who has never seen them before. Is it mind-boggling? I wonder how many people in the world have as extensive a collection of journals as mine.

December 1, 1999

Joan, who writes in journals constantly, told me she uses code, so no one but her will understand. She fears someone will read them, so she doesn't put everything down. Unfortunately, she doesn't have the privacy and safety to be blatantly honest on paper as I am.

December 12, 1999

In the middle of the night when I awoke, I was thinking about my 50th birthday and how I had completed two hundred journals by then. Here it is, my 55th, and I'm on #274 plus the few other morning page journals which I've filled. That's an average of fifteen a year—a significant number.

January 18, 2000

I don't even want to commit to paper some of the things Evelyn told me that no one else knows. I rarely hesitate to write something in my journal, but this is all so incredibly delicate it would be wiser to leave some of it unwritten and unspoken.

September 8, 2000

Recently, I've been having some uncomfortable feelings about my journals. I'm not sure I want Rebecca and Michael to read them after all. Hopefully, I have lots of years to make these decisions. I can't think of anything else in my life that has caused me to be so indecisive. Never have I changed my mind as many times as I have over what to do with my journals.

Part of the reason for this is because within the pages of my journals is my legacy. There's the yin and yang—that which I want Rebecca and Michael to have and that which I don't want them ever to read. So, at this point in my life, the dilemma remains. Someday in the future, I hope to read all my journals and decide based on what I discover—what is revealed, what speaks to me.

October 16, 2000

I'm facilitating a journal writing workshop in North Lauderdale. The prompt I've just given them is to write a dialogue between themselves and another person about an issue in their lives dealing with anger or an unresolved problem. I explained how it's like having a conversation with another person, but they have to be writing for both.

They're all busy writing away except for one man who is not in the flow. Instead, he's just sitting there staring at his paper. Since this is a valuable exercise, I wish I could get him to write, but I have no clue how to motivate him. In the meantime, it's time for me to write my dialogue.

November 19, 2000

Ted Koppel just mentioned he wished his grandfather and his great-grandfather had kept diaries so he would know what went on in their lives. I wish mine had as well.

May 14, 2001

We saw *Bridget Jones' Diary*, and I couldn't help but laugh. She was obsessed with her weight, diet, smoking, and drinking and recorded all those details daily.

It reminded me of my early journals when I recorded my weight and how far I jogged each day. It was important to me then but certainly is not anything I write about now.

July 20, 2001

Harriet talked about how she gets up two hours earlier, before anyone else in her house, so she can journal, meditate, and think—her centering time. She explained how her soul comes down on the page. I loved what she said and can relate, since this is why I got up early this morning.

August 14, 2001

May Sarton wrote that she only kept journals to be published at a later date. She explained she would never go through the hard work of keeping a journal otherwise. She believes that one who keeps a journal regularly (as I do) is narcissistic. I disagree with her about this. Don't writers use their lives as the basis for what they write? Don't we identify our universal truths and then find ways to share them with others? Perhaps some writers might be self-involved, but I consider the label of narcissistic to be harsh and unfair.

I might not always have gone as deep as I'm capable of, but I have committed my truth to the pages and continue to do so. Also, I am NOT writing these journals for publication. What happens to them later is yet another unanswered story.

November 2, 2001

I sent a journal to Sue Rosenblum, whose son was killed in the World Trade Center attack. I hope she'll find it somewhat helpful to write during this awful time.

November 16, 2001

My journals have a life of their own, and while in my possession, I'm in control—but only until I die, and then what? This is crazy, but here I go again.

December 8, 2001

Marsha and I talked about my will and the provision I've made for my journals. I told her I realized leaving journals to Rebecca and Michael would be a huge mistake. I've started to think about the possibility of destroying them. It was the first time I had said that out loud to anyone, but it seems my only solution. Burning them, while drastic, is the one way I can ensure they will be gone forever. Sadly, I am even considering this, but at the moment, I can't come up with a better alternative.

Would anyone ever understand the agony of this decision? It probably would seem crazy to someone else, but the truth is that my journals are my most significant possession and could be lethal in another person's hands. Ali recently suggested I have them buried with me in my grave when I die, but I'd probably need a double plot for that. I occasionally fantasize about someone discovering them a hundred years after I'm gone.

December 12, 2001

I have a lot to contemplate in terms of my writing, my journals, and what they mean to me. If I'm lucky, I have about thirty good years ahead of me to do something significant with them.

Once again, I've drafted a rewrite of my codicil. In it, I have requested that Adele, Marsha, and Lois extract my life lessons from my journals if I don't get it done before I die. This feels the most comfortable of any decisions I've made to date. Of course, I realize it would be an outrageous undertaking to ask of anyone. While each of them agreed to it, I am realistic and know I better get to work now.

December 28, 2001

I told the kids my decision about my journals. While we were having the conversation, there was a lot of joking around, which lightened up the discussion. They seemed okay with my not leaving the journals to them. Michael was bothered with my plan to have them burned after I die. Rebecca agreed with him on that. It was interesting to hear him object based on the book burning during the Holocaust. I don't love it either, but I don't know what other choices I have.

January 1, 2002

I took Michael to Bec's room and showed him my journals. He had never seen my collection in its entirety—drawer after drawer filled with colorful volumes of handwritten pages. I took out individual journals to show him. He wanted to see the one from when he and Sara got engaged. I knew exactly which one it was, since there are specific journals I can look at and know what's inside them.

It felt good to share it all with him. I'm happy I made my decision and told the kids, so I can move on from here. Knowing they will never read the actual journals completely frees me. FINALLY!!!

February 4, 2002

We talked about my journals at lunch, and Elisa begged me to promise her I wouldn't destroy them. She feels they'll be a valuable contribution to society someday. I let her know I can't promise that yet. It has been interesting to hear people's different ideas of what I should do with my journals.

May 18, 2002

Terry has begun journal writing, so we talked about the merits of that. She mentioned it's helping her get to know herself better. I'm always thrilled when someone begins to understand the value of journaling.

July 29, 2002

This morning pages volume goes back to January. So much has happened since then. I became a grandmother; Aemi and Steve moved away; I started volunteering with hospice; Daryl started to watch his diet; I began my massive journal project, and my life feels balanced and joyful.

September 30, 2002

Carolyn thought all journals I've written were quite an accomplishment and said it was something to be proud of. I don't think of my journaling in that way. It has naturally evolved out of my need to record my life, which I still don't completely understand.

December 28, 2002

When I am in my morning routine of journaling, walking, and meditating, I am much more centered, at peace, and mindful. My goal is to keep at this schedule and allow for it daily.

If someone were to ask me to describe my journals, I would say they're one woman's journey of self-improvement, growth, understanding, and exploration. My writing is primarily about how I live and negotiate life around me, what I think and feel about my relationships, my work, and my life in general.

June 26, 2003

Since Miami Dade Public Schools requires a project at the end of the institute for the teachers to get professional teaching credits, we thought the most meaningful assignment would be to have them journal during or after each day's session. I was moved by the emotions the teachers expressed and was impressed with their insights. I can't help but wonder if any of them will start to journal now, since none had before this. I wish I had thought to tell them to make copies to give to us so they could keep their original writing. Big mistake on my part!

July 16, 2003

I have been journaling more lately. It helps me cope with the ever-present pain I'm experiencing with Cookie being so ill.

March 17, 2004

Anaïs Nin kept journals since she was a young child. I've been reading one of her diaries, which is how she referred to them. In more recent years, a shift has occurred from labeling diaries to journals. I was curious, so I looked up both words.

The word diary comes from the Latin word *diarum* and journal from the root *diurnus*. Diaries are more a record of daily events, while journals include an exploration of ideas and feelings. I almost always write in complete sentences. Anaïs Nin uses phrases at times.

She is analytical, and I think I am too. She writes using more descriptive words; while I tend to use fewer adjectives and adverbs, thus hers is much more poetic. My writing style is simpler than her flowery one. We both write from our hearts.

She claimed that her life without her journal writing would be like a snail without its shell. I can relate to that. I've often thought that if I were on a deserted island, I would be fine as long as I had my journal and a pen. And if I didn't, I'd still be okay because I just would write in the sand.

I always have a journal with me and write no matter where I am — in line at the grocery store, stopped at a railroad crossing or a drawbridge, stuck in bumper-to bumper traffic, at Miami Book Fair taking notes, sitting at my desk on my lunch hour, and under a tree at the beach. Anaïs Nin carried her journal everywhere and wrote in cafés, on buses and trains, during lectures, and on trips.

She didn't write in her diaries to publish them. She wrote to explore her inner life, like most of us who keep journals do. It was in the sixties that she made the risky decision to share her journals with the public. According to what I read, she edited out much of the details of her romantic relationships.

February 20, 2005

On the day I became a grandmother last March, I began writing in a journal for Sophia. I've continued to do so and think it'll be a special gift for her someday. If nothing else, I encourage grandparents to at least get grandparent books they can fill out for their grandchildren as my parents did.

June 3, 2005

As I was going through the drawers in my safe, I took note of the beautiful collection of journals I have. Recently, I have been writing in plain, college-lined spiral notebooks to conserve space since my safe is filling up.

November 14, 2005

I finished my 300th journal today, not including the many volumes of morning pages.

January 4, 2008

Even though I might write ad nauseam about the same issue over and over again, at some point, I get to a place where I have integrated and understood my thoughts. It is helpful for me to digest, absorb, understand, and know.

April 30, 2008

In this journal, what sticks out as highlights were my cousins' visit while I was in Cleveland. Whether it's the mundane day-to-day happenings, the painful stuff with my brother, or this newest happening with my mother going into hospice because of her "failure to thrive," it's all here — recorded to revisit someday.

April 10, 2009

I honestly don't know how I would survive if I didn't have my journals to write in. I best express myself through journaling and let my feelings come out from that dark pit between my stomach and throat. Today, I feel vulnerable and afraid.

May 7, 2009

While I rarely talk to people on a plane, this time I did since the woman next to me was writing in a journal. She told me how she's been keeping journals since her parents got divorced many years ago. She explained how she worries about her writing because her grammar isn't great. The teacher in me couldn't resist. I told her a journal is the one place where punctuation and grammar don't matter. While that's true, I'm still pretty fanatical about both.

February 14, 2010

I spoke to Dan about his journal writing, which he's been doing since 1982. He shared how he works through emotional issues in his journals. I asked him if he had gone back and read them. He hasn't, but he has kept all of them from high school on and said he plans to someday.

December 26, 2010

There are times when I know exactly where my thoughts are going and what I want to put down on paper. Other times, I write something without having any idea what's coming next. It's like an out-of-body experience where I am trusting in something that is in control of my pen.

It used to happen when I was high, but it's certainly not that now. Maybe it's just my faith in knowing there is something that's guiding me along this path and is helping me to get down thoughts I didn't even know I had.

January 23, 2011

The woman from the Women's Jewish Archives, whom I met at the TED conference, talked to me about donating my journals to them. I'm not even sure I would want to, but the thought did appeal to me. Since she hasn't responded, it's no longer an issue. While I know 100% that I don't want to leave them to anyone, more and more, the idea of destroying them sounds awful to me. I am left with this quandary.

January 29, 2011

My cousin Raven keeps journals, and right before New Year's, she reads those she's filled during the past twelve months. After that, she creates a ceremony for herself, destroys the journals, and moves on. Maybe I could do something like that someday with my journals.

March 19, 2011

I shared an entry from long ago with all the Peikens and Sandbergs about having them here for Rosh Hashanah and noticing how the kids were interested in the adult conversation for the first time. The response I got back from Michelle was that it makes her want to keep a journal. I wrote back encouraging her to do so. Since she responded that she thinks she will, I sent her a journal. I'm always happy when I inspire someone to begin journaling.

December 9, 2011

The woman sitting next to me was writing in a journal most of the time we were in the air. When she took off her headphones toward the end of the trip, I asked if she had kept journals for a long time. The woman told me she began journaling when she first found out she was pregnant with child number one. She has six children and lots of grandchildren and writes strictly for all of them.

January 1, 2012

I bought this large, thick journal several months ago, especially for this day. Not only is it a new year, but it also marks the beginning of a new life for me as a full-time writer. It's fitting to start with a purple journal covered with butterflies. Just looking at it brings me joy.

May 14, 2012

Writing in my journal is the only place I can express a thought that is rambling around in my mind—something I could never share with anyone because it's either outrageous, self-centered, or shameful. This is a place to say it all—my safe spot and the best one I could ever dream of having.

August 19, 2012

I'm closing in on the end of this big, thick journal that I've been writing in since January 1. It has been quite a journey—certainly an important chapter in my life. It's filled with the beginning of my retirement, my mother's death, and the writing of *Room 732*—some huge, life-changing events.

October 14, 2014

Some days I feel compelled to write in my journal as if I have no choice. On those days, I could go on and on for hours at a time. On other rare days, I have little desire or need to write. The truth is that today for me, it's the latter.

January 1, 2016

I look at the blank pages in this journal and know they'll be filled with who I am and how I'm living my life. One day this will be yet another chapter. What I know for sure is that journaling is the greatest gift I've given myself.

Reflections on
Journey of Journaling

As I reflect on all I've written, many thoughts surface. Throughout these years, this journey has been an intensely personal one. Sure, people knew that I kept journals. Many would see me at the beach under a palm tree writing, but it wasn't something that I spoke much about. On occasion, I would have a conversation with someone who journaled or who was interested in beginning this practice. Once in a while, I would facilitate a journal workshop. Each year during our teacher institutes at the Holocaust Center, I helped teachers understand the importance of having them and their students write in journals as they studied the Holocaust. However, for the most part, my journaling was a private endeavor.

The first time I publicly did anything associated with journaling was in 2017, when I attended the National Association for Poetry Therapy and co-facilitated a workshop with Dr. Beth Jacobs, a dedicated journal writer. The topic we chose was *Preserving or Dismantling: What to do with those old journals?* As a result of that experience, Kay Adams, the founder of Journalverse and the host of the *Live with Kay* podcast, interviewed Beth and me about our journal projects that we were each working on.

In 2018, Beth asked me if I would be interested in serving on the council of the International Association for Journal Writing (IAJW). At the time, I did not know what IAJW did, but it intrigued me. I spoke to Lynda Monk, the incoming director of the association, and agreed to become a council member, which was comprised of experts in the world of journaling. I was flattered to be included.

From that moment on, my life as a journal writer became less private and more public as I am now part of a journaling community. Through IAJW, I join together with people across the globe who share my same passion.

Early on, Lynda asked me to facilitate one of the IAJW's journal circles and also conducted an interview with me entitled *Reflections of a Lifetime Through Journaling*. That was the beginning of my journal world expanding in ways I never dreamed it would. For the past three years, I have been attending monthly IAJW writing circles on Zoom and bi-annual council meetings where we gather and share information about our work, resources, and so much more.

Also, in 2019, Rebecca Kochenderfer interviewed me for her podcast, *The Power of Journaling*. The title of that interview was *Discover Legacy Journaling*, which is what I consider my journal project (this book and the next one) to be.

Toward the end of March 2020, just as we were hunkering down and sheltering in place, I received calls from the Greater Miami Jewish Federation and Gilda's Club of South Florida. Both asked if I would facilitate journaling circles online for each of their organizations. I was also asked to do journaling sessions with Campowerment, an organization founded by my friend Tammi Leader Fuller, which provides women with the opportunity to learn, connect, and grow to be their best selves.

I readily agreed to all three because I knew that journaling during the time of COVID would be helpful and meaningful to those who chose to do it. Since then, I've been meeting weekly with one of the groups and occasionally with the other two. As I write this, one journaling circle is about to join together for our 95th week of writing in community. It brings me great joy to know I've inspired individuals to journal.

I have been thinking about the conversation I had with the man at the beach in 1989 how the poet MacLeish claimed that by the year 2000, few would be writing letters or keeping journals. For sure, I have proved that theory wrong. I still do both and probably always will.

Losing those two journals left me feeling sad and concerned. Although I never put my name in any of my journals, the regulars at the beach would know who they belonged to. Had they ended up in the wrong hands, it might have been a disaster. At some point, I needed to accept both losses and let them go. While I write that now, I must admit that in some ways, it was like losing a chapter in my life.

When I read over these excerpts on the *Journey of Journaling*, I was struck by my process of deciding what to do with my journals after I die. I wondered if a reader might have found me to be incredibly indecisive. However, as I consider it from my current perspective, it makes sense that this decision was such a difficult one.

While my journals hold many thoughts for my eyes only, they are also filled with pieces of my life which I want to leave behind for this and future generations. And so, it took me a long time to figure out how I could use my journals to bestow my legacy to my loved ones and beyond.

Journal Prompts

For those who already journal:
- In what way has journaling helped you?
- What might you be afraid to write in a journal for fear someone would read it? What can you do to ensure that they won't?
- I find that when I journal, I . . .
- How do you feel after you have written about something difficult? What changes within you?

For beginning journalers:
- In what way do you think writing in a journal might be helpful?
- When I think about writing in a journal, I . . .
- If I open myself up to writing, I might . . .
- After reading the Journey of Journaling, I . . .

Prompts for everyone:
- Who am I? Who am I not? Who do I want to be?
- What do you do with secrets people share with you?
- What issues do you need to face and deal with?
- What brings you happiness? Peace? Joy?
- Before I sat down to write today, I . . .
- As I put my pen to paper, I . . .

Joining the Workforce

Whatever you decide to do, make sure it makes you happy.

— Nelson Mandela

January 27, 1976

I've been toying with the idea of getting a job but haven't found anything which interests me. Unless I am doing something challenging or meaningful, I doubt that I would ever be happy.

If I had my choice of any job, at this point, I'm not even sure what I'd want to do. The idea of going back to teaching keeps floating through my mind.

September 6, 1977

I'm excited to begin teaching again and am more than ready. It'll be a completely different experience for me since I'll be with two-and-a-half-year-old children. While I love being home with Rebecca and Michael, I've needed more of a daily commitment and stimulation outside of the house. It'll be helpful to be on the same schedule and at the same preschool as Michael.

December 29, 1977

Temple Sinai's two-week winter camp is over. They had asked me to organize and run it, and now I've been asked to direct Camp Sinai over the summer. While I've never done anything like that, I'm up for the challenge. From what I understand, last summer's camp had around fifty kids. I have no idea how many will register this year.

May 19, 1978

Teaching nursery school at Temple Sinai has been a far cry from elementary school—mainly because the children are still so young. I'm glad I am moving up to a pre-kindergarten class in the fall, although I did enjoy those little ones.

Now, I'm knee-deep in planning for the start of camp. My focus has shifted from teacher to director, which means I'll become "boss" to my colleagues. Since we're all friends, I don't anticipate any issues, but it could become tricky at times. My goal is to make camp fun for everyone, including the staff.

August 12, 1978

Since I had no prior experience in administration, this has been a summer of firsts. Being organized helped the camp run smoothly. Luckily, from day one, I have had everything well under control without much stress.

Barbara, who is the executive director of Temple Sinai, and Leslie, who is chairperson of the camp committee, took me out to lunch one day in the early part of the summer. I was working much longer hours than I had expected. They told me I was doing a fantastic job and gave me a $50 weekly raise after taxes—retroactive two weeks before camp began. I never expected that.

Working with the parents in this capacity has been enlightening and, at times, disheartening. From them, I have learned so much—mostly good but not all. Sadly, I discovered one woman who hates being a mother and doesn't think twice about telling others. Another mother called to find out why her son, "who is such a bastard," in her words, won a good camper award. Seriously? Another parent never once all summer picked up her child on time. It was miserable for her poor son, who was always the last to leave—long after all the other campers had gone home. It infuriated me, and no matter what I said to the mother, it made no difference. I believe it's pure selfishness to be late each day and not show any consideration for others.

I have grown to love being a part of Temple Sinai. My staff of high school and college students as well as several teachers whom I had previously worked with felt the atmosphere was a comfortable one. Consequently, it was easy to continue being their friend.

I fired two people—a new and challenging experience for me. Since I knew it was for the betterment of the camp, I did what I had to do. I was nervous at first but immediately felt better when it was over.

One was a teenager who was outspoken and didn't seem to be enjoying her job. Because of her poor attitude, no one liked her. Plus, she made life difficult for those she worked with.

The other counselor turned sour on his campers and became mean to them. After firing him, I went to his group of ten-year-old boys and gave them a few messages I hope they'll remember. One was that even if they are young, their feelings count. I wanted them to know we honored them by letting go of their counselor, who was not kind.

I also told them if they're having problems with someone, as I discovered they were with this counselor, they need to share it with an adult rather than keep it inside. I encouraged them not to harbor negative feelings. I also stressed that camp should be fun.

June 28, 1979

After a long day with lots of demands, I got a call tonight from a camper's mother. She was upset because her son came home with his bathing suit on under his shorts. Needless to say, I was not happy and could hardly believe that would merit a phone call to me at home after camp hours. The woman needs to get a life if this is all she thinks about. After that call, I told Daryl I didn't want to talk to anyone else, regardless of who called. That mother put me over the edge!

August 17, 1979

Camp has been the best working experience in my life. I've made every effort to create a closeness among the staff and establish a lively-spirited, joyful environment. Seeing the children playing and watching the counselors also enjoying themselves thrills me.

In reflecting on this summer, I faced a significant challenge. When I found out that one of the junior counselors was stealing not just money but food, jewelry, and even clothing, the clergy and synagogue administration advised me to fire her immediately. However, with the tremendous support of Aaron Podhurst, the temple president, who told me he would back me regardless of how I chose to handle the situation, I went with my gut. I called in the girl's mother and spoke to her—not as a professional but as mother to mother. I allowed her daughter to stay with the provision that she went for counseling.

I let her remain at camp because she is young, and I felt she could be helped. Even though others tried to convince me otherwise, I'm glad I followed my instincts.

From that point on, the mother kept checking in with me and telling me how her daughter's therapy was progressing. I told her there was no need to share that with me, but to her, it was necessary. My only disappointment was that neither the girl's parents nor the therapist made her return what she had stolen, which would have helped her learn an important lesson. Perhaps I should have made it the other stipulation for the teen to remain working at camp. That was my mistake.

Once again, all summer long, the most challenging part was dealing with some of the parents. Often, I disagreed with how they thought and felt about a situation. Yet, I was able to listen to them and react in the best way possible. All the while, I worked hard not to judge them. At times, I was frustrated by certain women who coddled their children and were unreasonable in their requests.

I have gotten excellent feedback from the community. I know I've done a good job because Camp Sinai has become a happy place to be for campers and counselors alike. Our numbers this year were up to two hundred and fifty campers from eighty-five last year.

August 19, 1979

My camp job was ideal. I worked hard on it for a total of eight months, including camp itself. Now the rest of the year, I can do everything else I enjoy.

The perfect climax to this summer was the staff pool party. Within fifteen minutes of its start, everyone was wild with water guns and water balloons galore. Each of us got thrown in the pool multiple times. We were like kids at play. I noticed a few temple administrators and one older counselor standing off to the side watching. I made the decision right then, never to be like that. When having a choice to play or be serious, I would much rather be young at heart. The next day, one of the women told me she felt so old that night. It did not have to be like that.

Daryl joined right in with the fun. Barbara let me know she'd like to have him as a head counselor. For sure, it would probably be more fun than taking care of people's feet all day — although he loves what he does.

The moving part of the evening was when the staff presented me with a lovely director's chair with my name on the back. They also gave me a huge card which they signed with notes. As I read what they wrote, I began to realize the impact I had had on them. Throughout the summer, I did my best not to act like a boss but gently and firmly let them know what I expected of each one.

I loved the staff meetings every Monday morning when we gathered and talked — a time we learned, shared, and became a cohesive group. Of course, safety was always the first item of business. With the pool and field trips, I needed to stay on top of that and remind them camper safety is paramount. The meetings themselves set the tone for the week.

January 17, 1980

Camp planning has begun — something which I genuinely love. Besides the meetings, I like the idea of creating and planning. At yesterday's meeting, they offered me $4,125, which is a decent raise from last year.

February 29, 1980

I am excited about camp and am amazed at the feelings I experience when I face a good challenge and constant decision-making. I know the camp will be bigger and even better than last year. We just opened registration and already have over one hundred campers with one of the groups filled. This is a big step for us. Only two years ago when I began, we were hoping for one hundred campers in total.

The interview process is one of my favorite things to do. I love meeting all the teens and college students and learning about them and their lives. I'm almost done hiring everyone and have lots of repeat counselors, which should make for an easy summer.

I always chuckle to myself when I hire guys who are over six feet tall. At the interview, I jokingly tell each one that if I need to speak to them, they're going to have to get down to my level—eye to eye!

June 11, 1980

With camp only a few days away, I'm looking forward to another great summer. One of my goals is to connect to everyone on the staff and get to know them well.

June 14, 1980

Yesterday was the staff orientation at camp. From the moment we began, I knew I was doing what I love best.

On Thursday, I went to an employment agency just to see what the world out there was like. The woman I met with advised me to buy a suit and become more sophisticated with my clothing, jewelry, and shoes. She described corporate work as a dog-eat-dog world. It all sounded rather unappealing, competitive, and not for me. I can't imagine what I will be doing in the fall, but I don't plan to teach preschool anymore.

June 16, 1980

I had to fire someone today. One of the groups walked over to Greynolds Park. There were eighteen campers and three counselors, so they divided up into three subgroups. About an hour and a half after they left, the CIT from the group strolled by my office. I went out to ask where the rest of his group was, and he casually mentioned he had left them at the park. What the hell? I was outraged and horrified to think that he left his little group of seven-year-old campers completely unsupervised. I immediately gathered a few others to run over to Greynolds with me to find the six campers. Fortunately, the young ones were sitting on the hill, but until we found them, I was a wreck.

As soon as I got back to camp, I told the CIT to leave for good. Then tonight, as I was just settling down, my doorbell rang. It was the CIT's mother who brought along her friend, a bus driver for Miami Dade Public Schools. For whatever reason, she must have thought the woman might have some clout. They tried to convince me to rehire the teen, but that wasn't going to happen. It was not a comfortable moment, and I wasn't thrilled they were in my living room. I let the mother know her son is just too immature to be responsible for other children. Truthfully, he acted more like a kid than the seven-year-old campers in his group.

July 10, 1980

The only downside to camp this year has been personnel problems within the groups. My biggest challenge is getting counselors to talk to one another when they have an issue. Today, I had a session with a counselor my age (thirty-six) and a thirteen-year-old CIT and helped them communicate with each other. After we finished, the older one told me she had learned more about communication in the past two weeks than she had learned all her life.

Some overprotective mothers hang out by the fence, hoping to catch a glimpse of their darlings. I stand firm in my policy of keeping the parents out. I'm doing my best to be kind and understanding, but it's hard. Over a carpool issue today, I had one mother roll up her window in my face and later slam the phone down when I called her. Obviously, she's used to getting her way. Eventually, I called back, got her to listen, and worked through the issue, but that was a tough one.

All day, there were minor problems. A counselor came running into my office because a camper fell, cut his head, and was bleeding. Someone else ran in yelling and begged me to come to kill a big daddy-long-legs spider creeping around in her room. Another camper threw up during lunch. And if all that wasn't enough, between the peacocks screaming and squawking all day long and staff constantly calling out my name for one reason or another, I was done in.

A little while ago when I got home from camp, I told Rebecca and Michael they were not to disturb me unless someone was dying. I went one step further and told them to tell Daryl not to come into the bedroom when he got home. I let them know I'd be out in time to make dinner. So, I shut my door, took the phone off the hook, and am sitting on my bed decompressing in the best way I know how with my journal in hand.

August 2, 1980

Seven weeks down—one to go! This has been a tremendously successful summer, with all three hundred and fifty campers and the staff of seventy-five having a good time. I knew it would be good on June 14th when we had our staff orientation. The former counselors seemed happy to be back, and the new ones were enthusiastic and ready to go.

One of the head counselors, who is loud, obnoxious, and a bully, unbeknownst to me, was constantly picking on his junior counselor, a shy, sensitive, fifteen-year-old boy. The poor kid came into my office this week in tears—his confidence shattered. I sat with him for hours and helped him feel better about himself and learn from the experience. The counselor will not be coming back for the remainder of camp.

Also, this year, I have had to work with counselors, helping them in the area of discipline. Some are quick to lose their tempers with the campers—probably handling the behavior issues as their parents did with them. My goal is to have them discipline with a positive approach. It takes more work, but it beats yelling and punishing. For sure, whistles are out of the question. Some would be blowing them all day long.

August 3, 1980

I have accepted a job at Temple Or Olom as the director of their nursery school. I met with the school board, and after one interview, they hired me.

Because it was so close to the start of the school year, I immediately began to dive in and get busy preparing for the first day of school. Last week and the week before, I would come home from camp, clean the house, make dinner, and then immediately sit down to prepare for my new job. The pressure of working round the clock mounted, and I felt as if I was about to explode. As a result, I've had to put off the school work until I finish camp. Yesterday was the first time I found a few minutes to journal, which is most unusual.

August 22, 1980

Camp ended in a beautiful and successful way. Our reputation has become widespread. I love that I made both young and old friends, and everyone left as happy campers.

September 6, 1980

At Kol Nidre services Friday night, Aaron Podhurst got up and gave the annual president's address to the synagogue. He began by talking about the rabbis. From there, he said something like, "I can't forget about little Merle Saferstein, who is sitting right up front." He continued talking about me and the camp program which I've established. He raved about it, saying how it's the best of its kind. He mentioned that we have a waiting list and how it's like a school in a camp where so much good is taught. His kindness touched me. On Rosh Hashanah, he had personally told me that he has never heard of a camp, except ours, where there is only positive to be said about it. Several people over the weekend commented about my being a celebrity—"little Merle" is now my nickname around Sinai.

September 7, 1980

My first week as nursery school director ended, and it was strange. I'm a figurehead with almost no impact on the functioning of the school. Some of the staff, who have been there forever, resisted any suggestions I made. Mainly, I laid low and blended into the walls, wearing beige. It isn't easy to be the new girl on the block, especially when some teachers are my mother's age.

I need to break in gently and be patient. In time, the staff will learn who I am and see what I can do to enhance the program. It desperately needs changes and some new blood.

October 8, 1980

I'm so pissed! In the last few weeks, it has felt like there's a beehive in the school. Periodically, I would hear murmurs of what seemed like gossip. Occasionally, I'd see two teachers off in a corner on the playground whispering. Someone was stirring the pot. It has taken me a while to figure out who the culprit is. Now that I finally have, when I get to school, I will tackle the situation.

Later. I arrived at school armed and ready for confrontation, something I would rather run from. Yet, as the administrator, it's my role to handle situations like this. I called Dee in for a meeting as soon as I walked in the door—unfortunately, later than I wanted, but the traffic was brutal.

The conversation was not easy; however, I had decided I had no choice but to make sure her behavior stopped immediately. There is no room for that in our school. She immediately got defensive and denied she was the one starting rumors. Luckily for me, I caught her in a few lies—enough that it was apparent she had been the one who was causing the buzzing among the staff and eventually had no choice but to admit it. She now knows I have zero tolerance for her actions. I'll be paying close attention.

November 4, 1980

This year has been the busiest of my life, going from camp into the nursery school job. Plus, starting back to school to renew my teaching certificate has come at the worst time. Suddenly, I have this added pressure of writing papers, studying, and taking tests. I thought beginning my master's degree in educational administration made sense, but it's challenging and a lot of busywork.

November 14, 1980

Fortunately, my job at Or Olom is going well. I am slowly bringing sunshine into the school. A few teachers are still resisting, but I fight for what I want and get it when it's important. For instance, many put up the same bulletin boards they've used for probably ten or more years. I can tell by the holes from all the thumbtacks, so now they are expected to add one completely new bulletin board each month. This means their rooms will look much fresher in four months.

January 11, 1981

Last week, I had a meeting with the board at Temple Or Olom, followed by a meeting with the staff and the board combined. The teachers desperately deserve salary increases but have never asked, since it didn't occur to them. I made sure to position myself at the head of the table for the meeting. I paved the way and stood up to the board. It consists of all men, who were probably shocked to see how prepared and in control I was. They considered my points, and the staff will receive hefty raises. The teachers can't believe it!

April 9, 1981

Being an administrator is not always easy. Some mothers make unrealistic demands and have expectations that make no sense. A few are petty. Still, others try to play games with me, which I refuse to do. On the flip side, for the most part, I am enjoying my relationships with the parents.

This week, one mother caused a stink over buying a Passover item for the school *seder*. Her problem was the item the teacher asked her daughter to bring in was $1.50 more than someone else's. I wonder if I will ever get beyond some of these parents' demands and *mishegas*.

Because I am indirectly responsible for their children's education and pleasure, I want to do it right. My goal is to bring order to the school, create a loving and educational atmosphere, and make sure each child is happy.

June 8, 1981

I just finished my first year at Temple Or Olom. It went well, especially considering the circumstances. Some teachers continued to fight change up through the middle of the year. The parents gradually opened up and showed their acceptance of me. The school needed refreshing, which is what I provided. The year has passed, and I learned how important it is to be patient and give people time to adjust to a different way.

July 10, 1981

This week our campers played soccer against a JCC team and won 10-1. Our boys were great. On Wednesday, another team from the JCC was supposed to play them, but they canceled. So instead, our female counselors played against our boys' team. The campers put up a good battle, but the counselors were hellbent on winning and did.

Some kids went all out for polka dot day and covered themselves with dots from head to toe, reminding me of a chicken pox outbreak. Last week was clown day. I'll have to come up with something different for next week. I'm trying to be original, but it's getting a bit old already after all these years.

The field trips this week were fun for all. The Seaquarium, Omni Amusements, and Venetian Pool seemed to be the most popular. The little ones loved the pony rides. After each excursion, what matters most to me is that the buses come back to camp with every camper safe and happy.

October 9, 1981

Ruth asked me if I ever wrote anything negative in any of their lesson plan books. Jean answered, "Sure, she tells me to be more specific." Sylvia said, "She only gives constructive criticism." I told them I aimed to be positive and teach them as best I could. I see their plan books as the vehicle to accomplish what they must and help a substitute when the teacher calls in sick.

Mr. Boytar, my principal at Adrian Elementary School, was a stickler for complete lesson plans. I learned from him.

November 1, 1981

We had an open house this week. I had written a speech but instead talked from my heart when I got up in front of everyone. I spoke from parent to parent rather than as an administrator, and my remarks were more passionate than I had planned them to be.

November 12, 1981

Today, I took over Ruth's class for a while and later Bonnie's just to give them a break and allow me to get to know the children better. I figure that relating to them personally is the best way to accomplish that.

It didn't take long to remember what drove me away from teaching three and four-year-old children. They're darling and sweet, but their chatter and noise level are over the top. The one positive is that I haven't lost my love for children and for teaching them.

November 27, 1981

Last week, Gloria called to tell me the school board recommended we have one additional week of school. Evidently, three parents had complained that we would be ending the school year too early.

I was furious that the board excluded me from negotiations and discussions on the subject. Yesterday, I wrote a letter to the board members in which I expressed my feelings regarding the unprofessional way they handled this issue.

Then I met with the teachers—some of whom didn't want to make waves but didn't want the extra week of teaching. I told them we need to stand up for what's right, so I intend to do just that.

December 11, 1981

Yesterday I received a call from one of the board members. They want me at a meeting next Tuesday night, which means I have to drive the twenty-five miles in the a.m., go back home for a camp meeting in the afternoon, drive carpools, shop, and then go back down to Temple Or Olom at night. It wouldn't be so bad if I didn't have our big *Chanukah* program at school on Wednesday, with the teachers' luncheon at my house following that. What a week ahead I have!

December 17, 1981

My meeting with the board turned out to be positive. I took the position that I was in charge and should be included in the decision-making process. They need to know they can no longer bulldoze me. I have learned how to handle these business issues in a polite but professional manner. When I encounter a hassle, all I want is to go off to the beach and write, but I knew I needed to fight for what was right.

I feel confident that I know what I'm doing and intend to take advantage of that in pursuing a new job. As much as I enjoy working at the preschool, the long drive on the Palmetto Expressway to the temple and back in traffic has gotten old. I need something closer to home.

January 29, 1982

A lot of shit has been going on around camp so far. There have been a few mothers who went to Barbara during registration with suggestions. One woman had the nerve to tell her she tried to talk to me at Publix, but I didn't respond well. It burns my ass because she made that up. I never even saw her.

February 8, 1982

My letter of resignation to the board at Temple Or Olom is in the mail. I plan to have a meeting Friday morning with the teachers to help them process it all. I have a feeling it won't be easy for them. My gurgling stomach and edgy nerves will feel much better when this is over. It's a big step to resign, yet, a necessary one. The drive has done me in, and besides, professionally, I'm ready to move on.

February 12, 1982

I am happy with how I handled the Temple Or Olom situation in a straightforward, honest way. I went to each teacher individually and shared my thoughts and feelings about my leaving, and then the entire staff met. They were understanding but expressed hating to see me go. I promised to work hard to help make the transition with a new director as smooth as possible.

February 27, 1982

It's time for me to look ahead and think about what comes next. I have until the end of summer because I'll be busy with camp. However, once September comes, I want to be situated in a new job. Since I am good at organizing, maybe I can work with people to get their lives in order. I wonder what it would take to become a professional organizer.

March 4, 1982

I had a good camp meeting. I hired the art and music counselors, so most of the staff is now in place. My salary for camp will be $5,825. Registration is going exceptionally well.

March 10, 1982

Our *Purim* program was this morning. The children sang so well and looked adorable dressed in their costumes. I'm always glad when these programs come together. The part I don't like for the children's sake is the extensive rehearsing. I feel they could spend their time in more productive ways, but this is what the parents are used to and want. They like to see their children on stage performing.

March 21, 1982

Leslie told me Barbara is worried that I might not come back to camp next year. All I said was, "She should be. I may be moving on." This very well could be my last summer.

March 27, 1982

The state attorney's office called in response to the resume I sent them. Based on the ad in the paper, I might be a good fit for the position. The woman I spoke with seemed interested in me and said the job was for rewriting procedures and training new personnel. It was the most exciting phone call I have received in a while.

April 21, 1982

School has been a hassle this week, starting with our salary meeting with the board Monday night. The teachers were infuriated with the five percent increment, and I don't blame them. It isn't equitable considering their hours have been increased. I'm happy they have finally learned to stand up for themselves and realize their worth. I'm supporting them in their fight for what they deserve. Perhaps if the board had a few women on it, things might be different.

April 22, 1982

Today I had an interview at a private high school with the principal, Mr. Harris. I felt more like the interviewer than the interviewee. Because of how often I interview individuals for camp positions, I've become a natural. I was completely in control the entire time.

By the end of our meeting, his words were something like, "I can definitely see a place for you here." He told me to go home and write my goals and objectives for what I'd like to accomplish at the school. I'm not sure exactly what the position would entail, but I believe a job there is possible.

Public relations might be one of the areas they would want me to take over. They're in dire need of someone who can "sell" the school to parents of prospective students. Since it's only been in existence for almost two years, they desperately need publicity.

April 24, 1982

I've been busy all week at school, plus I had several camp interviews. I hired all my staff and now need to work on planning the schedule and grouping the campers. I go from one thing to the next without much of a break. Today was a full day. I interviewed someone at Or Olom to replace me.

May 7, 1982

The teachers made a lovely goodbye luncheon for me at Jean's house—lively and fun. We sat out by the canal and chatted while they all drank lots of wine. They bought me a dainty gold bracelet, and each wrote a touching poem as a farewell. I cried when I told Daryl about it. I'll miss them but not the drive to the school.

May 15, 1982

Another teacher turned in her resignation today. That means two are leaving with a possible third who might also be going. Ruth is upset that no one is displaying any loyalty, but hers is stronger than most people I know.

May 18, 1982

I finally reached the principal at the high school. We spoke for a while, and Mr. Harris made it clear he wanted me to work there. He indicated there are definite areas in which he needs administrative help. In return, I laid out my thoughts and let him know I wanted contact with the teenagers. I also said I didn't want to work on Fridays, and he was okay with that.

When I go in on June 9th, I will know better what he has in mind for me. I just have to decide if it's what I'd like to do. Again, it's an educational setting in which I'm comfortable. There could be a possibility for growth and learning.

Like any job I tackle, it doesn't have to be forever. I could never lock myself into one spot unless I'm doing something I love. The only "forevers" I want in my life are Daryl and the kids, writing, and the ocean.

May 23, 1982

I wonder how it will be working with Mr. Harris. The high school might offer me enough of a challenge that I could leave camp. I feel ready to move on after five years.

Today, the new director for the preschool came to see the school in operation. She asked lots of questions and listened carefully to all I shared. I don't know how she'll do, but hopefully the teachers will like her. I felt strange thinking about being replaced.

The dinner the board made me was pleasant. They gave me a ceramic bag with an inscription on the bottom. Each board member also wrote sweet thoughts about how they admire me, so I'm leaving on a positive note. Someone once told me it's always best to leave the party while you're still having fun.

May 26, 1982

I've decided I will call Mr. Harris on Monday morning and ask to see him. I want the job but need specific details, which he has not given me yet. I'm feeling excited inside, knowing what possibilities lie ahead.

May 27, 1982

Today was the end of one phase of my career. After two years, I completed my tenure at Or Olom. I hope to spend some time reflecting on the day, the year, and my feelings.

We had a "Small World" graduation program. I watched the little kindergarteners, each one glowing with pride, as they marched down the aisle in their caps and gowns. It's a tradition they've had at the school since its beginning.

I hadn't planned on giving a goodbye speech, but once I got up there, I knew I wanted to say something. I thought about what it all meant—an end and a new beginning—and shared that with the parents. Each little accomplishment becomes a momentous occasion in a child's life.

I asked them to look back at their own lives as children and think about what it meant for them to either have their parents or not at their side. I encouraged them to be present at their children's significant events as they move forward—that this is the beginning and establishes a precedent for sharing in the future.

Then I introduced Eleanor, the new director, trying to make the transition as pleasant and positive as possible. I am hopeful they'll embrace her as they eventually did me.

Each of the teachers, the people in the temple, Rabbi Rudy, Leona, Shirley, and even Steve, the custodian, bid me a fine farewell. The parents told me they were sad to see me go, but each wished me life's best. I was feeling upbeat as mothers and fathers expressed their heartfelt feelings. Over and over, I heard how I infused spirit into the school. I kept listening, smiling, and even shed a few tears.

One parent told me she would miss the "casualness and comfortableness of my regime." I did my best to set an example and show up. I made myself available to teachers, parents, and students. Part of my philosophy is that each person, no matter how big or small, counts.

One of the students gave me a big hug, the tightest I've ever had at that school. I thought about what's in a hug. I want to remember how that felt and what it means.

June 8, 1982

This morning I had an appointment with Mr. Harris. We spoke for two hours, and the job is mine. I'll begin in September when the kids go back to school. I requested a salary of $17,500 for a ten-month job. He has to consult with the board for that. I'll be working from 8:00 a.m. until 3:00 p.m. four days a week—perfect hours for me. My office will be in the front where I'll have direct contact with the parents and students.

My responsibilities will be:
- To organize and coordinate a parents' group.
- To supervise the students' extracurricular activities.
- To help students create a student council and a newsletter.
- To be involved indirectly in any fundraising efforts through the parent organization and how they decide to raise money.
- To connect with people in the community.
- To promote the school through public relations.
- To be a liaison for the teachers and administration.

I'll be dealing with teenagers in a positive, loving way, promoting their self-confidence, maximizing their potential, creating activities for them, and passing along smiles as I go. Earlier, I made a long list of reasons why I would like the job. I'd be a fool not to take it.

June 21, 1982

The first day of camp has ended. All went well as far as everyone being where they belonged—doing what they should be doing. I'm glad I have the energy for this job. I sometimes feel like I am non-stop, going up and down the stairs all day and running around the fourteen-acre campus.

The only problem was with the parents, who are entirely off the wall when it comes to their darlings. Immediately as we began the day, I had a line-up of unhappy mothers who wanted their children in different groups. I can barely understand why people get so consumed with their little ones that they lose total perspective. I did my best to maintain my calm, but it wasn't easy. Madeline, Barbara, and I worked together rearranging a few groups and are hopeful that we made the right moves. It's impossible to satisfy everyone.

At the end of the day, one of the mothers, who had given me the hardest time, brought me flowers. Her note said, "Just to let you know, your hard work and understanding are appreciated." I had switched her son's group.

This afternoon at 4:45, a father called me at home to discuss moving his child to be with her friends. A few years ago, he had come into my office saying his daughter had had a concussion at our camp. Back then, he yelled at me and was out of control. This time, I didn't give him a chance. Instead, I hurried him off the phone and told him to call me at camp tomorrow.

June 22, 1982

Day number two is over. The schedule ran smoothly, which is always a relief. I loved walking around and seeing how everyone was where they belonged, participating in activities and having fun.

Carpool was done in twenty minutes—record time. By 4:05, everyone left. That's pretty incredible for the second day. Barbara stood at her window admiring the precision. I was smiling, knowing that because the camper whose mother never picked him up on time in past summers is no longer at Camp Sinai, we will be done on time. I also couldn't help but think of the summer when one little camper got put in the wrong car on the first day of camp. It was horrifying when the mother driving carpool came back and sheepishly claimed she took the wrong child. Fortunately, his ride hadn't arrived yet to pick him up, or we would have panicked.

I should go to sleep. God only knows what tomorrow will bring. I hear that more rain is in the forecast, so all activities must be indoors (except maybe splashing in puddles).

June 23, 1982

I'm waiting for the chairman of the board from the high school to come to my house. He wanted to meet me somewhere, but after a day of camp, I said I couldn't go anywhere but home, so I asked him to come here. My friends and Daryl couldn't believe I did that, but I honestly didn't care. I'm not exactly sure what he wants to talk about, but I will stay open.

June 25, 1982

It's now Friday at 4:30. The first week of camp is over. I feel wonderful knowing we are a well-oiled operation and love seeing the campers and my staff having a great time.

June 29, 1982

Mr. Harris called me again and let me know he's hopeful that I'll get the job. It's up to the board now, since the president felt I was a good fit.

June 30, 1982

It's been a long day beginning at 7:00 a.m. when one counselor called to say she could no longer work at camp. She doesn't feel well enough. The problems never stopped from then on.

I ended up working on communication skills with one group of counselors. The three of them couldn't relate to each other at all and were experiencing significant issues. I had them each talk about what was bothering them and insisted the others just listen. It was hard to know who was telling the truth, but what mattered was they could express themselves, listen to each other, and move on to a resolution. They made some progress, but this might take additional work.

July 8, 1982

Today Mr. Harris called me at camp to tell me the board approved my position. So, the job is mine. He said I wouldn't have to be involved in the solicitations at all. Thank goodness for that! I didn't want to touch the job if it entailed my being responsible for any fundraising.

Now, I have to meet with the president and principal together to firm up my job description. I was hoping I'd get the salary I asked for, but I won't. I'll have to settle for a little less. It's too bad, but I can't have it all. At least, they approved the days and hours I requested.

July 13, 1982

I rearranged some of the counselors in different groups since some weren't working well together. With a few switches, people seemed much happier and more productive. Let's hope that lasts. It's an exercise in being flexible. One of the counselor's mothers called to find out why we switched her teenage daughter's group. Parents do their children no favors when they step in over something like this—especially when the girl is sixteen.

July 15, 1982

Today was Western Day at camp and also our third annual water gun fight. What a massive free-for-all with 425 campers and counselors on the front lawn! It's so much fun for everyone to let loose. I didn't let them touch their water guns, balloons, etc., until exactly 2:00. At flag raising this morning, I declared that I would be walking around camp all day, and if I saw anyone with their water "weapons," they would become my property. They knew I meant it, so it was not an issue—but the excitement built up all day long, and then it was crazy wild. Everyone got into the action, which made it all the better. A reporter and photographer from the *Miami Herald Neighbors* came out and covered the event. They could hardly believe what was going on!

Besides that, today was also the first of two talent shows which Allison organized. Each group performed original music and skits from *Sweet Charity, Rocky III, MASH,* a TAB commercial, and *Grease* and had the best time. I felt great about the whole day.

July 17, 1982

Last night in book club with my dear friends, I spoke about my new job. The more I talked, the more excited I became. Now that I've decided this is my last summer at camp, there's bound to be some resistance. However, I'm looking forward to the start of a new career.

July 23, 1982

What a day! Three counselors had a terrible fight on the steps outside the temple. After they resolved the problem, a little girl had a nasty case of diarrhea. As I cleaned her off with the hose, I got an emergency call from the skating rink. Someone had fallen and needed stitches (twenty-two, it turned out), so they were off to the hospital. Right after lunch, a boy got hit in the head with a toy and was bleeding profusely. Then two second-grade boys got into a fight. We ended the day with another camper having a bloody gum with stitches required.

And so, when I got a call about signing a contract at the high school, I immediately said I would. I agreed to sign a three-month contract and told Mr. Harris that I'd want to negotiate for a higher salary after that. He told me it was wise because, at that point, I'd be familiar with everyone and would have proven myself.

July 28, 1982

What a day this was at camp. I'd never seen a broken arm before it was in a cast. Today, I saw two of them. The first was a little boy's. He tripped over someone, and while his arm was hanging in a strange position, he was incredibly brave. It took a while until I reached his family, who came and took him to the hospital. Later in the day, one of the girls was doing a cartwheel and landed on her arm. The strangest coincidence was that her arm hung just like the boy's did earlier.

I feel like I've been through the wringer. The responsibility of all of this is frightening and weighs heavily on me. I am definitely on the warpath as far as safety's concerned. I've warned counselors and campers alike. I sure as hell hope they'll be more cautious, although these were all accidents.

July 29, 1982

Earlier today, one of the counselors came to tell me a boy was bleeding at the pool. As I was running there, I asked the counselor who it was. When I heard it was Michael, I started shaking instead of staying calm inside like I always do in an emergency. It was strange to react that way, but I suppose my motherly instinct had kicked in. Somehow, while swimming, Michael bumped into another boy's front teeth. He had two fang marks on his hairline. He bled a lot but was a good patient. Daryl came over to check him out.

It was weird because I had a bad premonition about the pool today. Once Rachelle told me it was *Tisha B'av*, an annual fast day in Judaism on which many disasters in Jewish history occurred, I felt like I wanted everyone out of the pool. My mother had never let us go swimming on this day when we were kids. Besides the normal lifeguards, I had people on watch at all four corners of the pool. I was nervous about everything. I wanted the campers to be done with swimming and was relieved when they were.

July 30, 1982

My new job will entail less personal responsibility and pressure than I have at camp. With all the accidents we've had this summer, the stress hangs over my head on any one given day.

August 11, 1982

I'm first sitting down after a long "hobo" day at camp. Today is the last time I'll ever have to dress up for a special day.

Barbara, Leslie, Madeline, and I met to evaluate the summer. One mother told Barbara the other neighborhood camps were having three three-week sessions next year and that we should as well. There were a few additional complaints and parental demands—none worth writing about.

As I sat listening to the list, I didn't take any of it personally. That's big for me, since I never did well with any type of criticism in my earlier years. I know the time has come to be done with camp. Besides, after five years as the director, maybe the program needs new blood. Now, I have to get up the nerve to tell them.

August 12, 1982

After meeting with Mr. Harris yesterday, I'm ready to move on to this new challenge. I am especially thrilled that I'll have two months off next summer.

August 14, 1982

On Thursday, I announced to Barbara that I wouldn't be directing camp anymore. She wasn't prepared for that. She thought I'd want additional help but that I'd still be the director. It took me a while to convince her that this was it for me.

The last week of camp ended in such a great way. We had a wonderful Shabbat singalong yesterday, followed by the play *Free to Be You and Me*, which Allison beautifully arranged. Rebecca and Michael were both in it and did great. I had a grin plastered on my face the whole time. Following the play, we did color war cheers. The spirit filled the social hall!

The night before was our staff party, which turned out perfectly. We had our usual shaving cream fight, which is always a trip to experience. The counselors covered me from head to toe.

Daryl spent the night fighting off teenagers, who all ganged up on him. He loved it, but he could barely move by the time the evening was over.

I'm thrilled that camp's finished. No longer will I have the pressure of jumping when Barbara calls, the unnecessary parent phone calls in the evenings, counselors calling in sick in the mornings, and the responsibility of safety and security for each child. I won't miss having to please some of the overindulgent parents either. What I will miss are the good times with the campers and staff.

August 15, 1982

As I look ahead, I am ready to embrace my new job. This morning, I sat in a meeting and listened as Mr. Harris directed and oriented the staff. He ran an excellent meeting and seemed professional in every way. I'm going to learn so much from him. He's astute, concise, bright, creative with lots of ideas, and someone to respect.

August 20, 1982

Now that camp is over, I can concentrate on my position as the administrative assistant to the principal. I have high hopes for this job. The change in grade levels and responsibilities is a natural step for me.

Today in my meeting with Mr. Harris, we each had our lists and crossed off items as we discussed them. Much of what he had in mind was similar to what I had been thinking. I can see that the two of us will make a great team and will work well together. I'm ready to get started and make an impact.

August 30, 1982

Today was my first day of work at the high school. I got there early enough to get my office set up before anyone else arrived. My list of tasks is long, and I hope to tackle many of them by the end of the week. There is so much Mr. Harris wants me to do. I will never be bored.

I was floundering a bit as I went from one assignment to the next. When I asked Mr. Harris about assemblies, he told me he would teach me a crucial trick of the trade—probably the most important in my success, according to him. I wonder what it will be.

September 1, 1982

Gerry suggested that I number my projects. She told me to keep an accordion file with an individual slot for each day of the month. Then, whenever I have a deadline, I need to make a note to ensure everything is ready three days before that. I'll be checking the file daily to see what's next for the day and those that follow.

She also advised me to record every meeting—who is there and what we talked about. That way, I can always go back and refer to it. The better the system I organize, the better off I will be.

September 3, 1982

I've chosen a job I'm going to love. When I reflect on how this all came to be, the best part is that Mr. Harris pursued me. He wanted me to work with him, and now I get to do just that.

September 10, 1982

When I took this job, I made it clear I only wanted to work four days a week. Since they couldn't pay me more, it ended up being ideal for both of us. I need Fridays for my second career, which I hope will one day be my writing. From here on in, whatever job I have, I need to find a way to have Fridays off. I wonder if that's possible.

When Mr. Harris and I were discussing evaluations, I asked if he does self-evaluations with the staff. He said he hadn't, so I explained what I had done with my former staffs. He liked the idea and wanted to see a copy, so I immediately wrote up about twenty questions and gave them to him. He felt they were thought-provoking. Then he told me it's apparent that I know what I'm doing.

I'm sharing an office with George, whom I like and respect. We get along well and fill each other in about what's going on around us. He has studied Carl Jung, so I'm constantly learning from him.

I helped the students launch the flower project, where they sold carnations to raise a little bit of money. Now, I must get the parent association off the ground. I told Mr. Harris I needed his guidance, helping to steer me in the right direction. I am still somewhat at a loss because there's so much to learn. I plan to collect my thoughts over this weekend and figure out my next steps. Once I do, I'm sure I will be fine.

September 13, 1982

I'm noticing a great deal of apathy within the student body. There's much that needs to change. Slowly, I will be able to make my mark; however, right now, I am still a tiny cog in the wheel.

Yesterday, Mr. Harris asked me if I let the students call me Merle or Mrs. Saferstein. It's one thing at camp to be called Merle, but I don't think it's appropriate at the school. He told me I was in a pivotal position. It's true as I see my role evolve. I intend to quickly become an essential part of what's going on there.

September 21, 1982

Mr. Harris is getting a feel for what I can do. After a meeting we attended, he asked my opinion about busing. He suggested if I see something not being handled properly, I should let him know, which I already have in a few instances. George told me Mr. Harris respects what I say.

I enjoy the job because it's diversified. I never have a clear desk. I work hard and feel challenged. The parent association is my number one priority, yet getting the parents involved is not easy. Many of them seem indifferent, like some of the students.

September 23, 1982

Red flags are waving. Many faculty and students are upset and dissatisfied for a variety of reasons. I'm detecting some discontent about the way decisions are made in a rather haphazard, disorganized fashion. I am hearing a lot that is upsetting and have seen several situations being mishandled.

I get the feeling that Diane, Mr. Harris' secretary, believes I'm stepping on her toes. She quickly gets bent out of shape, yells at me, and becomes nasty when she sees me helping students. She feels it's her job and not mine and expects me to step back. Since part of my role is to work with the students, I'm not sure what Diane is thinking. She's making each day at school more difficult because she's constantly on my back about something. It helps to write about this and let off steam.

September 24, 1982

Mr. Harris gave me a lecture on how he'll measure my success. He wants two hundred students enrolled at the high school by next fall and wants $100,000 raised through the parent association by the end of the year. It sounds thoroughly unrealistic, but then he tends to be idealistic in unreasonable ways.

When I spoke to him about Diane feeling like I'm usurping her role, he told me he's surprised it isn't worse. He expected her to be more threatened by me than she is. I told him I was handling it and let it go because I don't want to appear petty. It's her problem, not mine, but it aggravates the shit out of me.

September 29, 1982

I've officially resigned from camp and am feeling relieved. It'll be weird not to be the camp director, but it's time to move on. I promised to make myself available to help with the transition. What I won't do is hang around and be in the way. It's important to give the new director space to grow into the role, and my not being there will make it much more manageable.

October 1, 1982

Yesterday was an exasperating day at school, since there was significant unrest among the faculty. Mr. Harris has made lots of promises which he hasn't fulfilled. I went out on a limb in our meeting and let him know the teachers were tremendously frustrated. He doesn't seem to be taking it seriously enough—a mistake, as far as I'm concerned.

Being new puts me in a challenging position. I am not sure how much I can or should say. What I do know is that I don't think I'd ever let my staff get to the point of such discontent over promises made and not kept. It's unhealthy and needs to be remedied. Mr. Harris seems blind to the facts.

October 4, 1982

Diane is moody. Any time I go anywhere near her territory, she gets upset. For example, there was a call for Mr. Harris, and since he wasn't available, I took a message. She screens his calls and was not happy that I didn't pass along the call to her. How ridiculous was that? Also, he dictated a letter to me, which infuriated her. What am I to do? Grin and bear it, I guess.

I asked George about my talking to Mr. Harris concerning how the staff is feeling. We decided it would be best for me to say as little as possible because I'm too new. All I told him was he needs to handle it as long as there's discontent or frustration. Mr. Harris told me he doesn't want the meeting with the staff but knows he has no choice since they are demanding one.

October 5, 1982

Today was a much better day than yesterday at school. I was as sweet as sugar to Diane. I'm working hard not to get in her way.

Mr. Harris told me the way I'm doing the inquiry phone calls to the parents is excellent. He wants me to connect with every parent and find out what their feelings are about the school. The good news is that he seems pleased with everything I'm doing.

I had my third parent association meeting tonight. It, too, went well. The organization is finally coming together.

October 6, 1982

Today was a camp meeting. They asked me to stay on as a consultant, help out as needed during the summer, and be involved in the camp committee. I made no commitments except that I would be there to advise when necessary.

Later, on behalf of Barbara, Madeline asked me if I definitely didn't want the job. She said Barbara wondered whether it might be a matter of money, and, if so, they were willing to negotiate with me. I told her I would have been up front and let them know if money were the issue. No, time and other responsibilities are.

October 9, 1982

One of the bonuses in my job at the high school is the relationship George and I are developing. We close our door on occasion and have some great talks. Things said in our office stay there. I'm grateful to have made a friend who understands all that's going on at the school. He gives me great advice, listens well, understands the dynamics, and sees the situation as I do.

October 13, 1982

Today something upsetting happened at school concerning the calls I had been making to the parents. Mr. Harris had asked me to write up a report on each call, which he promised would be kept strictly confidential and shared only with him.

At some point late this afternoon, he came in and closed the door to my office. He told me the guidance counselor had shared one of the reports with a teacher. My heart sank, since I felt betrayed. Unfortunately, there were negatives in the report about this teacher. The guidance counselor accepted the blame for what she had done. Actually, the initial responsibility is with Mr. Harris, who never should have broken his original promise and shared the report with anyone.

I am furious and plan to tackle this first thing tomorrow, since today he had to leave in a hurry and didn't give me the chance to have my say. It leaves me wondering just how much I can safely commit to paper and whom I can trust. It sure makes me wish I could erase it all and wipe the slate clean, but it doesn't work that way.

October 15, 1982

Yesterday Mr. Harris was finally available to speak to me about the incident with the report. I told him I was most unhappy that he violated our agreement of confidentiality. He listened but took zero responsibility. I could hardly believe it and am not happy.

The teacher who was involved came into my office yesterday to say good morning. It was big of him to do that. We talked it out, and I apologized for any problems I caused him. He did not fault me, since he completely understood who was responsible for what happened. I was grateful.

October 21, 1982

Today was a hectic, crazy day. Mr. Harris got the word that a big shot is coming to the school in two weeks. My task is to plan separate seminars with this individual for the students, the parents, and the organization that helps sponsor the school. I have so much to prepare and will write my first press release this week.

On Tuesday night, we had a parent association meeting with the executive board. I'm feeling lucky because a few parents are willing to work hard to get the organization where we'd like it to be. They're enthusiastic, which makes that part of my job much easier.

October 27, 1982

I am concerned with the commitments and agreements that aren't being honored. In that regard, I'm not content with my job. I woke up thinking about school and the unrest that exists there. Unfortunately, I'm feeling like what we're trying to accomplish hardly gets done because of the disgruntled students. While I understand the source of the issues, I'm not sure how to help the situation. Today I have rather gloomy thoughts about it all.

November 2, 1982

George asked me a question which he had thought about for a long time before speaking.

He wondered whether, in my experiences, talking out of both sides of one's mouth was the way of all administrators. He's as bothered by the "untruths and lack of promises fulfilled" as I am.

I told him how upset I was over the phone call project, which I hadn't mentioned to anyone at the school. Then, he shared some unfortunate happenings he's also experienced. In both cases, we see how it all stems from the top.

Both of us felt a sense of relief at the end of our conversation. George said the whole staff feels the same way as we do. It isn't easy to work for someone who isn't upfront or honest. I will have to be aware and cautious about what I say and do.

November 4, 1982

I feel troubled and disheartened. In many ways, I'm a much stronger administrator than Mr. Harris. I've only been at the school for over two months, yet I see so much that isn't working. It seems to be more difficult with each passing week.

Disenchantment has set in. Everyone around me feels cheated. I'm working hard to keep the negatives from blocking my productivity. The honeymoon is over!

November 8, 1982

Mr. Harris never showed up for our meeting today. That pissed me off, but it's his loss if he chooses not to meet with me. Last week Mr. Harris told me I'm not being clued in on everything —partially because of Diane and the rest because he wants me to concentrate on his main priority— the parent association. Mr. Harris expects them to be bringing in money! This is all so unrealistic.

November 10, 1982

Mr. Harris had a necessary meeting with the students today. He expressed some of his gripes with them and let the students do the same. It appeared as if he was correcting some of his mistakes and discussing some problems occurring within the school. I would have handled much of it differently. However, Mr. Harris wanted me just to sit there and listen, so that's what I did. It wasn't easy.

November 19, 1982

Last night was one of the parent coffees. The co-president talked about what I've accomplished by starting the parent association. One of the teachers today told me he never expected the parent association to get off the ground and gave me all the credit for making it happen.

November 24, 1982

Today I heard Mr. Harris introduce Diane as his assistant in charge of administration. She is his secretary, so that isn't her title. I'm the administrative assistant. I realize that's just the way it is— Diane needs to be appeased and in a position of power. I'm not at all threatened as she would be. I just think it's pretty interesting that he would do that.

November 30, 1982

I had a fairly decent day at school. Mr. Harris wasn't there, which made a difference. I got all the press releases done and mailed and feel good that I completed the project. It's also the completion of my third month at the school. I'm supposed to be up for review as of now, but we'll see if that happens. And by the way, he never did tell me the one crucial trick that would lead to my success as he had promised before I even started. I'm still waiting.

December 3, 1982

Mr. Harris had been out of town, so I've had the space to catch up with myself. He barely makes time for me. He came back yesterday and seemed so bogged down that we never met as we were scheduled to do. That happens more than I would like.

Yesterday I gave the other secretary, who works with Diane, a birthday card to give to Mr. Harris. Diane found out that I didn't go through her and lost it. She has such a need to be his clearinghouse. I can't handle that absurd bullshit. After all, it was just a personal card to him. I should have put it on his desk, but she insists that anything for him goes to her first. I've given up fighting.

I can't believe how I feel when I think about work. When I'm at school, I enjoy doing the work and interacting with the students. I've developed a wonderful rapport with many of them—especially those on the newsletter staff and student council. My disillusionment with Mr. Harris and the general attitudes in this school leave me discouraged.

December 7, 1982

Last night was the parent association meeting, which was beneficial in putting my position in perspective. Mr. Harris mentioned he hired me instead of a professional fundraiser. He explained that my long-term purpose is to establish an organization that will raise funds but that I don't have the personal responsibility to do so. I would never have taken the job if I did.

Today, Mr. Harris finally gave me my job description back. It puts absolutely no direct pressure on me regarding fundraising, which is in black and white.

December 10, 1982

Mr. Harris read my three end-of-the-month evaluations and wrote that I was "an energetic gal, quick to learn, and efficient."

He told me any frustration I'm experiencing is something I must blame on myself. He said I need to take the final responsibility for anything that doesn't work or succeed, be it with the students or parents. According to him, "You can't blame the economy or other factors, as true as they may be.

"Instead, you have to focus on how to get things to work." He has unrealistic expectations and no clear understanding of the reality here at the school or what it takes to build a parent association.

Mr. Harris also said he considers the time he spends with me as an investment. I don't know how long I'll be there and, as of now, have no long-range plans to stay forever. So, when he said that to me, I didn't say a word. Eventually, I want to be writing at the ocean. With that in mind, the rest is semi-tolerable.

December 11, 1982

Yesterday my press release was in the *Neighbors*. That was a big first for me.

December 13, 1982

Leslie told me that Diane told her that instead of Mr. Harris, I should have been the one to go to the meeting on Friday with the eleventh graders. All I can say is that number one, it isn't her place to decide, and number two, if he wanted me to be there, he should have asked me. He was the one who made the arrangements without informing me about it.

Today was a continuation of last week's evaluation. Mr. Harris felt what I've done was good but feels I'm frustrated. He told me not to be intimidated by the parent association. He believes I should be the facilitator and produce most of the work to keep it going, but raising the money is up to them.

He said that even though working with the students is more gratifying for me, he wants me to do what he wants and needs. I think he forgets that a considerable part of my job description focuses on students, their enrichment programs, the newsletter, and the student council.

I've accomplished a great deal in those areas to date and have lots more I'd like to do. The bottom line is that Mr. Harris expects me to spend my time building a strong parent group, so that it can bring in the dollars. That's all he cares about.

December 21, 1982

Yesterday the parent working on fundraising told me she might go back to work full-time, and if she does, she won't be able to help out anymore. I'm not going to worry until I have to, but it was my first thought when I opened my eyes this morning.

I hate to be dragged down by the bullshit. However, now more than ever before, I've found some benefits of a four-day week, insurance coverage, etc. So, for these reasons, I'm not as quick to give it all up. I also can't imagine where I'd go from here. I'll have to wait and see what happens.

December 23, 1982

While driving to school this morning, I made a decision. This is going to be the only year I work at the school. Maybe it's because today is the last day before vacation, and I desperately need a break, but also there are too many unsolvable problems that make working there unpleasant.

I will have to plow through all the issues and endure. There's little I can do, if anything, to control this situation. I am capable of giving so much to this place but am not given the opportunity. I'm stifled from doing what I do best, which leaves me constantly frustrated. I'm not alone in this. Hardly anyone was even in school today. I heard that one of the kids wanted to call in a bomb threat so they could all leave. That's pretty pitiful.

Yesterday one of the board members came in to talk to me. She's sweet, although I was upset by her visit. She lectured me about my job here and how she wonders what I've accomplished. She went through a list of things that the board is taking over, which she feels should be my responsibility—not one is on my job description.

Besides that, she said the board is under the impression I was hired to raise funds. I told her I was not a fundraiser but, instead, an administrator. I made that clear. Somehow, my role has been misrepresented. I later mentioned to Mr. Harris what she said about me as a fundraiser. He agreed that I'm not, but I wonder what he has told them. So, that's where I stand.

Mr. Harris let me know he is not taking a vacation because he has so much to do and indicated that I do too. I let that slide because in no way do I plan to give up my time off. I need it more than I've ever needed a break from a job.

January 4, 1983

First thing this morning, the school counselor came in to say good morning. She asked me whether I was happy here. I told her I preferred running my own show or having more control over what I do, and she agreed. I also told her that some of the personnel problems concern me. My biggest complaint stems from the negative atmosphere created. We discussed some of the items, and she said many on staff feel it's fruitless to even hope for change because so little gets accomplished. I wasn't at all surprised.

January 5, 1983

What a great way to start the day. I just got a call from Ron Miller of *Community Newspapers*. He received the article I wrote about the computer program at the school. He liked it and wanted to make sure he could use my name in the byline. He went on to say it was a well-written article and hopes I'll write more.

January 12, 1983

I had the publicity pamphlet deadline of tomorrow morning on my mind when Mr. Harris called Diane and me into his office to tell us what we have to do for recruitment. He keeps piling on the work. I felt pressured. Diane must have read my face and asked me if something was bothering me. I said nothing in response but just smiled. She then asked me how I thought it was for her because of the enormous amount of work she had.

January 20, 1983

This day changed drastically. As it happened, the electricity went out at about 11:30. I continued to work in the copy room because, without windows, I had no light in my office.

At about 12:30, I went into the teachers' lounge and found two-thirds of the staff there bitching like crazy. They were commiserating and discussing how the students feel about the school. Mr. Harris is oblivious to what everyone is saying. Today he let the kids do whatever they wanted   totally indecisive. He should have just let them all go home. It was chaotic and ridiculous.

January 24, 1983

When I spoke to Clara, the representative from our sponsoring organization today, she told me that a few board members said I sometimes seem frantic and question if I know what I am doing. She feels it's just that I am busy but, regardless, told me I need to take my time and slow down. I found her assessment of me not at all how I picture myself. I have a feeling I know what board members said that to her. She explained that if I'm with a board member, I should stay with them, give them my full attention, and even be late to my next meeting if need be. In any case, I wasn't offended by her because she also said the school needs the likes of me.

Today, there was an incident with Diane and the custodian. She was badmouthing him to someone, and he overheard her. There was lots of yelling. Mr. Harris stepped in and said he couldn't have this at the school because it isn't good for those listening. He should hear half of what goes on. The atmosphere is a disaster.

January 25, 1983

I feel miserable each morning when I wake up well before the alarm and dread going to work. It's getting harder to have good feelings about my job. I'm not two-faced and can't pretend to be happy with all the craziness and so many unhappy people around me. It's impossible to try to "sell" the school feeling as I do.

I know I have to work. We depend on my salary, but does it do us any good if I am miserable? I'm sure I take some of this despair home with me.

January 26, 1983

I talked to several faculty members today, and everyone is disillusioned and out of sorts. No one is happy to come here. What a sad commentary and certainly not the way I envision a school to be. George and I spend time consoling each other, which is what gets us through each day.

February 1, 1983

I put Mr. Harris on such a pedestal before working here but have lost all respect for him. I need to get out of there. The longer I'm at the school, the more I see wrong with it. Too much is done in a hurry and is not thought out, not honestly done, and not what I'm proud to be part of.

February 2, 1983

I had a long, obnoxious meeting with two board members. June, my nemesis and a trouble maker in every way, is impossible.

I met with Mr. Harris late in the day. He wants the parents to be more involved and do more to raise money. Also, he was upset about a rumor going around regarding the boys and girls and some of their interactions. He didn't feel I gave a strong enough answer to the parent who complained.

February 3, 1983

I handed out the t-shirts to the students for the program downtown. Diane wanted the kids to return them to use again for other events. I couldn't believe that. I told George I was getting the hell out of there before that happened. I retyped the newsletter, gathered all my materials, and then left for the day.

February 7, 1983

Mr. Harris told me one of the board members is upset that the parent association fundraiser is a few weeks before the big fundraising dinner for our umbrella organization. He said word is out that if people come to our event, they won't support the other, and as he put it, "You'll get the blame for it." Lovely! I told him the way I see it, it's a no-win situation.

I let him know I was not happy with this woman's actions and accusations. She has so much power and is like a poison that permeates the atmosphere. If I leave, I'm sure she'll spread negatives about me, but she may just be one of many reasons why I would.

Mr. Harris asked me how much I could take of this. I told him I'm confident she can't and won't ruin my reputation based on what I have done to date in the community, but I certainly don't like it. Get me out of there—fast! Five more long months to go.

February 9, 1983

Yesterday was a frustrating, aggravating day with everyone miserable and complaining. George and I sat cloistered in our office for over two hours, talking and commiserating. I feel better, and so does he, knowing that everyone feels this way. Sadly, we aren't sure if the absolute truth about this place will ever be known.

I won't let this happen again with another job. I feel locked in and will do my best to make it work until I get out of there. My frustration is consuming.

Mr. Harris isn't thrilled, nor is the board because I haven't done "my job" of building the parent association as they had hoped I would. I've worked hard, but there is only so much I can do. This is not a priority for the parents. I can't drag them in.

Also, Mr. Harris let me know that I will be successful in my job when I have a four-page spread on the school in the *Miami Herald*. Until then, according to him, I will get no credit for what I have accomplished. Lovely!

February 10, 1983

It's now 5:30 a.m., and I've been up for hours. I don't want to bring my work issues home with me, but it's all I seem able to do lately. It has taken over my every waking thought and makes me most unhappy.

I'm racking my brain to see if there's anything I can do to get every parent involved, but honestly, it seems I'm up against a wall. Many of them work full-time or have other obligations. Those I've spoken with who haven't joined in feel they're paying a lot for their children's education and have no interest in joining the parent association or raising school funds. Since the school lacks the spirit necessary to be a true success in anything we do, I have no idea how to entice them.

What's bothering me is that, according to some, I haven't met their expectations. It doesn't matter that they haven't come close to meeting mine. I will crank out the articles and see where that gets me. I sure as hell don't want to have my mental or physical health suffer over this, although I'm beginning to think it already has.

Mr. Harris sees the school as a miracle, but I think he's delusional. Most of us on staff believe he's completely unaware of what's happening around him.

So, I'll put in my time and do what I can. If I fail, I'll have to accept that. In so many ways, my disillusionment more than counters theirs.

I just wish I didn't have so many more months to think about this. I hope I can get through these next four months without too much anguish. Is that possible? I hate to rush away my life, but Fridays never come soon enough, and at the moment, June 30th seems light-years away.

February 16, 1983

Work was a bitch today. While in the Xerox room, I bumped into June (the awful board member who talks about me behind my back all the time). She told me how unhappy she was about a letter that Diane sent out. She's nothing but a troublemaker. Mr. Harris showed me the devastating letter she wrote to him. I let him know I was having a hard time handling all this aggravation from her. I think he heard me, but who knows whether what I say matters at all.

February 18, 1983

Yesterday was a day I'm not sure I want to remember. In the morning, Mr. Harris called Diane and me into his office before our scheduled appointment. He asked her to verify something she had included in the letter that didn't belong.

As it turned out, both of us had made mistakes. Diane hadn't gotten permission from Clara to sign the letter. What I did wrong was not include the envelope for return checks.

Mr. Harris then told us that Clara was furious. She let him know that someone from New York had called and said my job was now on the line as a result of this letter. She told him she was going to call for my resignation at the board meeting on Monday night. Needless to say, once I heard that, I decided it was the end for me there.

Mr. Harris asked Diane to leave the room. As the two of us talked, I heard things from him that were surprising. He said these women, for whatever reason, have a personal vendetta against me. He felt this whole situation was a no-win for me, which George has been saying all along.

He thinks that although he knew I needed a great deal of on-the-job learning, the board was expecting miracles from the start. Now, no matter what I do, it isn't going to be enough.

I realized my choices were limited. I could have stuck it out and taken the risk of having my name be slurred more than it will be at the board meeting. If I were to have let them ask for my resignation, I would have had to live with that. Or I could have written my resignation and gotten the hell out as soon as possible.

Even if my name weren't brought up for resignation, which was iffy at that point, I would have had to work with these women who felt I wasn't performing as they would like. This job was not a good fit for me, after all.

So, I decided to quit and let Mr. Harris know. I cried a bit and couldn't believe I was going to leave. I have never quit anything in my life.

However, it made no sense to stick around at that point. I left Mr. Harris' office and walked down the hall to mine. George had gone home sick, so the only one in there was one of the students working on the newsletter. I asked him to leave, sat down at my desk, and sobbed.

Just as I composed myself, there was a knock at my door. It was Alan, the executive director of the agency the school shares grounds with. He was coming to check out which offices needed to be painted. He asked how things were going, and I told him I had just quit my job. I usually would have kept my mouth shut, but I needed to tell someone at that point.

Before I said another word, Alan immediately asked me if I wanted a job. He needs someone to run their camp and early childhood program. I could do it—no doubt about it, but I wouldn't walk into that position for anything in the world. With the school on the same grounds, it is just way too close for me. Plus, if I were to run a camp or preschool, I would just go back to Sinai. I must admit it felt good to be offered a job, and I certainly appreciated him being there when I needed a shoulder to cry on. Unfortunately for him, he left with his gray suit jacket wet from my tears.

The rest of the day was a series of discussions. I began by calling Daryl. He came right over, and we talked and walked around the track. His reaction was one of anger more than anything else. He wanted my resignation letter to list all the reasons I was leaving — total defense, which he's been saying all along. It's not how I want to do it, but I appreciated that he was supportive and kind.

As we were walking, Mr. Harris came out of a classroom. We went over and asked him a few questions. I wanted to know if I had to give a two-week notice, but he told me I could leave when I wanted. He said I should do what I needed to do. I guess my going will be a relief to him.

Mr. Harris told me I shouldn't treat this as an emotional issue. Then, he let us know he doesn't let good people go and recognizes my energy, creativity, intelligence, and capabilities. He said, "Don't worry. Somewhere down the line, we'll work together again." WRONG!

What truly surprised me was that he seemed concerned about how I viewed him and our relationship. He kept telling me that he's a people person, not a politician. Do I believe that? Not for a second.

He asked where he failed me, if he did. I told him he never wanted to hear when I used to come to him with problems, so I stopped. I also let him know I had hoped he would curtail June's actions from the start when I first told him about the havoc she was creating.

I didn't go on and talk about all the other ways he failed me — especially by giving me the title of administrative assistant but never letting me be one. There are so many areas which don't work in the school. Since I've already written endlessly about all of them, I don't need to elaborate now.

Mr. Harris wanted me to capitalize on why I wasn't happy — that I wasn't using my strengths to their maximum. He also thought my resignation letter should read that my relationship with him was good and that my loyalty to the school would remain solid. Of course, he would want that.

I spoke to several friends after that. One told me the letter I write would be an important one. Another was concerned I would not get the money I had earned. Yet, another felt it best that I walk out with dignity and grace. That is the approach I plan to take.

My parents both think my decision to leave is a wise one. Everyone does.

Once I get over the shock of it all, I'll be relieved not to have to go into the school again. I'm better off just getting out of there now.

Word that I quit seemed to have spread through the school in record time. Jodi, one of the students, stopped by the house late yesterday afternoon and told me that lots of people (and especially the students) need for me to come back and let them have a chance to say goodbye, or as she said, to tell me how much they love me.

I'm saddest about leaving George. Les said he was green all day and on the verge of tears. I feel much the same. I am moving on, but he'll still be in that rotting pit. It could have been wonderful, but it wasn't. How unfortunate.

I must think positively. From now on, I don't ever have to get up at 5:30 a.m. and feel sick about my job. That counts for a lot.

The hardest part in all of this was telling Rebecca and Michael that I quit. I don't want them to have the message that it's okay to leave a job in the middle of everything. I hate for them to see me as a quitter. Up until now, I've always loved my jobs, but lately, I've been so miserable that I'm sure they know that.

Hopefully, somewhere down the line, I'll be able to show them the importance of self-care. I now know for sure if we're not moved by what we do, it's not the right job for us.

While I once again venture out into the community to look for a position, I find myself feeling confident and optimistic. I plan to look into service fields and educational opportunities. I need to read want ads and rework my resume.

February 19, 1983

Several of the high school faculty members have called. One told me I was a brave woman and was wise to get out when enough was enough. It was helpful to hear all of what he said. He let me know I made a mark on the school by contributing in significant ways. He warned me that I might have people criticize my failures — that it's happened there before, and it could happen to me.

Another teacher was furious. She felt it would be better to have gone down fighting. When I called Les, she told me that someone had called her at home and that June was on the phone with the other woman. Supposedly, June wanted the word spread that she certainly hoped she hadn't been the one to say or do anything wrong. She said, "I liked her and wanted to be her friend." What a lie!

The network is buzzing. The issue has become hot and heavy. I'm not sure how it will all work out. I only know that it's bound to get out into the community in no time, if it hasn't already.

February 20, 1983

I woke up pissed that Mr. Harris let me go so easily. What a weak man not to stand up for me and do the right thing.

Getting out of that pit of negativity was a relief. I worked hard and accomplished so much but not enough for the assholes who should only know I was misrepresented from the start. In the beginning, someone told them I'd raise funds, even though it was not my direct responsibility or in my job description. So, those who expected miracles need to see the truth, but that will never happen.

February 21, 1983

I went to school to turn in my resignation. Fortunately, I didn't see anyone. I just dropped it off and left immediately. I am curious to know what happened at the board meeting.

February 23, 1983

Today, I went back and cleared out my desk. I saw most of the faculty and many students, not all, but enough to know I'll be missed.

I feel good when I look back on this morning and realize that people care about me. Several said they'll miss my smiles, posters, and positive messages, which they let me know brought something special to the school. It was weird to be there but also good in that I could adequately say my goodbyes.

February 24, 1983

One week later and I feel fine knowing I did the best I could. I just didn't work well in a dysfunctional organization. I am set free! Robert, who is on the school board, called before to tell me he heard what had happened and wanted to know how I was. When I told him the story, I was all choked up.

March 1, 1983

Tonight, Robert called to tell me he received the minutes from the board meeting. He read the part that mentioned me. It stated that one board member said they were investigating a PR firm to get publicity for the school. They were "going to use the leftover funds from the salary of Merle Saferstein, who resigned because she was overwhelmed by the position." Robert was disturbed by the way my resignation was announced. How nice that he cares.

March 3, 1983

At the beach. I looked over at a woman on the bench across from Nicky's, where I was eating lunch. She looked just like June from the high school. Within minutes, she saw me and walked toward me. That's when I knew for sure it was her.

She told me she heard rumors that she was the reason I quit. I said, "No, you weren't the reason—just the last straw." June turned to her daughter and told her I was hired for fundraising and PR even though it wasn't my skill or expertise. Of course, I let her know that that was not in my job description.

June also told me she's heard I'm wonderful working with kids. I said, "Yes, I feel fortunate that I have that reputation." Then she said, "Oh yes, otherwise, this could have been a devastating experience for you." I could hardly believe she said that.

I let her know I could have done a lot more for the school, especially for the students, and wished I had had the chance to accomplish what I was hired to do. It felt good to say that I got out when I realized I wouldn't have that opportunity.

March 14, 1983

Robert told me he wrote a letter to Mr. Harris about the board minutes. In it, he suggested that there was verbal maneuvering. Robert asked that the words "overwhelmed by the position" be stricken from the minutes. He said it was untrue, unfair, and unbecoming and mentioned that no job was too big for me. Robert went out on a limb, which I greatly appreciated.

And so, the record has been set straight. Now I need to figure out what I want to do with the rest of my life.

Reflections on Joining the Workforce

Many emotions surface when remembering this time in my life and reflecting on these excerpts. Leaving teaching to become an administrator was a pivotal moment in my career.

Initially, what I never considered when I first accepted the job as director of Camp Sinai was the tremendous responsibility of it all. I was only thirty-four years old and was somewhat naive to the realities of life. Now, in retrospect, I realize more than ever what the safety and well-being of each camper meant. These excerpts brought me back to the enormous relief I felt when everyone made it through safely at the end of each summer.

My five years at Camp Sinai were a joyful time in my career. What could be better than doing a job in which the ultimate objective was to create an atmosphere where children gather to have a good time—to forget about school and simply just play? Sure, for me, there was daily pressure. Not only did I have a large staff answering to me, but, in turn, I had administrators to whom I reported. Scheduling, finding substitutes, accidents, irresponsible counselors, difficult parents, and behavioral issues were all part of the experience. Yet, when I reflect, it's the good times I remember—the joy, smiles, and laughter each day. Of all the positions I've had through the years, directing the camp remains the one that was the most fun for me. To this day, when I run into campers and counselors from back then, we often share stories of the good times we had during those summers. Reading about it brings back happy memories for me.

As I read the excerpts about Temple Or Olom's preschool, I thought about the challenges I faced when I took over the position of director. I had no idea what it would be like to walk into a school where my predecessor and many of the teachers had been for twenty-five years. They liked doing things one way and resisted anything new I presented. I had never been in that position, and as I reflect, I can still remember those difficult moments when I had to be firm and confident, despite what it felt like inside. That turned out to be a good life lesson. I wanted the teachers to like me, but I knew what mattered more was their respect for me. I learned to take my time and let them get used to my ways gradually.

Directing a preschool was easy and delightful. I was especially pleased because the teachers' philosophy was to keep it child-centered rather than stressing academics. And so, the atmosphere was more of an organic one where each child could grow and learn based on their curiosity and interests.

When I look back on this, I am grateful to have been part of children's early education in a way that they learned through experience. I have always felt there is too much academic pressure on little children. It seems many forget that a young child's work is play.

Reading about my job as administrative assistant to the principal of a high school took me back to a most challenging time in my career. I began that position with great enthusiasm. I was looking forward to working with teenagers and felt it was a tremendous opportunity to use my skills and add to a relatively new school.

It didn't take me long to feel the disillusionment. The experience was unlike any I had ever had and rocked my world in many ways. Reading about it brought me to that dark place within—to the feelings I had toward the end when I could barely crawl out of bed in the morning—something that had never happened to me before or since.

As I read the excerpts, I noticed my willingness to share my truth, even if it was painful. I could feel so many of the awful feelings surfacing once again. Throughout the compiling of excerpts for this book, it's been important for me to protect others and make every effort not to hurt anyone. And so, while I am hopeful that this will not be hurtful to anyone, I knew I needed to tell this part of my story—the truth as I experienced it.

Up until then, I could have never imagined quitting a job in the middle of a school year. Yet, I left in February after only five months of being on the job. I had weighed the pros and cons, but I knew I needed to be done. It was a risk—mostly because I was fearful of the message I would give to my children.

Eventually, though, I realized there was a more important message to impart. Above all else, if we don't enjoy our job or if the atmosphere makes it unbearable, it's time to leave. I believe that doing work we love feeds our souls.

Finally, while I relished being in administrative positions, what I know for sure is that my first love has always been teaching. I did my best in both my camp and preschool positions to take the opportunity to teach my staff whatever and whenever I could. That's where I experienced my greatest joy. Since retiring and teaching adults in my legacy classes for these past nine years, I know it's what I love doing above all else.

Journal Prompts

- What has your favorite job been and why?

- How have you or do you handle conflict at your job?

- Have you ever worked in a dysfunctional atmosphere? Were you able to effect change? What was it like for you?

- If you could have any job, what would it be and why?

- Have you ever been in a position that has turned sour? What happened? How did you handle it?

- Have you ever left a job because you were unhappy? How did you do that? Did you have another job before you left?

- Would you rather be an employer or an employee? Why?

- Write about a work accomplishment.

- Write about a time when you have grappled with leaving someplace because you were unhappy but were faced with insecurity to do so. What barriers did you face? What were your fears?

The Joys and Challenges of Marriage

To be fully seen by somebody, then, and be loved anyhow —
this is a human offering that can border on miraculous.

— Elizabeth Gilbert

January 22, 1975

In the lecture I heard today, the speaker shared significant thoughts on what to pay attention to in marital relationships. She suggested what's most important is to respect and trust one's spouse. She also mentioned being authentic, identifying one's feelings, sharing them, and not being judgmental toward one's partner.

April 10, 1975

A few years ago, when we moved to Florida, I found myself wanting more of Daryl's time. Some of that was because I was home with two babies while he was at work. I desperately needed the adult company and was depending on him for it.

At the time, I had a much-needed conversation with Daryl which changed things for both of us. When I told him how I was feeling, he listened and replied by letting me know he felt I was being "possessive" and was "strangling" him. I was surprised. Then when he went on to say he was going to join a gym, which I never expected to hear in response to what I was telling him, I was even more shocked. That's when I decided if he was going to do that, it was time for me to get out of the house and do something I would enjoy.

Registering for the adult education classes at Miami Dade Community College was the best thing I could have done for myself. I loved the transactional analysis classes (TA) and am grateful for all I learned. Plus, the sculpting class I took was great fun.

Now, I'm enjoying the Gestalt class and feel like a different person knowing I have Monday nights to look forward to each week. Daryl is in great shape and is going to the gym regularly, so it has become a positive for both of us.

Once I had a taste of that freedom, everything changed for me. As a result, today, I feel we're much more independent of each other. It's better and healthier.

November 25, 1978

I am lucky to share my life with Daryl. We're good friends, laugh with each other, and enjoy parenting Rebecca and Michael together. Luckily, we're growing as a couple as we continue to embrace one another's differences.

August 14, 1979

Daryl and I have been upset watching our closest friends go through difficult times in their marriages. We know they haven't communicated their true feelings and issues with each other. I am afraid for their marriages and, selfishly, our relationships as couples with them.

Our marriage becomes stronger the more Daryl and I talk about this. We've been closely looking at what makes our relationship work, which has proven to be a positive for us. I doubt we would otherwise be examining our marriage in this way at this point in our lives.

Last night we talked about how we believe that when people have affairs, it's almost always the result of some issue in their marriage they aren't addressing. I may be wrong, but I don't think people just go out and find lovers unless they have unmet needs.

April 23, 1980

Sometimes Daryl and I do a fabulous job communicating, but then suddenly, for whatever reason, and I have no idea what it might be, there is a shift. It seems as if we lose momentum or forget the skills we've been practicing up until then. I've noticed that's the case lately.

It seems whenever I tell Daryl I need to talk to him, he inevitably says something like, "Oh no, here goes another one." or "Here we go again." It's done sarcastically and never in a way where he indicates he's open or wants to hear what I have to say. I guess it's a trigger for him thinking I am about to say something negative. His words and attitude cause me to want to shy away from communicating. I don't, but it puts up a barrier, since he begins on the defensive without my even having said a word.

I know he would rather not have these discussions, but that isn't an option if we are going to have the kind of marriage where we can discuss the good and bad in our relationship. He definitely does not want to hear anything that isn't positive. That doesn't stop me, though, because I know what I need to say and do to maintain a healthy marriage.

Daryl often feels my timing is off when I choose to have a serious conversation with him. While I know the right moment makes a difference in how our discussion plays out, there are those occasions when I can't wait to say what's on my mind. Of course, if it were up to him, there probably never would be a good time.

But today as I expressed my true feelings, he listened to what had been bothering me. He cared that I was hurting. That led to us talking things out, which eventually took on a new dimension. Just being heard felt great.

September 21, 1980

I watched an older couple play together in the ocean. Their love for one another was evident. They later told me they'd been married fifty-four years. As I thought about that, I knew if Daryl and I were fortunate to live out our lives together, we would continue to love and enjoy each other playfully and humorously, just like them.

Last night, Daryl told me how well he knows every inch of me. He seemed proud to say, "I know you better than anyone in this whole world."

October 2, 1981

After all these years, I sometimes feel frustrated because Daryl isn't meeting all my romantic needs. Earlier, I made a list of what I wish Daryl would have caught onto without asking him. If I have to tell him what I want, even if he responds, it won't mean as much as if he figures it out on his own. I know that's stupid, but it is how I'm feeling at the moment.

My dilemma is whether I should be obnoxious and nag him once again. Or do I resign myself to no flowers and candlelight dinners? I don't think I've succeeded in teaching him a thing about romantic gestures. We've battled about this for eighteen years since the first Valentine's Day when we started dating, and he didn't buy me a valentine.

October 3, 1981

By the end of last night, I decided to speak to Daryl about how I felt and what I needed from him. He listened and seemed a little surprised, since he thought he had been doing much better through the years. Admittedly, he has, but he often slips back into old ways. That's what seems to happen with him. He makes an effort initially, and then, gradually, that behavior fades away.

Today, he came home with two cards for me—a funny one and a serious one. It didn't matter what he brought me. It only mattered that he heard me. I learned a big lesson through taking action—unless we tell people how we feel or what we need, they will never know. It often has to be reinforced in different ways and at different times. Then, what's most important is that the other person hears and responds. How lucky I feel tonight and how glad I am I spoke up.

October 11, 1981

This weekend, Daryl and I came up with three words of advice for newlyweds: communication, compromise, consideration.

October 20, 1981

I heard a great line on the radio today. The commentator said, "Neatness counts but not enough to cause a cold war!" He was discussing husbands and wives sharing chores. I listened and realized I am guilty of wanting my surroundings to be a certain way — something that doesn't matter to Daryl. I know he gets upset when I comment on his mess. It's a challenge for me to look the other way. In this situation, it's all about picking my battles — what is truly important and what I can tolerate. I suppose it depends on the day.

December 6, 1981

I've been protecting myself from the blustery fifteen miles per hour winds here at the beach. I'm behind a stack of lounge chairs which does a fair job of keeping me sheltered. Some man, who looks to be in his sixties, just discovered my hideout and asked me to go fishing with him tonight. I thanked him but told him I was happily married and not interested. He responded with, "But no one is happily married." I picked up my beach bag and moved on.

June 11, 1982

After being married for fifteen years, we have plenty to celebrate. I loved surprising Daryl with the book I wrote for him. I'm sure it was something he never expected I would do, but I've been happily writing it all year. I was delighted to spend several hours reading it together. We had some great laughs and loving feelings as we enjoyed remembering special moments in our marriage. Daryl loved that I divided our twenty years of being together (including the almost five of dating) into four quarters of a football game. I needed to add something to the book that he was interested in to make it more fun for him.

I'm just lucky to be married to a man who shares a similar, positive outlook on life. Our relationship continues to grow as the years pass. There are days when it feels like we are a fairy tale come true. Of course, it isn't all roses, and we have had to work plenty hard to get where we are. We have made it happen and now can celebrate these fifteen years with joy in our hearts.

January 9, 1983

Joanne, whose marriage is in crisis, called today. After talking and listening for a long time, I suggested she do something in return if she wants her husband to be good and do nice things for her. We must be willing to give and take but know that nothing will be one hundred percent. It just doesn't work that way. Sometimes, it seems like I am giving a lot more than my share. I'm sure Daryl probably feels the same way, but it all evens itself out in the end.

April 11, 1983

One of the reasons why two of the couples we know got divorced was that the wives were too dependent on their husbands. They didn't have enough outlets in their own lives, and their spouses could not give them all they needed to be content.

Watching them and learning through the years made me realize it's unrealistic and unfair to expect Daryl to meet all my needs. Slowly, I have been expanding my circle to include others who can fill the gaps.

April 27, 1983

Yesterday I read an article about husbands complaining about unsexy wives. The columnist suggested that it takes two to tango. So, I left it on Daryl's dresser. When I got home, he greeted me at the door with his clothes off. This morning, he told me how I'm the love of his life. I was thrilled and saw that if changes are to occur, people need to want to change and then do something differently.

May 5, 1983

After hearing that another couple is separating, I can't help but wonder why this keeps happening. Marriage takes work and energy—sometimes more than I ever could have dreamt would be necessary. When one of my friends recently had marital problems and talked to me about them, I asked him if he had ever considered divorcing his wife. He told me that would be the easy way out. Yet, I imagine that some can't take any more of whatever isn't working, and divorce is their only solution.

June 28, 1983

Roles in marriage need to be clearly defined. Now that I have quit my job, I am suddenly reduced to a different position—that of cook, laundress, maid, chauffeur, personal shopper, and so much more—some of which Daryl and I used to share. I was shocked when he said, "The chores are yours since I bring home the bacon." Where does that leave me? I must address this issue.

July 23, 1983

Allowing one another space is something we have finally mastered. Daryl lets me go off and do whatever I want and vice versa. We trust each other, which counts for everything. Maybe that's why we have nothing to worry about. I'm grateful that I can branch out and do my own thing and never feel stifled, unchallenged, or bored. Daryl gives me the space to spread my wings and soar.

He grounds me and keeps me rooted in my life. The security and love which I receive from Daryl nurtures me. Because of this, I have total freedom to do what brings me fulfillment and joy. I consider myself fortunate.

August 4, 1983

Tonight the two of us went on a picnic at the beach. While sitting in a lifeguard stand after dinner, I told Daryl how much he means to me. I also explained some of what I discovered while writing today. I've probably said it all to him before, but not in this way. He's learning along with me who I am, what I fear, and what makes me happy.

August 21, 1983

In an article I read about letters Harry and Bess Truman wrote to each other, it said, "A wife who is loved as an equal can endure almost anything as long as she knows that the direction of her husband's mind is toward her. They keep their identity by sharing their minds."

October 8, 1983

Unfortunately, we have been privy to many awful marriages. From my viewpoint, the downfall in each was a lack of communication. I saw the pain involved, so that will be helpful to me when I write the novel I am about to begin.

Meeting Lionel and hearing his story of marriage, divorce, and remarriage to the same woman gave me the underlying thread. Getting back together is exactly one of my fantasies when thinking about a few of our friends, but I doubt it will ever happen. So, if I base the book on Lionel's story, at least in some small way, I can realize that dream for someone — even if it is fiction.

In my Pollyanna way of thinking, those who married for the right reason — love — could have worked it out if both had stuck to an agreement saying, "I will not go to sleep until we solve each problem as it arises." They might have been up for days, but I believe they could have resolved their issues by communicating (including both talking and listening), whether through compromise or just learning to understand the other's needs, concerns, and viewpoints.

If I were to give any advice to newlyweds, I'd tell them not to let a problem go unresolved — to tackle it head-on as it occurs.

October 16, 1983

Last night we went out on Dave's boat and saw Julio Iglesias' home. We rode around Indian Creek Island and drifted under a star-filled sky. Daryl was into checking out the beautiful homes and the kind of gas mileage the boat gets. I preferred to check out his lips — so typical of each of us.

November 5, 1983

I remember walking across the Oval at Ohio State and telling myself that I would be making a big mistake if I didn't marry Daryl. At that moment, I knew he was the man for me — the one I wanted to live with forever. With him by my side, life is good.

July 26, 1984

There is something wonderful about knowing I have a partner who loves me and stands beside me through everything. We have in each other a companion and a lover, one who knows and understands. Today, Daryl is doing crossword puzzles, and I'm writing, so we sit side by side at the beach, each doing our own thing.

December 27, 1984

Our sex life seems to revolve around when the kids aren't home. I wonder how other couples manage. The last thing I ever want is for either of them to hear us. I can still remember hearing my parents in the room next to mine—something that always led me to hide my head under my pillow.

June 22, 1985

As I walked down the Broadwalk, I saw Dennis, the Hollywood bicycle policeman, talking to Doc. Dennis looked at me and said to Doc, "It's too bad she's married." I jumped in and said, "Actually, I'm thrilled to be," and kept on walking.

December 1, 1985

At the beach. Walking along the shore in front of me is one of our neighbors with the same woman he was with a few weeks ago. They look rather cozy and appear to be engaged in an intimate conversation. I'm pretty sure that I'm witnessing an affair. How sad for his wife and her husband.

If people have marital problems, I don't understand why they just don't devote their energy to working through them or ending their marriage before getting involved with someone else. I believe one owes their spouse (and the vows they exchanged) at least that much. I know I'm being judgmental, but to me, that makes the most sense.

Anyway, at the very least, I can't help but wonder why they are so brazen to be out in public. I've seen them together at Bagel Bar and elsewhere as well. Do they want to get caught?

I plan to keep my mouth shut and not say a word to anyone about seeing them, but at least I can write about it in my journal. This helps me process what I think and feel.

July 31, 1986

Sometimes Daryl and I speak a different language. We fit into the category of how females and males approach an issue differently. I want to vent, and he wants to fix it. I have to keep reminding myself of that, although at times, it's not easy. Lately, it seems we view so much in our lives from opposite perspectives. It is becoming more apparent to me as the years go by.

September 14, 1986

Last night one of the women told me the statistics about those who got married in 1986. The forecast is that close to 50% will end in divorce. Seven years together is the average length of a marriage these days. These are frightening statistics, and I only hope they aren't true.

Daryl and I can't help but wonder what will happen to our children when they get married. Hopefully, having grown up surrounded by love and seeing a solid marriage, our children will seek mates who bring them true happiness and fulfillment.

April 12, 1987

After all these years of being together, the tingling intoxication of what was once a new relationship has worn off for us. However, the reality is in letting go of some of that "excitement," we instead embrace the stability, comfort, companionship, and a hell of a lot more. Too many people opt out of their marriage instead of finding new ways to add that extra spark to their relationship.

The longer we're together, the more we learn how to make it all work. Luckily, our marriage is probably as good as the best. We are compatible and in love, and while we are so different, we have become masters at compromising.

November 19, 1987

For sure, I know what I can expect from Daryl. However, there are still times when I find myself wishing he would do something, which is probably close to impossible for him. I have to learn to drop those unrealistic expectations, since it is unhealthy and gets me nowhere.

December 13, 1987

This weekend allowed us to spend uninterrupted time together as we laughed and chilled out. It was great to be by ourselves without the kids and the pressures of daily living. Every couple needs this once in a while.

The time away gave me some perspective on our lives. Of course, being at the beach added to the joy of the weekend, and honestly, I could not have asked for a better birthday celebration.

December 26, 1987

Gregg asked me a strange question. "Is your marriage with Daryl a sanctuary?" I described it as being safe and secure, so my answer was yes.

He talked about the multiple sexual experiences he had with others. I listened and thought about how I've only had one other boyfriend besides Daryl. I explained that we were seventeen when we started dating, so Daryl is the only man I've ever "been" with. I admitted that, in retrospect, I would have liked to have had other experiences. However, that didn't happen, and, of course, I'm not going anywhere now.

January 16, 1988

Suddenly, yet another family we know is splitting apart because the husband had an affair. I feel a pit in my stomach as they face the pain of divorce and feel sad for the wife and kids.

I have seen so many children become pawns as they suffer from being bounced back and forth from one parent to the other. There are many shattered dreams on everyone's part. It is a harsh reality. There are times when I take Daryl for granted or am not as kind as I could be. Our friends' separation has once again forced me to look at what I have and make sure I treat Daryl well.

May 26, 1988

Last night, Cathy asked whether Daryl and I ever fight. I know to the outside world, we have something that looks wonderful, and in most ways, it is, but we have our share of arguments.

I hope our children get a realistic picture of what it means to communicate, which includes arguing at times. They've never really seen us in a big battle. Those fights are rare for us, but when they happen, we keep them to ourselves. I'm not sure if that's a good thing or not. Should children see their parents fighting? Would they be better off learning how to resolve conflicts if they saw how we work through our issues? Or is it best for them to be sheltered from it all?

Looking at many other marriages, I understand I am lucky to have what I have. So many people split up because of their unwillingness to accept what is and realize that nothing is perfect. I don't know of a marriage that doesn't have stuff. No one has the whole pie.

August 26, 1988

This has been an important time for Daryl and me without the kids around—a rare occurrence. We aren't used to being together as much as we have been this week. In general, we could spend more time together, but Daryl thinks how we've been in our lives is enough. I guess I've spoiled him by giving him a lot of space as I run off to the beach. Now, he's used to his time alone to watch TV and unwind. So, he is content. I am not complaining. It gives me more time to write!

October 22, 1988

I asked Daryl the question I had heard on the radio when I was jogging. "If you could change your spouse, in what way would you?"

He thought for a few minutes and answered that he hates when I get in my primping mode—meaning when I insist on him dressing a certain way when we're going somewhere or when I give him a disapproving look because he has a spot on his shirt.

He told me he also doesn't like when I become relentless on an issue. I understand that. I know it drives him crazy. I am glad he could verbalize all that he did. Whether I can change and let go of these behaviors is another story, but I am willing to make the effort.

January 19, 1989

Daryl has his priorities in the right place—family, work, friends. How I knew this was the man for me, I'll never know. Looking back, I was so young and inexperienced.

April 27, 1989

Living with a man like Daryl, who is content and easy and who asks for little, is terrific in many ways. It means he is on "middle C" most of the time and rarely fluctuates to any extremes—highs or lows. Of course, that eliminates the excitement and adventure which I would love. We aren't often on rocky ground because we both remain on an even keel most of the time.

September 9, 1989

I went into a candy store and bought Daryl a chocolate football and a small balloon heart that says I love you. I brought them home and made a big deal about football season starting—something he always looks forward to. He was happy but surprised because early on in our marriage, I dreaded when he would get lost in football all weekend. That's changed as I have finally accepted the fact that Daryl will not give up watching football.

October 29, 1989

Today in Ann Landers' column, a woman wrote that she was tired of hearing about people getting so wrapped up in wedding plans they forget what matters. She expressed how her wedding had to be cut down to marriage by a justice of the peace. Their parents had dessert at their house after. Then they went on a honeymoon—a camping trip with the bride's mom and gentleman friend.

The woman explained how her marriage, with that humble beginning, has lasted for sixty years. She said people put too much emphasis on a lavish display, and all that's left are bills and pictures in an album. She went on, "Also, too much hullabaloo is made about sex. That doesn't last forever either. What makes marriage stick is mutual respect, loyalty, patience, willingness to share, a sense of commitment, and most of all, being really good friends."

September 10, 1990

Sandra told me they're under tremendous financial pressure. Since I understand how money issues add stress to a relationship, I could sympathize with her. We've certainly lived with our share for most of our marriage. I can only hope that somehow things turn around for us. So far, I feel we are continuing to struggle and cope as best we can. For sure, it is not easy and is the cause of most of our arguments.

December 20, 1990

In the car on the way to the airport, my in-laws and I talked about how Daryl and I have simple needs. My mother-in-law said it's the secret of our success. I told them I planned to retire at sixty, write for the rest of my life, and live on the beach. My mother-in-law asked how Daryl felt about all of that. Before I could answer, my father-in-law said that as long as Daryl has a television and football, he'll be happy. Bingo!

March 7, 1991

We talked about how one shouldn't say certain things to a spouse—that which crosses a line and causes great pain—words that cannot be taken back once spoken aloud. I began to think about whether I had ever stepped over that line in our marriage. I guess if I ever had, it would have been related to our financial pressures, but so far, I think I have been sensitive enough and have not said everything to Daryl that I have felt.

I could never be married to a man who doesn't love me, who cheats on me, or who beats me. That would never be Daryl. Our problems are minor in comparison to any of that.

June 18, 1991

I talked to an adorable father who has been here at the beach with his two children all week. Somehow, we started discussing the subject of marriage, which he feels is life's biggest challenge. He also said he has realized that sex, while important, is not the most crucial factor in a good marriage. The guy told me he would never have thought that when he first married his wife, but in time, that has changed. I agreed with him.

February 3, 1992

Daryl and I are okay with one another having platonic friendships. It seems some couples can't tolerate their spouses being friends with anyone of the opposite sex. I'm so glad that isn't an issue for us. Maybe it's because we were friends first and shared so many of the same relationships with the guys and girls in our class. Whatever it is, I am thankful we have room in our marriage for this.

Daryl makes it clear he has no problems with Tom as my close friend. There are times when I am in the mood to get into a deep conversation and approach Daryl to talk. He inevitably says, "Why don't you call Tom?" That's when I know that Daryl is probably relieved I have someone in my life who is willing to discuss topics like spirituality and existentialism with me, so he doesn't have to. He told me it doesn't matter what anyone else thinks about me going to New York to see Tom. He feels strongly that no one else's opinion but his matters in this situation, and he is right!

I'm also grateful that I can branch out and do my own thing. Of course, Daryl knows I would never be happily married if he demanded I sit by his side and watch television with him or simply stay at home and not venture out. He understands I'm a free spirit and knows better than to hold me back. If he were needy and wanting more of my attention all the time as some husbands do, our marriage wouldn't work.

June 4, 1992

We're starting to pick up the pieces from our financial fiasco last week. Slowly, we are talking more and even laughing again. Since we're usually playful with each other, I missed that and so much else, including cuddling and more. So, this is a good, healing sign, which I appreciate because I was frustrated and miserable. I knew it would get better eventually, but I sure had my moments when I was ready to explode, and in some cases, did.

June 8, 1992

I remember when Daryl and I were first married, and his father discussed love with us. He told us we don't know what love is yet — that we will have to wait until we're married twenty-five years, and then we'll understand.

I disagreed with my father-in-law then and still do. I loved Daryl from the minute I committed to be his girlfriend. Granted, we've experienced more through the years to bring us closer together, but in reality, we've always known what love is.

Not a lot has changed in the last ten years, although we've had our share of challenges as all married couples do. We've had to pull together and pool our resources to deal with some rather rough moments. Somehow, we have created a bond that feels like it's so strong that nothing could destroy it. Of course, a week or two ago, I was singing a somewhat different tune, but I was upset and needed to go through that tirade. And so, I am learning to take the bad with the good.

One thing about our marriage that makes it all work is that, in many ways, I have taken the pressure off Daryl to be something he isn't or to expect him to provide me with something he can't. He needs much less in his life than I do, since he is easily satisfied. I am a much more complex individual. My world is fuller and more varied than his. But without the stability I have with him as my husband, I'm not sure what I'd be like. Ours is a relationship based on friendship, followed by doing for each other, and filled with caring and compassion.

June 10, 1992

Tonight while we were eating at Corky's, *Moon River* sounded throughout the restaurant. The band played that song for our first wedding dance — how synchronistic since this is the eve of our anniversary. Daryl has had enough of my romance and sex talk, but I haven't let that stop me. I intend to make this a special anniversary celebration starting now.

June 11, 1992

Neither of us can believe we've been married twenty-five years. I was looking through the wedding scrapbook I've kept with all my shower invitations, cards, announcements, lists of gifts, etc. Daryl wasn't at all interested in any of it. He continues to view me as a hopeless, sentimental romantic. Some things never change.

At the beach earlier today, we went into the water and played for a while. Of course, even trying to convince Daryl to "mess around" in the ocean is unthinkable—except for one day years ago. Today, he did pull down the top of my bathing suit when I suggested it, but that was only for a short moment just to humor me.

I'm excited to go to San Francisco to celebrate. It's someplace I've always wanted to visit. I'm grateful our family and friends gave us the trip as a gift. While they first thought to make us a party, and indeed, that would have been lovely, memories from our forthcoming trip will last forever.

July 17, 1992

There are times when I flashback to my parents, who were probably around this same age and stage in their lives as we are. I'll never forget the day my mom said she wanted to leave my father. She was always ready to go out, take classes, meet friends, and stay busy, while my dad would come home from work and collapse on the couch. She would get so frustrated. I think she found him unexciting and maybe way older in his actions than she was. I honestly believe she stayed because a few of their male friends died around the same time. My mother must have realized what a special man she had, regardless of all that bothered her. I know she loves my father, as well she should.

In a way, it's sometimes how I feel about Daryl. He's like my father when he lies around a lot, watches television, and lacks the energy or desire to get up and go. His parents are much the same way, so it comes to him through genes or learned behavior. At times, I become sad and even a bit concerned to think this is the way he is and probably will be from now on. What I know for sure is that I will not let his actions hold me back from living a full life.

June 10, 1993

Our twenty-sixth anniversary is coming, although I am in no mood to celebrate. Our financial issues have taken a toll on me, leaving me feeling pressured and upset. The realities slowly sink in. It is not an easy time for us. We will get through it and out the other end, but I feel we have a long road ahead. I'm doing all I can to stay sane and focused.

July 6, 1993

I thought about the woman who went from one love to another. I had to wonder what she gave up and what she got the second time around. What are the trade-offs in all of this? Who loses and who gains, and what is the loss or the gain?

Daryl and I share a rich and wonderful history. I don't think I would ever be willing to throw any of that away for a new, thrilling, romantic relationship. Marriage is based on trust and the vow of monogamy. I know if I ever crossed over the line (which I have no intention of doing), it would be like Humpty Dumpty. We'd never be able to put the pieces of our marriage back together again.

Life undoubtedly presents complications in even the best of relationships. Sometimes we need to stop and take stock. To start over or give up hardly makes sense.

July 16, 1993

This continues to be a trying time for us. We are only first beginning to climb up from the hole we have found ourselves in. Until now, we held back some of what we've needed to say for many reasons—none of them particularly helpful in our situation. We can only begin to heal since we have opened up, said a lot which was extremely difficult, and shared from our guts.

July 19, 1993

We have had a lot of wonderful years together, but now we must face the reality that we have both made some serious mistakes. I see that our financial problems will chip away at our marriage if we don't adequately address them.

Now that I'm aware of what's happening, I will no longer look the other way. I did that for too many years believing it was not my job to concern myself with our finances or be involved in any aspect of them. When we first got married, from what I knew (which wasn't a whole lot and was never discussed), the men were in charge of the money. And for sure, that was fine with me. I had no desire to bother with finances except to earn money and help ease the burden.

I take equal responsibility as a result of my non-action. I intend to work hard and give to our relationship whatever it takes to get through this nightmare. I am done burying my head in the sand.

Today, I feel a little bit wiser. The time has come for me to wake up. This is one of those hard lessons learned.

July 24, 1993

I believe it's important in a marriage to have some space from one another occasionally. In our case, this break will do us both some good after all the pressure we've been under. I need the time to write and process and am grateful I had this opportunity to stay at Lorene's mom's apartment here on South Beach for two weeks without it costing me a penny. Daryl is probably happy to be by himself with no demands from me or anyone else.

October 10, 1993

Daryl and I got pinned in 1964 on this date. While it was many years ago, right now, it feels like a lifetime since then.

October 28, 1993

We are fighting more than ever over our finances. However, I am determined to get through this. I'm forcing Daryl to communicate and explore the issues. The key is to get beyond the anger and address our feelings. We have certainly done our share of yelling, which is not typical of me. In some way, though, this arguing is helping us focus on the core issues rather than skirt around them. We must and will keep talking and working toward a viable solution.

This has been our most challenging year ever. We are being tested. Somehow, we are getting along the majority of the time, and I feel the love is somewhere—buried deep down. Someday, I hope that all we are going through will become the basis for a stronger, better relationship, but right now, it is still too painful to accept.

November 7, 1993

We have bridged the gap by sharing our feelings. It has not been easy, but I was determined to push us along and resolve our problems. We have a long road ahead of us, which we have to make work.

Daryl is reluctant to discuss many of his inner thoughts unless forced up against a wall. When I insist on him communicating, it often leads to a significant battle filled with resistance on his part. We must keep talking and moving toward a viable solution. It is essential to our marriage.

November 14, 1993

No matter what, the two of us can get through anything. Since April, we have endured a lot of anger and frustration as we have uncorked our feelings. We have let them spill out in the messiest of ways. It has been an ongoing, painful, and arduous task.

Daryl needs lots of reassurance because I have shown so much anger—the kind he has never seen from me before. Now, it's time to come together and be as positive and embracing as I can be so that we can solve this situation together. This is not something I can do alone, and he can't either. For him to budge from his stubbornness, my support is crucial.

We must join forces, although running away seems like it would be easier. However, I am much too determined to right our wrongs and handle our situation. If we can have everything set in motion before turning fifty, we will have passed the test. We've been slow learners and have had to hit rock bottom to climb up, but it isn't too late. That's the good news.

December 9, 1993

Daryl was open about admitting his mistakes and his shortcomings. He let me know I have been right most of the time through all of this, which in itself was surprising. But this is not about right and wrong. We needed to go beyond the blame and find ways to live with and tackle our issues.

When Daryl came home, we showered and then made love. It felt fantastic to be in his arms and close to him again. We both appreciated and needed that.

December 18, 1993

I have experienced many emotions and have come a long way in understanding the financial situation and what makes Daryl tick. He is frustrating to me on some levels since he resists change. It is how he has always been. Somehow I have to work with him and help him break down his barriers. I'm not giving up and am determined to get beyond this.

I hope that by next year at this time, we will be managing our lives in a much more stable, productive way. We are fortunate to have the support, help, and knowledge from Jeff. He has made it possible for us to work together on a plan of action, which we desperately needed.

January 2, 1994

We are holding on for dear life, love one another, and want our marriage to survive. We need to get back on track, even though it is difficult since we're both fragile.

It's no surprise there are so many divorces. Through the years, we have seen many couples run from their problems. Daryl and I, each in our own way, are determined not to allow that to happen to us—hard as it might seem at times.

We have the resiliency to make this work. No matter how much we've battled and how hurt we've been, we seem able to accept what is and continue to love one another. I know he would prefer if I were the kind that repressed my feelings, but in reality, I must always let him know where I am and how I feel. To do otherwise wouldn't be honest for either one of us. Not to mention that had I not pushed our communication this past year, we would be in a hole with no way out. In reality, once we started to peel off the layers, we began to uncover so much.

What has been eye-opening is that I was always under the impression we communicated well. It has been a rude awakening to see how much we hadn't said. I realize it is hard for Daryl to bare his soul and closely examine issues, which he only does when I force him. Plus, while I am quick to see a problem and immediately change to rectify it, Daryl needs a lot of time to process before taking the next step. That makes it all the more difficult. We are holding on for dear life.

January 6, 1994

Years ago, when I took the course at Ohio State on family and marriage, I saw a movie about going to bed angry and vowed I never would. At the beginning of our marriage, I was insistent that we address each problem as it arose. Lately, I haven't always been ready to verbalize what I was feeling, so I am no longer holding on to my self-imposed edict. While the concept is fine, in practicality, it's not always plausible. I now understand that sometimes one needs time for processing, understanding the problem, and figuring out a plan of action.

I also know we must always take care of one issue before another one surfaces. Otherwise, there may be too many to deal with, and then it becomes overwhelming.

From the movie, I learned to address the issue at hand and not skirt around it. The examples they chose to demonstrate were of different couples fighting. In each case, the problem itself was flashed on the screen. I can still remember how the couples argued. While one husband and wife seemed somewhat calm, in the way I choose to fight, they never addressed the issue itself.

Another couple was screaming at each other, sounding awful. Yet, they were the ones who were getting to the root of the problem. I've never forgotten this, and while Daryl yells and I am generally much quieter, I make sure we are focused on the actual problem and are not running from it.

January 8, 1994

Daryl has finally made some necessary concessions to move us forward. I'm now concerned with his feelings, since I have been hard on him. He needs some TLC. So, I will make him a good spaghetti dinner tonight and turn my energies toward being kind to him. I want him to know I appreciate that he is doing the work. His favorite foods always make him happy.

January 9, 1994

I told Daryl I think we are on our way, have hit bottom, and can only go up from here. This whole process has taken us back to the basics of our relationship. We have explored it all and have completely exposed ourselves to one another. We are waking up to our realities.

I knew I was right not to give up and instead continue pursuing our situation. I am forcing Daryl to communicate and work through our problems. I know it will all be worth it one day.

January 16, 1994

The dynamics in our family have been off-kilter. Our kids knew something was cracking under the surface, but they never asked any questions. Maybe it was easier for them not to know. We spared them as many details as possible and saved them from our hell, but the heat singed their feathers. Now that they know we are okay and are healing, all will be fine.

I am married to an impossibly stubborn man. Daryl was like a steel door, refusing to let me break through. I used every communication tactic I knew. I was so frustrated but refused to stop. That frustration drove me on and caused me to take action — to find another way inside. I forged ahead on an uncharted path. I knew I couldn't stop because I would have never succeeded in keeping us whole if I had.

Daryl probably had no clue as to what was coming next. I only paused to muster my strength and find a new way to say what I had said over and over and over. I hounded Daryl until he finally woke up. We pushed each other to our limits. I felt as desperate as I would be if someone were to take away my journal and pen. I was on the edge, about to tip over.

I thought my hysterics would surely get to him, but that was not the final straw. It was those notes I wrote him one night that said it all—one after another until my pen went dry and my mind went blank. There was nothing more to say. It was then that Daryl finally chose to hear (or see) what I was saying. Perhaps it was the first time he realized what I meant and how serious I was about our marriage being in severe trouble. It's done now, and we can move on and heal.

January 26, 1994

This is a pivotal time for us. Daryl and I have a second chance and know we will do it right. We have a lot yet ahead, but I feel as if the two of us are ready to tackle it together. We have been brutally honest with each other. I don't believe in our 26 ½ years of marriage, we have ever done as much work. We are slowly carving our way out of the tunnel and are beginning to see the light again. Somewhere in the back of my mind, I have reminded myself that, as my dad would always tell me, any job worth doing is worth doing well. So, that's what I've set my mind to do and have begun to turn things around.

February 14, 1994

Daryl bought me two valentines. On one, he wrote something very loving about how I am his one and only and how much he loves me. I guess the way Daryl looks at everything, the past is the past. I'm sure he will not ever want to go back and rehash any of what we have recently experienced.

February 28, 1994

We've been sitting together and talking during dinner in the last few days—something we hadn't been doing much of lately. We had both been unhappy and were avoiding each other as a way of protecting ourselves from more hurt.

Now, there are many subtle ways I see we are changing as we move in the right direction toward healing. This is one of those periods where we are carefully working hard to get some stability and balance back into our marriage—what a huge relief.

March 6, 1994

Last night at the Fun Fair with the kids from the youth group, Daryl and I decided to go into the boxing ring and put on these huge helmets and boxing gloves. It was fun but not easy to box. At one point, I punched Daryl. All I could think was that this one was for all the anger I've experienced this year. It felt kind of good, actually.

April 18, 1994

After Daryl returned from his card weekend with the guys, he told me three times how much he had missed me. I told him I was surprised since he was away with his friends, but he said he thought of me a lot and then said, "After all, you are my best friend."

Later in the evening, he told me that starting today, he wants us to get back together in the way we used to be—or something like that—indicating our sex life. Then he said, "Am I saying the right thing?" I smiled and nodded with approval.

May 6, 1994

What a difference. Daryl and I are back to playing again and having fun. We're going out of our way to please each other. The tension and anger are gone. What's left is all the good stuff, finally!

This has been one of those experiences which I will remember forever. It was a time in our marriage when we were at a serious crossroads. I feel like we have jumped every hurdle set before us and are now walking peacefully down the lane hand in hand.

I was not about to let us slide off into oblivion. I knew enough to know there could be a happy ending. Deep down inside, we still loved each other, and that was all we needed. I have always believed that if one marries for the right reasons, there will be a way to work around the problems. It sure isn't easy, but it's worth it in the end.

I baked Daryl his favorite chocolate cake to show my love for him and my appreciation for how he has come around. Before I let him have a piece, though, I made him sit and talk to me. I think he's afraid of what will come out of my mouth now. However, he didn't have to worry. I just wanted to tell him how much I love him.

August 22, 1994

I called my parents to wish them a happy anniversary and decided to ask them the secret of their successful marriage of fifty-seven years. They told me it's important to keep on fighting as a way to communicate. My mom said when they fight, all the anger comes out, and they feel better.

It wasn't exactly the response I was looking for or the pearls of wisdom I expected. In retrospect, what surprised me was that I seldom saw my parents angry at each other and certainly did not witness fights between them. I guess I was oblivious, or else they were careful not to fight when I was around.

August 26, 1994

My being here at the beach, writing and away from home, has been a romantic time for us. There is something to be said for courting, coming together from time to time, and allowing one another a tremendous amount of space. We are both going out of our way to be thoughtful and show kindness toward each other.

Daryl and I realize that what we have built in our relationship up until now is sacred and needs to be treated that way.

All of this is a testament to what we have created in our marriage. The past few months have been a healing and revitalizing time for us. We certainly needed to rejuvenate.

I've gone back in time and have seen how strong our love for one another always has been. We have the right ingredients. I don't think two people could be more different than we are, but we keep finding ways to make our marriage work.

August 30, 1994

When I met with the two vice provosts at the University of Miami today, one of the men told me he got married when he was twenty-one and his wife was nineteen. When they met with the minister before their wedding, they talked to him about their love and bliss. After they finished, the minister said to them, "So, who will take out the garbage?"

September 4, 1994

The football game is about to start. Daryl will be watching a 1:00 game, one at 4:00, and then another at 8:00. 'Tis the season!

As time passes, we seem to become more focused on our passions. With Daryl sitting in front of the television lost in football, I'll have more time to spend at the beach writing. It works for both of us.

September 10, 1994

Some guy offered me a glass of wine. I politely said no. He asked about my t-shirt—a concert shirt from Mike. I don't even know the group. He said it doesn't seem possible that I have a son old enough to be going to concerts and was surprised when I told him I'm about to turn fifty. I also let him know I have been married for twenty-seven years. That was enough to send him on his way.

September 29, 1994

We are in such a different place than we were last year at this time. To get here, we had to step back, take stock, pick up the pieces, learn lots more lessons, and move ahead. The struggle was worth it because we are finally getting our act together with our finances. A whole new phase begins.

October 2, 1994

The two of us have done a remarkable job making this summer work well with my staying at the beach to begin reading my journals. I don't know too many men who are that secure within themselves, who trust their spouses, and who are independent enough to allow their wives the kind of space I had.

On the other hand, I know several women who would love to spend the time away as I did. I've seen their eyes light up with a wistful gaze when I described my three months of solitude at the ocean.

December 4, 1994

Daryl just called me into the den to give me a bite of the middle of his peanut butter and jelly sandwich. Now, that's love!

December 11, 1994

We're in a motel room at the beach. I would rather have no lights on, the windows open to catch the ocean breezes, and no TV. I'd love for the program Daryl is watching to be over, but he needs his television and air conditioning. I am in a sweatshirt because I'm cold. He's happy, though. As always, someone must give in and compromise. It's my turn.

Spending my fiftieth birthday weekend at the beach was just what I wanted. I could not be happier. Tomorrow morning, Daryl will head to work, and I'll get to spend my birthday writing under my favorite palm tree.

May 20, 1995

Polly came to me sharing her concerns about getting married and wanting some advice. The first thing I told her was if either of them had any doubts at all, they needed to explore those before walking down the aisle and making the commitment to their sacred marriage vows. I let her know if she isn't true to herself, she will never be happy.

We talked about some of her fiancé's behaviors that she wishes would be different. Based on my experience, I'm learning we cannot change another person. I let her know I've dealt with this since even before our marriage and realized I need to accept Daryl as he is. Still, I sometimes find myself trying once again and hoping he will somehow change. I'm not proud of this, but I do believe this information is important to have from the start.

The more we talked, I could tell she wanted to hear everything I was willing to share. And so, I went on to say every marriage has its highs and lows. No marriage is perfect, and there are generally trade-offs. No one has it all. Of course, because it has been such a huge lesson for me, I also told her no one person can ever fulfill all of our needs.

It seems as if she is in the stage now where the intoxicating sensations of new love and romance have begun to fade. This generally happens in a long-term relationship. Somehow, though, even without the excitement as the reality sinks in, I let her know that love can deepen in countless ways.

May 25, 1995

Today, on *Good Morning America,* Dr. Judith Wallerstein spoke about what makes a successful marriage. I was glad I had my journal nearby to jot down some of what she said. Her advice seems solid to me.

- Separate from your family of origin. Reshape relationships.
- Your spouse must come first.
- Build togetherness. Create autonomy. Are these both living side by side? Cope with crises like a job change, illness, death.
- Become parents and include the child.
- Make a safe place for conflict. Welcome it.
- A happy, good marriage leads to being able to deal with conflict.
- Express love. Enjoy sexual intimacy.
- Maintain humor.
- The worst enemy is boredom.
- Provide emotional nurturance.
- Be able to read each other.
- Remember the feelings and memories that you felt early on. Keep them alive.

May 28, 1995

Daryl is starting to get connected with the HMOs. His practice is coming alive again. He has survived and is going to be all the better for it. Slowly, we're picking up the pieces and moving on. The hard work, pain, anger, and frustration have paid off.

I have learned what makes our marriage strong and secure. Tom told me he doesn't know anyone else who stands as two solid individuals, and yet when we come together, we are a tight, well-functioning unit. We've done it!

June 11, 1995

A dozen roses sprinkled with miniature yellow orchids from Daryl were just delivered—beautiful and sweet. Daryl knows I love flowers, and when he gets them for me, I'm always happy. It's a lovely way to begin our 28th anniversary.

July 21, 1995

I told Daryl when I write full-time, which will happen, this will be what it's like—a greeting at the door when he walks in, dinner in the oven, a clean house, and a happy wife. What could be better for him?

I'm sure he appreciates my being an attentive wife—cooking for him, getting someone to cut the grass so he doesn't have to, doing all the yard work, including even cutting off the croton branch, which I had asked him to do. So, I am taking care of him, and in turn, he is taking care of me. It is a pleasure to see a well-tended plant blossom.

October 8, 1995

I saw *Moonlight and Valentine* today and cried through the whole movie. The husband dies right at the beginning. I spent part of the time thinking about Daryl and how devastated I would be if anything happened to him. During the movie, I thought about how lucky I am to have him as my husband.

February 24, 1996

We had an excellent discussion about marriage with Michael. As he gets closer to marrying Sara, I decided to ask him if he has any idea what to expect in marriage. His answer showed me he is ready because he has his thoughts in proper perspective. He understands that it takes commitment, love, compatibility, compromise, and so much else. I am glad he has found someone to love and to be loved by in return.

March 23, 1996

It paid off to hang in there and do what had to be done. Daryl needed a few good, hard, swift kicks, but it was worth it. I showed him I was there for the long haul but there was only so much I was willing to accept. I let him know that he made me happy when he listened and took action.

In retrospect, I learned plenty. I understand how complicit I was in our downfall by running away from reality. Assuming that all was well was a huge mistake. I must always be vigilant and involved with our finances. It's a pivotal time because we have both accepted responsibility and know what we must do to stay afloat from now on.

May 3, 1996

Daryl enjoyed his rubdown last night, and I was glad to give it to him. I am doing everything in my power to take good care of Daryl. I know that my giving to him means it will come back to me in some way. The more I give, the more I get. It makes a difference, and I'm glad we both recognize it.

May 5, 1996

A quote from the rabbi at the wedding last night: "Spend less time worrying about who is right and more time with what's right."

Another three words of advice he gave to the newlyweds: "Respect, respect, respect."

May 18, 1996

Daryl needed help at the office, so I went there yesterday. It's not my favorite thing to do, but he had a busy morning, and his secretary wasn't going to be in. When all his patients left, I called him into the surgical suite. I decided I might as well enjoy myself while I'm at his office. It almost felt risky, but I didn't care. I doubted that any patients would walk in without an appointment. It was worth it.

October 24, 1996

At a lecture by Rabbi Harold Kushner
"Romantic love needs to see perfection. The essence of a happy marriage is forgiveness — not for what a person does, but for what a person is.

"We have been physically and emotionally naked with each other and have been intimate in every way. I know your faults, and I know your good points. I accept the package."

December 15, 1996

I listened as Lynette bitched to me about her husband the first hour we were together. When he came up to us after, she asked him to get her a drink, and he ignored her. Yet, a little while later, he brought one of the guys a slice of lime, club soda, a glass of ice, and some liquor. I wanted to ask, "Why don't you do that for your wife?" Of course, I know the answer. They are not treating each other well — no kindness and caring, thus, not doing for one another. While it might seem easy to fix in order to have a happier marriage, their ways are deeply ingrained in their relationship. They are into blaming each other and not looking at their own actions.

September 20, 1997

Stan says that men marry women with the hopes of them never changing, and women marry men with the idea that they can transform them. I think that rings true for us. It is slowly sinking into my brain that generally, people will not change unless they want to and make a concerted effort to do so. Will I ever learn?

October 31, 1997

When we marry, for most of us, the only example we have of what marriage looks like is that of our parents. That means how we act with our spouse might be a total reflection of what we've seen and lived with growing up.

For sure, when Daryl and I married at age twenty-two, all I could think about was finally being able to live together. At the time, because we had dated for almost five years, it never occurred to me that we were coming from two different worlds. We were in love, and that was all that mattered to me and all I thought about. Luckily, our values were much the same, making a big difference in how we began as a married couple.

We were not necessarily prepared for what might float up in our marriage. We needed more tools than we had. It has taken many years to figure out what works best for us.

December 16, 1998

I have comfort, security, understanding, love, depth, acceptance, caring, predictability, friendship, nurturing, warmth, fun, and a future in my marriage. What more could I ask for?

July 3, 1999

As Ruth and Tim's wedding approaches, I am excited to be the one officiating. In creating the ceremony, I've listed some advice I've come to understand and value through my marriage. Before reciting the list, I plan to say this:

A good marriage must be created and sustained. It requires time, effort, patience, tolerance, and forgiveness. Marriage is one of those things in our lives that we learn by doing. Together, you must and will create your way. Above everything, know that the most significant value is to believe in the importance of your marriage. Understand that as long as your flame of love remains lit, your marriage can and will endure whatever presents itself.

January 1, 2000

I am thrilled to be in New York City at the turn of the century. Yesterday, Daryl and I went to Times Square early in the day to get a feel for what it's like. There were masses of people already gathering, but it was not nearly as crowded as we figured it would be at night. Later, we ushered in the year 2000 from Tom's rooftop. From there, we couldn't see Times Square, but we could hear the roar of the crowds as midnight struck.

For us, it was one of those special moments when we were embracing and kissing the minute 1999 ended. I always insist on spending a little time on New Year's Eve talking about what we dream of for the coming year. I'm sure Daryl could do without that, but it is important to me, so he goes along with it.

We are both ready to welcome a new year, a new decade, and a new century. It's time to look at how we will fill the empty pages of our calendar.

February 15, 2001

Yesterday was Vince and Sarah's seventy-second anniversary, which is mind-boggling to me. I have never met anyone who has been married that long. What an inspiration they are. The fact that they are happy, constantly hold hands, sing to and with each other, and are still in love takes it to another level.

When I was alone with Vince, I asked what advice he would give to a newlywed couple. He said, "Be nice to each other." Later, in a different room, when I asked Sarah, she said the same thing.

I have to laugh at how simple their advice is and yet so wise. It doesn't take all that much of an effort, but it makes a huge difference. I need to be more conscious of my behavior toward Daryl.

February 13, 2002

Yesterday my mood was so different from the day before. As hard as it had been to fight with Daryl, it was one of those difficult discussions we had to have to clear the air. As a result, I know exactly where he stands, how he feels, what we both should do when we are with each other.

As always, it's all about communication and how we must say everything. Once out in the open with our fears and anger expressed, we are different. Saying what's so during a good fight eases the tensions. It's a fresh start with new information behind us. Of course, going through it is miserable.

June 11, 2002

Relationships don't just happen. They require constant vigilance, hard work, and concern for one another. They take commitment and everything else that comes from the heart and soul. I guess if I've learned nothing else, this is what stands out for me on our thirty-fifth anniversary.

November 23, 2002

Diane Rehm from NPR at the Miami Book Fair
"We are woefully ignorant of our partners before we enter into a long-term commitment. What questions do we ask or look into? What do people think marriage is all about?

"Sexual attraction is a big deal, but it ain't the whole deal." Diane and her husband were at ten weddings in the last ten years. All of them have ended in divorce.

"Money and sex have been the toughest topics we have dealt with in our marriage. The in-laws were the hardest to write about. My mother-in-law told me she married to have a child and loved him more than her husband.

"What makes a good marriage? Persistence, sheer stubbornness, love, respect, intimate attraction, and communication of feelings.

"Rarely did I know of a marriage made in heaven that didn't have to be lived on earth."

October 29, 2005

Hurricane Wilma hit five days ago. The two of us have been spending more time together than we have in years. Not having electricity for all these days leaves us with little choice. Without the TV for Daryl and the computer for me, we now have big chunks of free time.

We've spent countless hours in the yard cleaning up after the hurricane. We aren't afraid of hard work, are a good team, and do what is necessary to get the job done.

Besides that, we're getting used to eating a lot of peanut butter and jelly sandwiches. So far, we are managing. By 9:00 each night, we've been crawling into bed. Daryl has been playing solitaire, while I've been reading by candlelight.

Life is so much simpler than the way we usually live. We have eliminated all the frills and realize how little we need to be content. It makes me wonder if we'll do anything differently when we once again have electricity and get back to work.

November 6, 2005

What took place between Daryl and me today was most interesting. We had done surprisingly well for the thirteen days in the dark. We rolled with the punches and made the best of not having electricity. We were never short with each other and were having a great time together.

Then, as soon as the power came back on, we started bickering. I couldn't believe how we were acting. Once we recognized what we were doing, we quickly stopped. I'm not sure why that happened, but maybe we both had pent-up frustration, which we needed to be released.

I now think I could live simply and do without so many modern conveniences that come with power. The most positive takeaway in all of this is that Daryl and I spent such quality time together, which was good for our marriage.

December 31, 2006

Marlene told me that, in retrospect, she would rather have shared this life with one man and lived with the good and bad than to have started over and had to deal with all the issues that a second marriage encounters. She's currently living with the difficulties that stepchildren and ex-spouses can bring.

She isn't the only one who has told me that getting divorced was maybe not the wisest move, although, at the time, it seemed it was. What I've heard from many of my friends is that while they are happier than they were in their first marriages, in many cases, they traded one set of problems for another. It makes sense to me since nothing is all good or all bad.

June 9, 2007

And so, as we approach our fortieth anniversary, I realize more than ever that life is filled with ups and downs. While most of the time during these past ten years, we have been in a good place, financial problems continue to surface periodically. Plus, I am concerned with Daryl's health and his not taking care of himself. It frightens me. I would be lying if I didn't admit to feeling frustrated at times.

Yet, despite it all, we are a solid team. When we set our minds to it, we can accomplish a lot. We work well together and enjoy the partnership when tackling a project. We love our family and relish our moments with them.

We sat on the couch before, and I read Daryl the book I had written for him for our fifteenth anniversary. We both laughed and enjoyed walking back in time to the memories we've created throughout our lives together.

We have such a full and rich history—one we can tap into at any time and thoroughly appreciate. We have certainly shared many happy and sad moments. We've achieved something quite special—being married forty years is a long time.

June 25, 2007

We heard that sunrise at Lake Louise is supposed to be spectacular, so we decided to get up early to experience it. We had requested a wake-up call for 6:00 a.m., but we were both too excited, so instead, Daryl got up at 3:30, and I woke up at 5:00.

Aside from one other person, we were the only ones out by the magnificent lake. The temperature was around thirty degrees. We bundled up and held onto each other to stay warm. The mist rolled in and floated from one area to the next, weaving through the tops of trees, occasionally exposing a mountain peak, and sometimes skimming across the water. Seeing the breathtaking sunrise was a fantastic way to begin the day.

June 29, 2007

Daryl and I had a great time on our trip to the Canadian Rockies. We were eager to be someplace we had never been before and delighted in seeing the beauty that surrounded us.

Being on a group tour meant we spent a lot of time with others and some quiet moments alone. Always when we chose to relax during our free times, we fell into our standard patterns—Daryl content to be in our room watching TV, while I found a beautiful spot outdoors to write or explore.

The more I talked to people on our bus and observed them, I saw that each relationship mainly had good moments with occasional disagreements sprinkled among them. Nothing can be ideal all the time, even on vacation, regardless of how much two people love one another.

April 1, 2008

My record still stands. For forty-one years, I have pulled off a joke of some sort on Daryl for April Fools' Day. Without fail, I have succeeded even when he tells me in advance that he will not fall for anything. Regardless, each year, I manage to find something different to do or say that fools him.

When he came home today, he asked how my Student Awareness Day was. I put on a sad face and told him it was a disaster—that only two schools showed up—about seventy students in all. He fell for it and felt awful for me. After a bit, fortunately, I could then tell him it was a terrific success and, once again, I got him!

One of my favorite tricks I pulled on him was when I moved his car down the block, so when he walked out the door to go to the office, his car was gone. Another was when I banged pots and pans around the kitchen as if I were cooking.

I spent about a half-hour in there and then called everyone to dinner. Of course, when they came in to eat, there was no dinner. Daryl was not too happy since he thought we were having spaghetti. The kids loved that instead of our dinner, we ended up having Carvel ice cream followed by Krispy Kreme doughnuts.

January 9, 2009

Because we were high school sweethearts, we have many of the same friends from way back. So, when Carolyn, Lynn, and Margaret stayed here before we left for Carol's, Daryl could join in the fun. When we got into bed, he commented on how happy I must be. Our friends have always been important to both of us, and I was glad he could enjoy being with them too.

January 31, 2009

We've experienced some pretty wild evenings together—tonight being yet another one of those. We were at Mo's Deli with Ron and Eileen. While we were waiting to be seated, we overheard someone in line say that Jackie Mason, the stand-up comedian, was there.

Sure enough, we ended up sitting right next to him. At one point, he came over to our table to talk and asked Ron if his meat was good. He then picked up Ron's knife and cut himself a piece of brisket. We were hysterical. Throughout the rest of the evening, we talked back and forth with Jackie and the person he was with.

When I saw they had a big plate of rugalach, I asked if I could have one. After all, if he could take a piece of meat off Ron's plate without asking, I figured I could ask him for a piece of pastry. He ended up giving us the whole plate full. Daryl and I are still laughing over it. We can add this to our list of crazy memories.

April 3, 2009

Amid all the pain over the issues with my brother, Daryl is feeling shut out. I know he wants to be there for me, but he doesn't always get that I don't want advice or for him to fix anything. I just need him to listen, hug me, and understand I need some space to write and absorb my feelings.

I'm convinced that most men don't understand that women aren't looking for solutions when we vent. We just need to say how we're feeling and want nothing but to be heard. After all these years, I have not succeeded in getting that through to him.

August 1, 2010

Daryl and I are on the plane on our way back from Peachfest. One of the best things we do together is enjoy our family. Since we've been with each other for what seems like forever, Daryl is as much a part of the Rothenberg cousins as I am, even though he is a cousin through marriage.

Somehow, maybe because we were so young when we started dating, we have always felt welcomed and grateful to be accepted by each other's families. From the beginning of our marriage, we both called our in-laws Mom and Pop. These days, it seems many young couples call their in-laws by their first names.

September 18, 2010

Daryl was not happy when I told him that everyone was concerned about his health and weight. He did not want to hear that and let me know that enough was enough.

Meanwhile, he keeps talking about expecting and wanting to live a long life, which is great, except that if he doesn't take care of himself, I'm not sure how that will be possible. It affects our marriage and our lives together, although he doesn't see it that way. It's maddening to me.

March 10, 2011

Unfortunately, the side issues of divorce never go away. Kids are often the ones who are affected the most—mainly because they have to divide themselves between both parents. I have heard from many how they have struggled with what feels like living two separate lives.

Rebecca's friend told me that when her parents separated, they both disappeared. They were into themselves completely, wanting to experience new lives, and left her and her sister on their own. She said they had a lot of freedom but no longer had a family.

She told me almost all her friends' parents were divorced, and we were the only ones who showed her what was possible in terms of a solid, loving marriage. It was surprising to learn that unknowingly, we greatly influenced her.

June 11, 2011

Today is forty-four years we've been married. That's a long time. Miraculously, I stayed in bed and slept in, so I was still there when Daryl woke up—something that rarely happens, since I have become such an early riser. We lay in bed and talked about our marriage. He asked me what I thought about this past year. I told him there had been good years and bad ones, and that thankfully, this last one has been exceptionally good.

June 11, 2012

Forty-five years and counting—another milestone and reason to reflect on our marriage. Almost all of our high school friends have stayed married. Each couple has had its challenges. Like so much in life, I realize it's not necessarily the issue itself, but it's more about how we handle it—our attitudes in facing adversity.

Every marriage is so different. I sometimes wonder how those who work together and are with each other 24/7 manage without having much space. I doubt that Daryl and I would do well with that.

As the years have passed, our different interests have become more and more apparent. I continue to be out there learning new things, seeking adventure, traveling, and meeting people, while Daryl seems perfectly content to go to the office, play cards, and hang out in the den. Luckily, it works for us.

October 5, 2012

Daryl left me this note: "Mer, I am extremely proud of you as you embark on your author-filled days and also your newest teaching endeavor. I stand there amazed at my wife of forty-five years and relationship of fifty. With all my love, Me."

I feel fortunate that Daryl has always supported whatever I've done by showing an interest in my work and creative endeavors. He has never once felt threatened by my successes and has always been proud of me. I know many husbands who could not handle their wives being in the spotlight. How lucky I am! I get flowers. Some wives get a cold shoulder.

November 14, 2012

At the Miami Book Fair, Jeff Tobin said that four states voted for same-sex marriages after thirty-three losses. Ten states are now legal for same-sex marriages. I'd say it's about time the country is moving toward this.

I cannot imagine what it must be like to love someone and be a life partner but not have the same rights that married couples have. I recently heard from a gay friend whose partner was in the hospital. Unfortunately, because they aren't married, he was not given any significant information from the doctors. I'm hopeful that one day we will live in a world where this is no longer an issue.

February 7, 2013

Daryl ate the entire devil's food cake (his all-time favorite) I made him yesterday. He looks forward to it every year and has since we've been married. While it kills me to bake it for him because of the ingredients, I know he would be crushed if his birthday came and there was no cake. Of course, with his diabetes being what it is, one stick of butter, 1½ cups of sugar, 1½ cups of flour, and ½ cup cocoa is not what he should be eating! Next year, I think I'll cut the recipe in half.

February 11, 2014

Sarita told me about the affair she had and regrets it because she broke her wedding vows. Yet, she's glad for the experience. When she and her husband went to an event recently, Sarita looked around at everyone there and realized their whole world would drastically change if she were to leave her husband. At that moment, Sarita knew it was time to end the affair and decided to be true to her marriage. Her husband will never know. Is it better that way?

May 10, 2014

I had asked Daryl if he would come to synagogue with me, and he said yes. It's okay if he doesn't want to, since I know it doesn't mean anything religiously to him, but I am always glad to have him by my side.

At the dinner after services, we sat with a few people new to the congregation. Daryl talked to one of the women and ended up selling her one of my books. He went out to his car, where he has kept a ready supply of *Room 732* and brought one in for her. At least a few times each month, he comes home and tells me he has sold my book to one of his patients. How sweet is that?

June 11, 2014

Gone are the days of romantic anniversaries. Daryl is playing cards tonight. I knew he didn't want to miss his weekly card game, so I told him I was okay with him going. We instead celebrated by having an early dinner. I think Daryl was shocked that I let him go, but I figured it would make him happy. So, that's my gift to him this year.

June 19, 2015

This vacation in Italy is a dream come true. I'm so glad we went to Switzerland first, though, since it was a country Daryl has always wanted to visit. Being there was everything he dreamed it to be and seeing him that ecstatic made me smile.

Today was yet another full day of touring. We began with a fabulous breakfast at the hotel. Because it was a buffet, Daryl was in heaven. After eating, we piled on the bus and left to go to the Galleria dell Academia, where we saw the statue of David—something Daryl said he has always wanted to see in person. From there, we went to the Uffizi Gallery. After, Gorgio, our tour guide, gave us free time to walk the streets, eat lunch, and shop. The two of us walked to the National Library and then searched for the Florence synagogues, where guards carefully watched whoever entered.

Most often in our marriage when we've taken trips, Daryl is not all that adventurous. I like to take the detours, and he is interested mainly in getting to our destination without any stops. So, this time around, he is stepping out of his comfort zone to please me. I'm grateful. It took us a long time to walk back, but, of course, we stopped and had gelato, which we've done at least once every day. I must say as much as Daryl hates walking, he has not complained at all. Right now, though, he's on the bed napping and snoring away.

September 27, 2015

I have written about this ad nauseam. It is an issue that surfaces for me periodically and has since the beginning of our relationship in 1962. There have always been little things about Daryl that I wished would change. I don't know if everyone feels that way about their spouses, and I'm not proud that I do. I need to let go of this desire to make him into someone he isn't. Regardless that I thought I could effect change, I have been unsuccessful. I now know I will never change Daryl. I can only be responsible for myself. The time has come for me to wake up and be realistic. He is who he is, and I am who I am.

Bottom line: It is unfair of me to expect him to be anything different. It has taken me fifty-three years to finally let this go. I guess I'm a pretty slow learner. As of today, I commit to being done with this!

December 3, 2015

It's insane that I am awake at 4:00 a.m. Daryl has been in the hospital for four days with cellulitis. At first, he refused to go, and I had to drag him there. However, he was so out of it that he didn't even know what was happening. I've canceled my trip to Boston, since I need to be here for him. I also canceled all my classes this week.

I am hopeful this is a warning sign for Daryl and that he has finally awakened to the dangers of his diabetes. He says he is on board and plans to start taking care of himself and eat the right foods. I can only hope he will, and if he does, it will make a difference in his health.

As angry and frustrated as I have been with him through the years about not taking care of himself, all my anger melts away, and fear takes over when I see him in the hospital bed. I love him and want him to be healthy.

December 8, 2015

Daryl is better! He went back to work. His energy level and his mood are more regular, and his leg looks much improved.

Yesterday he left me a note before he headed to the office. "Thanks, as always, for all your help. I love you." It's lovely to be appreciated. That goes a long way.

April 17, 2016

I met a woman today at one of the conference sessions, and we ended up walking out together after it was over. She told me she was getting married on June 11th and talked to me about her upcoming wedding.

One thing led to the next, and she told me her fiancé is fabulous but doesn't make a decent income. She also said that their sex is not fulfilling enough for her. I gave her lots of advice, starting with suggesting she buy a vibrator, write or talk to him about her concerns, and above all, make sure she is marrying him for the right reasons. By the end of our conversation, she told me she realizes she has much to think about before saying I do.

June 11, 2017

Fifty years is a long time to be married. When I think back to us beginning to date in our senior year of high school, there is no way I could have ever imagined we would spend the rest of our lives together. We have a long and wonderful history—one that we can tap into at any time and thoroughly appreciate. We've shared family and friends and have been together for countless milestone events in our lives.

We have shared the whole gamut of life, from experiencing both significant challenges and the most heart-filled moments. Today, we have reached an enormous milestone and have achieved something quite special—a time of joy and celebration.

I feel blessed to have made it to this point in our lives together. I look forward to celebrating this milestone anniversary with our family in South Dakota at the dude ranch. It'll be a new experience for all of us, and I like the idea of doing something we've never done before. It makes for a more exciting life and is a great way to create new memories.

Reflections on
The Joys and Challenges of Marriage

When I look back on my marriage to Daryl through the excerpts I've chosen to include, it's clear that ours has been one with peaks and valleys. Gratefully, the good has far outweighed the bad, but I would be painting an unrealistic picture were I not to share some of the most challenging times we've experienced.

I have learned no marriage is without its struggles, and none is perfect. How could it be when we, as humans, each have our flaws? No matter how similar our backgrounds might be, no two of us are the same. How we differ and what we have each brought to our marriage might have seemed minor at first, but there have been moments when I have felt like I wedded someone from an alternate universe. While our values are similar, who we are as individuals could not be more different.

Throughout our marriage, Daryl and I have learned how to negotiate our contrasting ways of being. For us, the saying that opposites attract is undoubtedly the case. I've always had a lot of energy and a drive to accomplish something constructive and meaningful constantly. My list of goals is long, and I find myself not wanting the clock to run out before I finish everything on it. When I retired, I had a plan.

When Daryl retired, he had none. Once COVID hit and we were together 24/7, I realized the gap in how we spend our time continued to widen. Despite this, we co-exist well side by side and always have.

More recently, when Daryl was in the hospital with a valve replacement followed by seizures, I thought about how we had stood together under the *chuppah* in 1967. On our wedding day, we were excited to finally be getting married after first being friends for two years until we were almost eighteen and then dating for four-and-a-half years. We were all smiles, and while we declared our vows and heard those words "for better and for worse," we had no idea what they truly meant. We were young and clueless about what our future would bring. How can anyone know?

One thing that stood out for me as I read the excerpts was how playful we were in the early years of our marriage. When I read about watching the couple in the ocean who had been married for fifty-four years, I thought about that.

Here we are, having just recently celebrated our fifty-fourth anniversary. Back then, in 1980, when Daryl and I were only married for thirteen years, I had wondered how we might be years later.

Now, I imagine how we might seem to a young couple if they were to see us together in the ocean. Yes, we have our playful moments and love each other, but I'm not sure we would appear in quite the same way as the couple did to me all those years ago.

Figuring out my needs and what it would take for me to be truly happy took a while. I grew up with the idea that marriage was like a fairy tale. That's how it was in the early sixties for many women. We believed that our prince charming husband would sweep us away and take care of our every desire. There were years at the beginning where I expected Daryl to be the be-all and end-all.

In the seventies, when I read the book, *My Needs, Your Needs, Our Needs* by Jerry Gillies, I became enlightened. That's when I learned that no one person could completely meet another's needs. I then realized I would have to find ways to fulfill my own life, not expect Daryl to provide it all for me, and not solely depend on him for everything. I came to understand the importance of being independent, which has served me well in my marriage.

Despite our differences, I am incredibly thankful that Daryl is supportive of my work and my writing. He's always been the first one to listen to what I've written, help me with word choices on occasion, and let me know he's proud of me. I feel fortunate because I know not all husbands would be as generous of spirit. For that and so much else, I am grateful.

In June 2019, I officiated at my great-niece Elysha's and now great-nephew Cory's wedding. Before writing their ceremony, I went back and read the original one hundred fifty pages of marriage excerpts I had taken from my journals. For me, it was an excellent way to reflect on all I had learned about being married and helped me decide what would be best to share with Elysha and Cory. I knew this was a sacred responsibility, one which I took seriously.

I have since shared the shortened but unedited version of this chapter with Rebecca and her husband Dave, and others who have recently married. I am hopeful that something I've written on these pages will be helpful in better understanding all that marriage encompasses.

Journal Prompts

These prompts can apply to anyone in a relationship. One does not have to be married to respond to them.

- What matters most to you in a relationship? What are the qualities you look for in another person?

- If you have different spiritual practices, how do you make them work?

- What are your expectations of your partner?

- What did you see growing up that you would like to replicate or copy in your relationship? What would you like to do differently?

- What are your common interests? Values? Beliefs?

- What strengths do you and your partner each bring to your relationship? What weaknesses?

- What do you need most in a relationship? How do you make sure to meet them? What about your partner's needs? Are you meeting those?

- What do you fight about, and how do you fight? How do you resolve conflicts?

- How do you communicate about financial issues? What are your financial goals?

- Of all of the people you have met and could be with, why have you chosen each other?

- What attracted you to your partner initially? Is that same spark there? What has changed since the beginning of your relationship?

On Being a Woman

*It took me quite a long time to develop a voice, and now that I have it,
I am not going to be silent.*

— Madeline Albright

June 18, 1976

Through the years, I have often looked to others to meet my needs. I am beginning to realize that it's important as a woman to find fulfillment within myself. The more I understand that my happiness can't depend on someone else, the better I will be as a wife, mother, friend, and whatever other roles I may have going forward.

July 7, 1977

I can't put my finger on what it is that is causing these awful feelings. I'm restless, discontent, and basically out of sorts. A few of my friends have mentioned that their moods change, days and sometimes a week, before they get their period. So, maybe that's what is happening. It seems to be my pattern lately.

October 26, 1979

I'm at Hollywood Medical Center waiting to have a tubal ligation. I hope I never regret my decision. I was put to the test recently when my period was late. I knew then I didn't want to have another child and didn't want to face having an abortion. That's when I realized that getting my tubes tied would be the right decision for me.

Having had cholestatic jaundice when I was pregnant with Michael was enough to know I never want to experience that again. The doctor assured me it would reoccur and would get worse with each pregnancy. Besides, I am approaching thirty-five and feel I am past my childbearing years at this point in my life. I feel confident about my decision.

December 14, 1979

When I graduated high school, women had few career options. We could have become nurses or teachers, and those who didn't go to college could work as a secretary.

I was programmed at a young age to get a college education, become a teacher, find a husband, get married, and have children. I didn't even realize there could be choices. While I have no regrets about the path I took, I am grateful that women today aren't limited the way I was.

March 10, 1980

More recently, there has been a revolt in the women's movement. I'm reading about how women are standing up to men and fighting for their rights. It hasn't translated to my community yet, where so many men I know think women should have fewer rights and opportunities. Some seem to want their wives to stay home and not venture out into the world. Most don't even want the women to have credit cards in their name, which seems pretty crazy to me.

I'm getting messages from a few of my friends' husbands that I'm a rebel and am causing trouble in their homes because I'm raising the consciousness of their wives. Seriously!

At a party recently, two of my friends' husbands (whom I'm friends with also) came up to me and said, "Just be aware when you're jogging because we might be kidnapping you. You're causing too much trouble for us with all your women's rights bullshit." Of course, I knew they were kidding about the kidnapping, but I believe they were letting me know I needed to stop feeding their wives ideas about equal rights. And so it goes.

July 2, 1980

I'm outraged at those men in this world who won't accept women on equal footing and who treat us as second-class citizens. I doubt I'll ever understand.

I'm also frustrated with a few men in my life who don't express their feelings. It's hard to relate to them on an emotional level. For that reason and so much more, I feel fortunate to be a woman.

August 4, 1980

Since taking the job as the preschool director and preparing for the school year, I have so much to do. Suddenly, more than ever, I'm aware of all the responsibilities that are mine here at home.

I feel resentful of the inequality of my roles versus Daryl's when it comes to our household chores. I must let him know how I feel and hope he'll understand. Things have to change. I don't want to walk around being angry all the time. Right now, I feel like I have two jobs—one outside of the home and one inside.

November 14, 1981

Some men seem threatened by me. Maybe I come on too strong for them. All I want is fair and balanced recognition and equality. It seems so many women struggle for that. To date, it appears to be an ongoing fight that results in our continuing to be held back in society.

My desire for equality continues to rock the boat in the neighborhood. Most men preferred things the old way when they could get away with doing little and having few responsibilities. Who wouldn't want that? It's time for a change.

January 16, 1982

It was interesting to hear Daryl express his thoughts about women versus men. He claims women are too emotional and not at all practical. In general, I know women are more open, sensitive, and caring, while men seem focused on concrete issues and facts.

I mostly listened. My feeling about this subject is that by nature, women are opposite from men. Daryl's and my thoughts couldn't be farther apart on the spectrum of women's and men's fundamental beliefs on many topics. We speak a different language.

There is nothing like another woman to talk to when I need to be heard. They understand me as no man I know ever does. I'm not sure what I'd do without my female friends.

April 17, 1982

We have no cleaning woman unlike most of my friends. I assume the greater part of work in both the house and yard.

I do my best not to complain constantly about the inequality of men's and women's roles, but it's hard to keep my mouth shut. Will the time ever come when we even up the scorecard?

May 9, 1982

It seems as if more and more people are talking about the Equal Rights Amendment. When Congress introduced it in 1923, there was little hope of our country ratifying it. By the late sixties and early seventies, the feminists saw the amendment's ratification as the only way to eliminate discrimination against women. Unfortunately, ERA didn't happen then. I'm hopeful that times have changed, and it will be ratified by the deadline next month. How could it not be?

July 1, 1982

It is hard to believe that only thirty-five of the thirty-eight necessary states ratified the Equal Rights Amendment. I don't understand how that is possible in this day and age.

I'm sure that Phyllis Schlafly, who campaigned against the ratification, must be happy today. She had argued, among other things, that the ERA would take away privileges like the "dependent wife" benefits under Social Security. She is for women staying at home, yet I'm pretty sure she goes to work each day. I don't think I'll ever understand women who are opposed to ERA. What am I missing?

July 20, 1982

After my interview today at the high school with Mr. Harris, the principal, and the board president, I left feeling unnerved. Mr. Harris told me he hopes ERA never passes. I was shocked and disheartened. Don't men get it? Do they believe they're superior?

We discussed my role as a woman coming into the school. Mr. Harris talked about a woman's place in America and said, "If ERA had passed, America would change and not for the better." The president's comment was just as bad — something like, "I hope it never passes! Nothing good can come from it." And so, I am walking into the working world where women have to know their place, accept it, and endure. I hope I'm ready for this.

When I state how I feel about women's rights, some men become belligerent. It is upsetting and frustrating, and although I hate to view men negatively, in some ways, when I listen to what they say, I feel disgusted. So many men don't want to recognize us women and our capabilities. They seem threatened by us — as if we're too competent. I'm not sure what it is. I only know that it upsets me.

It's almost like I have to keep my feelings quiet and secret. It's hard for me to do, but I know better. I would not get a welcoming reception if I shared all of this with a man right now — not even Daryl, who has thankfully become somewhat more understanding.

I wish I didn't have to fight for my rights, but if I want change, I must. I long for a more equal, balanced system for everyone. I dream of a world that is just and peaceful. In doing my part for equality, I am working hard to erase my prejudices and open myself up to listen to others.

August 7, 1982

The other night, we watched *20/20* on television, and one of the segments featured something called premenstrual syndrome. Finally, after all these years, there is a name for the outrageously awful feelings I get before my period. I think all women will be pleased to hear that what we've suffered is an actual condition that has been studied scientifically. It's about time! Perhaps if there were more women scientists, it wouldn't have taken so long to get to this point.

October 3, 1982

It's a good thing no one is here with me at the beach today. My PMS (so glad it now has a name) is in high gear. I'm edgy and moody and sending off messages like, "Don't come near me. Don't touch me." At times like this, I can't stand to be with myself. I feel unbalanced.

My hormones are playing havoc with my emotions. I don't even want to subject others to who I am right now. No wonder Daryl said I looked like I had fire coming out of my eyes when he walked in the door yesterday.

These moods are beyond my control. I am usually reasonably even-tempered, but I start to feel like I'm crawling on the inside near the onset of my period. I'm better off not being around anyone else. Thus, I am in the car at the beach, waiting out a severe thunderstorm. There is no one else in sight except for one woman who is jogging on the Broadwalk. Maybe she is as desperate and crazed as I am!

November 29, 1982

Today, six of my closest high school friends had lunch together as we gathered in Cleveland for our twentieth-year high school reunion. The last time we had been together like this was when we were in college. Now, we've all been married for about fifteen years, give or take a year or two. All of us but one is working, and each of us is juggling schedules daily, trying to find the perfect balance.

First, we each caught everyone up on our personal lives and then discussed marriage, work, and life in general. We talked about how we are as mothers and how we sometimes take our frustrations and moods out on our children. It was reassuring to know we all pretty much felt the same way about parenting.

Somehow, the conversation led us to talk about our fantasies and what we thought would be the excitement of having an affair—some more than others longed for someone else for variety. Fortunately, we are all in solid relationships with our husbands and happily married, but that doesn't mean we can't fantasize on occasion. Being able to do that with my girlfriends was so much fun and reminiscent of when we were teenagers imagining what was then unknown to us.

January 11, 1983

After a long day at work, I went grocery shopping. Daryl has a meeting, and the kids are at a party. I put the groceries away and then straightened up the house. I don't seem to be the one who makes the mess, but I sure as hell am the only one who cleans it up or who even cares. Why is that?

A family of four requires a significant time commitment on the part of the woman. Demands pull me in every direction—carpools, shopping, cleaning, cooking, planning, coping, wiping tears, giving hugs, and balancing.

February 19, 1983

After leaving my job at the high school midyear and discussing it with a few of our male friends, I am shocked at their response and support. Some of them might even view me as an equal in the working world. We've come a long way.

August 31, 1983

I recently read an article from *Vogue* about women working at home instead of going off to a job. Very few men see what I'm doing with my writing as having any validity at all and certainly not as a job. I was shocked when both rabbis at synagogue commented on just that—them being scholars of the book and all. I wonder how it would be if I were a man who would choose to stay home and spend my time writing a novel.

In our writing group, we discussed our roles as mothers and homemakers. We talked about the way others view women who stay home and "do nothing."

Anyway, there's always so much to do around the house. I am constantly cleaning the kitchen, washing the floors, picking up stuff everywhere. Not to mention that I am expected to run all the errands, since I "don't have anything else to do!" Ha! Oh, the plight of the housewife!

I just drove my first carpool of the season. The good news is I have managed to "fit" it into my schedule. The bad news is I probably have about two hundred more trips to make this school year.

September 5, 1983

I never expected to have a women's lib conversation with my niece Judi at her age. We talked about the variety of neat jobs available to women. She's amazingly aware—a raised consciousness at age eleven. It's encouraging to know that young girls understand all their options in our world today.

September 20, 1983

I'm at a breakfast listening to Gloria Steinem. Before she started to speak, the woman next to me, who had just turned sixty-eight, told me the best of life was yet to come. She said when one is in her sixties, there is no competition—whatever that means. I wished I had had time to ask her, but we were interrupted at that moment. Competition with other women, with men, in the workplace? I wonder.

Gloria has just said that it's the system that's crazy, not us. She feels we need to come together to discover hope, change, and dreams. A sign of progress is that we have new names for experiences and are trying to make language accurate. "Imagine," she said, "if a man graduated with a spinster's of arts degree or had to work as a sistership instead of a fellowship."

Other great quotes and thoughts: "A pedestal is as much a prison as any other small space.

"If women could raise themselves to wealth and power, as 'they' (men) say they do, there would be more of us there.

"Working women—a phrase that is a curse. Feminists try to give words like working in the home and working out of the home.

"When we speak of human rights (like Soviet Jewry), we aren't speaking of women's rights. What about women all over the world who are trapped by their husbands and who need to acquire their permission to do anything? We must fight for all people to be free.

"When a woman feels she's missing a man, she may just be missing the rest of herself."

Gloria Steinem is powerful in that she has given women the confidence and security of knowing that others feel the same way. She left us with the following. "Do one outrageous act. Make an impact. Make someone aware."

Later. Since hearing the lecture today and realizing that Gloria is not married, I've given lots of thought to what it would be like to be a single person with no responsibilities to a spouse and children. It takes a great deal of energy to raise kids and be a good wife. Sometimes, I wonder if there's much left for anything else.

I would guess that without having to divide oneself and then devoting one's energy into a single focus, that individual could more easily become accomplished in a particular area of concentration. With a family and other responsibilities, I am like a wheel's hub scattered in many directions.

One thing that was apparent today was how much further we women must go in this struggle—sisters—abused women in the world with no country of our own—a different breed than any other minority.

I liked Gloria Steinem's sophisticated, non-combative approach and her inspiring words to keep up the fight for what's deservedly coming to us and nothing more. She left me with a lot of food for thought. Her important messages from earlier this morning are slowly sinking in.

When Gloria talked about women needing permission from their husbands to do anything, it reminded me of an incident that happened after my first year of marriage. I wanted to get my ears pierced. For whatever reason, Daryl's family always thought pierced ears were barbaric, so he went along with that thinking.

I had gained twenty-five pounds that year, so one day when I again begged him to let me pierce my ears, he consented with the stipulation that I first had to lose that extra weight. I immediately went on a diet, and on the day I weighed 107 pounds, I made an appointment for that afternoon with the doctor who was going to pierce my ears.

I can still remember walking in the house with little gold posts in my ears. I took one look at Daryl and said, "That will be the last time you'll ever tell me what I can do with my body." That was the day I became a feminist, and he's paid the price ever since.

October 8, 1983

Tonight some of my teacher friends from the preschool had dinner together. Bernice, who is quite the actress, shared about a lecture she recently heard on rape. She had my attention when she described how to pull out the rapist's eyes or slowly slip a hand under him, then grab and turn his testicles.

As we were leaving, she walked up to me and whispered in my ear, "Tell me, do you think a sixty-five-year-old woman would be crazy to be seeing a thirty-two-year-old man?" I replied, "Not if she's happy and having fun!" Enough said.

November 11, 1983

Last night, I listened to the ladies (all around my age) wishing for fewer wrinkles and lines, hating their extra fleshy necks, and complaining about the dark circles under their eyes. I wonder if anyone is ever totally happy with the way she looks. Based on last night's conversation, I seriously doubt it. Fortunately, I don't get too carried away wishing for what can't possibly be.

December 10, 1983

While in synagogue this morning for a bar mitzvah, Donald, one of my former camp counselors, now about to go off to college, took me aside and confided in me. He revealed that the mother of his girlfriend had fallen in love with him and had seduced him. He told me the experience drove him into therapy. According to this good-looking eighteen-year-old kid, the episode was right out of *The Graduate*—except it happened to him in real life. It sounds to me like this woman took her fantasy one step too far.

February 5, 1984

In one corner at the party last night, five women sat discussing Danielle Steele's most recent book and then changed the subject and talked about their children's after-school activities. These are the same women who have always had little to say except about their kids. While I love my children and can tell lots of wonderful stories about them, I enjoy a more stimulating conversation when I'm out for an evening.

I quickly vacated the scene and moved over to the bar where one of the men was ordering a glass of wine. He had one too many drinks, and while talking to me, he reached over and touched my breasts, which shocked me. I immediately stepped back, turned around, and walked away. What right did he have to fondle me? It was an uncomfortable and upsetting moment. I should have slapped him but was too surprised to think clearly. It isn't the first time he's come on to me, but he was more blatant this time than ever before. If only his wife knew what he was doing. Daryl certainly heard about it on the way home and was furious.

This incident brought me right back to years ago when Doug thought nothing of coming on to me and grabbing my breast at a party. What's with these men?

March 30, 1984

I feel strongly about the importance and necessity of women taking a stand and stating their needs in our male-centered society. Females have been repressed for too long. Many years ago, when I began to fight for my equal rights, I felt resistance from Daryl.

Fortunately, he has gradually realized that sharing some responsibilities (like doing some of the laundry that he used to regard as "woman's work") makes much more sense for everyone. Of course, I'm sure he preferred when I did it all. Who wouldn't?

My novel will make a statement about men's changing roles. As of now, each of my characters feels differently on the topic. Barbara is slowly evolving into an enlightened being. Suzanne remains many steps behind. She's still in the dark ages, always catering to her husband at the expense of her happiness. Martin's head remains buried in the sand, but he will soon learn—if I have anything to do with it—which, as the author, fortunately, I do!

April 7, 1984

Earlier, the writer Logan, staying at the Riptide, told me he thinks women novelists do a better job on character development because they are more tuned in to understanding people's feelings. "In general," he said, "women tend to be more emotional and sensitive." How great it was to hear that from a man and know he understands.

April 10, 1984

This morning, Rosemary, Lorene, and I sat in my kitchen and talked. I sensed the strength of the collective power of women. It's difficult to describe, but I feel there is so much we can accomplish when we join together for a common cause. We discussed how stifled females have been through the ages and how much it will take for our society to alter how it views women. We also agreed that we could at least start the process by making changes in our own homes. If we teach our sons to treat women with respect, consideration, and equality, we will at least be making a difference for the women in their lives.

April 15, 1984

Adele and I have been talking about needing to find the time and space for our creativity. It isn't easy and often means that I write, and she paints in the middle of the night. No wonder most famous artists and writers have been men.

Today, my roles consisted of being a maid, a laundress, a chauffeur, a gardener, a cook, and a sympathetic mother. Somehow, I'd rather be writing.

April 28, 1984

Before our conversation ended and Gail walked on down the beach, we talked about child-rearing and how sometimes parents satisfy their unmet desires through their children. She told me she had always wanted to be a Girl Scout, but her mother felt it wasn't ladylike enough. So, when her two boys reached the proper age, she enrolled them in Cub Scouts and became the den mother for the troop.

That leads me to think about Suzanne in my book and what her outlet will be. We all need one or more when raising children. Until recently, most women I know didn't during their children's early years and had to find ways to be stimulated. That was true for me. My creative endeavors saved my sanity while the kids were young, and I was stuck at home.

I did macramé, pottery, and stained glass, refinished furniture, sewed my clothes and Rebecca's, painted wall graphics and pre-made ceramics, sculpted, and took gourmet, Chinese, and general cooking classes.

May 10, 1984

Tonight, I bought Rebecca her first pair of heels. Even though her ankles keep turning in, she's parading around the house in them. It brings her one step closer to growing up and being a woman.

July 19, 1984

The Democratic Convention ends tonight. I love the idea of Geraldine Ferraro being the first woman as a vice-presidential candidate—a sign of the times and a hope for the future. She is changing our lives by setting an example for women of all ages. What a boost for the women's movement.

Shirley MacLaine wrote about how women with unfulfilled lives remain second-class citizens. The majority of my friends work or volunteer. The few who don't look to their husbands for their fulfillment.

That inevitably leads to a relationship with too much dependency and unhappiness. Indeed, if nothing else, it puts the women in a powerless position. I've seen marriages break up in some instances because of the wife's unrealistic expectations and unfulfilled existence.

July 27, 1984

Min, who is now eighty-nine, asked me whether I found a job yet. She couldn't fathom why I would want to work. I guess it's hard for a woman of her generation to understand. She told me the only time she ever had a job was before she was married. Like so many women back then, both she and my mother were secretaries. According to Min, there were no other choices, and for sure, once she had children, working was not an acceptable option for her.

At some point, my mother knew she needed more and went back to school to study to become a Hebrew school teacher. When I was young, I always felt proud that I had one of the only mothers of my friends who worked.

August 1, 1984

I spoke to Chris, a woman who gave me some interesting facts on Miami's NOW chapter. She had been the president and was an excellent resource for the information I needed for *A Slice of Life*.

She is an ardent feminist and talked about constantly questioning the way life has been for women. Chris has been studying religion and was talking about ancient religions, pagans, and witches. She said there is a school of thought that believes human society was once matriarchal. It's almost hard to believe that was possible based on the way things are today.

August 19, 1984

I overheard Frank telling his son to stand up for his rights. "All women are the same. If you don't speak up, they'll take off your pants and put skirts on you." Really? I'm glad he's not my husband.

September 15, 1984

Earlier, I spoke to Fred. Being a chauvinist, he feels women shouldn't have any brains and minds to think independently. He would prefer we just be outer shells that men can penetrate.

November 15, 1984

I was at the SHE Center doing research for my book. While there, I overheard a young teenager crying in a nearby room. She wanted to have an abortion and kept saying it was her body, and therefore, she should be allowed to do whatever she felt was right. Her mother, on the other hand, seemed dead set against her having the abortion. She refused to listen to her daughter and instead proclaimed, "You are still a child yourself. You're too young to realize the impact this will have on your life if you kill the fetus growing inside of you. I am your mother, and therefore, the decision is mine, not yours."

Whose life is it anyway? Who should decide? The counselor has her hands full.

November 24, 1985

Bob asked me what comes after the Anne Frank exhibition is over. I told him I hoped to become the educational consultant for the exhibit and travel around the country. He suggested it was time for me to become a homemaker again. We joked about that, but I quickly realized he was serious. He said a woman's place is in the home. I couldn't help but ask, "Oh, so it's okay for you to travel all over the world on business but not me?" He didn't know how to answer me, so he said nothing in response.

February 21, 1986

There are many older women, including my mother, with whom I enjoy spending time. To me, it's a matter of valuing their wisdom from a life well-lived. Their experiences have taught them lessons I have yet to learn. How fortunate I am to have elderly women in my life who are excellent role models.

June 22, 1986

I had a strong reaction to Nora writing Mrs. Daryl Saferstein and not putting my name instead of Daryl's. I suppose some don't understand why this would bother me. I'm about ready to drop the Mrs. altogether and use Ms. instead.

When I was signing all the letters I had written for the Anne Frank exhibition, I realized by writing Merle Saferstein, somehow there was no "credit" given to my parents. It was then that I decided to add an R for Rothenberg into my signature. So, since then, I have been signing my name as Merle R. Saferstein.

January 14, 1987

I'm glad to be a woman living at this time. Last night, I spoke to my Aunt Janet, who talked of women today being out in the world and not having only to endure the drudgery of housework as she did. She said she was jealous because her life was so confined, with no choices once she had children.

Then this morning when I talked to my mother, we discussed what it was like when she was premenstrual and didn't understand why her moods darkened, and she became so mean. In those days, no one talked about things like one's menstrual cycle. I can't even imagine what it was like to keep it all inside. I'm glad to be a woman of this generation and am even more hopeful for the generations to come.

January 16, 1987

I'm waiting to have my mammogram. This place is an experience in itself, with women in hospital gowns walking around with low-hanging breasts. I guess drooping breasts are what happens as one gets older, although from what I'm noticing, even the majority of the young women's breasts don't seem to be any too perky. I guess we're all more alike than different.

February 6, 1987

While I was jogging today, I made a decision. I'm going to color my hair. Lately, each time I stop at a red light, I look in the side-view mirror and pull out another gray hair or two. It's time to officially get rid of the gray that seems to be popping out all over my head. It feels like a big step in helping me to look younger.

May 6, 1987

I decided it was time to dole out some responsibilities, so I did a smart thing and gave everyone in the family a job to do. Daryl has to wash the floors. He was pissed about it, but I told him I'd get a cleaning woman if he didn't want to do them. Daryl quickly shut up but was still upset—tired, not in the mood, blah, blah.

I told Mike he had to cut the grass and trim the front, and I gave Rebecca the backyard to clean up. They were all complaining, but I had to laugh—like I love doing any of these chores.

September 10, 1988

At one point, after everyone at the table had finished eating, and I had washed all the dishes, I called Daryl over to help dry a few pots and pans. He said something like, "With all these women here, I can't believe I have to do this." At which point, I said for that remark alone, he could wash and dry everything that's left. I then walked out of the kitchen and left him to finish up.

January 15, 1989

I woke up with a backache and menstrual cramps. I decided to go out and jog, hoping it would get my mind off how I felt. It is not always easy to be a woman.

The upside of this is that most women innately have a nurturing instinct that fewer men possess. So, as with almost everything in life, no one has it all.

March 8, 1990

I'm feeling lucky that Daryl has finally come around and is being helpful in the house. He has now totally taken over the laundry and is entirely responsible for it. That alone is such a pleasure. He also helps prepare dinner if I ask him. It is no longer my job alone to do all the household chores. I remember how resentful I used to be, but fortunately, that has finally passed.

It makes me think about the role my father took on when I was growing up. With my mom teaching Hebrew school late every weekday afternoon, my dad was responsible for putting dinner on the table when she walked in. She always prepared the meals in advance, but he made sure dinner was ready at 6:15. I can remember my father making great lunches on Sundays after Sunday school each week. He also washed dishes and anything else my mother asked him to do.

My father told me that when we lived upstairs of Uncle Rube and Aunt Helen, my uncle called my dad a traitor. The reason for that was because Uncle Rube felt my father was setting a bad example by making sure dinner was ready and by doing dishes. According to my father, Uncle Rube said, "After all, you're going against 'the code of husband rules' and are setting a bad example."

January 25, 1991

Bella Abzug was just on TV. She spoke about the importance of bringing women onto the scene to care for our world and think of the future. She's strong and is someone who makes a difference for many. In the seventies, her slogan was, "A woman's place is in the House—the House of Representatives." While she is out of office, she continues to further her vision of equality. We need more women like her.

February 9, 1991

Last night, we saw *Not Without My Daughter,* based on a true story about an American woman who married an Iranian doctor. He wanted to go back to his home country to visit his family. Once they got there, he decided not to go back to the States and kept her hostage.

I can't imagine being a woman in that kind of society. How can they stand being treated as they are? What is their daily life like? It makes me all the more grateful to live in America.

March 20, 1991

At dinner last night, we were discussing the Equal Rights Amendment. Michael was putting me on when he said he was against it. He knows what buttons to push, so I have to believe he was teasing me. In my heart, I know Michael is for women's rights. Besides, how could he be otherwise? Not with me for his mother!

April 20, 1991

I was shocked to learn that Annie was one of those women who works from home, taking calls from men who pay her to talk to them in a sexy way. I can't imagine what that must be like, but I would guess it would be pretty degrading. However, what she told me is that she speaks to these guys while she's ironing. That's pretty funny, considering what the men on the other end must be doing.

September 15, 1991

Barbara has her Ph.D. in fine arts and teaches art history at the University of Miami's Center for Fine Arts. When her husband walked away, we had a good talk about women artists. She told me how feminist art is often different from men's because it depicts the fragmented artist's life and women's lives in general.

October 14, 1991

I just watched some women who spoke on behalf of Clarence Thomas, the nominee for the Supreme Court Justice. He's under attack for the sexual harassment of Anita Hill, who was his aide. He had been her supervisor at the Equal Employment Opportunity Commission.

The coverage has been constant. For sure, I don't believe Judge Thomas because why would any woman put herself up for careful and painful scrutiny if it weren't the truth? People in the public sector must be accountable for their actions just like everyone else.

June 28, 1997

In the prologue to May Sarton's biography, she writes about how mothers have a hard time as writers. While I understand this because I have lived it, reading it was validating. The interruptions on an average day with children around make solitude impossible. Tom has always told me that interruptions are my life. He's right because time and space are necessary to stay in the flow.

June 29, 1997

Daryl and I discussed how some men don't want to hear what women are feeling. In that respect, I am fortunate because Daryl finally truly listens to me.

November 22, 1998

Judy Collins at Book Fair: "You can't blame women. We live on an emotional level and have to have a mammogram every year. It's no wonder we have trouble deciding whether to take estrogen."

June 4, 2004

They found cancer in nine of Steph's lymph nodes, which was awful after her chemo treatments. She told me she cried for two days and tried to talk to her husband about her feelings. He only wanted to help by fixing things in any way possible but couldn't listen to what she was saying. She felt frustrated. As a result, Steph found herself not wanting to share with him because it didn't feel good. She needed something he couldn't give her. So, she has turned to her female friends, who provide her with the support she's craving.

April 19, 2007

I was reading an article about working women and the pressures they experience. Balance is the main issue. The author of the article suggested that each day women find one hour in which to do their own thing—whatever it is. Carving out the space is a challenge but is necessary.

October 18, 2007

Tonight, I saw Eve Ensler and her play about women in prison. It was heavy, and I could barely sit there at times because it was painful to watch. The physical and sexual abuse that these women spoke of was bone-chilling.

All of this led me to think differently about people in prison. Most of the women in the play lived lives filled with anguish, abuse, and neglect early on. Many were victims their entire lives and only turned into perpetrators when they could no longer contain their rage. Some ended up in prison for killing their abuser out of self-defense.

About half the women in the show had been incarcerated. After the play, the actors sat on the stage with Eve Ensler and answered questions. Many of them shared that they needed support when they were released from jail but didn't necessarily get it. A few women talked about freedom and how they will never feel completely free because of those they left behind in prison.

Eve Ensler mentioned the significance of women telling their story—that nothing is more important than that. She believes it's the only way to heal. She was raped and feels her writing and talking saved her. Eve also said we need to teach men to be tender.

October 7, 2010

When I was young, and my mom was doing something for herself, I sometimes felt she was selfish. It took my being a mother to understand that she could be a wonderful mother because she practiced self-care. She filled her reservoir to be able to give to us. She has always been a wise woman.

I've been fortunate to have my own identity, in addition to that as a mother and wife. A few women I know seem to have little else except being their children's mother and their husband's wife, and for them, I suppose it's enough. Who am I to judge?

My journals have been the only place where I can say some of these things. As a mother and a wife, I wasn't sharing my frustrations with others in the earlier days. Women didn't talk about what it was like to be a mother and be at home with no outlets—at least none of my friends did. It took many years before we could speak of these feelings. I'm not sure how it would have been for me if I wasn't able to write.

When I was in the writers' group with Adele and Cynthia in 1984, I was writing *A Slice of Life*. I had put many of my feelings into the book, although I was completely unaware that I had done that. The two of them pointed it out to me. That's when I realized I was transferring many of my emotions and frustrations onto my characters. So, Suzanne, the housewife, was pretty miserable at times. Like me, she needed more stimulation in her life.

December 7, 2010

I am excited to be at this TEDWomen2010 conference here in Washington, D.C. The TED book they gave us begins with this: "There's a conversation we sometimes have with people we trust: the real differences between men's lives and women's lives."

The introduction focuses on women around the globe—the mixture of cultures, ages, and different stages and sectors of their lives. It credits women as innovators and leaders who are forging new directions in their communities and beyond. It stresses the importance of education and how it makes a difference.

December 8, 2010

Sheryl Sandberg did a fantastic job giving her TED Talk yesterday. Watching her up on stage in itself was thrilling. Some of her main points were: Women are not making it to the top of anywhere. How do we change these numbers?

She also spoke about how women both at home and work often feel guilty. She suggested women make their partners real partners—meaning having more equal roles in the home. She also pointed out that society puts more pressure on men than women and makes it hard for stay-at-home fathers.

One of the phrases she used was "Sit at the table." Women underestimate their abilities and don't negotiate for themselves. They often attribute success to others. Her suggestions: "Believe in yourself. Own your success."

Another message she gave was: "Don't leave before you leave. Women start thinking about this before they even have children. Stay in before you need to leave."

December 25, 2010

The other day when I came home and cleaned, Daryl asked me why I was doing spring cleaning in December. I realized he's rarely around when I clean the house and has no idea what I do every week. When I told him this was my regular cleaning routine, he was surprised. I'm guessing it never dawned on him that the dust just doesn't disappear on its own.

June 30, 2012

I'm at a lecture given by a woman who is speaking about women and *mitzvot*. She just said that God had given women three *mitzvot*: challah, purity, and lighting Shabbat candles.

She's an Orthodox Jew and has different views than I do — especially when she explained that the natural place for women is in the kitchen. According to her, "Women belong home raising children." Need I say more? The concepts about a woman's role were different in my family.

Help! What am I doing here? It is hard to listen to this, since it is the antithesis of what I believe. I can't leave, though, because it would be rude to walk out, although I would like to!

November 12, 2012

Junot Diaz at the Miami Book Fair
"We live in a culture that feels as if women are not fully human. On the other hand, women grow up believing that men are fully human." According to the author, men treat women as second-class citizens. In many cases, he is not wrong.

June 24, 2014

In preparation for my trip, I've been reading the materials on women in India. So far, I've read that Modi, the new prime minister, has passed a bill stating that 33% of the government seats must be for women. They have some laws protecting women, but most have been put aside in their society in many cases.

I have learned about rape in India and how most women are afraid to report it because they will then be shunned. Recently, one woman was so brutally raped, including iron rods stuck up her, that after multiple surgeries, she died. People reacted, and thankfully, new laws are now in place.

Some statistics and quotes about the women in India: Women probably accomplish two-thirds or three-fourths of the work. Women earn about twenty percent of what men do and are the center of the home and community. All of this information has prepared me for understanding the plight of women in India.

June 25, 2014

Here in Dubai, I have been fascinated with women wearing black, long-flowing gowns and burkas with only their eyes showing. Most of them that I've seen seem young. It reminds me of the

Orthodox Jews in many ways—incredible to see how the men usually dress, but not the women. I can still remember walking down the Broadwalk at Hollywood Beach one brutally hot summer day and noticing a couple who were Orthodox Jews. She wore a long skirt, tights, a long-sleeved shirt, and a wig. He had on a bathing suit and nothing more. While I know that the woman is to be covered so no men besides her husband will desire her, why should she have to be the one to suffer?

June 26, 2014

When I walked along the shore, I noticed a woman in her burka sitting in the water. The poor dear is trying to cool off since it's 108° outside. It reminded me of when I was a young teenager in Cleveland. I was riding on a bus in the summer and empathizing with the two nuns sitting near me in their black habits with multiple layers of heavy fabric. They had to be miserably hot.

As I ate lunch today, I watched a woman who was completely covered. She and her husband were eating, and each time she took a fork full of food, she lifted her veil just enough to put what she was eating in her mouth. It may be a way of life for the devout, but it sure doesn't look like the way to enjoy a meal. Like all observant Muslim women here, their eyes are the only part of their bodies that other men besides their husbands are allowed to see.

This way of being for women who must cover up crosses many cultures and religions. I can't help but wonder if a woman doesn't feel invisible when she's all covered up. It seems so much of what's expected of women around the globe is still archaic, with incredible restrictions imposed by men.

June 29, 2014

At a rural one-room school outside of Udaipur in Rajasthan, India. As the teacher and I talked with Ambrish interpreting, three other women joined us and listened intently. We asked each other questions about education in our respective countries and also about our personal lives. When I told the teacher I had written and published a book, Bwandi, one of the women listening to us, looked particularly interested. After some coaxing, she opened up and said she had always wanted to write a book. That led to a conversation through the interpreter, which I will remember forever.

I learned that while Bwandi desperately has a story she wants to tell, she cannot read or write anything but her name. I invited her to write it for me, which she laboriously did in Hindi on the back page of this journal. She beamed with pride when she finished. I then asked about her family. Since her three children went to school and completed their primary education, I inquired whether one of them might be willing to teach her to read and write. She explained that her sons no longer live at home, and something was wrong with her daughter. She didn't explain but looked sad.

As I listened, it occurred to me that maybe the teacher would be willing to teach Bwandi, so I asked her. She immediately said she would. Bwandi's eyes filled with tears. So did mine. I then asked Bwandi if she would commit to learning and eventually write the book. She enthusiastically agreed.

We shook hands as I taught her the popular Nike phrase, "Just do it!" Within seconds, the women sitting around us smiled and started to chant in unison, "Just do it!"

July 1, 2014

At the Kamoda Village in Rajistan. When we arrived in the village, the women were immediately separated from the men. We sat in a circle and began a discussion with a translator. We asked the women questions, and in return, they asked us what they were curious about.

Two of their most memorable questions were: Did our parents arrange our marriages, and did we work in the fields?

I was sure their chosen leader was close to my age, but instead, she was forty-three. I was clearly the oldest woman in the circle. The conversation was enlightening because we learned so much about their way of life. They were happy to share with us, and we were grateful that they did.

The women have formed a support circle of thirteen through the encouragement and education of the organization Me to We. They've each saved money, and every one of them bought goats for their family. This alone is a huge step and not typical of women in that area.

One woman has made sure all three of her girls are in school. One of her daughters recently had dropped out, and again the people from Me to We, who are helping them live a better life, had worked successfully to get her to go back for her education.

We had the opportunity to peek into their lives when the village women took us into their homes. The one I went into was a tiny room with limited supplies. We sat on the floor while the woman in my group began to make *chapati*, an Indian flatbread. She invited us to assist her, which was a lot of fun for the kids.

Later, in New Dehli, Sheryl spoke to approximately five hundred women about her book *Lean In*. Before her talk, there was a reception during which time I spoke to several women but mostly just observed everyone in their elaborate, exquisite, and colorful saris.

Before Sheryl walked onto the stage, Kelly came over and told me Sheryl wanted me to take a picture with her and three women ambassadors from Slovenia, Ethiopia, and Somalia. One of them, a Black woman about my age, told me she wanted to talk with me. She asked if I could make time to be with her, which of course, was more than flattering and exciting. The other two ambassadors asked if they could join in. So, after Sheryl's speech, I met with the three women.

They talked about how it is sometimes difficult to be a woman in their position—how people call their husbands Mr. Excellence and are shocked that it's the women who are the diplomats.

Somehow, the conversation led to how we need to learn to ask for what we want. By the time we finished, we all realized how universal so many of our feelings and experiences of being a woman are.

July 5, 2014

Deborah Lyons, the Canadian ambassador to Afghanistan, told me they are trying to get women on the high council. She talked about being a woman in a country like Afghanistan and in their government. For the most part, she does well and is respected. Deborah said there are things she won't do — like covering her face. She always has a bodyguard. Deborah is a feminist, and at lunch at the Oberoi in Agra, I listened to her describe the male-oriented Afghanistan society.

As I meet more women from other countries, I understand how we are all connected somehow. Suddenly, for me, new light has been shed on the idea of caring about women in our global world. It's up to us to decide what kind of citizen we want to be and how we can help make this a better world by opening ourselves up to others. What I know for sure is our bonds as women are strong regardless of where we live.

August 24, 2014

This next generation is still struggling to find equality in their jobs and beyond. While we have progressed and the woman's place in our country has changed for many, the fight is not yet over. Will there ever be a day when pay is equal for men and women doing the same job? Will the Equal Rights Amendment ever be ratified?

Fortunately, I do see many of today's young couples working together in sharing roles at home. It's refreshing to observe men being responsible for cooking and other jobs once relegated to women. This and so much else gives me hope that one day women and other minorities will find their equal place in our society — as it should be.

March 6, 2015

This quote by Maya Angelou says it all. "Each time a woman stands up for herself, without knowing it possibly, without claiming it, she stands up for all women."

Reflections on
On Being a Woman

In reading through the various chapters, I have noticed that, on occasion, my thoughts and ideas about a particular subject have changed considerably over time. I've seen shifts in both personal and cultural growth about specific topics.

As I reflect on these excerpts about women, I'm struck by how different life was for us in America when I began journaling in the seventies. Yet, we still have a long way to go to realize gender equality both here and abroad. With women discriminated against worldwide, the devastating implications on economics, health, food security, and governance remain.

When I began reading through these excerpts, I noticed how angry I was early on. I didn't understand the inequality between men and women. I still don't. Back then, I realized that most women around me, both in my neighborhood and at work, didn't seem to be aware of the vast disparity that existed. I was determined to wake them up to what was happening around us. Looking back reminds me of the resistance I received from the men in the community. Chauvinism reigned supreme in my world. Thankfully, over time, that has changed with most men I know.

What became important to me was my responsibility as a mother to teach my children a different way. We did not divide our home into pink and baby blue. Instead, we chose neutral colors like green, yellow, and red. I did my best to dispel all myths about the roles of men and women.

I wanted Michael to grow up treating women equally—household chores and parental duties were to be shared. Fortunately, he has a father who modeled that for him when he was old enough to notice. I pointed out women who succeeded in sports, academics, and business. I talked about the dangers of gender stereotyping early on.

With Rebecca, my messages to her were of a different sort. Sure, I taught her to expect equal treatment, but in addition to that, I wanted her to know that she could accomplish anything she set out to do.

There were no barriers or restrictions. She was athletic, so she went to a sports camp where most of her friends were guys. She was the one in our home who was best able to handle technology challenges, so we let her set up our answering machine and computer, among other things. With that and so much more, we broke the mold of expectations from men and women.

There are several significant differences between when I wrote early on and now. It's almost hard to imagine that there hasn't always been a name for PMS. Also, I well remember when Ms. was first mentioned.

Many of my friends were surprised when I decided to use that personal title instead of Mrs. It just felt right to me, and Daryl was okay with it. I still carried his last name, which nowadays many women choose not to do.

Another difference was what many of us considered to be appropriate childbearing years in the seventies. Somehow, at thirty-five, I felt I was too old to have another child. I couldn't even imagine it. That certainly is not the case for women today, and I'm happy that it isn't. People are now thinking about becoming parents in their thirties unlike so many of my generation.

Probably the most significant movement that has affected our society today is the Me Too movement. I didn't realize until recently that the phrase Me Too was initially used by Tarana Burke on social media in 2006. She was a sexual harassment survivor and an activist. Me Too didn't become a household term until 2017, when the sexual-abuse allegations against Harvey Weinstein surfaced. Since then, men in all walks of life have been rightly accused.

And then there was the Brett Kavanaugh hearing with Christine Blasey Ford. Reading my excerpts about Anita Hill reminded me of how upset I was when she lost her court case. Once again, in 2018, I sat glued to the television watching the proceedings and feeling a tremendous sense of frustration and anger. In my entries about Anita Hill, I had written how I couldn't imagine any woman going through a trial like that unless she had been violated in some way. I felt the same way all these years later.

I also thought about the two men who didn't think twice about putting their hands on my breasts. I've considered exposing them all these years later. I know how it would devastate their wives, although perhaps they might not be as surprised as I think.

What I feel above all else is how grateful I am for the changes toward women today. I have witnessed Lean In circles all over the country and the world. Women now find tremendous support for one another in all areas of their lives. Thankfully, no longer do we have to keep silent about what we're experiencing. I am counting on more positive changes down the road and continue to be hopeful that women around the globe will be treated equally to men one day.

Journal Prompts

- What changes have you noticed in our society concerning gender over the past ten years?

- What do you like best about being a woman/man?

- What were the messages your parents gave you about gender roles when you were growing up?

- Write about a woman who impacted your life. What did you learn from her?

- What are some differences between men and women?

- Write about a significant contribution a woman has made that has inspired you.

- What does feminism mean to you?

- If the Equal Rights Amendment were to pass, what difference would it make?

- "Never limit yourself because of others' limited imagination; never limit others because of your limited imagination." What does this quote by Mae Jemison, the first black woman to travel in space, mean to you?

- What challenges do women face today? What challenges do men face?

Parenting Forever with Love

The two gifts we can give our children are roots and wings.
— Carol Bernstein

September 7, 1974

When I got pregnant with Michael, people seemed surprised and thought we were crazy to want our children so close together in age. However, we knew what we were doing. For now, of course, we have two little ones running around and lots of diapers to change. Yet, it was a wise decision since they will have each other to play with as they grow older.

December 12, 1974

Having Rebecca and Michael eighteen months apart means we have lived in "babyland" for a long time without a break. All this extra equipment in our small space is crowding us out, plus toys are everywhere. For someone who likes order, this is a challenge. I have lots of years of this ahead, so I had better get used to it.

However, today on my thirtieth birthday, I am counting my blessings knowing I have Rebecca and Michael, who have given me a feeling of completion in my life. The love, happiness, and laughter we share brighten my days.

January 10, 1975

Mostly, I love every moment of playing with the children, but there are those times when I get restless. I miss accomplishing something more than just entertaining two little ones all day long. Most women I know seem perfectly content to be at home raising their children and not needing any outside stimulation. I need more in my life, but I must wait until both kids are in school before I venture out and get a job. Of course, none of this is anything I would admit to anyone.

February 5, 1975

I just finished reading *Parent Effectiveness Training*, which made me more conscious of treating the children as individuals who deserve to be carefully listened to. When I get down to their eye level and pay close attention, I am astounded by how much they know and say. They may be little, but they are constantly teaching me.

April 10, 1975

One of my favorite things to do with Rebecca and Michael is take them to the library for story time. I enjoy watching as they absorb all that's going on around them. It reminds me of my teaching days when I would read stories to my first and third graders. Now it's even more gratifying to watch my children soaking it all up.

August 8, 1975

I've been able to get out a little this summer and have some time for myself. Recapturing a sense of my identity, which seems to have been absent the past few years, makes a difference in how I feel and act with the kids.

May 19, 1976

Some of the best moments I have as a parent are when I immerse myself in Rebecca's and Michael's worlds. If I put aside my chores and just spend time with them, I get lost in the wonderland of children. I cherish their innocence and find myself often looking at all that surrounds them through their eyes. Their perspective enlightens and delights me.

February 12, 1977

If I weren't teaching pre-kindergartners at the nursery school and entrenched in "child chatter" all morning long, I would probably have more patience for Rebecca and Michael. Sometimes, I just want to escape from the multitude of questions that four-year-old children ask.

November 10, 1977

This morning was a perfect example of my having no patience. For the first time, I screamed at Rebecca as she schlepped her blanket through the pile of dirt I had gathered while sweeping the floor.

It was raining, and everyone was stuck inside. I had just gotten my period, felt awful, and could barely tolerate the kids and their friends as they took over every corner of the house. I craved having my own space, but I never had a minute to myself.

August 12, 1978

After my first year of directing Camp Sinai, I was shocked at how many parents give in to their children. So many of them with young campers initially came to me and begged that their little ones not have to swim because they had cried all morning before coming to camp. I know that is anything but pleasant, and I felt for them. However, my mantra to the parents became, "If you give in to your two-and-a-half-year-old child now, good luck when he or she becomes a teenager." I know it's much easier in the moment to let the child have his way, but the consequences are too significant. Many parents don't get that. Children thrive on structure and rules. When the parents cave in, the child gains power.

January 19, 1979

I wonder if I'm living up to my parents' expectations—whatever they may be. And then, I wonder what expectations, if any, I'm going to have for my children when they grow up. I intend to experience a full life, so I never have to sit around waiting for them to entertain me. I'm lucky my parents don't rely on me for their happiness. I am learning from them.

April 25, 1979

Long ago, I learned that a child shouldn't have to be responsible for a younger sibling. It's the parents' job to take care of the children they bring into the world. I'll never forget when my Aunt Janet had a baby later in life and made Dolly, her fifth-grade daughter, come home from school every day and take care of her baby brother. It wasn't long after that when Dolly's grades tanked, and she started to get into trouble. Months later, my aunt sent Dolly to live with my parents.

Initially, that turned out to be a positive for my cousin because my mother and father gave her the attention and love she needed. Unfortunately, my aunt couldn't tolerate the idea that Dolly was thriving away from home and had my parents send her back. It's almost as if she had been sent to live with them to prove to others that Dolly was the problem. I felt awful for my cousin and wondered what her life was like after that.

June 18, 1979

In our staff meeting this morning, aside from telling the counselors about the importance of safety, I made a point to talk about the camper who might be problematic or unlikeable for some reason. My point to the staff was that these children are someone's precious jewels. The parents have entrusted us with them, and our job is to make sure we treat each child with kindness, caring, and respect.

December 12, 1979

No one taught us how to be parents. What we learned was the result of observing our parents. So, if we were lucky to have a mother and father who did a good job raising us, our chances of doing the same with our children would be a lot better.

Rebecca and Michael will grow up having their ways of doing and thinking and won't necessarily follow ours. Above all, I just want our children to be independent, honest, empathetic, and authentic. I'm hopeful that they will be conscientious about whatever they do and share their goodness with others. The way we parent and model these behaviors will play a role in who they become as adults.

Recently, I talked to Stella about how she was physically abused as a child. She told me she's heard that those who were abused, in turn, abuse others. Her greatest fear is that she would repeat the behavior with her children, which is one reason she's afraid to have any. My heart goes out to her since she is left with scars that are difficult to heal.

July 28, 1980

In directing the camp, I have sadly seen some awful parenting. Some smother their children, while others are neglectful. While I try not to judge them, in certain situations, it's just so obvious.

Then there are the parents who complain about everything. Since camp began, a few have called me at home to find out why their child's socks or a Tupperware lid weren't in their camp bag. Those calls put me over the edge. Do they have nothing better to focus on? Do they have any clue that there are 350 campers, that I might have something a bit more important to think about, or that I need some downtime after a full day of camp?

October 10, 1980

Dinner is the one time every day when we sit together uninterrupted by the outside world. To ensure that, we take our phone off the hook. We each talk about what happened throughout our day, mentioning something positive that we experienced and at least one thing we learned.

I'm hoping to teach by example as well as by instruction. I let the kids help me cook whenever they ask and have encouraged them to prepare their breakfasts and lunches. Cooking is becoming a joint responsibility, unlike the way my mother raised me. She never wanted me in the kitchen because she was afraid I'd make a mess, and therefore when I got married, I never knew how to cook anything.

Daryl and I don't always do what our parents did. That isn't to say that what we experienced wasn't good. We just have other ideas which work better for us.

November 8, 1981

I hope the kids grow to understand that my need for solitude to write has nothing to do with them, and therefore, they won't look at me as selfish. I just need the time and space to create.

November 22, 1981

With Daryl away this week, the children challenged my authority several times. I've been surprised by how boldly they have defied me. I've had to lay down the law, and each time they've stomped off to their rooms.

This hasn't been easy, and I have no reason to believe it'll change. Who said parenting was a breeze? For sure, nobody who has been one!

February 21, 1982

In a discussion earlier today, I mentioned how children use manipulation to gain control. As parents, it's up to us to draw boundaries and demand certain standards. I am a firm disciplinarian as a mom and was as a teacher. I learned from my mother, who had a reputation of being strict. Our students always knew what to expect from both of us and acted accordingly. Most of the time, my kids do as well, but there are those moments when they try to push the limits. They never win, although I'm sure they keep hoping they might one day.

April 9, 1982

Our friends who have teenagers are paving the way for us. I wonder how our kids will turn out. We've done our best. Hopefully, that's good enough.

A key ingredient in child-rearing is consistency. When that's coupled with love, trust, and a proper amount of attention, children stand an excellent chance of growing up to be well-adjusted, happy adults.

July 18, 1982

I wonder about those parents whose children are dependent on them and vice versa. How will those kids function when it's time to leave home? What happens to those parents who center their entire lives on their children?

The dependency often starts early on. Other times, it happens because of circumstances. I've noticed that since Laura's divorce, she and her daughter are enmeshed. Even coming to camp becomes an issue because her daughter doesn't want to separate from her mom. They appear to be glued to each other—never leaving one another's side. It can't be good for either of them.

July 23, 1982

I thought I had seen the epitome of parental neuroticism, but today won the prize. A couple, who had just enrolled their daughter in camp, came to the synagogue, followed the bus their child was on to Circus Playhouse, sat in their car for two-and-a-half hours while their child was inside, followed the bus back to camp, and then went home. I wonder what that child will be like when she grows up.

August 11, 1982

Today, a mother complained to me that because her daughter "has learned so many songs this summer at camp, the kids couldn't have possibly done much else or had any fun." Really? In my opinion, a child who is singing is a happy one.

August 26, 1982

Last night Rebecca and Michael put us to the test. A few days earlier, we told them there would be no dinner waiting for them if they were late again. Sure enough, the clock ticked away well past the designated dinner hour. They were upset when we stuck to our word and didn't have a meal for them when they came into the house over half an hour late.

I doubt they understand that, as parents, our responsibility is to discipline, set rules, and stick to them. I guess they'll never be late for dinner again. After the fact, I admit we wished we hadn't set such a drastic punishment. They didn't starve, though. They managed to find something to eat.

December 13, 1982

I let the kids know I was hurt that they ignored my birthday yesterday. They were focused on Chanukah and their gifts and did not remember what day it was. While they're only children, they must learn to think about others. It's never too early for that lesson.

January 29, 1983

Rebecca and Michael broke our most beautiful and treasured tree by climbing on the ponytail palm, which is off-bounds. Although I was furious, I handled the situation by talking about trust, responsibility, love, caring, and appreciation of nature. I was tough in my approach but gave them the messages they needed to hear. Their punishment is to do yard work.

Daryl felt they would have learned more with the old-fashioned approach to disciplining – that of a "spanking" rather than the mental "beating" I gave them. We don't always agree on the method, which makes it more difficult. Most important to me is that Rebecca and Michael appreciate nature and not abuse it. Which way will best teach them that?

February 24, 1983

Now that I quit my job, Rebecca told me she likes having me around all the time. I'm not sure I will be a great stay-at-home mom, but at this point, I think our kids could use a good, old-fashioned dose of mothering.

April 9, 1983

Above all else, my parents are the two people on this earth who want to hear any details I am willing to share with them. Even as an adult, I still feel their deep love and sincere interest in what I do. I understand that not everyone is as fortunate as I am when it comes to parents. I only hope Rebecca and Michael will say the same about Daryl and me someday.

May 2, 1983

Harvey, who is eighty years old and wise, told me he believes children reflect their upbringing. He said if they see good examples, they'll turn out fine. According to him, what we give to a child growing up lasts forever. While I agree with much of what he said, I believe that sometimes outside influences affect children's development and who they become as adults.

June 22, 1983

A red flag always goes up for me when I hear parents talk about their child and use "we" instead of he or she—like "we" took our medicine, or "we" will start school soon. The message I hear is the parents are identifying a bit too closely and are not naturally separating from their children.

August 7, 1983

Tomorrow Rebecca and Michael return after being with their grandparents for eight days. I will be glad to see them arrive home safely. At times, I may want my freedom, but I would be miserable without the kids. They mean everything to me. I anxiously await their arrival. I can think of little else.

However, with them around, I cannot be a full-time writer. Even though I get what I want, I must give up something I don't want to let go of. I need to find the delicate balance once again. Do others experience this parenting challenge?

Meanwhile, Daryl just found Frosty, who had escaped from his cage while the kids were gone. He's going back into confinement. I still can't believe we ever agreed to let Michael bring this little mouse home from school. What were we thinking?

August 11, 1983

I stopped by camp today to see how the summer went. One of the women counselors told me she had received a $50 gift certificate as a tip. She said she was going to buy her daughter something with the money. I quietly told her she ought to consider getting something for herself. Big tears welled up in her eyes as she said, "I never do!" I kind of figured that.

December 15, 1983

Last night was sad for Michael. Some of his friends teased him, and he got cut from soccer because he missed two practices. I wanted desperately to protect him from the hurt, yet, I knew I couldn't take away his pain.

Why is it that when my kids are hurting, I often feel worse than when I have my own problems? I suppose it's just natural—the mothering instinct—to want to protect our young ones from pain. I doubt that part of being a parent ever goes away.

Kids are tender, and what we do and how we handle situations will have a lasting effect. In this case, Daryl and I listened to Michael, shared our feelings of understanding his hurt, and gave him love.

January 10, 1984

I heard that Sal got a court order to have his son put into Jackson Memorial's ward for his drug use and behavioral issues. How did it come to this? What must it feel like to have a child talk of running away at age fifteen? I feel for both the father and son. They're obviously in a difficult relationship, which is why it ended sadly with the son being Baker Acted.

May 20, 1984

One of my greatest joys is watching the kids play and laugh. Their giggles remind me of all the good in the world. Is there anything better than the sound of a happy child?

June 20, 1984

Spare me! Sometimes I wonder if I am fit to be a mother.

November 21, 1984

I'm beginning to understand firsthand how raising teenagers is as challenging as I had heard it was. I will need a lot of patience, empathy, and tough skin to do this right.

December 7, 1984

I just read an article that said unconditional love is the most important thing we can give a child.

What do parents do when they have a child who does something terrible or is just an impossibly difficult person? Are they still able to love that child unconditionally?

January 15, 1985

Rebecca is sick with a high fever, sore throat, cough, and cold. I took her to the doctor, but I am worried because she still feels awful. Are we doing enough? Is what we are doing right? It's not always easy to know, and it's hard to see her like this.

February 15, 1985

Jared shared with me how his son has been acting out. Since he asked my advice, I told him the bottom line is that we, as parents, are in charge. We have to stay firm and be in control. It means hard work, but there can be no giving in. He had all kinds of excuses, so I'm not sure if he even heard me.

April 18, 1985

I spoke to a woman who was complaining about where she is in her life. She told me how difficult it is to be a parent of teenagers and then deal with her elderly parents, who are not well and need a lot of attention. She couldn't decide which was more challenging. Indeed, being the sandwich generation presents issues on both ends.

May 26, 1985

Darlene is upset because some girl is picking on her son, so she asked my advice. I know she wants to handle the situation, but I suggested it would be better to help her son deal with it by showing him how he can work through this issue. By doing so, she would empower him, which would be a gift.

There is no iron-clad rule against it, but in general, I feel parents shouldn't interfere. Hard as it might be, we need to step back and let our children fight their own battles and learn from the experience.

Parental interference in situations like this is seldom in the child's best interest. I know it's so hard to see one's child being hurt. However, these tough life lessons teach us and give us tools to navigate our lives.

June 30, 1985

A psychologist recently suggested that parents read their teenager's notes to and from friends to know what's going on in their lives—things kids don't always talk about with their parents. Since trust and respect for one's privacy are highly valued in our home, I'm not sure how I feel about this.

I do not go snooping in Rebecca's and Michael's rooms. Since I have made it clear I don't want them to read my journals, I feel it would be wrong to go through their drawers. It seems a violation to do so. Is it our role as parents to check on our children in this way? I know lots of people who do.

July 15, 1985

The kids in the seat behind me are whining, which I have no patience for. All it takes to cure that is for someone to say to them, "Use your words" or "I won't listen to you when you are whining."

August 28, 1985

I'd feel a lot better if the kids were home. We were so disappointed last night when we waited for them at the airport only to learn their plane had been delayed and then canceled. We had our hearts set on spending the evening together and hearing all about their visit with their grandparents. We miss them.

Now we're back at the airport again, waiting for their plane. We both feel anxious. Just let them be here already!

October 13, 1985

The woman who comes to the beach often with her severely handicapped child is incredibly devoted to him. It must be challenging to be on call 24/7 with no breaks—to have a child who cannot function on his own. It's beyond anything I can imagine. My heart goes out to the mother.

October 20, 1985

There is a baby nearby who reminds me of Rebecca at that age. Babies make people happy—a hope for the future—the reassurance of the continuance of life cycles. I'm enjoying the memories as I watch the mother, who appears to be gazing at the wonder of her child.

November 28, 1985

I'm shocked at what I just heard. What must it have felt like to find at age nineteen that the man he thought was his father was his stepfather? On the other hand, how did it feel for the stepfather? And then what about the birth father who learned he has a son? Each scenario is life-changing for these three individuals.

June 14, 1986

Now that we officially have two teenagers, Daryl and I are holding our breaths. From all the stories we've heard about raising teens, we can only pray that ours will be easy and loving without any issues. I know some of it is luck, but not all of it. The role we play definitely will make a difference.

I am convinced that parenting is the most demanding job I have ever had, but it is also the most rewarding. I have experienced the full range of emotions from days when I have wanted to run away to a deserted island and be alone with no one to care for to those days when I have wanted nothing more than to spend hours on end with Rebecca and Michael.

September 5, 1986

Katherine told me her father was an alcoholic and was ruthless and abusive. It's hard to imagine what it would have been like to grow up in fear of a father as she did. The impact of all those awful years has left its mark. It's probably the reason why she hates to be touched. I've seen her flinch when people come too close to her. I never understood why, but now I do.

September 14, 1986

The two of them are off the wall from all the trouble their son has gotten in. They let him get away with so much because they wanted him to be their friend, so he now has the upper hand as a teenager. Some of that probably stems from the problems the dad had with his father. So, their son keeps fighting them until they give in when they don't necessarily want to. I'm concerned about how this will end. I have a feeling it's not going to be pretty.

November 30, 1986

It seems so many women I know talk about how critical their mothers are. While my mom has been wonderful in most ways, to this day, she still lets me know my hair is too short or too long, my shirt is too tight, I need darker lipstick, and on and on. While I suppose she does it because she wants me to be as close to perfect in her eyes as possible, it's hard to take.

As a result of how awful it feels, I compliment Rebecca and Michael whenever possible. When there are things I don't particularly like, I keep my mouth shut.

January 1, 1987

There are moments when I find myself wanting something for Rebecca and Michael that isn't always what they want for themselves. When that happens, I need to remind myself this is their journey and not mine. That's much easier to say than to do.

April 16, 1987

We had a discussion about nature versus nurture. Since one of Ann's children is adopted and the other is not, she is convinced genetics overrules.

What I didn't agree with was when she said, "We raised them exactly alike." I don't believe one can raise any two children in precisely the same way. The position in the family, for starters, makes that impossible.

August 23, 1987

Arlene is in therapy and is experiencing emotional pain. She's facing the need to let go of her son as he gets ready to leave for college. The empty nest looms ahead for her. She feels she now has no purpose in her life, since she gave so much to her son and did almost nothing for herself.

January 29, 1988

At one point during the evening, I had an overwhelming feeling of love sweep over me. Having my kids beside me felt terrific. It doesn't get better than this.

June 19, 1988

Yesterday Daryl and I discovered we had a philosophical difference over Rebecca paying for her gas. Because Daryl was raised with his parents constantly giving to him, he doesn't believe our kids should use their own money to pay for items like gas. He'd rather them save whatever money they have.

I, too, believe in them saving money. I've insisted that half of what the kids earn go right into their savings account. The rest they can spend as they please.

If Rebecca pays for the gas she uses, it will help her become more responsible and independent. In my opinion, it will make a difference in her relationship to money in the long run. Where do we go from here to figure this one out?

July 8, 1988

I have been thinking about the four boys who desecrated the synagogue. When we met with their parents, I better understood why these kids acted as they did. Except for one mother, the couples openly showed their prejudices, which is obviously where their sons learned it from. Children absorb the messages we give them, whether verbal or through our actions. They watch us and most often mimic our behavior. These parents are now living with the results of that.

One mother seemed horrified that her son had engaged in such despicable behavior. I don't believe she is a racist as the others appeared to be. From the way she talked about their family and their values and then her son's friends, I got the feeling she believed her child was influenced by his peers. Yet, since he went along with it, she understands he is responsible for his actions.

She is ashamed of her child, feels tremendous frustration and anger, and is unsure what steps she needs to take. She told me how this incident had turned their lives upside down. I cannot even imagine what this must feel like as a parent.

August 10, 1988

Some woman came and sat right next to me while I was having lunch at Oasis by the Sea. Her toddler was crabby, so she bought him a fruit bar and gave it to him. Then she took off his dirty diaper and put it on the chair. She was going to change him on the table, but I leaned over, and as nicely as I could, suggested that she not do that since this is a restaurant. Seriously!

September 16, 1988

I gave Rebecca and Michael cans of food to take to school for the Jamaicans who lost so much because of Hurricane Gilbert. We're doing our best to raise their consciousness, teach them social responsibility, and show them how important it is to take care of those in need whether we know them or not.

February 6, 1989

My parents let me know I was special and loved when I was growing up, but I also understood that I wasn't the center of their universe. They made it clear that while we mattered to them, they put each other before Jerry and me.

Years ago when the kids were little, I had read an article by John Rosemond, a columnist and expert on parenting, who strongly influenced my thinking. He talked about how important it is that one's marriage comes first, that kids exist because of the parents, and that they will thrive if they grow up in a stable family. He believes that a strictly child-centered home creates kids who feel a sense of entitlement.

May 5, 1989

No one ever said that parenting was a piece of cake, but neither is being a teenager.

June 28, 1989

I am excited for both kids and know that this summer away will be one they'll never forget. Now that they're gone, I feel a bit empty and lonely and am not sure I'm going to like having them out of the house. They are such a big part of our lives and have certainly taught us so much we would never have learned in any other way.

We are in no hurry to rush our children away. In fact, we'd like to be able to stop the clock a bit. We'll have many years together alone without them. For now, I want as much time with Rebecca and Michael as possible.

August 4, 1989

We didn't hear from Rebecca, which hopefully means she made her connection from Boston to New York. I don't like the idea of her traveling alone, but the experience is certainly good for her and is a great adventure. Besides, by next month, she will be away at college and on her own. My parents would have never let me do what she's doing. They wouldn't even allow me to go to Niagara

Falls with friends when I was in college, but I feel differently. Kids need to gain their independence. They need to learn how to be on their own. This experience will add to her collection of memories.

August 7, 1989

Right before we left to go see the movie *Parenthood*, we got a call from Rebecca. She missed her bus to take her back to camp and was at Penn Station in New York City with twenty-five cents to her name. She was pissed because the camp in Pennsylvania wouldn't send another bus for her, which meant she'd have to wait until the next day. We were beside ourselves and anything but happy with her.

Since she had no money and was all alone, I gave her my phone card number and told her to call the people I could think of who lived in New York—Aunt Rhea, Jane, Tom. The first two weren't home, but Tom was. He couldn't believe she was at Penn Station—in his words, "a dangerous place"—and told her not to move.

He went to get her but first called us. By then, Daryl and I were so upset with her and told him to teach her a lesson in responsibility. Instead, he took her to his office, ordered Chinese food and a bottle of wine, sat at Peter Jennings' desk, and had a great time with her. Need I say more?

The movie last night showed how parenting never ends—how one has to deal with kids' problems from early on up through adulthood. It captured the many issues that arise in raising a child. For years, I've heard the saying, "Little kids, little problems. Big kids, bigger problems." I am beginning to understand that more than ever.

My friends and I notice how the issues intensify and change in scope as our kids get older. One was telling me that her seventeen-year-old nephew is doing cocaine. Another friend's son just tested positive for drugs. Someone else's son has herpes. Help! Where does it end? It makes me a little nervous to think of all that's potentially ahead for us as parents.

August 26, 1989

Taking Rebecca to college this weekend has not been easy, especially since she had just gotten back from being a counselor at sleep-away camp all summer. It's going to be hard to say goodbye to her in the morning. Where has the time gone? How is it possible that she is ready to be away on her own? I already have an empty feeling inside and know I'm going to miss her—probably more than I can even imagine.

Leslie told me that sometimes when the children are at college, they call home and dump their problems on their parents. Then they hang up feeling better and happily go off to a party. The challenge is for us to move on as well. It's probably good advice to have in advance.

October 3, 1989

Robert complained to me about how his wife is too lenient. He said she often calls the kids several times before they come to the table. Also, it drives him crazy that after putting them to bed, they keep coming out with various excuses before going to sleep. He feels unsuccessful in his plea to set down the law. According to him, she won't hear of disciplining them because she's afraid to be too strict. She feels the kids won't love her as much if she is. I believe children know we love them when we set boundaries and enforce them.

October 9, 1989

The double standard is maddening. I listened as John talked about what he told his daughter about sex and then said something opposite to his son. I don't get it. To me, they both need to be careful. The guys must respect women and vice versa. Gender shouldn't be an issue here, but in our society, it appears to be.

November 21, 1989

Michael, Daryl, and I watched a TV show—a sitcom about a fourteen-year-old girl who disobeyed her dad. He had grounded her, so she snuck out of the house. We talked about what kind of punishment would have been effective. I've often wondered what would happen if we let the kids determine their punishments. Occasionally, I did that with my third-grade students and was often surprised that they were harder on themselves than I would have been.

On rare occasions when I've been upset with one or both of the kids, I doled out a punishment that was too severe and didn't fit with what they had done. In those moments, my anger got the best of me. When I stepped back, I realized my mistake and was being too rigid or unreasonable. It was then I explained I was wrong and why. I hope that by doing that, the kids have seen that I could be flexible and fair.

December 19, 1989

Rebecca arrived home for winter break this afternoon. She came into our room earlier and said she wanted to talk to us either tonight or tomorrow. Because of how she said it, I asked her if it was bad, and she said yes.

I immediately knew we should talk right then, so I called Daryl into our room and closed the door. She told us she had been molested by someone who often babysat for us. He was about fifteen at the time, and she was ten or eleven. Since we had a daughter and a son, we would rotate having girl and guy sitters. I'm still in shock. Rebecca asked us how we felt, and I told her I felt like an observer looking in. Certainly, this could not have happened to my child. Plus, he was someone whom I loved and trusted.

I'm sad, upset, confused, angry—betrayed. It is painful that Rebecca wasn't able to come to us long ago to tell us. I always felt she could talk to us about anything, but I realize how difficult it must have been for her. She said Shani had called us once and planned to tell us for Rebecca, but that was right when Bonnie had died, and she realized it wasn't the right time.

Rebecca explained that she had told her roommate, who was the one who found her a therapist. Because Rebecca saw her a week before her eighteenth birthday, the counselor told her she was obligated to report it to HRS the next day. When she did, they sent a male HRS worker to talk to Rebecca. I was appalled to hear that they'd do that. How hard it must have been for her to speak to a man about something as delicate as having been sexually molested over a period of a year or so.

She told us she had blocked a lot of what had happened. She shared some of her painful feelings, which were heartbreaking to hear. I'm glad she's home with us so we can give her the love and attention she needs. Luckily, she has had friends to share all this with through the years, but I am hopeful she will feel the safety of our love since she's told us.

Now, there's the issue of whether to press charges. Rebecca has mixed feelings about taking him to court, which I can understand. Facing him would not be easy. We'll be getting a call within the next week from an HRS counselor and hope we'll get some guidance then.

December 20, 1989

I hardly slept, as it all felt like a bad dream. We want to help Rebecca in every way and know we need to figure out the right thing to do.

Hopefully, Rebecca will find some inner peace in working through this. So far, she doesn't feel as relieved as she had hoped she'd be. I suggested this will be a process and may surface from time to time. I let her know if it does, she can always go to counseling.

Meanwhile, anger and outrage are building up within me. I will have to come to terms with all these feelings at some point, but for now, I just want to make sure Rebecca feels supported.

We can give our children all the right tools and guidance to help them grow up emotionally and physically healthy, but we cannot insulate them from the outside world. Others touch their lives beyond our home and realm, and most often, we have no control over that. Unfortunately, in a blink, a child's innocence can be taken away.

As parents, we do our best to protect our children. Sadly, something can happen that will change a life forever. It's painful when we see our children suffering through no fault of their own. It leaves us powerless a place I do not like to be.

December 21, 1989

We called Rebecca's therapist in Gainesville tonight. She apologized because she had to report what happened to Rebecca to HRS. The therapist told us she doesn't think the guy is a first-time offender from what Rebecca described. She also feels Rebecca doesn't need long-term therapy but has to work through what she has blocked, so it doesn't surface later when she least expects it.

The therapist said part of the reason Rebecca didn't tell us was that it was too humiliating, and then, as time went by, it just became too difficult. She thinks Rebecca is a great kid and that we are blessed to have a daughter like her. We sure know that!

December 28, 1989

Last night I took Aaron to the mall. Because he has Williams Syndrome, some of his features draw attention from others. I noticed people staring at him and then looking at me. It occurred to me how painful it must be for the parents of handicapped children to have their child be the object of others' stares and so much else.

Sitting near me is a baby whose face is disfigured. I can only imagine what her parents will endure for the rest of their lives. My heart goes out to them. Probably the only ones who could ever understand what these parents go through are those in the same or similar situations.

December 30, 1989

Today was an important day. Rebecca decided she did not want to face her abuser in court. I support that since it would be difficult and maybe even traumatic for her. Instead, she let us know she wants to make sure he never works with kids again.

Since his current position involves working with children, we took the necessary steps to have him fired. He will now be listed as a Florida sexual offender. I can only hope this will save other children from his abuse.

January 12, 1990

On an emotional level, being a parent teaches us how to give and share time, energy, money, expectations, emotions, and lots more. It also teaches us how to put someone else before ourselves, and that's no easy task at times.

Usually, I'm able to give to my children and do whatever I can for them. Once in a while, I'm not in the mood to do anything for anyone else - selfish as that might sound. However, I realize the importance and value of being a loving and giving parent and the joy it brings.

March 2, 1990

I just watched some woman struggling with her eighteen-month-old son over a drink. She gave him a sip of something from her straw. He loved it, so she poured some in his plastic cup.

He didn't want that. He wanted the big cup with the straw, but she didn't give in to him. She gave me a frustrated look, and all I could say was, "Good for you." To myself, I said, "But wait, it doesn't get easier."

May 31, 1990

As I sat with Jeanne, I remembered back to what it's like to parent a baby. Her thirteen-month-old demands so much attention. It's a constant chore—a full-time job to take care of a baby's needs. While it is physically demanding, in some ways, it's harder to be a parent of older children.

I am slowly becoming aware of the changes in my role as a mother. No longer are Rebecca and Michael dependent on me as they were when they were little. However, raising a sixteen and an eighteen-year-old has its challenges too. As with almost everything in life, it's a trade-off.

June 1, 1990

It makes me cringe when I hear people say things like, "I'd kill my kid if he ever drank or smoked"— especially when the parents are drinking or smoking. We set the example for our children, who learn by what they see us doing. That old expression, "Do as I say and not as I do" holds little weight in reality.

October 23, 1990

Tonight is our last school open house ever as we rapidly move on to a new phase in our lives. How is this possible?

One of the women in the row next to us has her baby with her. I can't even imagine what it's like to have a senior in high school and another in diapers.

Dr. Marshall just said, "Babies are the best toys ever invented. Too bad they grow up." I don't feel that way. I like it just the way it is.

November 16, 1990

Next to me sits a Haitian girl whose mom had given birth to her when she was fifteen years old. She told me sometimes her mother seems more like a peer than a parent. It's a classic case of babies raising babies.

July 20, 1991

As I sit in the back seat with Michael up front on his way to orientation at the University of Florida, it reminds me of when my parents took me to Ohio State. How has it happened that it's time for us to be taking Michael to college? I'm feeling nostalgic.

College is exactly one month away for Mike, and we are looking ahead to what our lives will be like without him and Rebecca at home. Time is creeping up on us, and there's no way of pushing it back. I have such mixed feelings. On the one hand, I'm glad Mike is going off to school. He'll love it, and it's what he should be doing with his life. On the other hand, it makes me sad to think this is where we're at in our lives.

August 25, 1991

We are officially empty nesters. After 19 ½ years of having kids around, we are on our own with no children in the house. We have given them the tools to negotiate their lives. They've grown up and have become young adults. Now, they are off spreading their wings.

November 6, 1991

Rebecca told us that in her sociology class, they discussed their upbringing. She listened to those around her and said she felt lucky for the family she has.

She also told us she's grateful for the way we raised her — how we always said yes to the right things and no at the appropriate times. She told us we gave her so much of what she needed. I was thrilled and realized that some parents wait a lifetime to hear these words.

January 5, 1992

Patty has to go back to work soon. She'd love to be home parenting her baby, but her financial circumstances don't allow for that. So instead, she'll be taking her daughter to daycare.

In retrospect, I'm grateful I was able to stay home with my kids when they were babies. Of course, it was not always easy to be with two little ones without any adult to talk to. There were days when I wanted to be out working and feeling stimulated. Yet, from a parenting standpoint, I feel fortunate to have had those early years with Rebecca and Michael.

March 6, 1992

Liz talked about how her father physically, sexually, and verbally abused her as a small child. Luckily, she had neighbors who were aware of what was going on and rescued her. Liz lived with them until she was sixteen and was in therapy from kindergarten on. It took years before she even told her husband, since she had repressed a lot of it. Now, Liz writes poetry and shares her experiences with others. All of this has led her to work with children and help them cope with their difficult situations.

It's hard to imagine how one's life is framed with a father like that. I'm guessing the issue of trust becomes a huge factor. How can a parent do that to a child? I will never understand.

May 10, 1992

It's a weird and sad feeling to have a Mother's Day without Rebecca and Michael around. It could very well be this way from now on.

Each Mother's Day since we left Cleveland, I've called my mother early in the morning. Many times, she's told me that the day isn't the same because I'm not there. At least she has Jerry's family there to celebrate with. Is this a "what comes around, goes around" moment?

I've listened to and watched parents interact with their children all day here at the beach. I keep thinking of Rebecca and Michael and remembering how it used to be with all of us. So much triggers my memory, especially when I see children frolicking in the water or digging deep holes in the sand. We had a great time, and always, it was a gift to have the ocean and beach as a playground for our family.

July 21, 1992

Michael was curious, so we spent some time talking about the merits of tough love. Bill Milliken, the author of the book *Tough Love*, says the message to the child must be something like: We as parents don't care how what we do makes you hate us. We love you, which is why we're doing this.

There are those kids who dropped out of school, left home, got in trouble, and then came back expecting their parents to give in to them as they previously had. In some cases where the parents can ascribe to the tough love philosophy, there might be hope. Now that their son or daughter has no money nor a place to live and needs his/her mother and father, the parents have to take control.

I explained to Mike how sometimes parents must say no once and for all. He told me how he watched his friend's mother give her kids all the essentials—food, shelter, and money but no discipline or rules. He said that as if he knows what matters most in parenting.

March 13, 1993

Rebecca had gone to South Beach and hadn't come home yet, so I was concerned. She got home at 3:00 a.m., and Daryl and I had woken up and had been up for at least an hour waiting. During that time, I thought about how parenting has its highs and lows—like so much else in life.

When the kids are away, there's no daily contact—everything is long distance, so we can't touch, feel, and experience the joys in the same way. On the other hand, we also don't agonize when they are out in the middle of the night.

May 2, 1993

Earlier at dinner, Rebecca asked if we would be embarrassed if one of our kids was in jail. Neither of us knew exactly how we would feel and hoped we'd never have to face that. I told her the messages we wanted her and Michael to know. You can always come home. We have faith and confidence that you will succeed in whatever you do. We will always be there for you. We love you unconditionally.

June 17, 1993

When I was walking on the Broadwalk, I saw a father and young son on rollerblades. The little boy was behind his dad and had taken off his knee pads. The father reprimanded him, and the child said, "But, Dad, I don't need them!" The next minute, he fell flat on his face and badly scraped his knees. It was one of those "I told you so!" moments that happen so often in our lives as parents.

July 3, 1993

What was I saying earlier about parenting? Sometimes I feel like we, as parents, are pushed to the limit. I generally can handle almost any part of being a parent, but I've had moments when I wish I didn't have to deal with a particular issue or problem.

I still maintain that the most difficult times for me are when my kids are hurting. Maybe it's just natural, the motherly instinct, to want to protect our young ones from pain. I don't think that ever goes away.

July 19, 1993

Rebecca has asked us to write a letter to her for after we are gone. What are the areas to include? Personal? Professional? Goals? Hopes? Dreams? Life lessons? What is it that I, as a mother, want to pass along to my children?

As a parent, we have a great responsibility. We bring children into this world, and it's up to us to guide and teach them what they need to function in our society. I hope by the time she reads the letter I plan to write her today, there will be nothing that she hasn't already learned or heard from us. Maybe I just need to concentrate on my love for her and why having her as a daughter has brought me joy.

July 20, 1993

Today in Ann Landers' column, there was a question about functional families. Ann's response was as follows: "A functional family is one that works. People respect one another's right to be different. They don't impose their values on others. They help each other when they're in trouble. They are non-judgmental and supportive. They refrain from jealousy, back-biting, and tale carrying. And most of all, they honor that old Ann Landers' axiom, 'Mind your own business.'"

July 21, 1993

I was reading about six boys who were involved in killing another one. It happened that the boy who did the actual killing had been a lifetime best friend of the one he murdered. I couldn't help but think about the parents of the boy who was killed. And what about the parents of the other boys? How must they be feeling? How does this happen? A father of one of the kids said he didn't raise his son to do bad things.

Today's political cartoon in the newspaper was of two boys out on the lawn in front of a school. While they were eating lunch, one asked his friend what his mom had packed for him. The other had a gun in his hand. Yesterday, I read that a high percentage of school-aged children could put their hands on a weapon in a matter of one hour.

Innocent children are killed daily by being in the line of fire. In many cases, the parents are to blame for not locking up their guns.

July 22, 1993

I noticed that several of the parents in a large group yelled at their kids as soon as they arrived here at the beach. What should be a fun experience looks like it might turn into a nightmare for these children. And this is just the beginning, since I see a few adults pulling beers out of their coolers. I can't even imagine how the parents will be if they get drunk. It's no wonder some children grow up to be angry citizens ready to fight and kill.

Later. The large, rowdy group of families is packing up after the parents have been drinking all day. I wonder which of them will be driving home and whether the kids think about their dads driving and drinking. Will any of them dare to stand up to their fathers and refuse to get in the car with them? There is so much wrong with this picture.

August 24, 1993

I tend to want to continue guiding Rebecca and Michael with advice, but those days are over. I will have to let them do what they will—as hard as it may be for me to stay quiet. The most challenging part is letting go of my control. It is their lives, and they have to live them as they will—despite what I think. This is yet another part of parenting that's a challenge for me.

October 17, 1993

I remember when, after the fact, Bonnie discovered her father had had surgery while we were at Ohio State. She was distraught, and it impacted her tremendously—feeling as though her parents weren't forthcoming with her. It was then I made my parents promise always to tell me when something was going on with their health or just simply something I should know about.

I think we should tell Rebecca and Michael about Daryl's tests next week. He disagrees with me, and since it's his body, I will honor his wishes. I just know that I'll always be upfront and tell them what's happening with me.

March 29, 1994

I heard Ken say he doesn't think children care at all what parents say. He believes our generation was a lot different. I disagree. While there are differences in each generation, I think basic human nature doesn't change all that much. I sure wish I had kept journals back then!

It reminds me of Socrates' quote about children: "The children now love luxury; they have bad manners, contempt for authority; they show disrespect for elders and love chatter in place of exercise. Children are now tyrants, not the servants of their households. They no longer rise when elders enter the room. They contradict their parents, chatter before company, gobble up dainties at the table, cross their legs, and tyrannize their teachers."

May 8, 1994

Rebecca and Michael seem to be vying for who is the favorite child. We joke about it, but I do my best to set the record straight. There is no favorite. I wonder if most kids, at one time or another, question who their parents love more. Jerry and I went through phases where we thought the other was our parents' favorite. It wasn't so with them either. Of course, there might have been days when one of us was misbehaving, and the other came out looking like the angel in the family. But for the most part, I think they had different feelings for each of us but never one over the other.

Both my mom and dad talked to me about how they felt their parents had favorites among their siblings. For my mom, she was number seven of nine siblings. Aunt Lil had rheumatic fever when she was young, and often a sick child gets more attention. Plus, my mom was one of five sisters in a row, so when Uncle Mel was born, he received a lot of attention from his parents as the baby boy. In my dad's family, Grandma once told him she hadn't wanted to get pregnant with him because his sister was only eighteen months old, and she wasn't ready to have another baby. Growing up knowing that had to have been difficult for my father.

I believe my parents took what they had lived with and were determined to be different with Jerry and me. Despite how they were raised, my parents have given me their blessings throughout my life, have shown genuine excitement and pride in my accomplishments, and have supported me in my endeavors. I know that I can count on them. What more could one ask from parents?

August 22, 1994

Estelle told me about all her physical and mental blocks. She mentioned that her problems began in the womb with her mother smoking one to three packs of Camels a day. She felt her mother poisoned her before she even entered the world.

September 16, 1994

We shared a lot with Mike about how we trust him to make his own decisions, how we are here for whatever he needs, yet we won't tell him how to live and what to do. I shared with him what my dad had said to me right after Daryl and I got married. "I've raised you. I've given you whatever I can and have taught you the best I know how. From now on, it's up to you. I won't be giving you any unsolicited advice, but I will always be here if you need me." He kept his promise.

Michael then wanted to know if Daryl had asked my dad for permission to marry me. I let him know my parents were more than ready for us to get married. Since Daryl knew that, it wasn't necessary. Michael wanted advice on how to approach Sara's father.

September 19, 1994

Rebecca is on her way to Atlanta, and Mike is traveling to Gainesville, so until they are in their respective homes safe and sound, neither of us will relax. I'm always happiest when everyone is where they belong and not on the road. I am doing my best not to worry—to block it, but it isn't working. Do all parents feel this way?

September 28, 1994

Rebecca just called to see what to use since she ran out of bread crumbs and was making eggplant parmesan. I like those kinds of calls—no problems, no pressure!

November 1, 1994

We were talking about the feeling of losing it with kids—the contorted face and pointed finger, lack of control—the cutting edge—the moment you realize that you could harm your child with your anger, rage, frustration. That's when it's time to step back, walk away, take a deep breath, and count to ten.

December 11, 1994

A runner just passed me with his daughter in an athletic stroller. She is about seven years old and was eating an ice cream cone at this hour—6:00 a.m. Boy, did she get lucky.

My mother would never have let me start the day in that way. She was so conscious of my weight and what I ate that she might not have let me have an ice cream cone at the end of the day either!

I am grateful that I didn't end up with an eating disorder. I easily could have with how my mom handled food issues with me—always watching and commenting on what I ate or giving me small portions when Jerry's and my dad's plates were full.

March 27, 1995

Andrea told me her mother has hit bottom with her drug use and needs a job and a place to live. She asked if I had any ideas. I acknowledged how hard it must be for her to play mother to her mom. Life isn't fair for kids who have to worry about their parents and deal with these situations.

June 3, 1995

Shelly agreed that unless one is a parent, there is no way to truly understand what it means to wake up in the middle of the night for sick children, provide for their needs, and be there for them even when one can barely manage her own life. Parents learn what it means to give of themselves. Of course, parents have needs as well. If we don't take care of ourselves, no one else will.

June 11, 1995

A couple with their child just walked by. The mother was spelling half of her sentence to her husband, so their son wouldn't know what she was saying. It reminded me of how my parents would speak Yiddish when they didn't want us to understand. Daryl and I never found a "secret" language to use, but we did our share of talking behind closed doors. Rebecca and Michael found their own way to communicate with each other by speaking gibberish, which was maddening because we never caught on to it.

July 8, 1995

Katherine talked about how her mother never felt she had been a good daughter. No matter what she did, she didn't measure up. If she called three times, according to her mom, she should have called four times. To live with knowing that one's mother never approved of her had to have been difficult. It's no wonder her self-esteem is so low.

July 13, 1995

I just read an article on not refereeing children's arguments. When I directed camp and a counselor brought two children to my office who couldn't get along, I did not resolve their conflict. Instead, I explained that they had to work it out themselves. I suggested some tools to help and reminded them to listen to each other. Then, I left my office and let them go at it until they worked through their issue. They walked out as friends—arm in arm.

I did the same at home. Rebecca and Michael would get frustrated because we didn't let them tattle on each other. I knew having them solve their problems would better serve them in the long run. Hopefully, in the end, it taught them better conflict resolution skills.

July 20, 1995

I told Rebecca she could call me any time, day or night. I realize how important it is to be available 24/7 for our children when they need someone on the other end.

In the same conversation, I asked Rebecca if she felt I was ever a selfish mom. She said maybe in her lifetime, she might have felt that for a fleeting moment or two but now understands that if I was, it was only because of my own overload and that I needed my time just to be. I'm grateful that she feels this way.

September 2, 1995

A nine-year-old girl is sitting at the next table complaining about her babysitter having a Turkish accent. The stepfather said something about his accent being the same as the sitter's. The girl responded, "Let's hope she learns how to speak better than you do." That's the moment to have taught the child an important lesson about respect as well as diversity.

The dynamics between them seem troubling. I have a strong sense that something is not right there. The stepdad appears to be a hot-blooded individual who keeps kissing his wife in a sexy way—definitely inappropriate in front of the child and in a restaurant. I can sense a battle going on between the girl and her stepfather. She's angry, and from what she's saying, she feels tricked by him.

The mother seems torn between her husband and child. I wonder how often that happens in relationships where kids are involved.

October 31, 1995

Susan congratulated me on Mike's engagement—then said, "So, you are going to be a mother-in-law." I asked her if she had any advice, and she replied, "Keep your mouth shut."

November 12, 1995

When I told Betty how positively my mother reacted to my writing, she said some people wait all their lives to hear "well done" from their parents. Again, I know how fortunate I am.

February 17, 1996

Lana had some questions about proper gift etiquette and asked if I would help her. I'd never thought much about this and always assumed everyone learned these kinds of things from their mothers.

I've recently discovered others who didn't grow up with the same social norms as I did. And so, while knowing when to give a gift or how to buy the right one seems entirely natural for me, it is not so for some whose mothers did not set the example.

April 7, 1996

A little while ago, a six-year-old boy walked away from his mother here at the beach. Two women who noticed went with him looking for his mom and thankfully found her. What an awful, panicked feeling both the little boy and his mother must have had. I remember those anxiety-producing moments when one of my children would momentarily disappear from my sight.

I just learned from one of the women that when young children meander off at the beach, they will always move with the wind at their back. The women were smart enough to turn him around and go back to where he came from.

April 11, 1996

When I asked Millie about being a mother-in-law, her advice was to remember that when you talk to your child, you might as well get used to the idea that you are also talking to their spouse. So, according to Millie, "When you talk to one, you're talking to two." She also told me the difference between a daughter and a daughter-in-law is that you can go into a bathroom when your daughter is on the toilet.

May 22, 1996

I know that from this weekend forward, Michael will be putting Sara first. I'm sure it will take some getting used to, but that's what he should be doing once he gets married. I have faith and belief that we have given Michael all he needs to be a good husband. He is ready to marry Sara.

So much of what I've been feeling is new to me. I've never had a child get married, so I need to get used to the shifting family dynamics. A part of me fears losing some of what Michael and I have shared through the years. While I don't think that'll ever happen, I need to work on it so that it won't. Our mother-son relationship has always been wonderful, and I'm hoping nothing changes — although that's probably unrealistic.

We invest so much time and energy in raising children. What do parents do with that energy when the child marries? I guess I'm about to find out.

June 8, 1996

Men never seem to get a bad rap from their children. Fathers tend to get away with so much more than mothers do. Why is it okay for mothers to get the brunt but never fathers? I don't get it.

Mothers learn that to meet someone else's needs, it's necessary to become somewhat selfless — to put the children first and give in every way imaginable — even when it's the last thing in the world we might want to do. In some strange way, society seems to expect much more from mothers than fathers.

August 14, 1996

There's a mother near me with her son, who's about twelve years old. It reminds me of how Mike and I used to spend countless days at the beach together. We were always compatible and loved our time here. I want to call over to that mother, "Enjoy him while you can."

November 15, 1996

I'm guessing that most mothers struggle with needing time for themselves — especially working mothers. In the eighties, when I was working on my book, I would write in the middle of the night when I found total solitude without interruption.

I knew it was the only way to balance my role as a mother and my desires as a writer. Most often, on weekends when Daryl was home, I would escape to the beach where I could be by myself and write.

October 22, 1997

Rebecca is supposed to move today. The landlord hasn't called her back, so she is up in the air, which is stressful. I hope it works out for her. It doesn't matter how far away my children are. What's going on in their lives is always front and center in my mind. Once a parent, always a parent.

January 19, 1998

I hope and pray that this knee surgery goes well for Rebecca and am grateful I can take care of her at this time. I want to do whatever I can to alleviate her pain. Being here in Atlanta for her is where I want to be. The anesthesiologist was telling us about his fourteen-year-old son and how hard it is raising him.

He said it's incredible how his child acts as if he has a direct line to God and knows all the answers. Nothing the father says is ever right, according to his son. The doctor's final comment on the subject was that at least he'll get time off from purgatory for being a good father. Ha!

January 26, 1998

It was hard for me to come home. I didn't want to leave the cocoon which Rebecca and I had woven together this past week. I was comfortable, content, and cozy with her and wished I could have stayed in that space. Of course, it's unrealistic to expect to do that. She's already up and around and no longer needs my help.

June 11, 1998

In my dream, I was locked out. I was going to go to the hotel desk to get a key, but instead, I saw my father, who had the key and gave it to me.

As I wrote that, I thought of the metaphor of that sentence. In life, we teach our children by giving them the tools to make their way in the world—to handle things and learn by observing others. And in many ways, that's what my parents did for me.

October 31, 1998

Olivia told me she wishes just one time her father would admit he was wrong, that he worried too much, or that he made a mistake. She believes she would have become a different person if he had. The two of us decided it's better to appear human and let our kids see our flaws.

December 27, 1998

Irene's dissertation is about divorced couples who parent well together. She listed the essential ingredients, including respect, trust, compromise, and a sense of family. It is great for children whose parents can co-parent peacefully, regardless of how they feel about one another. Unfortunately, I've seen too many who battle, and, as a result, the kids suffer. It's especially sad to me when one parent badmouths the other. No one wins, but it's the child who gets hurt the most from that.

June 3, 1999

Two of our friends' fathers are well-known doctors. Both have countless awards and plaques for their professional accomplishments plastered all over their office walls. However, the two of them have their priorities upside down. For both fathers, work always comes before family. In both cases, they haven't been around for their children. So, they have notoriety and fame, but neither will receive the father of the year award.

July 24, 1999

Andrea still has not told her children they are adopted. We talked about it, and I expressed how important it is that she tell them. Learning something like that once a child is no longer little can be devastating. It will most likely backfire if she doesn't let them know. It is possibly too late already, since the kids are now teenagers. When parents keep secrets and taboos, there are bound to be negative consequences.

August 1, 1999

Since Emily is a psychologist who works with young children and their parents, I asked her what she suggests about parenting. She said her first words of advice are to look at one's parents and see what they liked, what felt good, and what didn't. Emily then tells them to do those good things and make sure not to do those that didn't work. She also mentioned the importance of connection and giving unconditional love.

November 20, 1999

Marilyn Segal, from the Mailman Center, is speaking at the Miami Book Fair
"Play is important because kids make up their own rules, cooperate, collaborate, and have camaraderie. It prepares them for life.

"From the moment your baby is born, play with your child and continue to do so throughout his life.

"Hang in there for the full ride—continue to be involved regardless of how old they are."

January 17, 2000

Rose was telling us she was feeling parental guilt. I asked more about that, and she said she didn't allow her son to make decisions for himself. He is now all over the place and not succeeding at anything he has tried.

Another thing Rose admitted is how she enabled her son in many ways—doing everything for him he was capable of doing for himself. That continued throughout his teenage years into adulthood. Now, he can't seem to do much without help from her. While her intentions were honorable, she realizes it would have been better if she had given him the tools to learn and do for himself. Nothing she did led to his becoming independent. In fairness to her, we all do the best we can with what we know.

April 15, 2000

At a relatively young age, Ada heard her father ask her mother why they had to have such a dumb child (meaning her). He was always kind to her siblings, but he was never nice to her. Later, Ada's mother came into her room, drunk as she always was. When Ada cried to her mother about her father, she received no words of comfort.

Years later, she, of her three siblings, was the only one there for her parents when they needed her. On an unconscious level, she was probably looking for their approval and love, which she hadn't gotten from them during her life. Don't we all strive for that?

August 11, 2000

Nancy told me she's thinking of breaking up with her boyfriend. She said doing so reminds her of her father's death—the loss, pain, abandonment, and aloneness.

When Nancy talked to her mom about this, her mother told her how hard it was to hear. She let her know she was struggling with her grief. After that, her mom didn't call her for days. That must have been awful for Nancy. No matter how bad I might feel, I hope I will always be there to support Rebecca, Michael, and Sara.

September 6, 2000

Darci's "behavioral" guru told her that daughters sometimes need to "throw up" on their mothers, so what her daughter did is not unusual. After hearing that, both her sons told her she wasn't a "perfect" parent. We all know that no one is, but somehow when kids dump on us like that, it's tough.

February 4, 2001

Suzanne had a hard time when she learned her daughter was gay. She told me she can't tolerate the idea of her daughter loving a woman and is ready to write her out of her life. She even took her to a therapist to see if he could get her daughter to change and be "normal." I feel for both mother and daughter and hope she will accept her daughter as she is one day.

July 14, 2001

I only wish my mother would have sat me down and told me about her journey with my dad and their finances. Had I known she took care of the money when they were having difficulties and then began to pay close attention thereafter, the message would have been helpful to me. Instead, my parents felt that money was an issue never to discuss with anyone but one's spouse.

My life might have been different in some areas had I known that it's okay for a woman to be involved with the finances and maybe even take charge. Since I hated math and thought the finances weren't my responsibility, it was easy to look the other way. Huge mistake.

I'm glad women know differently in the generations after mine. I would have loved to have been taught more about my role with finances by my parents. I learned so much from them—this just wasn't one of those critical messages they gave me.

August 6, 2001

Louise's daughter Jayne feels sad because she can't understand why her birth mother didn't want her. My friend told Jayne how her biological mother wanted her to have a mom who could love and care for her. Louise promised that she'd help Jayne contact her birth mother when she turns eighteen if she wants to. While adoption can leave children with lots of questions, it's so much better the children are told they're adopted when they are little.

September 13, 2001

I have a great need to be with Rebecca, Michael, and Sara now. With the World Trade Center attack this week, everything seems unpredictable, frightening, and off-kilter. As soon as the planes begin to fly again, which will hopefully be tomorrow, we will be on our way to Minnesota so we can all be together. There's little I can do for my children right now except provide them with love and the certainty that I care about them. Unfortunately, with the tragedy in New York, everyone is hurting.

November 8, 2001

I saw a movie that touched me deeply. When the mother hugged the son goodbye, I felt the pain of having to let go—the separation process seems so difficult but necessary.

After the woman left her son, she called her father to come get her. In the car, they sang, *All I Have to Do Is Dream*. She cuddled with her dad for comfort. That got to me, and I felt myself missing my father and his love in a way that I haven't in a long time. My father has been gone five years now. He remains in my heart as I think of him with every sunrise and sunset that colors the sky.

March 14, 2002

I've often wondered what it's like to have your child become a parent—to watch him go through the process and experience the evolution of life. I'm guessing it will be emotional to observe. I'm ready to see for myself. Becoming a grandparent is a dream come true for me. We should be hearing from Michael any minute now since Sara has been in labor for a long time already.

Later. The feeling of becoming a grandmother has overwhelmed me with gratitude. Sophia Naomi has entered our world, and now we must wait patiently to hold her in our arms. Sara described her tiny button nose and rosebud lips to us. A photo was on the way. I cannot contain my joy!

June 7, 2002

Yesterday in talking to Sara about Sophia going to daycare and sometimes staying an extra hour so Sara can exercise after work, I let her know I think it's a great idea. She needs to take care of herself. Too often, new mothers get consumed and never have the space they need for themselves. For working mothers, it's incredibly challenging.

November 8, 2002

Mike and I talked about Sophia and how she's been crying to be picked up. He suggested that maybe I could "cure" her when I come to town. I reminded him that grandparents are supposed to spoil their grandchildren. So, whatever I do, I'll do it with love.

November 23, 2002

Diane Rehm at the Miami Book Fair said the best gift we can give our children is love. Secondly, we should provide them with faith in themselves—letting them know they will succeed.

February 15, 2003

Sheila spoke to the school psychologist because she wanted to shield her children from their grandmother's pending death. The therapist told her it would be a disservice to do that. When Sheila said she was afraid she would be harming them, the psychologist suggested that she should look at it as an opportunity to teach them about life and that we all eventually die.

The therapist let her know she should give the children options — to see their grandmother, make her cards, call her, etc. She said that no patient of hers has ever claimed they were scarred by visiting someone in a hospital or going to a funeral — but many experienced anger because they weren't given a choice to go.

April 1, 2003

In compiling the profiles for our fortieth-year high school reunion book, I noticed several classmates wrote almost entirely about their children and little or nothing about themselves. While I love Rebecca and Michael dearly, and they are tremendously important to me, they don't define who I am. I don't look to them to feel fulfilled or meet my needs. Yet, of course, I included them in what I wrote because they are an important part of my life.

June 2, 2003

Johnny asked me to explain what it was about grandchildren that was so special. He wondered where all the incredible feelings come from.

I'm not sure I explained it well, but I talked about my maternal instincts and how they remain even when my kids don't need me or when I'm not a priority in their lives. Then along comes a baby born to my child, and, in some way, is a small part of me. Suddenly, another flame is ignited. I also think it has to do with the continuity of one's life and bloodline.

June 5, 2003

From the book I'm reading *Wholeness of a Broken Heart* by Katie Singer, I love this quote. "As I understand it, being a mother means having an unzipped heart twenty-four hours a day for the rest of your life."

January 4, 2004

Saying goodbye to the kids was tough. Jeff said it best tonight. He isn't sure which feeling is more intense — the anticipation of seeing our children or the sadness of saying goodbye to them.

January 27, 2004

I had a great conversation with Sara, Mike, and Rebecca, each individually. I was happy to connect with them. When that happens, and they're all in a good place, I feel peaceful. They are part of my barometer reading. Interesting how all the external forces surrounding me impact my state of mind. I wonder what it would be like to be self-contained and not let outer influences affect my mood.

September 7, 2004

I loved taking care of Sophia, feeling I had her parents' trust. Sara and Michael didn't seem to worry at all and hardly called. I was glad they could go away and spend some time together without anyone else around. Fortunately, I had no problems with Sophia this weekend.

I had made up my mind long ago when I babysat that when parents called to check on their children, I would be upbeat, so they could relax and enjoy themselves. Whatever issues there were, it was up to me to solve them while I had the responsibility of their children. My thinking about this hasn't changed.

February 3, 2005

Michael said he's concerned about Sophia getting tubes in her ears. The idea of putting her under anesthesia makes him nervous.

He told me he now understands more about what we went through as parents. It was great to hear him say that and talk to him about it. I felt a new connection with Michael as we related parent to parent.

April 15, 2005

Yesterday, a most insistent mother called the Holocaust Center about the visual arts contest. She was upset that her son's entry didn't win. It was a collage on a huge Jewish star that hung on this big, heavy stand. The piece was uncreative and not at all related to the Holocaust. The woman wanted to come to the office and see the other entries.

She gave me a hard time and couldn't figure out why her son's piece wasn't a winner. I hung up thinking how some mothers get too involved in their children's work and lives. I wonder how her actions impact her son.

Another parent recently called to ask if I could find a survivor for her sixteen-year-old daughter to interview. I told her I would be happy to do it, but her daughter would need to call me first. A teenager is certainly old enough to make a call like this, especially if she wants to speak with a Holocaust survivor.

May 11, 2005

My mother, who has filled her life with activities, has been my role model. When I watched the video of her ninetieth birthday party and was reminded once again of all she did, it was evident that she has stayed young by being active. Her mind remains sharp through all of her studying, reading, volunteering, and being out there in the community. I know that's what I want for myself.

Like her, I am hopeful that I am modeling this for my children, nieces, and nephews. Hopefully, the more they see what's possible as we age, the more they will structure their lives in a productive, meaningful way.

September 21, 2005

We had a wonderful conversation about grandmothers based on the book I'm reading called *Mother of My Mother*. The author focuses on how girls are generally closer to their maternal grandmothers. They usually aren't with paternal grandmothers unless both parents are close with the mother/ mother-in-law. I feel fortunate that Sara makes every effort to have a wonderful relationship with me as I do with her.

January 24, 2006

Sandy has significant issues with her son. He's cutting school, is disrespectful, and constantly takes the car out in the middle of the night. She's the "bad" guy, since her husband is way too soft. Yet, they aren't making him face the consequences of his actions. They didn't ground him after the court situation where she ended up lying for him so he wouldn't face two felony charges.

It was upsetting to listen to her. I know from others' examples that all of this is going to lead to more trouble. We can't protect our children from themselves unless they change their behaviors. For sure, we do them a disservice in trying to save them when it isn't justified.

January 29, 2006

Yesterday I spent time journaling about my mom and whether to tell her about my brother and everything that has been going on. She knows something is up, since she's asked me several times already. I mentioned it to Rebecca, and she responded with the question: When do we stop protecting our parents? She wrote about how she protects us from things that might be hard to hear, and I then realized that I do the same with my mom. In truth, I bounce between protecting my mother and my children.

January 31, 2006

Aemi told me about a new parenting technique Jake's teacher suggested. It takes the place of barking orders and reframes the thought for the child. Instead of saying, "Sit down so we can eat," one might say, "When you sit down, we will eat." It's part of the philosophy of Jim Fay's *Love and Logic*. It gives children the opportunity to take some ownership of their actions.

April 1, 2006

Today was Isabella Sue's baby naming. What moved me the most was seeing her wrapped in my father's *talis*, the very same one he wore as I sat next to him in services all of my life. Isabella is, in part, named after him, which makes it all the more special to me—having the continuity. Seeing yet another granddaughter brought into the fold of Judaism warmed my heart in a way that's almost impossible for me to describe.

June 9, 2006

Yesterday, in our teacher institute, Dr. Pan, the president of Broward Community College, talked about how society sometimes rewards children for something that doesn't merit it. He gave an example of how some parents give their children money for good report cards. Praise yes, money no. He explained how doing that creates unrealistic expectations for our children. This information probably belongs in a parenting 101 manual.

August 25, 2006

When Beth was a child, her family had meetings around the table if any issues were brewing in their home. They were allowed to express their opinions and had long discussions that only ended when whatever was bothering someone was resolved. They then had to agree not to carry around the anger or have family discord. It sounds like her parents were ahead of their time, or they knew something that most people didn't.

October 7, 2006

This week, a man in Pennsylvania went into an Amish schoolhouse and killed children. Even the Amish, who live secluded, aren't immune to society's sickest people. It led me to think about how we, as parents, do all we can to protect and shelter our children. Yet, we can only go so far, and then there are times when others come along and take away the safety net we created.

January 27, 2007

Today when Michael disciplined Sophia, I watched but remained silent. At some point later, he asked me if I thought he handled the situation correctly. That permitted me to say something. He had given her a time-out and then went to get her. He asked her if she was ready to get off the steps. I later suggested he might have said, "When you are ready, you can come back to the table." That leaves it up to her to get it together.

I try my best to teach by example and rarely say anything unless asked. Most parents want and need to do it their way. I must honor that, even though I know I could teach them something valuable. If one is open to learning other ways, I'm right there, willing to share what I know works best.

May 1, 2007

There's a father with a two-year-old across the aisle from me. He has given her about four lollipops to keep her quiet.

Also, on the plane is a young child who has been hysterical most of this trip. I heard his mother tell the flight attendant that both she and her son are petrified of flying. My guess is he has picked up on her fear. The poor boy is sobbing. Oh, the challenges of parenting.

November 19, 2007

I watched a boy around six years old run away from his mom in line at Disney World. She chased him and tackled her son on the ground to stop him from getting away. Another woman helped to hold him down once he was caught. The kid was kicking and fighting and needed to be physically restrained.

Then when I looked over a few minutes later, the three of them were back in line for the ride, with both women giving the boy a ridiculous amount of positive attention. Everyone around us looked a bit surprised at that. If he were my child, he would have sat out that ride and even more. He won!

May 21, 2008

Why is it that some men who marry after their wives die completely discount their families? Often, they do this with no regard for how it hurts their children or grandchildren.

I'm not sure I will ever understand how a man walks away from his family for a woman. Does it have to be all or nothing? As a parent, I don't get it and doubt that I ever will.

April 12, 2009

I was lucky in so many ways, although I admit I would cringe when my mother was angry. I never was good at confrontation, and when she yelled at me as a little girl, I would do anything to get back on her good side. I became a people pleaser growing up.

In some ways, my fear of her anger impacted my behavior to this day. I continue to avoid conflict in relationships and especially with the narcissists in my life. I am convinced that what happens to us in our early years with our parents and families affects us for the rest of our lives.

September 30, 2009

The three of us strangers have had an intense conversation during this plane ride. We've been discussing how it has taken this long for the two of them to understand that their mother's anger was about their moms and not about them. They wished they had known long ago what they know now. Of course, it doesn't work that way, but both decided they would have become such different people if they had.

October 18, 2009

Sue Monk Kidd wrote, "It was like observing a conflict at the hub of my existence. Baby or book. Children or writing. Motherhood or career."

June 17, 2010

A teacher in our institute is pregnant with triplets. I keep wondering how she is feeling with the anticipation of giving birth to three lives simultaneously. Is she fearful of being overwhelmed? Is she ready to have her life changed forever? Knowing all that she has learned this week about the Holocaust, is she considering what kind of world she is bringing her children into?

Of course, that brings me to think about most Holocaust survivors, who immediately after the war found partners, got married, and had children. They were ready to embrace life and repopulate the world.

December 8, 2010

The only choice we had to make at the TED Conference was which chef to hear at lunch today. I chose Alton Brown, who talked about kids and food. His suggestion was to cook with your children because they will take ownership and be more inclined to eat the food. It's also an excellent way to help them make wise choices about what they eat.

Some of my best memories from raising Rebecca and Michael were cooking alongside them as they grew up. I loved teaching them and enjoyed that time of creating together. It also prepared them for cooking for themselves when they went off to college. I was especially pleased when Michael was getting married and wanted all my recipes of his favorite foods. Now I'm loving the times when I can cook and bake with Sophia and Isabella.

February 27, 2011

Sonia remembered that my childhood had been a happy one in comparison to hers. Her mom had told her how she shouldn't follow her dream because she had no talent. She said that once she learned about my mother, she thought, "Merle's mother would never say that to her!" She was right. How must it be for children when they get such negative messages from a parent? What a way to foster low self-esteem.

January 30, 2012

There are moments when the sadness that my mother is no longer here overwhelms me, yet I treasure the memories. There is something about parents and who they are in our lives that is irreplaceable. Even though my mother was almost ninety-seven, I still wasn't ready for her to be gone forever.

The recent article about me in the paper this week was the first time in my life I couldn't share something positive about myself with my mother. She had always been my number one fan and supporter who took pride in what I did—as only some mothers do.

September 16, 2013

Someone in our community needed a bone marrow transplant, so Temple Sinai asked me if I would organize the effort to find a donor. Today was the day we held the drive in the hopes of finding a matching donor. As the parents were swabbing their cheeks for the bone marrow testing, I watched them with their children. Only a few carefully explained what was going on. If they didn't, I asked the children if they knew what their parents were doing. I wanted to make sure it was a learning lesson for them. The teacher in me tends to do that.

Above all else, I hoped the children would learn by example. It was a perfect way for the parents to show their kids the importance of doing for others less fortunate than they are.

December 20, 2013

Since Michael is now a parent to both Isabella and Sophia, I find myself smiling when I see a situation with the girls that reminds me of when he and Rebecca were young. Somehow, history repeating itself in this way is reassuring and, in some cases, is the ultimate payback.

September 30, 2014

I gave the women in my legacy class an exercise to think of people who impacted their lives. One of the women wrote TRUST on the page and circled it. She went on to tell us how her mother told her never to trust friends—only family—and made it clear that friends will stab you in the back.

She admitted that since then, she has always been guarded in her relationships. The messages we get from our parents when we're young make a difference throughout the rest of our lives.

January 6, 2015

Marsha and I have been talking about how she grew up—how she had to go elsewhere for role models—how she learned about families from being at her friends' homes and watching their parents interact with them.

Growing up, I thought everyone's life was like mine. It shocks me to hear these nightmare stories about how some parents neglected their children.

April 9, 2015

Rebecca and Michael have taught me so much about who I am. By being their mother, I have had the opportunity to love in a way I would never have otherwise. Equally as important, motherhood has brought me a tremendous sense of purpose in my life.

Seeing them as responsible, caring, and loving adults brings me joy. I am a better person for having Rebecca and Michael as my children.

December 12, 2015

I experienced unconditional love from my parents—a gift that is the basic foundation for who I am today. Having that in my life has given me a strong sense of self.

Looking back, I can remember being young and feeling heard by my parents. They paid attention to what I had to say as if there was value to my every thought and feeling. They believed in me, which helped me to thrive.

I was fortunate to have been raised in a stable, secure, and loving family. I know I can give to others as freely as I do because of how I was treated as a child. My parents gave me what I needed throughout my life for me to grow up feeling fulfilled.

I have a responsibility to be the best parent I can be. My parents taught me what a treasured gift it is to be there for my children and love them with all my heart and soul.

Reflections on
Parenting: Forever with Love

Reading these excerpts reminds me of a few lessons that have shaped how I taught and how I parented. Having had a solid, competent role model in my mother, a teacher herself, I learned how important it is to be firm and consistent in our expectations but always with love. What struck me when she died was how many of her former students showed up at her funeral and *shiva* and talked about what a fabulous teacher she had been.

I was lucky to learn from my mother and father, and so as a parent, teacher, camp director, etc., I understood how I could succeed by being consistent. I wrote about this in my excerpts and am clear that above all else, this is what works best in raising children. I'm convinced that they need structure and rules. They do best when they know what to expect. As I reflect on the excerpts, I see where so many children and young adults struggled because their parents were inconsistent and gave in to them—when they just couldn't say no to their child. Giving in to children always seems to backfire. So, if I were to advise parents of a newborn, I would say be consistent and shower your child with love.

Teaching for almost five years before having children helped me to be a better parent. I have to laugh when I recall this one incident from my first year of teaching when I was twenty-two. One sweet boy in my third-grade class was acting out. I called his mother in to talk to her about her son's behavior. I remember giving her advice, at which point she asked me the following. "Miss Rothenberg, do you have children?" When I replied that I didn't, she said, "I'd love to have this conversation when you do." Looking back, I now understand that there's a lot to parenting I didn't have a clue about. The more I worked with children, the more I learned so that when I had my own, I was a little more educated. Still, I had a lot to learn and did so by trial and error.

When Daryl and I were raising our children, we brought to our parenting what we knew from our parents. We parented as we had been parented. I think that's what most people do. In a few instances, I've known people who had unhappy childhoods and who have made a conscious effort to raise their children in a different way than how they were brought up. Fortunately for many, there are now parenting classes to help people learn positive parenting skills.

When I looked back at these excerpts, I noticed that I had repeatedly written the word challenge in various situations. There were times when parenting was just plain tough. Daryl and I had decisions to make, even though we were clueless about what to do.

Sometimes we would discuss what we thought was the best approach and then decide the most appropriate way to handle a situation. Our styles differed, so often we would deal with an incident in opposite ways. Other times, we just reacted immediately without thinking. Always, we did the best we could as we faced the challenges of being parents.

After completing this chapter on parenting and considering putting it out for others to read, I first shared it with Rebecca and Michael. I wanted to make sure they were comfortable with the excerpts about them. Initially, I had not written about Rebecca's traumatic experience from having been repeatedly sexually molested. However, after she read the chapter, she told me she felt it was important to include it. The fact that she wanted me to share this shows the incredible amount of work she has done to heal. As does anything that hurts my children, it significantly impacted my parenting.

Rebecca was young, and like many children in similar situations, didn't understand what had happened to her. It wasn't until she was a teenager and saw Oprah's show on sexual abuse that she began to make sense of this. Rebecca was grateful to Oprah for providing her and countless other innocent children with this vital information. Many decades later, I had the incredible experience of having lunch with Oprah in her home. Before I met her, Rebecca had asked me if I would be willing to thank Oprah and let her know what that show had meant to her. When I did, what touched me the most was Oprah's genuine concern and interest in how Rebecca was all these years later.

I can remember back to 1984 when Florida State Senator Paula Hawkins first spoke publicly about having been sexually molested by a neighbor when she was five years old. By then, I had worked in the field of education for many years. I had never before even thought about this issue, since it was not anything people discussed. Hearing Paula Hawkins opened my eyes to the reality, but even then, I never considered that this could happen to my child — and, in fact, by then already had.

The responsibility of being a parent never really ends. I used to think that once the children were out of the house, it would be smooth sailing. Fortunately, I have maintained a close relationship with both Rebecca and Michael, and so what happens in their lives, the good and bad, easy and difficult, often affects me. I believe that's true for most of us. The key is to find balance.

Above all else, what I know for sure is that I was extremely fortunate to have two parents who loved me. They gave me what I needed to set me on my path.

When they celebrated their fiftieth anniversary, we had a service at their synagogue in their honor. The rabbi asked me to write a prayer thanking God for my parents. Below is what I wrote on behalf of myself, my brother Jerry, Daryl, and Cookie:

To my parents with love,

As the sunrise of your fiftieth anniversary approaches, we give thanks to God for His presence in our lives, for the miracle of creation, and for all that you, our parents, have given us.

As the earth offers its inhabitants nourishment and shelter, so have you loved and nurtured us.

As the roots provide a secure and steady foundation for the tree, so have you furnished us with solidarity and stability.

As the cycle of the seasons fills our days, so have you helped us understand the ever-changing flow of life.

As the moon illuminates the night, so have you eased our fears during troubled moments.

As the mother lion teaches her cub independence, so have you patiently guided us toward becoming free-thinking individuals.

As the stars sparkle in the evening skies, so have you served as our guiding light of wisdom and inspiration.

As the willow bends in the breeze, so have you exposed us to the importance of flexibility in thinking.

As the sun shines on our bodies and souls, so have you shown us the way to count our blessings for the good that surrounds us.

As the creek overflows into the river, so have you taught us to live life to its fullest.

As the petals of a flower open, so have you encouraged us to blossom and realize our potential.

As the bird soars through the heavens, so have you challenged us to aim for new heights.

As the butterfly gently lands on a flower, so have you enlightened us to the joy of touching others' lives.

As the rainbow appears at the end of a storm, so have you bestowed upon us hope for a brighter tomorrow.

As the waves roll onto the shore, so have you devotedly given us endless, unconditional love.

Journal Prompts

- What was your relationship with your parents when you were young? As you got older?

- Did you feel your parents trusted you? Did they respect your privacy? Write about this.

- What is a message you received from your parents that you have incorporated into your life? Why is it important to you?

- If you are a parent, what have been your biggest challenges in raising your child?

- What advantages did you have as a child that your parents did not have? What about the disadvantages?

- How are you like your mother? How are you like your father?

- If you are a parent, in what ways have you raised your child (children) differently than you were raised? In what ways has it been the same?

The Search in the Interim

The only way to do great work is to love what you do.
If you haven't found it yet, keep looking. Don't settle.

— Steve Jobs

April 2, 1983

I'm floundering and have no clue what my next career steps will be. At the moment, I'm directionless with an open-ended future, staring at a question mark. I must acknowledge the journey I'm on and realize it might take a little while to find my niche again. The high school experience has done me in.

I told Daryl I might want to go back to school and eventually get my master's degree, which would enable me to teach on a college level. At the moment, I am exploring all options and am listening carefully to whatever ideas anyone suggests.

April 12, 1983

I can't imagine taking a job where I'm cooped up in an office. I need to be in a more open environment. While I'd like to find a part-time job teaching, I must first figure out what and who I want to teach. I have a few ideas: teaching student teachers, a course in writing for therapy, or adult education—maybe even facilitating a women's group. Unfortunately, at the moment, it's hard to actively pursue a job because my strong desire to write is constantly enticing me.

Adele and I talked about career choices. She suggested I become a psychologist. It's ironic since I had told my parents in my sophomore year at Ohio State that I wanted to change my major from education to psychology. At the time, my mother insisted I stay in education because, as she said, I'd always have a job if I'm a teacher—as if I wouldn't as a psychologist.

189

April 13, 1983

This journal has quotes at the bottom of almost every page. One says, "A caress is better than a career." When thinking about it, it may be true. I am aware of how important it is to be around for the kids. The atmosphere in our home has changed for the better since there are more hugs these days. I have so much more patience now that I am not working. I wonder if Rebecca, Michael, and Daryl even notice. Without rushing out each morning, being able to kiss the kids goodbye before they leave for school, and greeting them when they arrive home gives me a presence that's been absent for a while.

April 15, 1983

I had a meeting focusing on camp with Alan and Myrna at the JCC. While they knew before we met that I would not take the job as director, they wanted to pick my brain. They tried to convince me to work there, but I held firm. Instead, it felt great to be in the role of a consultant.

April 22, 1983

Earlier, someone gave me an idea for conducting a seminar centered on a topic. I could facilitate the group, serve refreshments, and charge a small fee. It would be like a class. Of course, what to focus on is yet another story, since I have no idea what I might teach.

I've been laid back in terms of what I may want to do in the fall. I plan to make some inquiry calls next. So far, I've used having lots of houseguests as an excuse. It's been a factor, but I must admit I'm enjoying this life too. I am satisfied being around more as long as I have something constructive to do.

At the moment, I'm thrilled not to have to think about work. I need this break desperately. Even after two months away from the high school, I realize how the stress, dishonesty, unrealistic expectations, and more did a number on me.

April 30, 1983

Tom believes I should concentrate on my writing and envision myself as a freelance writer or novelist. I'm a long way from that, of course, but who knows what tomorrow will bring? Is it possible that I could one day become a writer?

May 1, 1983

When we had dinner at the Rustic Inn, newspapers covered the tables instead of table cloths. Right in front of me on the paper was a listing of job opportunities. One ad read, "Blind college student looking for help with writing and work in classes." I tore it off and stuffed it into my purse. Yesterday, I responded to that ad. I had no idea what it might turn out to be, but in placing the call, I opened myself up to a new experience.

When I spoke to Marvin, the college student, we scheduled an appointment for me to meet him at his apartment today. As a romanticist, I created an image of Marvin and expected to find this young, vibrant, collegiate guy. Boy, was I in for a surprise! Marvin is probably fifty pounds overweight, tall, and old—most likely around fifty-five. Before becoming blind at forty-four, he was a travel guide all over the world. He was married twice, is now divorced, and has two daughters who don't talk to him. He had beautiful shells all over his apartment, which caught my attention. I wonder if he found them at some point in his life. I didn't ask.

There were some things I didn't particularly like about Marvin, but despite that, the experience might be enjoyable. I accepted the challenge of helping him: driving Marvin to school, sitting with him in his classes, taking notes, helping him prepare papers, and studying for tests. Hopefully, I will enjoy learning whatever he is studying. Just the idea of being on a college campus and in a class again excites me.

He became angry when he spoke about the woman who had worked with him before. He said she was selfish and thought of herself before him. He accused the woman of deserting him when he needed her most. As Marvin talked about her, he had an outburst that was uncomfortable to witness. He harbors anger about his bad luck in becoming blind, which is understandable. I just hope how he behaved today is not how he will be the next time we're together.

Although Braille has nothing to do with this, learning it when my kids were little may have been the first step to bringing me to this adventure. I might want to pursue becoming a teacher of the blind. Back then, I wanted to work with blind children. Unfortunately, that didn't pan out because the available jobs in the field all required a master's degree.

May 2, 1983

I can't even imagine what kind of door I'm opening by working with Marvin. I plan to contact the blind service agencies and see where and if I can get involved. This path may allow me to understand better those who live with a handicap. Wouldn't it be incredible if this led me to something else?

I want to embrace the experience with Marvin and concentrate on what I can give and what I can learn. It may well be an opportunity I can grow from and might just be a perfect place for me to begin my next step in this journey.

May 10, 1983

Well, so much for Marvin. I picked him up and brought him to Florida International University's campus. Fortunately, walking to his classroom was easy enough. He seems to manage reasonably well without much help.

So, that part was good, but the rest was a total disaster. He is a bitter person with no saving grace. He exploded at someone in class when they said something he disagreed with. As we walked back to our car, he bitched the entire time and continued once we were on the road. I just listened and kept thinking that this was not the energy I wanted to surround myself with. So, my short-lived job is now over.

May 27, 1983

I called the Division of Blind Services and found out they might soon have a position for which I'd be qualified. While it's not public knowledge yet, I learned it's for rehab teaching through the Lighthouse of the Blind. The woman told me she couldn't give me more information but said I should send my resume. I immediately began to rewrite it and eliminated administration as a personal and professional goal.

I'm not sure I'd be willing to work the hours she talked of (8:00 5:00), but it does sound like the perfect place for me to be. More details will follow as the situation unfolds.

Indeed, I have the desire to accomplish something significant and want all my days to count. I hope to write at least three days each week. Of course, if I find a job I love, I'd be willing to take it and save writing for the weekends.

May 31, 1983

I just received a call asking if I might be interested in working at Temple Beth Moshe in North Miami. The rabbi and his wife are leaving, so they need a principal for their Hebrew school and Sunday school. I immediately declined. While I felt honored that they thought of me, it is not what I want to be doing.

June 6, 1983

Daryl lit up when I told him I was seriously looking through the want ads. It will relieve some pressure if I start bringing in money again. Plus, I need to meet people, have a reason to get up each day, and challenge my brain.

June 22, 1983

I had an appointment at the Lighthouse for the Blind today. The woman I was supposed to meet was out sick, so that was disappointing. Instead, I spent time talking to two other women who work there. What they told me was enough to know I wasn't interested in the job. It's long hours, and most of the work is with people in their seventies and up. That won't do for me, since I want to work with a much younger population. I did get a few names of people in the field to contact.

June 23, 1983

I made a call about supervising student teachers at Florida International University. Unfortunately, they have more staff in the department than they do students, which eliminates that idea.

July 2, 1983

I talked to Carmela at Broward Community College, who may have some tutoring work available with students in the fall. She said she'd like me to work there and would call me in late August. The prospect of working with college students excites me.

Since I'm not working and there's no job yet, I've decided to write a book. It seems like an ideal time to get started. It's becoming clear that I am a writer, although I don't think I could say that out loud to anyone.

I have the storyline for the book and now need to spend time creating the characters and working on an outline. Even though I have zero experience in writing a novel, I know I can do this. I've decided to write the book through the characters writing letters to each other.

July 6, 1983

I called Miami Dade Community College and spoke to a woman who said she hand-delivered my resume to the right person, who was impressed with it. The job working with handicapped students won't be available until August 24th. She told me to call on Wednesday to set up an appointment. At least I know a possibility exists.

I also called the Division of Blind Services. Let's hope maybe I can find some work there.

July 14, 1983

I need more in my life than writing, even though that's what speaks to my soul. It's probably not best for me to isolate myself, especially when I feel vulnerable with my writing. I just can't put total stock in one thing that is so intangible at this point.

Today, I gave a seminar to the JCC camp staff on behavior and discipline. While I passed along valuable information, I have no idea what sunk in. If nothing else, I was glad to do something worthwhile.

While at the JCC, I offered to do rap sessions for teenagers—a place where they could come and talk. Since it might be something the teens would enjoy, I hope it happens.

July 20, 1983

I went to Miami Dade Community College and met with the director of the handicapped students' program. He suggested I look into the Change Center, but he's also putting me on the list to work with students in his department—especially in the more personal areas. He showed me a machine that takes a book, scans it, and speaks it out, which they use for blind students. It could easily take the place of Braille and would be so much easier. Of course, it's super costly, so that might make it inaccessible to most. I liked being on the campus of a college. The atmosphere was buzzing, even though it's summer.

July 21, 1983

I met with Larry Roberts, the head of the turtle hatchery project at Hollywood Beach. I offered to work on an educational, interpretive display for the hatchery and a slide demonstration. I have no idea where this will lead.

When I told Daryl what I was going to do with the turtle project, his first question was, "Will you get paid?" So far, it's a volunteer position, but it's a beginning.

August 4, 1983

Someone called me about an opening for the director of the JCC nursery school. The position is mine if I want it, but no way can I go back to a job like that now. My world is so different from when I was working. There is no comparison to the time and space I have. It's not going to be easy to stuff this jack-in-the-box back in.

August 8, 1983

I have given myself a huge challenge—to write a novel without any experience or education as a writer. It's what I want to be doing above all else, but it means a long road ahead. To be a writer is not one of the easier choices I could have made. And while writing is what calls to me and sometimes I feel so optimistic about it, at the moment, I am struggling with a ton of self-doubt. I wonder if that's normal or just because I don't have a clear idea of what I'm doing. Either way, I feel discouraged.

August 26, 1983

I had two job offers last night. One was to work in Temple Sinai's office. Barbara was so sure I'd want the money that she was surprised when I refused. I want to be writing!

For the other job, the man spoke to me in confidence because the person whose place I would take as program director has yet to be fired. I said no to that one as well.

These offers are tests along the way. As unappealing as they are at this time and as much as I should be working, I just know who I am and know what I can tolerate doing. I must feel good about a job, or I can't put myself in that space.

August 29, 1983

Today is the first day of a new school year. September will no longer be the "beginning of the year" for me as it has been for so much of my life. It feels strange on many levels.

August 30, 1983

I met Les at the high school for a walk and ran into Mr. Harris. As soon as he saw me, he said, "I could sure use you around here." I replied, "It's funny because just yesterday I was sitting at the beach writing and feeling completely relaxed as I remembered last year on the first day of school when I was running around." He told me what an awful headache he had last night, and although I could barely believe I said it, I looked at him and smiled, "Gee, I felt great last night."

September 1, 1983

Today, I was offered a job as the after-school program leader at the JCC. Even if they tripled the salary, I would say no. I know I sound picky and probably ridiculous to some, but the truth is that while flattering, once again, it just isn't anything I can see myself doing at this point in my life. A job needs to speak to my soul.

September 28, 1983

The more I work on my book, the more familiar my characters become to me. I finally have all their names and have begun to think about who they are. Each morning when I jog, I create another piece of their lives. I've got their astrological signs figured out, family trees, careers, and where they live. Slowly, they are coming alive for me.

Since writing is now my full-time occupation, job hunting is a little more challenging. The longer I spend at the ocean, the harder it becomes to picture myself working for someone else in a confined space.

October 10, 1983

I just received a call offering me a part-time teaching job at a private school. Unsolicited proposals continue to come out of nowhere, but I keep turning them down. The director made it clear that given the hours, I could teach and still write (which I know is possible), but nothing about the job appeals to me.

October 21, 1983

Last night, I dreamed that I would agree to be the director of Camp Sinai again. Maybe my unconscious is willing to give up what I have now for what feels familiar to me. However, it would be almost impossible for me to go back to something I've already done.

While there are days when I'm utterly content writing at the beach, other times, the feeling of desperation, of wanting to do something, anything other than what I'm doing, overwhelms me. Those are the days when I am experiencing writer's block —that awful feeling when I'm empty, and words don't come down on the page. Yet, I know there's only one way to travel on this road, and it's to forge ahead and not go backward.

October 30, 1983

I just got a call from Ned, the guy I met at Ron's party. He may have access to two charter boats to tie in with his drug program. He wants me to think about organizing a summer marine science program. I'm interested and love the idea! He will get back to me if he can work it out on his end.

November 8, 1983

Barbara told me there are serious problems with the nursery school. She wondered if I'd consider teaching one of the classes and being in charge of the afternoon program. I didn't accept the position. I just couldn't. She told me she respects me for my decision.

December 11, 1983

I ended up talking to some guy at the beach about our careers. As a result of our conversation, I began thinking about teaching adult education classes. That could easily fit in my life. What to teach is another question, of course.

In the meantime, I hope to publish this book someday and trust it will happen eventually. I just have to keep plugging away, have faith, and be patient.

I saw an ad about an autistic person needing help. I decided I would call and see what it was all about. Who knows where that might lead? I need to find my place in society where I can accomplish something meaningful. What is my mission anyway? What do I want to achieve in my life? Who am I, and what matters to me? I'm desperately in search of answers.

December 14, 1983

I made some calls about adult education, and while it looks like a possibility, it won't be any time soon. The new semester begins in January, and the community colleges have already arranged their schedules.

Ned called. He can't get the charter boats, so that dream is over. I'm feeling lost. I keep hoping the ideal opportunity will appear, and I have to believe it will when the time is right.

January 10, 1984

Cynthia came over, and the two of us discussed the possibility of starting a letter-writing business. We brainstormed and focused on what the next steps needed to be. We'll be writing letters for people who can't or don't want to write them for themselves. What could be more perfect, since I always write letters to family and friends and understand their value? Daryl complains that he's spending a fortune on stamps for me.

January 24, 1984

I went to meet with Julian today. He confidentially told me they wanted me to become director of the nursery school at Temple Sinai. The second part of the proposal was that I'd be his administrative assistant in charge of the Hebrew/Sunday school. I gave him my reasons why neither job would work, including not dealing with the bureaucracy.

He said he's kind of known all along what I want to do — to walk the beach, write, and contemplate. He told me he has none of that alone time and envies me.

I talked to Mom and Dad, who were proud that I was asked to do these jobs. My mother would have loved to have been the supervisor of such a school. As she said, though, "I wouldn't want you to do something because I wanted to do it." I was glad she understood and could say that to me.

Dad told me he'd like to see me back in education. I explained that I would have enthusiastically accepted being the director of the day school but not the nursery school. Unfortunately, they didn't offer me that job.

Tom told me to bask in the glory of all these job offers. It does feel good knowing someone looks to me as a suitable candidate for the various jobs, even if I don't.

February 16, 1984

Today marks the first anniversary of my not working. As I look back, I can't help but feel relieved. It has not been an easy year for me, but not for a moment do I regret my decision to quit.

March 1, 1984

Rabbi Kingsley offered me the job of editing the bulletin for Temple Sinai. I'd only be making $200 a month, but I suppose it's better than nothing — plus it involves some writing.

Being the editor of the bulletin, coupled with the cookbooks I've edited and a few newsletters, will undoubtedly improve my credibility as a writer. Maybe this will be the next step in my writing career.

As I walked out, Barbara asked me by a thumbs up or down if I would take the job. She and the rabbi were thrilled when I agreed and seemed happy to have me working there again. Barbara commented that I probably hold the record for the person offered the most jobs at the synagogue.

March 2, 1984

How is it that all these jobs have come to me? Mom said she's never known anyone to be offered as many different unsolicited positions as I have. Perhaps this is forcing me to look at who I am, why I am on this earth, what I need in my life to bring me fulfillment, and what it all means anyway.

Tom told me so much of the questioning I'm doing is part of existentialism. He talked about the pain of self-identity and individuation and the process as the emergence of self. He said as long as I am on this path of going deeper, I might as well be in a creative space like the ocean to go through it all.

Later. Well, this has been an interesting turn of events. I just got a call from Barry, who asked if I'd volunteer to work with schools on an Israeli 36 committee. I said I would since it'll bring me in touch with kids, which I love. As we talked, he said they might need someone in their teen program. I'd consider it if it meant planning and going on the teen safari across the country. Could I be on the road for a month? Would Daryl let me go?

Later when I told Daryl about the teen travel program, he said I could go if I took Rebecca. He'd be willing to take care of Michael. I couldn't believe it but was sure excited.

March 3, 1984

I just had a flash of what the teen trip would be like. I shouldn't start counting on this, but I hope it can happen.

A job for me will be there when the time is right. I need to keep exploring my thoughts and feelings and figure out what this means in the interim. I hope I'm growing and am moving in a positive direction.

March 15, 1984

The JCC wants me to do more leadership training with the CITs. If it happens, they also offered me the job of in-home teen travel on a three-day basis and the cross-country trip. The only problem is the cost per child is outrageous, so they don't know if enough teens will register. I wouldn't get paid if Rebecca came. If she stayed home, I could make a few thousand dollars.

Of course, I would love for her to come along. When I told Daryl the options, he said he'd be okay with both kids at home. That amazed me. So, if enough teens sign up, I'll be going. How will I do on a bus with twenty-five teenagers for a month? I would probably love it and can't help wondering if this is a dream — traveling around the United States.

March 16, 1984

I keep thinking about the JCC teen travel job and what a great experience it could be. I would most certainly write my way through it. It's a perfect opportunity for me — a change of scenery, a way to make some money, and the chance to be with teenagers exploring the country through their eyes. A break from this challenging year might be a huge relief.

I just thought about what it would be like to leave the family. Instead of kids' letters from camp, it would be my turn to go to "camp" and send letters home to my family.

March 18, 1984

I just got a call to judge the science fair at Temple Sinai's day school. It's lovely that they thought of me, but I said no. It seems as if everyone sees me as available because I'm not "working." My writing doesn't count as work for anyone but me.

March 19, 1984

Cynthia and I have put our business adventure on hold. We need too much money up-front to advertise, which is out of the question for both of us. The good news is that teen travel around the country is still a good possibility. As soon as they get the figures from Trailways, they'll be in touch.

April 3, 1984

"As far as I'm concerned, we are on! Welcome aboard," Myrna announced. The JCC has cleared it for the teen travel trip. Hopefully, we'll get enough kids signed up so we can be on the road, although I don't want to let myself get too excited. For now, I just need to imagine it happening.

April 10, 1984

Article from the *Miami Herald*: JCC offers summer travel for teens: Area teenagers will have a chance to beat the Miami heat during the summer months, thanks to a 31-day trip sponsored by the Michael-Ann Russell Jewish Community Center. The Teen Travel Trip, open to students in grades seven through eleven, will feature tours via an air-conditioned bus to Chattanooga, Chicago, Denver, Rocky Mountain National Park, Phoenix, Los Angeles, Salt Lake City, and other points of interest.

April 22, 1984

Last week I told Julian I would substitute, so he called me to come in today. The topic for this Sunday school class of fourth graders was death. I wondered how I would do that aside from reading Leo Buscaglia's book, *Freddie the Leaf*. That's all there was in the teacher's lesson plan, so I had to make it up as I went along. Talking to them about death was challenging at first, but I was delighted that the students were open, honest, and sweet. Being back in a classroom felt natural and great.

April 24, 1984

Unfortunately, so far, only seven teens have registered for the trip. I sure as hell hope the program takes off. I need to think positively, but it isn't looking good.

Two men, both uninspiring individuals, interviewed me for the ESOL program at Miami Dade Community College. They put me on the list to hire if they need someone.

May 2, 1984

I just came home from a long day of substituting for an unruly first-grade class. Even with a two-hour break, it was grueling. I couldn't believe how poorly behaved some of the kids were.

Never in my entire career as a teacher did I have to work to get students quiet and in order. I couldn't believe how agonizing it was. Have I lost my touch, or is it just what these kids are used to? At one point, I was thinking of how I used to walk into the social hall at the end of camp each day.

There would be a total of four hundred and twenty-five campers and counselors. All I had to do was get up in front of them, raise my hand, and like magic, they would stop talking and start singing. Today, I could barely control eighteen six-year-old children.

May 4, 1984

I now feel peaceful and glad to be at the beach. I got called to sub again today, but honestly, it wasn't worth the money or my time.

I would much rather have this day to work on my novel instead of trying to discipline a bunch of poorly-behaved children.

May 10, 1984

They had to call off the teen travel trip because not enough teenagers were signed up. I'm so disappointed and sad since I desperately wanted to travel. I had hoped to go off and be on my own to experience an adventure, but that won't happen now.

I went into my room and cried, but I couldn't wallow with our company here. My focus once again changes. Now, I must decide what in the hell I'll do with the rest of my life.

May 11, 1984

Tom was sweet when I told him the trip was canceled. He talked about how the space is now cleared for something new. God only knows what lies ahead. I feel like I am staring at a blank wall—never a good feeling for me. I guess I'll have to let this experience take me where it will. Obviously, I have no other choice.

May 12, 1984

I talked to Joel today. He wondered if I would take the job at the Israeli consulate, since it is most likely mine if I want it—which I don't. While I'm sure it's a dynamic place, it doesn't feel like a fit for me at this time. I just can't see myself confined to an office job. I'd be locked in, and right now, I get claustrophobia just imagining that.

May 16, 1984

I have been working on the bulletin all day. Slowly, I am getting it done and am editing tightly.

I got a call from the ad I answered about becoming a collaborator for a writing job. The man is in marketing and wants to write about fraud. He's looking for an experienced writer. I'm not that yet, but it's okay since I'm not interested in the subject for his book anyway.

May 17, 1984

I spoke to the rabbi about the bulletin. He said he had some minor corrections. I asked if it was okay in general, and he said it was but that we'd have to sit down and talk about style. I'm new to this and will take a while to adapt to what he likes. I tend to be so hard on myself, and currently, self-doubt is ruling me once again.

May 18, 1984

I'm torn now with the issue of work. I want to keep busy, do something productive, and make money, yet I cringe at jobs where I have to be confined to someone's hours or take orders from people. I understand all the more why I have always loved volunteering. I could do it on my terms and be stimulated at the same time. Of course, now I need to get paid for my efforts.

I wonder if I'll find a happy medium. Is this intense desire to write getting in my way? When I'm in the flow, it seems to be all I want to do.

June 7, 1984

I rechecked the want ads today. They are becoming more pitiful by the day—at least for me.

June 15, 1984

I talked to a woman at Miami Dade Community College North Campus about tutoring or note-taking for college students. They just finished pairing off people for the summer, but I can do it in the fall.

I need to have a focus and make an impact somewhere on someone. While being at the beach each day writing is satisfying in some ways, I am isolated and missing contact with people. I need more in my life, but I have yet to figure out what that will be.

June 21, 1984

Jerry from the Miami Beach JCC just called and offered me a job in charge of membership. Once again, I had to refuse. That position holds no spark for me and just won't cut it. Am I being ridiculous? I don't think so, but a few others in my life do!

June 28, 1984

When I came home from the library, I dragged out the phone book and made a few calls. I spoke to a human resource person at HRS, where I could possibly get a position doing house calls regarding child abuse. I'm going to get an application for that. Dade Schools and Dade County have a freeze, so anything to do with either is out for now.

I also connected with someone at the Museum of Science, and while they don't have any job openings, he told me to send my resume in case something opens up.

I was scraping the bottom of the barrel and circled back to something I had hoped could happen a while ago. I spoke to someone at the Division of the Blind, wishing I could find a way to work with blind children in some capacity. I learned that besides my Library of Congress Braille certification, which I received many years ago, I still need a master's degree even to be an aide to a teacher. Another wall I can't climb now. It seems ridiculous that all my experience with children makes no difference at all.

June 29, 1984

Madeline called. She told me her friend was working for an employment agency helping people write their resumes and teaching them how to interview correctly. That sounded like an interesting thing to do. Certainly, I've interviewed plenty of people in my life, plus I have had my share of interviews. It gave me an idea of another avenue to pursue.

I received the application for HRS. Once again, with my degree certification, I don't fit in any of the categories. I filled it out anyway, but it's a lost cause, I'm sure — another roadblock.

July 1, 1984

I'm now considering going back to school and becoming a child psychologist. I'll start investigating the field and learning what it'll take to guide and advise teenagers — maybe dealing with suicide since, unfortunately, it is becoming more common among this age category.

Let's see where this leads me. Perhaps it's time to get that piece of paper to give me the credibility to do what I already do so well. The positions I've been most interested in, aside from the teen travel, all require higher degrees than I have.

How else will I advance? I don't know another way except for luck. And how long do I want to keep holding out?

July 2, 1984

I have been unable to make any contact with the psychology department at any of the local universities. I have no idea what will happen to yesterday's thoughts. They're worth pursuing, but who knows what's involved.

I got a call from someone at the High School in Israel office. A friend had given the woman my name, and she asked me to come in for an interview.

July 5, 1984

My interview went well for the High School in Israel position. It entails a lot of out-in-the-field work. The drawback is that it would mean interviewing students every afternoon after school. Also, there are phone-a-thons every Wednesday night. The job seems perfect for me in some ways, but the hours are horrendous because I would have to work when Rebecca and Michael are around and need me.

At the moment, I am sitting on a bench on the bay about to be interviewed for the activities director position at the International Fine Arts College in Miami. I filled out the application and am waiting to see what's next. It's in a beautiful building—a historical museum site. I like the atmosphere here. Young instructors are walking around, which in itself appeals to me.

July 6, 1984

I never even asked about the salary during the interview at the art school. I can't believe I walked out without knowing. How crazy is that? Our conversation was inspiring and exciting. The job is strictly student activities work—exactly what I'd love to be doing. Plus, I like the idea of working with creative people and being on staff at a college. It was the first interview in over a year that I walked out knowing it was a job I would want.

I told Daryl I'm thinking positively about the position at the fine arts school. He asked what I'd do if I didn't get it, what kind of depression I'd be in. I told him I'd probably be on the next plane out of here—as if that is an option. I also told him I wouldn't take the High School in Israel job since the schedule would be too conflicting.

July 11, 1984

I went to Bauder College today for an interview. The job is to begin as soon as possible. The pay sucks—$11,000 for the year. The hours are anything but good—7:30 a.m. until 4:00 p.m., and it's a half-hour from home without traffic. There are no vacation days the first year, but there are ten days of sick pay after six months.

I loved the atmosphere, activity, people, art, and fashion. The environment seems alive, which I would enjoy. However, I'm not sure how ready I am for a schedule like that. While the pay, although shitty, is more than I'm making now, it is pitiful. I made $14,000 at the high school for four days a week, ten months, and no travel. I'm not sure this would be worth it. Plus, I would be an assistant to the director, and I've been there and done that already. At least, there are some job prospects ahead. I hate to sit around waiting for calls but have no choice. The future is not necessarily in my hands at this point. I'm at a real crossroads and wonder what will happen.

In the meantime, I went to this interview dressed up in my suit and heels. What no one knew was that underneath it all, I had on my bathing suit. After the interview, I went right to the beach, took off my clothes, stockings, and heels in the car, and headed to my spot under my favorite palm tree.

July 12, 1984

I just decided there's no way I would work for $11,000, not with those hours and that kind of travel back and forth. I talked to someone tonight who makes $25,000 in a similar job. The contrast shook me into reality. I would be nuts to sign on. Sometimes I wonder how and where I will find a job. At the moment, it hardly seems like the penny I saw yesterday, the first star I wished on last night, or seeing the rainbow this morning are going to do me any good.

July 13, 1984

I got a call from Bauder College. The woman said she had made her selection and was sorry it wasn't me. She said I'm so well-qualified for something and would keep my application—blah, blah, blah. It doesn't matter since I had decided not to take it, but regardless, the rejection didn't feel good.

Then, I decided to call the dean at the Fine Arts College in downtown Miami. He said he hadn't decided yet and mentioned that the former student activities director might return. He'll be away for two weeks and told me to call on August 1st when he'll know more. I can't help but wonder what's coming next. I'm conflicted because it's hard to live this solitary existence necessary to get the book written. On the other hand, I want to be out in the world touching people's lives. I'm a mess!!

July 17, 1984

I went to FIU to do some research for my book. When I got back, I sent out my resume for two jobs. One was for a teacher at a drug rehab center. The other is an assistant administration director at a human resource agency.

July 20, 1984

I'm working hard not to panic but instead to accept what is. In the book I'm reading, Shirley McLaine explains that things happen at the right time when one is ready. I've heard this before, have even written about it, and want to believe it. Yet, I have felt prepared for a long time, and still, nothing happens.

July 23, 1984

After my walk, I checked out the classified ads. A big zero, so I put on my bathing suit and headed to the beach where I wrote all day long.

August 1, 1984

I called about the job at the International Fine Arts College. It was given back to the person who had it originally. So much for that.

August 9, 1984

I am open to opportunities should they come along but looking in the want ads each day is depressing and leads nowhere for me. As of today, I am done with that. When the right position opens up, I now believe it will come to me.

August 28, 1984

I've been working steadily on my book. When I realize this could never have happened if I had a job, I feel grateful I can do this. I am setting a target date of my fortieth birthday to finish the novel.

November 26, 1984

Tom and I discussed this journey I'm on. The time I've taken to write has allowed me to learn much more about myself. Even though it's been difficult, I hope someday when I look back on it, I'll see how significant it was for me. I want to believe I will have grown into a better version of myself from the challenging moments. Isn't that what "they" say happens during tough times?

December 10, 1984

The moment I put the final period on my book today, I sat in front of my typewriter and thought, "Okay, so that's done. What's next?" I was surprised at my reaction since I expected I would feel exhilarated and want to celebrate. But that wasn't how I felt at all. Instead, I realized the experience of writing the book, the journey, brought me joy and not the actual completion of *A Slice of Life*.

The issue for me is whether or not I can become a full-time writer. What worries me about that is those times when my writing doesn't flow. In those moments, I feel vulnerable and wonder if I could ever succeed as a writer. Of course, when I am writing non-stop, creating, and feeling more alive than ever, I tell myself that I could do this for the rest of my life. Indeed, I'm torn and uncertain about my future.

Does anyone even understand what this journey has been like? I can't expect others to get why I haven't accepted the jobs offered to me. I suppose it doesn't matter. I know what I need. I am clear about only taking a job that will fulfill something within me. Otherwise, I just can't. It's as simple as that.

December 11, 1984

We'll be spending the weekend at the beach. My goal is to read *A Slice of Life* to Daryl. I have lived with these characters in my head for all this time. I'm now ready to share them. I'm curious as to whether it will read well. Hearing it aloud will be different from reading the words silently to myself. Of course, this is not the kind of book Daryl would ever pick up and read, so he might not respond in the way I hope he will. I have to brace myself for that.

The weather isn't going to be great, so I doubt that we'll mind being holed up in the Hollywood Beach Hotel. It'll be Daryl, me, and my characters Barbara, Suzanne, and Marty for three days.

December 15, 1984

I've just finished reading Daryl *A Slice of Life*. He loved the ending and said I deserve a pat on my back. He was sweet and told me he's proud of me for writing the book and thinks it's worthy of publication. My next job is to edit and rewrite. It's necessary for consistencies and also for a few parts that don't flow. Hopefully, I'll finish by the end of January. I intend to get the wheels in motion.

The most exciting part is now that I've read Daryl the book, I feel that I have something to show for this time when I haven't had a job where I've made money. Suddenly, my being a writer looks a bit different to him.

December 28, 1984

This has been the most solitary journey I've ever embarked on. It would be helpful to talk to others who have written books to understand whether my feelings are normal. What I know is that my emotions are like a see-saw.

While I'm grateful to have had the time to write, I also feel unconnected to my world. I am more than ready to get a job that holds meaning for me. I'm frustrated and unfulfilled.

January 16, 1985

Tonight Bennett asked me if I would be interested in teen travel for this coming summer. He showed me the itinerary of the trip, which looks inviting. Last year, it was my dream and what I thought was the answer to everything. This year, the responsibility of it all sounds dreadful. What a difference a year makes.

January 25, 1985

Ruth told me about Esther, an eighty-nine-year-old woman who wants to talk to someone about writing her life story. She suggested I call her, and when I did, Esther seemed like an interesting woman. We're scheduled to meet next month.

February 5, 1985

I'm at Esther's apartment. She wasn't ready when I arrived, so she is dressing now. I have no idea what this morning will bring. I just wish she'd hurry, since I would rather be at the beach editing my book. I have my bathing suit on instead of underwear and will head to the ocean as soon as I finish here.

February 6, 1985

Esther still has a sharp mind. At the end of our conversation, she told me her days were numbered, and she needed to get this book written. Lord only knows where this could go from here, but she has asked me to be the one to make it happen. For the most part, we seem to think similarly, so this may well be a meaningful journey.

February 8, 1985

Esther told me about her twenty journals, which she intends to share with me since she knows they'll help in writing her story. She feels this is the most important part—putting together all the pieces. As she said, "This is the end—my final chapter."

And for me, this is my next chapter. Just as I had begun to wonder if I will ever find something to do that is worthwhile and interesting, this has come into my life. There was nothing I could have done to make this happen. How is it that these things come together as they do? I believe it's the universe at work.

Next, I need to talk about money with Esther. I wonder how one goes about doing that. It's not my strong suit.

It wasn't until I finished the last of May Sarton's books that I realized just how much one could learn from older people.

I feel that Esther is determined to live long enough for me to finish this book with her. Our time together allows me a peek into how someone her age views the world.

I love the idea of being exposed to new ideas and viewpoints. Esther is a woman who thought and acted in ways well before most women of her generation. I find her fascinating, and in some ways, it helps me see myself as if a mirror were put in front of me.

February 10, 1985

I just finished reading what Esther has written about her life. Since her family was poor, she struggled and survived on bare essentials in her youth. Almost nothing in her life frightened her. She had a strong sense of self-confidence early on and was incredibly brave.

Her husband Julius, a brilliant chemist, created several flavorings, perfumes, and liquor. Some of Al Capone's men even bought Julius' unique formula.

Esther mentioned making money from the book's sales, so I may have finally found my eventual source of income. That in itself is worthy of a celebration. Being someone's biographer is not anything I ever expected I'd do, but I love the idea of it.

February 20, 1985

I have been asking Esther for her journals, knowing how important they are to her story. Up until today, she's been making up excuses as to why she couldn't give them to me. I was wondering if she just didn't want me to read them, which I can understand.

However, today she finally admitted that her nephew has her journals. For some strange reason, though, she seems afraid to ask him for them back. I'm not sure what that's all about since they are hers. It'll make a big difference for me to have her words, thoughts, and feelings. I need to find a way to convince her I must have the journals to write her story in the best way I can.

February 24, 1985

Esther is a healer with powerful energy. She's the granddaughter of a mystic, which might explain some of why she is the way she is. She has become my teacher. I was ready for her. Both of us are benefitting from the relationship we're developing. Esther told me that Miss Madison came into her life and remained for over a half-century. She likened me to her in the way I also walked into her life. I hope to get a few more years with Esther because I have much more to learn from and about her.

I suggested we create a family tree, so I have all her relatives in their proper place in my mind. She thought it was an excellent idea. She later let me know that her family was important to her, as were her friends Tom and Miss Madison. It isn't coincidental that she also had a Tom in her life.

February 27, 1985

I rushed like crazy, grabbed an orange and a few crackers, and left for Esther's. I got there and found a note saying she was sorry, but she had to go someplace. I can't even describe my disappointment.

At that moment, I realized that Esther could easily abandon this project, and then what? I want to write Esther's story and am counting on it. Yet, the reality is that I may not. As with anything else, there are no guarantees.

Questions I need to ask Esther:
- What is your final goal?
- Do you consider me your biographer?
- How much time will you devote to this book?
- Are you willing to make it a priority?
- Will I get the copyright?
- How does your family view this, and does it matter to you?
- What kind of financial arrangement can we make going forward?

February 28, 1985

Esther has canceled until next Thursday. I'm getting the feeling that she is in no hurry to get on with this project, and it may have to be put aside for the time being. I have no choice.

March 6, 1985

When I called Esther, she told me all her energy was going into her family at this time. I wasn't really surprised, but I was disillusioned. It looks as if I have to step back now because she isn't honoring her part of our agreement.

Since I felt her pulling away, I decided not to sit around and wait but instead shift my focus. So, I've been busy doing research for the book I hope to write on the Hollywood Beach Hotel.

March 12, 1985

Esther called and asked me to come back. I'm not sure what her deal was and why she was putting me off, but today we spent four hours together. I felt a real connection with her as we talked, and I filled seventeen legal pages. I didn't stop taking notes except when she told me about various family members, since there's no need to get too involved with their stories. Her nephew, who has her journals, has given her conditions for getting them back. She doesn't want conditions but doesn't know how to fight him for them. I could hardly believe he's doing this and cannot imagine why he thinks it's okay. It makes no sense.

March 15, 1985

Today Esther told me that she had just learned the real meaning of life at age eighty-nine. According to her, it's all about God. "God is life." She understands that God has provided and has given her all that has come into her life. Esther said that while she always believed in God, this revelation feels different and is important to her. I'm not even sure what she means.

Esther and I discussed the financial piece to all of this. I explained my concerns and how I felt like we needed to make some kind of financial arrangement. She was vague and told me the money would always be there. I feel apprehensive about pushing her further right now for fear she'll change her mind about letting me write her story.

March 16, 1985

Esther is teaching me about channeling and writing from spiritual sources beyond ourselves. She explained it as having a direct connection with a higher power for transformation, personal growth, and life-changing experiences. It reminded me of what I had read about Edgar Cayce and his channeling work in the seventies.

According to Esther, there are people all over the world who are tuned into this spiritual plane. Esther believes we'll all come together in the 21st century. She feels it would be the answer to a more peaceful world.

March 26, 1985

I just arrived home from Esther's, and as usual, I found it to be an enlightening afternoon—although we didn't talk about her life or the book. Instead, Esther's friend Dolores, who is a healer, joined us. She asked if I would be open to experiencing some of what they do with healing and balancing, and I said I would. Dolores told me I have a beautiful soul and am a true seer, for whatever that's worth!

She stood behind me and did something with my "soul star," although I have no idea what that is. She had me put my hands up, and suddenly, I started to feel hot and cold and felt some energy inside me moving around. She then had me spread out my arms and offer my energy to the universe. She said I would expand my writing if I kept myself open. While it all seemed a little out there, I went along with it.

March 27, 1985

I woke up dreaming about our appliances breaking. I am worried about finances but can't give up my writing for a regular job. It's difficult to explain what it is that pulls me to write. I feel possessed in a way that I can't do anything but what I'm doing.

April 4, 1985

I'm at Esther's. At first, Dolores told me Esther wasn't feeling well and was going to have to cancel. Then, just moments later, she said we'd do a healing. I went into Esther's room, and she asked me how I was. I told her I was in transition but was keeping busy. She said I should just let it happen. As she said, "You have planted the seed, but there's no need to examine it until it begins to sprout."

After a bit, Esther and Dolores invited me to join hands and pray. They then did a healing, which seemed strange to me, since I wasn't sure what it was all about. When they finished, Esther told me her book was no longer a priority. Right now, she has "other things to do," so I asked her why the change of heart. She simply responded, "I am just clearing myself." I have no idea what in the hell that means.

I left shortly after, feeling letdown and disappointed. Was all that healing and energy work in preparation for what Esther was going to lay on me? I'm shocked since she was hellbent on having her story put into a book. I don't understand why the sudden change. So, I face yet another hurdle, which I must jump over and move beyond. Of course, that's easier to say than do.

April 14, 1985

I've been thinking about Esther since my last visit to her home. I decided to call and make sure she was finished with me. She explained that in her quiet moments, everything has become more evident. Esther has been resting all weekend and told me she is listening to what God tells her to do.

She suggested that since we won't be working on her story, I'll have a better idea of what I want to do with my personal life and writing. Before I hung up, she said we could look forward to doing some good work together. From my viewpoint, we're done. I have no intentions of ever working with her. This call was the closure I needed.

April 16, 1985

Once again, I have an underlying current of panic brewing as I worry about money. At times, it makes me feel like I should give up writing and get a paying position. Of course, I know I would only be kidding myself if I thought I could now work in a 9–5 job. I have no idea where all this is heading or when and how to get my book published. I must be flexible and go with the flow, but it is difficult at best.

April 17, 1985

This morning, I helped out and took over for one of the teachers at Ojus Elementary for a few hours.

Passing out papers and giving instructions was routine and not too exciting. While there, I thought about what it would be like if I went back into the classroom and am positive that it's not what I want to do. Being at the school was an important validation.

May 6, 1985

I need to find a way to be content with what I'm doing now. I'll have to go deeper and see what it is I want out of my life. I may have to decide to put my writing on hold. Here we go again! I'm back in limbo and feel lost. I could scream. Why can't I just accept what is? Where am I heading?

Today as I walked the Broadwalk, my thoughts floated back to where I was last year at this time when the teen travel fell through. Immediately, my mind drifted to working with handicapped people. I wonder why I keep circling back to this.

I feel unsure about what comes next. It's a miserable feeling. I need something to happen soon, or I might lose my mind. I'm pretty desperate about now and cannot imagine what I can do that will satisfy me. I've hit bottom tonight. I am scared and sad. I don't think I've ever felt this unbalanced. This is not good, and yet, I have no idea what I can do about it. Help!!!!

May 7, 1985

Life is unpredictable, for sure. Just when I felt like my world was caving in, Tom called. He started telling me about his newest job at the Anne Frank Center and how he is now responsible for sending the Anne Frank exhibition around the country. I was not expecting what came next. He asked if I would be interested in bringing the exhibit to Miami. The catch is that this would be a volunteer position, which means I would not be earning any money between now and when the exhibition leaves Miami sometime in the winter.

I told him I'd have to talk to Daryl and think about it because of the money issue. I'm starting to absorb what this means and realize this could be huge. My mood has shifted dramatically. I can hardly believe his offer, and above all else, the timing of it.

May 8, 1985

When I spoke to Daryl about the exhibit, he was terrific. Of course, he wants me to bring home a salary, but he feels positive that I should be doing this. He understands how it all speaks to me and what a significant opportunity it would be to do something as exciting as this. How fortunate I am to have a husband who understands. So, I've agreed to be the exhibition coordinator.

Meanwhile, the timing on all of this is incredible. How is it that this presented itself when I was at the lowest point with absolutely nothing on the horizon? I feel like a completely different person than I did yesterday before Tom's call. Just thinking about all that the exhibition entails has me hyped up and super excited. I probably won't sleep tonight.

Reflections on
The Search in the Interim

This was definitely not an easy chapter for me to go back and reflect on. When I left the high school, I walked out without a plan. All that mattered to me was that I got out of what felt like a toxic environment. I did what I needed to do to save myself, but by quitting, my dreams of what might have been completely shattered.

What struck me as I read these excerpts was how many jobs I was offered. It's been years since I had thought about how I kept getting calls, going in for interviews, and sitting there wondering how I could ever take any of those positions. For me, each one felt wrong for one reason or another. Mostly, I knew I would be miserable if I said yes to any of them. I just kept imagining that the walls would cave in on me.

Of course, I was left with conflicting feelings. Money was an issue, and not earning any did not help our financial situation. In some ways, I was being selfish, and while that bothered me, I just kept thinking that were I to accept any of the jobs offered to me, I might be just as miserable as I had been at the high school. Daryl was patient with me, and for that, I was extremely grateful.

What also factored in was that my writing began to take over. Suddenly, it was all I truly wanted to be doing—at least when the words were flowing. There were also those moments when self-doubt crept in. I was vulnerable. When I told people I was writing a book, while a few understood that writing is a full-time job (and for me at that time without pay), most looked at it as a hobby and wondered why I wasn't "working."

In many ways, writing *A Slice of Life* was a lifesaver for me. With the job search less than successful, I spent my time doing something constructive that I loved. It didn't take long for me to realize that my dream was to become a writer, and the only way that could ever happen was if I wrote. It was a mixed bag of trade-offs, as is so much in our lives.

During this time, while I was job hunting, I was simultaneously on an inner journey. I was questioning and hoping to find answers to some of life's biggest questions, like what is the meaning of life? Who am I? What is my true nature/essence? I was learning that to be happy, I needed to be doing something purposeful. Touching lives and making a difference mattered to me. And yet, none of the job offers provided that.

These excerpts took me right back to that desperate time in my life. There were periods when it all felt empty and almost hopeless. I was struggling to stay positive and continue looking for the right job. Much of what I pursued and felt possible and hopeful about seemed to dissipate into thin air. I never stopped trying to find something that enticed me, but I felt discouraged over and over again.

Meeting Esther and working with her was the answer to my prayers at first. I was intrigued by her wisdom and life experiences. When that soured because she decided not to pursue the endeavor, I was once again crushed. Reading about it brought me right back to those moments of disappointment and sadness, as well as yet another blank slate.

At some point, long into my search, I began to believe that the only way I could get through it was to trust in the universe. Of course, that was easier said than done. I wanted to believe that the right job would come along that I would find what spoke to my soul, but it wasn't happening.

As so often is the case, it wasn't until I hit rock bottom that everything changed. As hard as it might have been at the time, I had to go through the struggle. In reflecting, it was during those difficult times that I grew. I asked the hard questions, and at some point down the road, the answers revealed themselves.

All it took was one phone call from Tom, and my world looked completely different. When I reflect on that time in my life, I feel grateful that there is a happy ending to this chapter.

Journal Prompts

· Have you ever been at a crossroads in your career? What did it feel like?

· Write of a time when you felt lost and unsure of what was coming next.

· Write about an urge or feeling you've had when you just needed to listen to what your gut was telling you.

· What has your career path been like?

· What's been your favorite job?

· Write about a time in your life when out of nowhere, an opportunity, a person, or an experience suddenly changed your direction.

· Who or what do you turn to when you feel desperate?

Anne Frank *in the* World

1929 - 1945

Where there's hope, there's life.
It fills us with fresh courage and makes us strong again.

—— Anne Frank

May 8, 1985

Tom said he thought of me because he knows I'm someone who will get the job done. He also told me he's sure this would be a perfect fit because I keep journals.

While I agreed to be the chairperson of the exhibition, I have no idea what that means. He let me know he would help, and in his words, "We'll make lovely music together." He left me with this thought. "You can make it as big as you want. This is yours to create."

May 13, 1985

Tom is planning an evening event in New York to unveil the exhibition, which just arrived from Amsterdam. I'm excited that he invited us to come and that Daryl feels we should go. Financially, it's a stretch, but passing it up would be a missed opportunity.

May 23, 1985

I just scheduled an appointment with Diane Camber, the director of the Bass Museum, to see if we could hold the exhibition there. I'm starting with the venue, since that's key to all of this.

In her letter, my mother-in-law said that organizing this exhibition might be too overwhelming a task and I should reconsider. The truth is I need to be overwhelmed, although I doubt she would ever understand that. My parents think it's fabulous.

May 24, 1985

I felt I should reread *The Diary of a Young Girl* by Anne Frank before going to New York, so I began yesterday. It's been hard for me to think of anything else since then. Last night, I dreamt about Anne.

June 11, 1985

We're in New York for the opening. I just saw Tom, who was busy with television and radio journalists covering the event.

Daryl and I have come into the James Chapel of the Union Theological Seminary, where a girl is playing the piano and is singing, "I want to write. I have to write—to write what's buried deep down in my soul." Daryl turned around to look at me. He knows this is touching something within me. I feel a connection to Anne Frank—writer of a journal—bearer of one's soul. It is such an important, necessary part of who I am and obviously of who she was as well.

June 12, 1985

Today is declared Anne Frank Day in the USA. It's the first of its kind to exist—all because of Tom's doing.

We're at the benefit, and I have just met Aranka Segal, a Newbury Prize winner, Dr. Ruth Westheimer, and Elie Wiesel, all of whom are Holocaust survivors. Each was down-to-earth and engaging.

When I took off my heels to show Dr. Ruth I was close to her height, she looked me in the eye and said, "You and Daryl have nothing to worry about in your relationship. I can tell you're a solid team." Being the noted sex therapist that she is, I'll take that.

Elie Wiesel is speaking now and just mentioned Tom in his remarks. I'm impressed!

"Is it her age, the indifference? Everything that can be said about the period can be found in her diary. The tragedy begins when the book ends. Anne Frank captures everyone because she was a child and appeals to the child in all of us.

"Why are people so concerned with Mengele? Why are people so into the killer? We're fascinated by him. There's that mystery in evil.

"Those who rescued—why did some have the courage to care? Why did they choose to help people in general? They were all simple people. Why were there so few? We learned that it was possible to help and that in spite of cruelty in the face and power of the killer, the victims maintained their humanity. The killers didn't.

"One must use words in order to sensitize people. Children became poets and philosophers.

"We don't want to mourn and create morbidity. We tell stories and sensitize people by knowledge, culture, art, and philosophy.

"When we sensitize self to one tragedy, we're sensitizing to all tragedy and in all places. There is so much injustice in the world.

"After the war, we had one question. What do we do with our knowledge? We were young, but we knew more than the oldest of my old teachers. We knew about suffering. We knew truth with a capital T. How does one transmit it? I still don't know how, but I know we must—otherwise we'd be crushed. We must have hope."

June 13, 1985

Tom, Bauco, and I talked about my being on the team with the Anne Frank exhibit. Since Bauco heads the Anne Frank Center in Amsterdam, he is a critical player in my involvement. He described my place in all of this as a lightning rod and a facilitator.

As a result of the conversation, ideas are exploding in my head. To be with two bright, creative, and idealistic men is a gift at this time in my life—especially after the long period of solitude I've experienced.

Tom is trying on his success and not quite believing it—the TV coverage, the *New York Times* article, and on and on.

June 14, 1985

A whole new world has opened up for me all of a sudden. I can hardly believe what three days in New York did for me. The possibilities are endless since Tom let me know that the sky's the limit.

When I talked to Bill Lehman, he already knew about the exhibition because he had seen it in the *New York Times*. He agreed to raise the money needed, which is tremendously kind of him. I can't imagine fundraising on my own and need to come up with a minimum of $11,000 just to bring the exhibit to Miami. So, I'm relieved and grateful, and now, thanks to Bill, I am free to make this happen.

How ironic that Anne Frank, a young girl who kept a diary, will now connect Tom and me in a new way. The journaling piece is what has hooked me in and probably him as well. Anne Frank's intimate thoughts and openness in her diary give us a peek into what it was like in hiding and what she was feeling.

June 21, 1985

The itinerary for Bauco's and Tom's visit here worked out well. We met with people from the Greater Miami Jewish Federation, the Bass Museum, and the Southeastern Florida Holocaust Memorial Center—all of whom had wanted to be involved in the exhibition when I contacted them.

I am suddenly sky-rocketing onto a new professional plateau. Tom is making it possible to bring me along on his exciting ride. He has confidence that I can organize the exhibition, which will enhance our relationship in new ways.

June 22, 1985

I am making a list of possible locations for the exhibition, including the Ft. Lauderdale Library, the Bass Museum, and the old Main Library. I also am collecting the names of people to contact. I plan to meet an assortment of individuals, explore new places, have a variety of new experiences, and make things happen. In a matter of a little over a month, my life has shifted gears from walking on the beach, completing a novel, and feeling lost with no clear direction, to something as thrilling as this — something I never could have imagined.

July 7, 1985

Daryl and I discussed the exhibit. I told him how glad I am that he's interested and willing to be a part of it all. He knows I'm going to be extremely busy, but he seems perfectly fine with that. There's so much positive to look forward to.

Ambassador von der Stul may do a major speech on immigration in Miami. Tom thinks having the exhibition here is going to be pivotal. He has begun to refer to the big opening event as "your opening." The fact that it is the first city on the tour makes it all the more special.

July 17, 1985

I've been asked to be on a television program to talk about the exhibition. First, we need to find the right location, but I'm working on it. One of the neatest things about all of this is where it will take me during these next few months.

I'm a little nervous about finding a venue. Plus, Tom informed me I must form the civic committee now. He wants me to include politicians, university presidents, community leaders, clergy, and city and state officials. The broader the base, the better. Where do I begin?

Bauco in Amsterdam has expectations which he is putting onto Tom. In return, he's passing along the pressure on me to raise the money for the cost of bringing the exhibition here. I don't like this part for a few reasons.

For one, any talk of fundraising rattles me after my experience at the high school. And besides, this changes the dynamics of our friendship. Tom guaranteed me that down the road, it will all be worth it; however, as a result, we've already experienced a few tense moments between us.

July 20, 1985

Flashes of ideas come to me as I begin to attack my first real job as an exhibit coordinator. Taking steps to organize this project and writing about it helps to dissipate my anxiety.

Someone suggested I look at the new Main Library downtown as a possible venue, so here I am. The library currently has Gleason Romer's photographic exhibit *Changing the Face of Miami* in the auditorium. Sol Hirsch, from the library, is checking the room's measurements to see if our exhibition will fit.

Tom keeps talking to me about how I must create an Anne Frank Center here so I can have a job after. I have no idea where this will take me, but I have a feeling it's going to be good.

July 21, 1985

Bill told me he'd write a check for the $750 deposit to bring the exhibit here before I even asked him. He gave me excellent advice and offered for me to meet with people in his dad's congressional office to help me get some politicians involved.

Each day new adventures surface. In just one month, I've gotten into offices of people whom I never dreamed I would talk with one on one.

July 24, 1985

I just spoke to a woman from St. Thomas University who sounded interested and offered her space to use in any way we might find helpful. She put me in touch with a newly-released Cuban prisoner, an ambassador to the UN from Cuba who might want to be involved.

The meeting at the Miami Beach Public Library went well. They, along with the Bass Museum, seem willing to do anything to have the exhibit, but neither appears big enough. The new Main Library downtown, if we can get it, would be the perfect location.

When Tom calls these days, it's always from the office and is all business surrounding Anne Frank. He isn't writing me letters anymore. I miss our personal connection and friendship. I no longer know what's happening in his life and need to tell him.

July 26, 1985

When Bill called today, I told him I set up a meeting with the director of the Main Library. He was surprised and told me I should take him with me to seal the deal. Since it was my personal challenge, I was adamant that I needed to do this by myself. Hopefully, by mid–August, we'll have a decision on the venue.

July 28, 1985

Sol Hirsch, from the library, just called me back with the measurements. The space is 3,400 sq. feet, and the exhibit will fit. Plus, they're putting in a new sound system next month. I feel hopeful.

This exhibit will be a major event in Miami. I plan to involve the entire community— Blacks, Anglos, Cubans, and everyone else who lives here. Since our city has experienced its share of racial conflict, my goal is to break down barriers of discrimination and bring together our diverse cultures. An exhibit like this focuses on the dangers of prejudice and what can ultimately happen if left unchecked and unleashed. Hopefully, I can bring the civic committee together as a testimony to what can be done with human rights issues.

I want to teach what I preach: to have respect for one another, to stand up and speak out against injustice, and to never judge someone based on religion, skin color, sexual orientation, or race. I have my work cut out for me. Anne Frank said, "In spite of everything, I still believe people are really good at heart." Like her, I feel the same way. It is what guides me and leaves me filled with hope for our world. Goodness can and will prevail. Education is vital, so hopefully, the exhibit will be a vehicle to that end.

July 31, 1985

I met with Ed Sintz, the Miami Dade Public Library system director, and covered my complete agenda. He had questions, which I answered and let him know they did not have to concern themselves with any funding issues. He then said, "We house Anne Frank's diary on our shelves along with other great writers. She has a special place in our library, so this is a natural all around." We both agreed on that. Based on the wonderful conversation we had, I know he wants to have the exhibit there. Now, I just have to wait to see if he can get it approved.

After my meeting at the library, I met with Jeff Mel and Todd Bernstein from Congressman Lehman's office. They were receptive, helpful, and enthusiastic about the exhibit. They're going to connect me with the political figures in Miami and all of South Florida. They even offered the use of their Watts line for my out-of-town calls, carte blanche to call anyone I feel would be helpful and interested, and the use of Congressman Lehman's name. Talk about doors opening. I can't stop smiling.

August 1, 1985

I just made ten calls to ask individuals to serve on the civic committee. I'm amazed at how easy it is to say, "Congressman Lehman's office suggested I call."

August 4, 1985

I told Tom I was concentrating all my positive energy on the library saying yes picturing and imagining it to come true. He said it's the only way to make it happen, and it will. This project is going to succeed.

August 5, 1985

The new Main Library is ours! It's the best news possible. I love that I did it all by myself and didn't need anyone else's help. I'm learning that we each have the power to make things happen and have dreams come true. It just takes determination, focus, desire, and hard work. I typed seven letters tonight to invite people to join our committee: two university presidents, the superintendent of schools, the library director, and three congressmen.

August 10, 1985

I got a call from Dr. Eduardo Padrón, the president of Miami Dade Community College. He told me he admired my noble effort and would help in any way he could. The responses from people add to my excitement. Superintendent Britton from Dade County Public Schools was delighted that we're having the exhibit at the library. Goldie Goldstein, executive director of the Southeastern Florida Memorial Holocaust Center at FIU, said they're happy to be involved. Sister Jeanne O'Laughlin, president of Barry University, Dewey Knight, first deputy Miami-Dade County manager, and county commissioner Barbara Carey agreed to serve on the committee.

Here's what Tom wrote in the book he gave me. "To Merle. My dear friend, who understands and hears the 'ever-approaching thunder,' is also a believer in the goodness of humanity. Like Anne, we are making it happen. Thank you for all that you are. Love, Tom."

August 15, 1985

The civic committee meeting was a success. There were sixteen of us, which included a great representation of Miami. I introduced the committee to the exhibit details, shared thoughts about the opening, and explained ideas for programming.

I can hardly believe that I am going to be involved in teaching about the Holocaust. For years, I heard about Leatrice Rabinsky, who teaches a Holocaust literature class at Cleveland Heights High School in Cleveland, Ohio. I've always admired her and thought it was such a noble profession. The time has come to join in her efforts and pass along the message. Of course, my experience will be different from hers since I will not be in a classroom. Instead, I'll be exposing others to the information through eight hundred black and white photographs which illustrate the personal history of Anne Frank and her family and focus on the historical events during the Nazi era in both Germany and Holland.

It intrigues me that someone found the Frank family photo album in a chest of drawers in Germany, recognized Anne Frank, and sent it to the Anne Frank Center in Amsterdam. The center then created an exhibition out of these photos for educational purposes.

August 18, 1985

Tom talked about how we have a lot to do to carve the jewel we have been given. He feels the work is going to bring us to a new consciousness and connection. "We have the opportunity to cut and polish the diamond of our friendship. Anne Frank has provided us with wonderful tools."

August 19, 1985

I have typed twenty-five envelopes and handwritten personal notes thanking people for coming to the meeting and being on the civic committee. For a while, my work will consist of writing letters, making calls, and planning for the exhibit's arrival and everything else surrounding it.

August 20, 1985

My meeting at Dade County Public Schools with Zelda Glazer, head of the English department, and Paul Hanson, from social studies, went well. They agreed to promote the exhibit throughout the school district, since they believe in its messages. I love going into these meetings with a clear plan of what I expect to accomplish. So far, it has served me well with whomever I've met.

Tom said I'd be able to name my position by the time this is over. I hope that's true.

I just recorded a new message for our answering machine. Between that, the post office box, my typewriter, pen, paper, and the Anne Frank stationery I designed, I have my office all set up.

August 26, 1985

Ed Sintz, Mickie Carden (assistant director), Barbara Young from the library's art department, and I accomplished a great deal and clarified many items at our meeting. Barbara loves the idea that this project will bring people together and teach them to think about important issues. Meanwhile, there is no end to the work ahead of us.

Mickie wants to hold a public grand opening two nights after the benefit opening and call it a preview party. The library staff feels it's important for the community to have the opportunity to attend a special evening event when the exhibit first opens. Besides, since the purpose of our benefit opening is to raise money, we need to have an event that is free and open to everyone.

Tom loved hearing that Mayor Steve Clark, U. S. Congressmen Bill Lehman, Dante Fascell, Claude Pepper, and Larry Smith accepted the invitation to be on the committee. Then, when I got home from my meeting at the library, I received a call from Governor Graham's office saying he also would serve on the committee. It just keeps getting better with each passing day.

I foresee exciting times ahead connecting with many more people from South Florida and beyond. This may just be the opportunity of my lifetime. I feel like I'm walking onto the next stepping stone. In Tom's letter he wrote on the way back from Miami, he said, "Very appreciative of your generous hospitality and confident of your abilities to do Miami. Hoping it will bring you enjoyment, renewed purpose, and prosperity."

August 27, 1985

Life is going to be different. After wandering the beach for the past two years plus and feeling lost, I have now entered into a new reality. I suddenly have people to see, places to go, and much to accomplish. My lists are beginning to dictate my days. My phone is ringing, and I have a direction again.

I've been reading *Tales from the Secret Annex,* Anne's book of short stories. She saw the world from an amazingly positive perspective, especially considering how she lived during her last two years.

I don't think the survival of her writing was an accident. How many would ever know what happened during the Holocaust had they not read her diary? Yet, I realize it is one story in millions—each telling an aspect of what went on between 1933 and 1945.

September 2, 1985

Adele agreed to handle the press for the exhibition. She'll do a fabulous job because that's who she is. Getting the word out to the public will be crucial to the exhibit's success. It's going to be a considerable undertaking, which means she'll probably have to give up her art to do the work. That's a sacrifice and one I truly appreciate.

September 3, 1985

The library meeting went well. Ed assigned a staff member as the liaison to handle school groups that call the library to schedule tours. I'll be managing the adult tours as well as evening events for organizations. We'll have docents, but many groups will want me to speak to them, so I'll need to coordinate all of that.

I left feeling a bit overwhelmed. As Barbara reminded me, I have a lot to learn.

September 4, 1985

I'm at the Holocaust Memorial Center taking their interviewers' class. I doubt that I'll have time to interview survivors, but I need to gain as much knowledge about the Holocaust as I can. Marilyn told me that attending this course was a most meaningful experience, so I feel sure it will be helpful on many levels.

What an intense experience. People on both sides of me have been crying. We just saw *Genocide*, a film about the Holocaust with Orson Wells and Elizabeth Taylor narrating. The footage of ghettos and concentration camps was difficult to watch. I am moved and see more clearly than ever the importance of the Anne Frank exhibition in making others aware of the Holocaust so that something like this never happens again.

September 12, 1985

Archbishop McCarthy, Rabbi Lehrman, Dr. Robinson, president of Florida Memorial College, and Reverend Ron Qualley agreed to serve on the committee. It's coming together.

September 18, 1985

I spoke to Bauco, who said he would like to move his whole office down here and become a subsidiary of mine—a great, fun fantasy for me. I was glad to joke around with him. But the truth is, he wants me to set up an Anne Frank Center. It would be a lot of work, and I'm pretty sure we don't need another Holocaust center in South Florida. However, he and Tom are not giving up on the idea.

September 24, 1985

This morning, I had an interesting conversation with someone at the library who wondered why the exhibit was opening around holiday time. She said the two didn't fit. It never occurred to me, but I think the timing will work in our favor. Peak tourist season in Florida starts in mid-December, plus the Picasso exhibit will be at the art museum right next door at the same time.

I'm working on organizing a writing contest for high school students. Thanks to the presidents from the universities serving on our committee, several English professors have agreed to serve as judges.

Students at North Miami Beach High School are putting on the play *The Diary of Anne Frank*. I spoke to the drama teacher, and she agreed to do some programming with me.

One way this exhibit will be a success is by involving the students. They are our future and while they are young, they'll benefit from learning the lessons from the Holocaust.

September 27, 1985

Tom called and left me frustrated because the ambassador can't come down to open the exhibit—too much politics. Plus, the catalogs aren't ready, the press release isn't completed, and so far, no one has organized the proper order for listing the civic committee. While it might not sound like a big deal, it has to be done correctly because of the politics and positions of the people serving. It's all frustrating and not the way I work!

September 30, 1985

John Dorschner, from the *Tropic*, called. They're going to cover the Anne Frank story. Wait until Adele hears this one. It is tremendously exciting and such a coup. She did her homework as she always does.

When I told Tom, he planned to immediately set in motion the process of getting the pictures from Holland for the *Tropic*, since they're critical to the article. Hopefully, that will happen.

October 9, 1985

I'm at the Holocaust lecture. During the break, I spoke to Dr. Jerry Goldsmith from Holland. Before the war, his girlfriend was friends with Anne Frank. He was in hiding for two years right down the street from the Frank family. I talked to him about the possibility of participating in an activity with students, and he readily agreed. Now, I need to think about how he can best fit in.

October 12, 1985

Most people in my life have no clue as to the magnitude of the exhibit or the impact it's going to have in South Florida. Meanwhile, it continues to grow in scope. I'm starting to feel like it can't be contained—as if it's almost impossible to summarize. Everything is happening so quickly and is expanding in many directions.

With each new addition to the committee, the composition changes. After I complete gathering the forces, I will then mobilize the troops into action. This exhibit is pulling the community together in a unique way.

I have set two goals for myself and hope to accomplish both before the exhibit closes on the 26th of January. First, I want at least 50,000 people to come to the library to see the exhibition. Then, I want an editorial about the exhibit in the *Miami Herald*. I wonder what it will take for either to become a reality.

I've been working on this exhibit for four months now. Although I don't know exactly where this will take me, I sense that I'm building a foundation for something important in my life. Only time will tell, but I am staying open to all possibilities.

October 23, 1985

I'm at FIU. I just did a lot of running around—picked up the embosser, got the stationery for the press releases, and went to the post office. I had a few exciting calls with a major donor and the rabbi from Temple Israel who wants to include his synagogue in the activities.

Then I spoke to Rick Hensler, from American Savings, who is working on the ads in the *Miami Herald* they are doing for us pro bono.

October 24, 1985

Today was my first interview. Going to *Diario Los Americas*, the Spanish newspaper, was an adventure which felt like I was in a different country. Of course, everyone was speaking Spanish when I arrived. Fortunately, they talked to me in English.

The background I'm getting in the interviewers' course I'm taking at the Holocaust Center is invaluable to me. I didn't realize how helpful it would be when speaking about the exhibition. So much of what I talked about today came from what I've learned through the class.

I got a call from Mickie at the library with big news. Even though it's a stretch for them, they have agreed to keep the library open for us on all Sundays in January. That will make scheduling groups a lot easier.

October 29, 1985

At North Miami Beach Senior High School. I brought Rebecca with me to listen to Jerry Goldsmith, who is about to meet with the cast of the Anne Frank play. By talking to the student actors, he will give them a better understanding of what it was like in hiding during the Holocaust. Hopefully, by learning from someone who lived in hiding, they will be more authentic in their roles.

Later. Jerry began by telling the students how he lived when he was a young teenager. "I was in hiding two miles from Anne Frank. There was always pressure on us to be quiet and not be discovered. Sometimes before people went into hiding, they would trust their best friends by telling them where they were going. Unfortunately, in many cases, those friends exposed them.

"We were in the attic of a house and couldn't wear shoes all day. Anne had a toilet where she was. We only had a pail. There was no one to cut our hair.

"We were there for two years from August 1942–1944. Being confined like that added to our feeling depressed at times. My parents and I played three-handed bridge. We depended on people to bring us food, books, and whatever else they could. If something happened to them, there was no one to count on.

"It was difficult to live in confinement together. Anne's space was more insulated.

"I always felt like I was going to survive. We didn't live in fear. The three of us listened to BBC and stayed optimistic. We didn't keep track of the days.

"We wanted to feel safe and believed we wouldn't get caught. Who could imagine there was a war that would kill millions and millions of people?"

Jerry did a superb job helping the students get a clearer picture of life in hiding. The student who plays Otto Frank asked, "Did you have problems with people fighting? It's always an issue for us in the attic." Others questioned him as though they were the characters in the play, which ultimately helped them better understand their situation.

This experience was invaluable, and as a result, the play will be all the more powerful. The teacher was blown away, and so was I! I hope these kids will never forget it. I know I won't.

October 31, 1985

These last four days have been a whirlwind with Tom, Jan van der Temple, and Bauco here. At each meeting, I took charge and got the job done. At the meeting with the Dade County Public Schools' administrators, I was excited sitting around the table with the heads of the English, social studies, and art departments and filling them in on all that was happening. The tiger on the shoulder of my dress was like a message not to mess with me. I am working with some of the school system's bigwigs, yet I'm the one calling the shots. It's a first for me, which feels kind of surreal.

Tom wants me to write a grant to fund the further work of the committee and form a center here. He isn't giving up on the idea, nor is Bauco, who said he would make me the director of the southeast region of the Anne Frank Center. While all that sounds enticing, I do not want to raise money. Writing grants is about the last thing I can see myself doing. All I want is to travel with the exhibition, and, hopefully, that will happen.

November 1, 1985

We've talked about my role if I become the educational consultant in the United States after Miami's exhibition. Since the Anne Frank Center has no money, the cities would have to cover my costs. Tom told me he'd like me to create a step-by-step guide. I told him I'd do it for pay and then smiled. I wasn't kidding.

Jan, a Dutch economist, came to the United States, specifically to Miami, strictly to see how much money the exhibit could generate to support itself. To them, this is a business. When it comes to finances and conversations about money, I shy away because the bottom line in all this for me continues to be on a different level. My primary interest is what we are going to teach those who come to see the exhibit. To me, it is a meaningful, educational tool that can change lives.

It won't be long before *Anne Frank in the World: 1929–1945* hits Miami. I want to find out how to place an ad on the electronic billboard near the airport. It's something relatively new and continuously rotates announcements. How exciting it would be to have Bauco and Tom see the exhibit advertised as I drive them from the airport on their next visit.

November 5, 1985

After the excellent response from the students for the contest, I'm giving more thought to holding a symposium for high school students from all over Dade County. It would be an all-day seminar at the library with the theme of discrimination and prejudice and, of course, focusing on Anne Frank and her diary.

I now have a star in the sky to reach for and a dream to make come true. Every morning when I awake, my first thoughts are of Anne Frank and the exhibition. The project is always on my mind.

November 8, 1985

Tom told me that Anne's actual diary would not travel with the exhibition as they had initially planned. Those in Amsterdam are now afraid there could be a terrorist who would find a way to steal it. So, instead, they are creating an exact duplicate.

Financial pressure permeates my work on the exhibition. Tom said he's a goner if we don't come up with $20,000. That, of course, adds more pressure on me since the initial figure I had to raise was $9,000 less. I can't stand when Tom and I talk money, and he feels the same.

November 16, 1985

Two years ago, Tom told me that something big would come my way when the timing was right. Neither of us had any idea it would be like this. The invitations to the December 15th benefit opening are in the mail. It's time to get this show on the road.

November 22, 1985

Things are progressing. The meeting for the volunteers and docents went well. I stuck to my agenda and was able to answer everyone's questions at the end. So far, we have a great group of people who will make a difference in how this all plays out.

Ingrid Roskin, a child survivor who was in hiding in Holland, attended and said she would help. When we talked about the crowded space around the television monitor, she reminded us how Anne lived with six other people in an area no more than four hundred fifty square feet. She wants us to make sure the docents talk about that.

The list of people, including government and community officials, coming to the opening continues to grow. Each day as the responses come in, I get more excited.

November 25, 1985

I just met with Ed Kilroy at the library and took care of more logistics. He brought me down to see the boxes filled with the exhibit panels, which arrived yesterday. Looking at them was enough for my heart to speed up and the reality to hit.

Lori Horne, who is covering the exhibition for the *Miami Herald*, just called. She mentioned how tying the exhibit to Chanukah would make a good slant. I told her this is much greater than a Jewish issue and encouraged her to think more broadly. Hopefully, she understood because my goal is to help people realize prejudice affects everyone, and the Holocaust was a human tragedy that left its mark on all of us.

November 26, 1985

Adele just called. She had talked to John Dorschner, who said they had planned to put an article about the exhibit in the *Tropic*. They had their layout and slant all arranged. However, because the people at the Anne Frank Center in Amsterdam didn't send the photos as promised, they aren't going to be able to do it. Adele and I are crushed. We have to move on, but it is beyond upsetting.

December 3, 1985

I had a call from Marge Saulson from Detroit and then from Enid Futerman in New York—both of whom are coordinating the exhibits in their cities and wanted guidance from me. It pleases me to share information that I've learned over the past few months. This is what I hope to be doing all over the country when I have the official title of educational consultant for the exhibition.

December 4, 1985

It's pouring outside unexpectedly. My suit, blouse, heels, and hair are soaking wet from running in the rain from the parking lot to the Metro Dade office building.

I didn't have an umbrella, and since I didn't want to be late for my meeting with the mayor, I didn't have much choice.

Despite how I look, I feel calm and excited. At the moment, I'm sitting in the reception room, where I am creating a puddle of water under my chair.

I pray it doesn't rain on December 15th. I don't even want to think about it. I need to concern myself only with that over which I have control.

Back in my car. I couldn't believe that Mayor Clark was chewing gum, using swear words like calling Hitler a bastard, laughing because my hair and clothes were dripping all over everything, and talking to me like we were friends. He was just a regular guy with no pretenses. I felt comfortable the entire time I was with him. He told me he was in high school when the war was going on and had no idea what was happening. He readily agreed to take part in the opening.

December 6, 1985

We're no longer counting months or even weeks, since we only have nine days left. This is it—the final countdown. Daryl has been terrific in taking over the last-minute logistics for the benefit. It's a huge load off my mind.

We have collected $18,837 to date. We're doing amazingly well, thanks to Bill's effort. In addition to that, the opening is bringing in money, as we hoped it would. I thought I had launched a long time ago, but in reality, maybe I was only preparing for this. I remember Tom's public moment. Mine is coming soon.

December 8, 1985

I just got a call from one of the exhibit installers, who said the team is working hard. Hopefully, it's all coming together as planned. Just seeing the PVC pipes laid out was a good start.

December 9, 1985

I'm on automatic, as Tom says. There is no stopping me. From now on, it's a matter of going with the flow, which is all I can do.

Joké, the researcher for the exhibit, did a brilliant interview with the *Miami Herald* today. She's responsible for all the research behind the exhibit and created the exhibition with the oppressors', liberators', and victims' countries in mind.

Adele has done a superb job getting more articles in the paper. In the *Miami Herald* alone, we're going to be in *Lively Arts, Living Today,* and the *Neighbors*. We just got word that an article will appear in the *Miami News*. Is this truly happening?

December 10, 1985

When I got back to the house after buying bagels, Bauco had just come out of the shower and greeted me in a towel. He kissed me on both cheeks and thanked me for all I was doing. His plane was late last night, and he didn't get in until 12:45 a.m. Daryl stayed up, but the rest of us were sound asleep.

By the time I got out of the 50 States Security meeting where I had set up everything for the next six weeks, I was pretty much on overload. Then, I came home to twenty phone messages and a lot left on my list to accomplish. Both Adele and I are wild at the moment. The pressure is on with so much to do in these last few days.

December 11, 1985

I'm sitting at a table on the plaza near the library. A huge banner with Anne Frank's picture as a young child hangs across the front of the building and gently flaps in the mild breeze. Buzzards float in the currents circling the uppermost part of the courthouse. Tom and Bauco are planning their schedules for the next few days. I'm catching my breath.

Earlier, I was infuriated to find out that the posters for the Miami exhibit weren't shipped here as planned. The person in charge of that never got it together in time to have them made. No one told me, and it wasn't like I hadn't asked enough times. All we have are the leftovers from the week the exhibit in New York was making its initial debut in the United States. I suppose they are better than nothing but not at all what I had planned for and wanted.

In the car down to the library today, Bauco officially offered me a job as the director of the Anne Frank Center in Miami. The only catch is that I would have to create the center, which means coming up with the seed money before beginning. I can't think about that now.

Just one month ago, the exhibition's opening was still behind the scenes in all kinds of lists on my legal pad—not even known to most people in Miami. Now, it's hitting the newspapers from Palm Beach County on down. Cookie called from Cleveland to say she read about our opening in the *Cleveland Jewish News.*

Tonight, I wrote a check for $10,250, the largest amount I've ever written, which means the exhibit is paid in full. Tom and Bauco had huge smiles on their faces when I handed it to them, knowing their salaries were now covered for a bit. My obligation to the Anne Frank Center is fulfilled, although I know they are still counting on a lot more.

A cold front is on the way for the weekend. They're predicting temperatures will dip down to around 50° on Sunday. We're going to freeze at the opening, which is scheduled to be held outside the library on the plaza.

Unfortunately, in addition to the posters, the weather is another area over which I have no control. It leaves me with no choice but to let it go.

Today, in separate conversations with the two contest winners, both told me they never thought about the prize money when they wrote their essays. Hearing that made the fact that they won all the more meaningful. Their essays were profound and impressive — especially for ninth-grade boys. However, knowing that about the money makes me wish Tom and I had never set the first-place prize for $500 and the second for $250. What were we thinking? When we decided, we were sitting on the beach feeling no pain and not thinking realistically. Meanwhile, the boys probably would have been satisfied with $50 or $25 respectively.

December 12, 1985

I awoke to a half-page article about me and *Anne Frank and the World: 1929-1945* in the *Miami Herald Neighbors* section. It begins with an anecdote about how I experienced anti-Semitism at Ohio State University. From there, it continues and explains what the exhibition is about. A big picture of me at my desk accompanies the article. Adele arranged it to appear in today's paper as a birthday present for me. I'm touched by that and all of her hard work.

When I went into the den, I accidentally pushed the wrong button on my answering machine and erased all my messages. I could tell the tape had been almost full because of how long it took to rewind. So much for the birthday messages, press calls, and whatever else might have been on it. I can't believe I did that. With the exhibit opening three days away, I have plenty to concern myself with, and since there's absolutely nothing I can do about it but beat myself up, I once again need to let go and move on. Easier said than done, of course.

Then Tom called to tell me someone from the radio station called him to say the interview he and Bauco did earlier today was accidentally erased. Now, they have to go back to the studio and redo the entire interview. Tom did not sound too pleased. I can relate.

I went over my press statement for tomorrow with Adele and Daryl. I'll let Tom and Bauco read it as well. Now, I have to finish my speech for the opening.

My parents just arrived a bit earlier than expected. They're reading all the articles from the various newspapers. News of the exhibit is popping all over.

December 13, 1985

I'm at the press briefing conference table with everything in order. I gave my statement. While I was talking, I heard echoes in my head, just like when I made my presentation at the Miami Beach Public Library. I'm convinced it's nerves. Joké is speaking now. I should be paying attention instead of writing in my journal.

December 14, 1985

Governor Graham sent the following letter today:

Dear Friends,

It is a special privilege for me to extend my congratulations and appreciation to the Anne Frank Exhibition Civic Committee of Greater Miami on the opening of "Anne Frank in the World: 1929 – 1945."

This exhibit affords the public an opportunity to reflect upon one of the bleakest eras in world history, yet marvel at the resilience of the human spirit and strengthen our resolve to never again allow such human misery, suffering, and persecution as that inflicted upon Anne Frank and the millions of other victims of the Holocaust.

I applaud the efforts of Ms. Merle Saferstein and the many individuals and organizations responsible for bringing this remarkable exhibit to South Florida.

With warm regards,

Sincerely,

Bob Graham
Governor

December 15, 1985

I'm at the library. It's 1:00, and there's not a soul around except for two security guards. Before I do anything else today, I must rewrite my remarks for this evening. Tom called me right as I was walking out the door to come down here.

I could hardly believe he now wants me to chair tonight's entire program. Tom thinks it's only appropriate for me to introduce all the speakers instead of him as initially planned. He gave me some ideas of what to say. Now it's up to me to get it all down on paper.

Today's *Miami Herald* has two huge spreads. Adele gets the credit for the magnificent work in getting all the press to cover the event.

Later. I'm now inside the auditorium sitting on the floor. It's 2:45. I'm the only one here surrounded by eight hundred pictures of Anne Frank, World War II, and the Holocaust. In the silence of this room, I feel enveloped by powerful spirits of the past.

I am grateful to be spending this time alone. When I left, our house was on wheels, and I knew I needed time to center myself, take a few deep breaths, and figure out all the introductions for tonight. The moment I've been waiting for these past few months moves closer.

December 16, 1985

It's now 2:30 a.m. Tonight was the closest I'll probably ever come to feeling like an Oscar-winning Hollywood star complete with flashing cameras, flowers, kisses, and praise. I felt glamorous, confident, and appreciated.

What an incredible day. To begin with, I was on the 6:00 news. I never feel nervous when I talk about Anne Frank—regardless of who is asking the questions, so the interview went well.

Before the opening began, I met with Archbishop McCarthy and walked him through the exhibit. Occasionally, we stopped and talked about one of the pictures that provoked something in either of us. He asked me a few questions about the Catholic Church and how I thought it treated the Jews during the Holocaust. Since they were delicate questions and required answers that I didn't feel qualified to give to the archbishop, of all people, I told him that Tom would be the best person to talk to. After all, he had been in the priesthood. As soon as Tom arrived, I warned him about what was coming.

As the crowds began to gather, I mingled and tended to a few of the last-minute details. Once I saw that everything was in place—the tables set, the wine chilled and ready to be poured, the sound system working, and the dignitaries in their seats, I made my way up to the podium. At exactly 8:00 p.m., I stood at the microphone and welcomed everyone to the premiere opening of the international exhibition *Anne Frank in the World: 1929–1945*. Then I called on Archbishop McCarthy to give the invocation. Cantor Shulkes followed and sang *Eli, Eli,* my favorite Hebrew song, written by Hannah Senesh, a paratrooper killed during the Holocaust.

Although it was probably only about 56°, the night was crystal clear with a star-filled sky. Each time I got up to introduce the next speaker, the breezes blew through my hair and my dress, but it didn't even matter. I was in another world.

During Tom's powerful speech, two airplanes flew overhead. He had to pause for a moment each time and let them pass. As usual, he spoke brilliantly. What an honor to be sharing center stage with him, Bauco, and all the other officials, clergy, and dignitaries tonight.

Ed Sintz spoke without notes. He talked about how I had convinced him that the exhibit belonged at the library and how right I was. He said they plan to shelter and protect Anne Frank. Ed described how the diary would continue to sit on their library's shelves surrounded by the literary geniuses of all ages—a glorified and profound declaration similar to what he had said to me originally when I went to ask him about housing the exhibition at the library.

The program ended with Mayor Clark reading the proclamation and officially declaring the exhibition open. That's when the partying began. We welcomed Anne Frank with a gala reception under the stars. Wine glistened in our glasses.

We celebrated the occasion of bringing Anne Frank—a wonderfully significant gift—to the city of Miami. Just knowing how important it is for our community makes it all the more special.

The night flew by. Every once in a while, Tom and I met up among the crowd of around three hundred fifty people. Whenever we passed each other, we would stop for a minute, exchange a few quick words of disbelief that this was happening, chuckle at the wonder of it all, and move on. The journey along this path has had its share of curves, but we've kept forging ahead. Tonight, we both feel as if our spaceship launched upward and onward.

When we finally arrived home at about 12:30, the following notes from the kids greeted us, each letting us know there would be no school for them tomorrow.

> *Dear Mom and Dad,*
>
> *I'm so tired. Don't wake me up (tomorrow either). Congratulations. Well done.*
> *I'm proud. I love you. Come and kiss me.*
>
> *Love,*
> *Rebecca*
>
> *Dear Mom and Dad,*
>
> *I'm very proud of you. You were great, and I enjoyed it very much.*
> *I'll see you at 12:00 p.m. tomorrow because I'll be sleeping till then. Please don't wake me. I love you.*
>
> *Love,*
> *Mikey*

Tonight, I experienced a moment of glory. I hope that the glow of this evening will last forever.

Later. About forty people are standing around watching the video. I've gotten about ten phone calls already this morning. Tom is interviewing with WNWS. I left my journal open before, and Tom wrote: "And it went very well thanks to Merle-Babe. Can you believe this? It's a long way from our hole in the sand. Thanks, Merle and company."

December 18, 1985

The response to the exhibit has been overwhelming. I haven't had the time to put it all down on paper. My life has been wild since my last moment of relaxation on the massage table last Thursday. Talk about a whirlwind! We've had great publicity—TV and newspaper coverage from all over Florida. I was just on Channel 10 news.

We've already had 3,500 people go through the exhibit, and it's only the third day. People are swarming downtown to see it. Last night was fabulous too. The library hosted the public party, and as everything else has been, it was a huge success. They were thrilled with the number of people who showed up.

Yesterday, I had a wonderful meeting with Tom and Bauco over lunch. They're trying to get $3,000 from Detroit, so I can serve as a consultant to the various sites. They have given me their vote of confidence. Last night at dinner, Bauco toasted me and welcomed me as part of the team. I'm on my way.

Bauco let me know that much of their future success depends on me. The pressure is on for the dollars. On the other hand, I am not pressuring anyone because those moved by what they see will be inclined to donate. Maybe I'm wrong, but it just isn't who and what I am and certainly not my reason for doing all that I have.

The TV show I did *Something on 17* turned out well. However, I felt a little out of it when I stood up to leave with my microphone still attached to me. What was I thinking?

I just had a run-in with a few people because I turned off the tape about Hitler and the Holocaust too soon and didn't let the credits run all the way through. They sure showed their displeasure. A few even told me that "the people in Miami are just disgusting." I could've done without that because I don't feel it's true. I apologized and moved on.

I had a good talk with Floyd Major from the Community Relations Board. He invited me to speak at two big county meetings. My life is heading in an interesting direction.

Bauco called this morning and was excited with the number of people who have come to see the exhibition. He loved his send-off on the new billboard at the airport the clincher that impressed him the most.

When I hear people talk about this exhibition's importance, I know I have brought something worthwhile to the city. The coming together of groups is just what I had hoped for.

December 20, 1985

Cookie has gone to deposit money in the bank. I'm figuring out how many books we sold and how much we collected. I don't like doing the bookkeeping end at all.

I can't believe how Anne Frank has come into my life. With her as my platform, I can break down barriers and teach children about celebrating diversity and respecting others—what an excellent opportunity to pass along these messages.

December 21, 1985

I'm at the library, and the auditorium is locked. We can't find anyone who has the key. People are waiting to get in and are starting to get upset. I'm not thrilled myself.

I just opened a letter from the archbishop, who explained how the church protected Jews during the war. I will pass it along to Bauco and Tom. Let them decide how to respond since I don't have a clue.

December 22, 1985

I feel as if my life is not my own. I'm not cut out for working seven days in a row. I wonder how people do it. However, I love what each day brings and don't want to miss any of it. So, this is ultimately my choice. I am not complaining!

Between the Picasso exhibit and ours, crowds are filling the plaza. Presently, in the library, we have one large group of people in the auditorium while others in the lobby watch the video of Hitler shouting to his followers. The total of visitors is 7,358 so far — not bad for less than a week. Somehow, from my dining room table, I have gotten all these people walking through the doors of the new Main Library.

No security guard showed up today. That's a problem. I feel much better when we have guards here, which is a sad commentary in itself.

I had an interview with a woman from the *Forward* today. She went to Hiroshima to see how people were dealing with life after the fact. She's doing something similar now with the after-effects of the Holocaust.

December 26, 1985

Today was a record-breaking day with unbelievable crowds. The Christmas holiday helps. I'm glad to see all the children and teens who are coming through the doors. I talk to as many of them as I can.

On occasion, I hear from strangers, "I saw you on TV and recognize you." Or, "I've read about you in the paper." I am not sure what to do with all that.

Ernest Nives called from New York to tell me that CBS wants to do a special on Miami. He feels we may break the Miami Dolphins attendance record. I see crowds of people in my sleep.

December 31, 1985

The exhibition has stirred so many thoughts, feelings, and lots of questions about how the Holocaust happened. As a result, many individuals who come here want to talk about what happened during that time. The exhibition is becoming a forum for conversation, questions, and a quest for understanding — just as I had hoped it would be. We're sweeping the city — a clear indication of how many lives this young child, Anne Frank, is touching.

January 7, 1986

We had several schools here this morning. One teacher had given her students questions to answer, and not only were the kids noisy, but they were using the exhibit poles as a surface to put their papers on and write their answers. I was horrified and found myself walking around disciplining, which was not exactly what I wanted to be doing!

Now a group of fifty Holocaust survivors is here. Talking to them choked me up. It has to be incredibly painful for them to walk through this exhibit and remember. I can't even imagine what it must take for them to relive their memories. I feel privileged to talk to them.

January 8, 1986

Some man just asked me if Anne Frank was still living. When I told him, his remark was, "No kidding." I've talked to a few people who had no idea what a concentration camp was. What world are they living in?

Each day, at least one thousand people go through the exhibition. Hopefully, they're thinking about discrimination and its effects on others.

I started thinking about my future, how the exhibit will end on January 26th, and wondering what I will be left with. What is it I want to do with my life? Where is all this going? What part will I play in the Anne Frank organization when the exhibit is over. Where will I fit?

Yesterday, Ernest called and pressured me for money. As a result, I was not happy and let Tom know. In turn, he gave strict orders to everyone from New York and Amsterdam never again to ask me for money. I feel better, and I know Tom does too. I'm relieved that he called back, and we talked further about all of this. It's essential that nothing interfere with our friendship and what we've created.

January 10, 1986

I'll be speaking to two groups today and love doing that. The questions people often ask prompt discussion. I am becoming an expert on Anne Frank and am learning plenty from people who walk through the exhibition. We've just hit 34,000 people.

I haven't had a chance to stand back from all of this. I've been here every single day since December 15th because I want to be. I generally leave around 6:30 p.m. and trust that the volunteers will handle everything until the library closes. Today was the first time I left earlier because I needed to be outside. With the beautiful weather, it's hard being cooped up listening to Hitler barking orders all day long.

January 11, 1986

So far, 2,200 people have come through the exhibit today. Sister Nöel, bless her heart, had it all under control until I arrived. Harriet Nash thinks what I've done will be good for me someday.

Hopefully, she's right. For now, I'm being quoted often and have become a spokeswoman for a worthy cause. I keep wondering if we will hit 50,000. Today one of the security guards, who has become part of our team, asked about the numbers. They are as invested in our goal as we are. In these next two weeks, I hope we'll see 14,000 people.

January 12, 1986

Tom called tonight to talk about the financial picture. Core and Bauco want more money. They want to see it happening. We discussed Tom coming here to pass out envelopes for donations. As it happened, he called back to say he was coming tomorrow. I told him not to — that it's too soon with my in-laws here. I made him wait until Wednesday. The whole thing has gotten me a bit crazed, and so not what I want.

I couldn't believe it when Tom told me I was not under pressure to raise money. I responded with a resounding "Bullshit!" That just isn't true. In addition to the initial cost of renting the exhibition, they've expected me to be raising money. That was not our original deal. The rules changed somewhere along the line without my knowing it. I am, after all, a volunteer in all of this. Plus, I need permission from the library to do any kind of fundraising there.

January 13, 1986

I spoke to Ed about Tom passing out fundraising envelopes. Since they are a public library, they can have no part in it. He saw how desperate I was, and he kindly told me that he had no intention of coming into the exhibit. In other words, he plans to look the other way.

January 14, 1986

While we have a short break before getting back to the teen symposium, I wanted to write for a few minutes and get this all down on paper. Two students from each high school in the county are here, in addition to the entire cast and crew from the Anne Frank play at North Miami Beach High School.

Earlier, I divided everyone into random groups to talk about discrimination in their lives. While this is not a particularly easy age for teens to put themselves out there and meet others, these students did not hold back. The conversations were deep and meaningful.

Goldie Goldstein and Rositta Kenigsberg from the Holocaust Memorial Center spoke. They told us a little about the process of interviewing survivors and liberators, which they have been doing since the center first opened in 1980.

I then followed with a piece on journaling and gave the students tips for writing in a journal. I talked about what Anne Frank's diary meant to her and how it has been a way for millions to learn about the Holocaust. As a prompt, I had each student write about what Anne Frank means to them in our world today — much like our contest theme.

Later. What a fantastic day this has been. The highlight for me was having the students from the play with us. Because everyone had name tags with first names only and nothing else, there was no way for the students to identify which schools others came from. So, it was a surprise to everyone when, after lunch, Peter got up from his seat and started to say his lines from one of the acts.

One by one, the characters each stood and performed an entire scene. It was a mind-blowing, awesome experience. No one could believe what was going on. Talk about goosebumps.

After that, we took the students (over 125 in all) down to see the exhibition. By then, they were well prepared and understood the context of what went on during Anne's life. The conversation following the viewing of the exhibit was insightful because they were knowledgeable and focused. They understood the dangers of prejudice in a way they might never have before.

Of all the programming I've done throughout the exhibition, this was by far the most powerful. It's a day to remember for sure.

January 15, 1986

Tom and the envelopes have arrived. I am feeling a little anxious about how this fundraising effort will end up. Tom has been standing at the door and handing out envelopes as people come into the exhibit.

I've been talking to groups all day. Some man who overheard me said, "Why don't you differentiate between Germans and Nazis?" All I could say in response was, "Good point." I will be aware of that when I speak from now on. Not all Germans were Nazis.

Bauco called and wanted to know how it was going with Tom and the fundraising piece. I told him it was working. In my opinion, the people at the Anne Frank Center seem to have lost total perspective of Anne Frank's messages and are too consumed with the financial picture.

January 17, 1986

Herb Karliner, a survivor who was on the SS St. Louis, is volunteering with me today. He first came to the exhibit because he was in the children's home in France with Ernst, who is on the board of the Anne Frank Center. Listening to him talk about what it was like to be on the ship at our shore and not be allowed to come onto land was heartbreaking.

We have hit 42,000. The numbers keep mounting. We'll hit over 50,000 at this rate.

Later. Tom told me tonight he does not expect that I will get total thanks or praise from the Amsterdam center until the dollars are in and accounted for. At least, I accomplished what I set out to do and more, which counts for so much. People in South Florida have learned and will remember Anne Frank. I'm proud that it has been a smashing success.

January 20, 1986

We've had huge crowds all day. With only one week to go, people are coming in droves. I can hardly believe this will soon be over. When the panels are boxed up and shipped out, will I fade into oblivion? Doubtful—very doubtful.

Yet, I can't help but wonder how I'll feel next Monday. I must believe there will be new beginnings.

January 23, 1986

Channel 10 is here taping panels of the exhibit while they wait for me to speak to another group. They just finished interviewing Ed Sintz.

We've had several groups so far this morning. I love being at the hub of the action and am going to miss this.

January 25, 1986

The editorial about the exhibition was in the *Miami Herald* today. They quote me as saying that the students came away with a better understanding of the seeds of discrimination. "They understand that if we don't start respecting our fellow human beings, this can happen again."

I have reached both of my goals. We have far surpassed having 50,000 people come through the auditorium to see the exhibit. I look forward to seeing what the final number will be tomorrow. It's such a satisfying feeling to reach goals, especially challenging ones like these.

Margarita told me about her life in Cuba. We talked about how each life affected by dictators is tragic. I also told her that when I speak to students, I talk about the oppression in South Africa, Cuba, and the Soviet Union. It's something young people lucky enough to live in America need to know. Unfortunately, there is prejudice and discrimination everywhere.

It feels great to have become an expert on Anne Frank. I have wanted a meaningful platform from which to speak and teach and have finally found one. Who knows where I will go from here?

In these last six weeks, I have:

- Spent more than four hundred and twenty hours at the library.
- Seen tens of thousands of people walk through the arches of the Main Library.
- Spoken to seventy-five groups of students and over one hundred groups of adults.
- Met people from all over the world.
- Talked with Holocaust survivors.
- Reached my goals and realized my dreams.
- Made a name for myself in the community.
- Learned more than I ever could have imagined.

I'm about to end a significant project in my life. I don't know that I'll ever have the opportunity to put on a show like this again. Making it all happen has been an experience of a lifetime.

January 26, 1986

The final total of people who came to see the exhibit is 60,365. It was a grand slam! People will be talking about Anne Frank for a long time here in South Florida.

Bauco told me he had hoped for 25,000 visitors and seemed overjoyed by the final number. Tom gave me credit and said it was all the work I did that made it a success. The truth is it was a team effort. Adele gets credit too, and without Bill, it couldn't have happened. Plus, the volunteers made a huge difference, as did the library staff. Above all, I love the idea that I connected with people who believe we can change the world through educating our youth.

January 27, 1986

My phone has stopped ringing. My calendar is empty. I have nothing to do and nothing to look forward to. It feels like the bottom has fallen out.

January 28, 1986

I was in Ed Sintz's office earlier today tying up loose ends. While there, we learned that the Challenger exploded. What an awful tragedy. Suddenly, nothing else feels important. The country is mourning.

February 1, 1986

The sadness of the space shuttle breaking apart and killing all seven crew members has permeated my being. I am not alone in this sorrow. I am sitting with my sadness doing whatever I can not to spiral down. I'm not being all that successful.

February 2, 1986

One week ago, I was knee-deep in the excitement of the exhibition. Phones were ringing, and crowds were gathering—what a striking contrast to the absolute silence I am experiencing now. I have nothing to do. I ripped apart our front gardens—tore everything out. I guess that was metaphoric enough for one day.

I missed having a celebration when the exhibit ended. It was a night of football, and everyone at the Super Bowl party was involved in watching the game. I felt the strong desire to share my success with someone, and since that didn't happen, I made my own private party. I bought myself roses, but sadly, even they drooped and died the day after. I guess that says everything.

I wonder if I will ever work for the Anne Frank Center. Part of me feels they might just wait too long to make it happen. Nonetheless, I'm keeping the space clear for what's coming next—whatever that will be.

February 12, 1986

I just found out from Tom that the boxes filled with the exhibit left today, and along with it, so did my dreams for the future. Boy, does it feel awful to no longer be needed. Very little is left but a crushed Anne Frank pin I found under my bed.

February 13, 1986

Today I got a copy of Ed Sintz's letter to the Greater Miami Jewish Federation. In it, he said, "Mrs. Merle Saferstein, local coordinator for the exhibition, worked tirelessly to ensure the success of the exhibit, and we are grateful for her efforts." It felt good to be acknowledged. It's way more than I received from those in Amsterdam whose salaries I earned.

Tonight I wrote something in my letter to Tom that I want to copy in my journal, so I have it forever.

"I'm glad for my involvement with the exhibit. It opened the door to where I needed to go next. It helped me lay groundwork I never knew was possible. It brought me closer to the kindred spirit of Anne Frank. It allowed me to better understand myself and what I've been saying, writing, and thinking for years.

"It was undoubtedly the most challenging project I've ever undertaken and brought me some important exposure. It helped me know what I want in my life. It provided me with an opportunity to grow. It drew us closer and gave us the platform to create together. It took me soaring, and its absence threw me crashing down. It taught me more about life and my life in particular. It showed me who I am. It was one of the most wonderful experiences and a true highlight in my life. I thank you for giving it to me."

Reflections on
Anne Frank in the World: 1929-1945

So many feelings surfaced as I read through these excerpts on the Anne Frank photographic exhibition. First and foremost, coordinating this exhibit and bringing it to South Florida has been the highlight in my career life. When I look back on it, I remember the many facets of the experience and what it took to make it a reality.

To begin with, the day before Tom called to ask me if I'd be interested in bringing the exhibition to Miami, I had hit rock bottom. I was lost, and out of what felt like nowhere came this incredible offer. When I reflect on that piece alone, I realize what an important life lesson this was.

There are times in our lives when we feel empty—when our dreams come crashing down—when we are hanging onto hope by a thread. The beginning of May 1985 was one of those moments for me. I knew I needed to forge ahead but didn't know how. What I knew for sure was that I was open and ready and had cleared the space for whatever would come next.

When Tom offered me the volunteer coordinator position, I had no idea what it all meant. I pretty much accepted on blind faith and instinct. While I knew my connection to Anne Frank and her diary was meaningful and that I would be teaching on some levels, I honestly didn't know what it would entail.

I started from scratch. In one of the entries, I wrote how I did it all with my typewriter, telephone, paper, and pen, and that was exactly how it was. Being organized helped. I felt my way through and knew I would only succeed if I put myself out there. I instinctively understood that it wouldn't happen if I didn't ask for whatever I needed—the venue, people to serve on the committee, volunteers, and so much more. What followed was a daily list of things to do—step by step, imagining the final result and creating it.

As with other subjects in my life, the financial piece continues to be a thread through my journals. With the exhibit, I was in a position where people expected me to raise funds above and beyond the originally agreed-upon fee for bringing the exhibition to Miami. The pressure of that weighed heavily. It was all too reminiscent of what I had just experienced at the high school. Going back to those negative excerpts made me realize that while it was part of what went on, I am happy to let go of those memories. There was so much positive about the experience that I'd much rather remember.

One of the most exciting parts of reading these excerpts was to relive some of the life-changing moments I had. Before the exhibit, I had read a few books about the Holocaust and had taken the interviewers' course at the Holocaust Center. Yet, I was walking into the world of Anne Frank and the Holocaust with minimal knowledge. I suddenly became a student soaking up as much information as I could in a short time.

In addition, I luckily had the opportunity to learn from survivors who had lived through the Holocaust. Before and during the six weeks the exhibit was in Miami, I met countless survivors who were willing to share their horrific stories with me. Talking to them and learning from them helped me better understand how best to share Anne Frank's story.

I had been searching for what I could teach, and the exhibit offered me a perfect platform. While I was unclear about what was to come after January 1986, the foundation was being laid. Sometimes when we're in a situation, we can't see how we are building and preparing for our futures. Nothing we do is lost. Somehow, it accumulates, ends up adding to the mix, and becomes part of what we do as we move along on our path. To this day, I find myself referring back to that time in my life when I coordinated the exhibit. It became part of who I am. That's how it works. From this perspective, it's easy to see. It certainly wasn't back then.

Above all else, reading these excerpts reminded me of the tremendous gift Tom gave me. His confidence in me and his willingness to help me create all I did around the exhibit was what I needed to succeed. While there were moments that tried our friendship, the two of us shared a common goal. We knew the importance of what we were doing, and together, we ensured that the South Florida community and beyond would understand how prejudice can lead to genocide.

Journal Prompts

- Have you read Anne Frank's *The Diary of a Young Girl*? How old were you when first reading it? Do you remember how you felt and thought about it then? What kind of impact did it make on you?

- What have you done in your life that was entirely new for you when you began? How did it feel? How did you move through it?

- Write about something you've accomplished that you feel proud of when you look back on it.

- If you could choose one event in your life that was a highlight, what would it be and why?

- Write about an experience preceded by a dark time—when you were empty and, out of nowhere, an opportunity arose.

- When you reflect on a most special career moment, what brought you to that experience?

- Can you remember a time where something was out of your control? How did you respond? What did you do to get through it?

- Have you ever had someone offer you something that changed your life? Write about it.

- Write about an experience (something you've done or learned) that you have brought forth from one job to another as you have moved on in your life.

- What seeds have you planted to get where you are?

- Have you ever had to let go of something? A dream? A person? A job? How did it feel, and what did you experience?

Holocaust Documentation
and
Education Center
Part One

If we want to reach real peace in the world,
we should start educating children.

— Mahatma Gandhi

January 27, 1986

Jeanette, who volunteers at the Holocaust Memorial Center and chairs the Holocaust Awareness Week committee, called me. She told me everyone has been talking about the Anne Frank exhibit, and, as a result, Goldie wants me to come to their planning meeting tomorrow and help them in any way I can. Of course, I said yes.

February 19, 1986

While at the second committee meeting, I suggested doing programming for high school students in addition to what they were planning for adults. Goldie and Rositta had seen what I had done with the student symposium at the exhibit. Since they were impressed with that, they were receptive to the idea.

After the meeting, Patricia called me into her office to talk about a book she wanted to create featuring Holocaust survivors. Her vision for this book is to photograph the survivors and write summaries of their stories from their testimonies. She asked if I would be interested in helping and told me I could co-author the book. Need I say more? I am ecstatic to have a project like that on the horizon, even as a volunteer.

February 28, 1986

Rositta called to tell me their new secretary had quit. At the moment, they are in a total panic and desperately need help. She asked if I would serve in that capacity until they find someone else. I said I would but also let her know that I wouldn't stay unless I was involved with the education department within three months. Unfortunately for me, they have already hired a woman with her Ph.D. in Holocaust studies to be the director of education. She'll be starting in August, so I'm not sure where I might fit in.

March 3, 1986

For my first day on the job, I was busy making reminder calls about a board meeting, proofing the ad journal, answering phones, and doing random tasks. I'm not sure how much I will like what I'm doing, since it is anything but challenging. However, it beats not having something to do or anyplace to go.

March 16, 1986

Working at the Center offers me much of what I wanted in a job:

- Being on a college campus (Florida International University)
- Seeing the water (Biscayne Bay)
- Working close to home (four miles)
- Surrounding myself with good people
- Touching lives and making a difference
- Learning new information
- Having a somewhat flexible work schedule
- Continuing with the work I began with the Anne Frank exhibition
- Working in an educational institution on this level

March 17, 1986

Goldie said she wanted me to fit into an administrative role. Later, I told Goldie, Rositta, and Rita, a Holocaust survivor who volunteers in the documentation department, that I'd like to be the one to organize the student symposium we've begun working on. Everyone seems in favor of my doing it. It's what I do best, so they'd be foolish not to let me.

April 28, 1986

Goldie and I talked, and she told me she wasn't happy with the new secretary. Goldie then asked if I would fill in once again and told me she recognized my programming strength. She let me know that they can't pay me more, but they hope to down the road. I do not want to be a secretary, but I do like working at the Holocaust Center. While it's a considerable comedown from my position with the exhibition, I might as well just say yes since there is nothing else on the horizon. I need to stay open and see where this takes me. Something tells me my journey there has just begun.

May 7, 1986

I just got home from the Student Day symposium. I felt somewhat responsible for its success, since, for starters, the idea to do it originally came from my suggestion to the committee. I planted the seed and helped it grow. I felt comfortable speaking at the podium and talking about Anne Frank, and the feedback I received assured me that they now understand what I can accomplish. Goldie said it was the best program they had ever done. It took a lot of work, but it was well worth it.

The students got the message. We charged them with the responsibility to go home and tell others what they experienced by meeting a Holocaust survivor. At the end of the program, many came up to the podium and talked about what they had learned. It was especially meaningful that they had the chance to speak with the survivors at their tables. It feels terrific to have contributed to something so significant.

From now on, I'll be looking for every opportunity to speak with students, as I did with the many groups of school children at the exhibition. I have identified what it is I want to teach. I understand how important it is to make today's youth aware of the dangers of prejudice, bigotry, and indifference.

May 14, 1986

After lunch, I told Goldie I had another job offer, which I wasn't taking. However, I did let her know about the salary I could have made. I'm sure Daryl would rather I made more money, but something about the underlying purpose of what we're doing at the Holocaust Memorial Center is too important to walk away from. It's one of those moments yet again where I ask myself which matters more—taking a job for money or for something that speaks to my soul? I know the answer, which is why I am staying right where I am.

I asked Goldie where she sees me fitting in the future of the organization. She told me that someday she sees me being in charge of the student department. She kissed me and thanked me for not leaving. Goldie also told me there would be a raise at some point when they can afford it. Before I left, she made me promise to always come to her if I received another job offer.

May 15, 1986

I went with Goldie to a speaking presentation she was giving. On the way, she told me they were expecting about fifty people to show up. I'm not sure what happened, but when we arrived, only one person was there. By the time she got up to speak, there were four people in the audience. I couldn't imagine how she must have felt and was embarrassed for her because of the low turnout.

On the way home, we had an important conversation. She told me it never matters how many people come to hear her. What she cares about is the impact she makes on whoever is there. She said if one person's life is changed because of something she shared, then she will have made a difference—and to her, that's what matters.

May 22, 1986

I am the right person to be a liaison between the schools and the Center. I want to be speaking at our programs and working with the teachers. Based on all I did to bring the exhibit to Miami, I know I am capable.

Of course, when Charlotte arrives and becomes the director of education, what I'm doing now will quickly change. Until then, I will continue. I'll also keep on imagining and envisioning the role I want to be in someday.

May 28, 1986

Jack, the volunteer who has been there since the inception of the Center, asked to meet with me. Goldie values his opinion, and I think she might have asked him to talk to me about my future with the organization. I told him of my other job offers, which keep coming to me. He suggested I stay at the Center because of the unlimited possibilities. He sees the organization as a growing establishment, which is getting bigger all the time.

July 10, 1986

Even though I'm still filling in as a secretary for now, I'm doing much more than secretarial work. I decided I'd like my title to be special projects coordinator because that seems to describe my position accurately. I'm overseeing much in the education department and helping out in other aspects of the organization. I approached Goldie with the suggestion, and she came up with the title of program director. I'm comfortable with that. Somehow, even though it isn't a big deal to have a title, our identities are often wrapped in them. In this case, it identifies and reflects more of what I'm doing.

July 23, 1986

I got a call at home from someone on the Dade County school board inviting me to join the Advisory Committee to the Superintendent on Intergroup Relations. The recommendation had come from Jim Highland from the Community Relations Board at Metro-Dade, whom I had met through the Anne Frank exhibit. He had no idea I was working at the Holocaust Center.

When I told Goldie, she seemed excited at the prospect and asked if I would serve as a representative of the Center and not just be an independent. I agreed, and then she went on to tell me not to get lost there. It was her way of letting me know she wanted me to stay. Later, at lunch, we talked about the student action committee and who to include on it. It looks like it is all going to come together as I hoped it would.

August 4, 1986

Charlotte started her job at the Holocaust Center today. She seems to exist on coffee, broccoli, and chewing gum. I wonder what it's going to be like to work with her. I will lay low and wait to see what happens.

August 7, 1986

I'm slowly watching the most cherished part of my job disintegrate as Charlotte moves in. She has already contacted the schools and plans to meet with various people at the county level. While I find myself upset about Charlotte and her "take-over," I am working hard to put it all into proper perspective as I must relinquish some of my dreams for my future here. I will continue with my work as best I can and let things happen as they will. Most important to keep reminding myself is that Charlotte is, after all, the director of the education department.

August 12, 1986

Goldie must have thought about Patricia's suggestion to include me with the executive staff because she asked me to come to their meeting today. She announced I would be in charge of the students and the student days as I had requested a while ago. I was surprised and delighted.

I will also be handling the teacher workshop at the end of the month for the Dade County schools. I've been working on it for some time now. Goldie and I went through the agenda and the timing of it. I can only wonder how Charlotte feels about all of this, though it's evident her skills are not in administration.

October 9, 1986

This morning, I went to the intergroup relations advisory committee meeting. I was glad to be there among representatives from various organizations like the Community Relations Board, Anti-Defamation League, the Miami Police Department, American Jewish Congress, American Jewish Committee, and a few Hispanic organizations. Sitting there with the superintendent and a room full of professionals all working toward a common goal of helping students develop respect for one another's diversity is what matters most to me in my work.

I volunteered to be part of a committee to help bring in other organizations. I'm not sure Goldie was thrilled when I told her, but at the same time, I wanted to get involved. She admitted that the exposure for our Center would be positive.

December 24, 1986

Yesterday in a conversation with Goldie, she told me she would put me in charge of the department of education without question if Charlotte weren't here. She recognized that I was doing the bulk of the work and was responsible for getting it all done. Goldie said when she talks to both of us, she is actually directing her conversation to me. I get the feeling she's not happy with Charlotte.

February 2, 1987

We had an excellent meeting for the Student Awareness Day committee, which I staffed. After the meeting, Goldie and I discussed various educators. She let me know she thinks of me as an administrator and not an educator—that I'm the only teacher she knows who is organized and can handle administrative work.

Goldie plans to evaluate Charlotte to set the tone for firing her. She told Abe Fischler, "Merle could do the job with one arm tied behind her back."

February 25, 1987

Rositta received a call from the rabbi at the Hebrew Academy, who was furious because Charlotte had canceled the programming, which she had scheduled with them. Charlotte hadn't told any of us she was planning a program with the school; however, Jean had seen a copy of the confirmation, which Charlotte had left in the copy machine. The shit hit the fan!

Later. Charlotte fell in the parking lot on her way to her car and broke her hip. She's in the hospital and will be incapacitated for quite a while. It looks like the education committee is now in my hands. This turn of events has shocked all of us.

Goldie was kind and said she was concerned about how much work I would have to do. She need not worry, since I'll have a much better handle on things now that I am overseeing it all by myself.

March 4, 1987

There's no doubt about the fact that I'm working hard these days. My salary is no reflection of that. It's the old story of loving what I'm doing versus not making money equal to my worth. Will I ever have both?

March 13, 1987

Charlotte called at 8:00 a.m. and wanted to know how the teacher seminar went. To begin with, she asked if there was much to do and if I felt she had done her share. I told her I was up working every night until 11:00 since she's been gone. She asked me if Goldie knew I was doing so much work. What she was asking was, did Goldie know how much she had not done?

March 15, 1987

Tomorrow is the Student Awareness Day meeting to finalize our agendas. I also plan to prepare the Broward teacher seminar before Charlotte returns.

March 24, 1987

The office is different now that Charlotte is back. As per Goldie, I have taken charge but need to be careful because Charlotte is still the director of the department. It's not easy since I find myself acting as her supervisor when she seems lost, which complicates life.

April 2, 1987

Goldie told me she plans to give Charlotte three months' notice after July 1. When she does, she's hoping Charlotte will leave quietly.

Goldie then wants to make me in charge of the department of education with a raise in pay commensurate with the position.

April 9, 1987

Goldie decided not to wait three months to let Charlotte go. So, with that in mind, I move closer to my dream job.

I can't help but think back to when I wondered how and if I would ever get beyond the level of a classroom teacher to make things happen. Life works in strange ways. In retrospect, the steps have led me here—as they always do despite how crooked the path may have seemed.

April 22, 1987

Goldie is under tremendous pressure and is giving me extra things to do, including going to the *Yom Hashoah* meeting with her. Jean needed me for something and called me Miss Organizer. Charlotte asked who that was.

Since I had mentioned how overwhelmed I was, Jean told me I was acting calmly compared to how I say I'm feeling. My head is going in many different directions as I keep switching hats all day long.

April 29, 1987

Yesterday's Student Awareness Day went well, except that the room was too hot, and the lunches came late. Thankfully, today's program was successful without any glitches. At each table, one survivor and one facilitator sat with ten students. We had decided to seat students from the same school at different tables, and thankfully none of them complained about not being allowed to sit with their friends. Conversations at the tables flowed. From the way it looked and the feedback I received, everyone was engaged.

The best moment of the day was when a tenth-grade boy from Puerto Rico came up to the podium at the end and said, "I'm ashamed to admit it, but before I came here, I didn't like Jews very much. After listening to everything I heard today, I have learned so much and have changed my thinking. I admire those survivors who spoke today and respect their courage." As he talked, his voice began to quiver. He eventually started to cry.

With three Student Awareness Days in the past week, plus the teacher seminar under my belt, I am accomplishing exactly what I had hoped to do. I'm grateful for this opportunity.

April 30, 1987

Goldie wants me to go with her on Thursday when she meets with Abe Fischler. She plans to ask Charlotte for her resignation but first must ask Abe's permission since he's the president of the Holocaust Center. She feels that because I work closely with Charlotte, I can fill in any information she needs.

May 5, 1987

I went to the planning meeting at the Federation for the Auschwitz exhibit, which will be held at the Main Library. I may end up being more involved than I have time for, simply because I now have the experience they need to make this happen.

The committee of several from the community relied on me to give them all kinds of advice. I admit it felt good to be the one who could guide the ship in what appeared to be unknown waters for those gathered.

May 7, 1987

Abe said to let Charlotte go! Goldie is so ready and will do that as of May 30th.

I'm going to talk to Goldie about what Abe said about needing to find someone with a doctorate to fill the position of director of education. We have one now and look at what has happened—absolutely nothing. In my opinion, advanced degrees don't always mean the person can do the job.

May 11, 1987

Goldie asked me to go to the Miami Dade County Council of Cultural Affairs to present a budget of $5,000 for Student Awareness Days and *Yom Hashoah*. She's putting me out there and exposing me to a variety of experiences. I was nervous but did fine.

May 27, 1987

Today, Goldie fired Charlotte, so tomorrow will be the last day I'll be working side by side with her. I feel for Charlotte, since she has no idea what she'll do. Personally, my life will be easier.

June 30, 1987

As of today, I am the director of educational outreach at the Southeastern Florida Holocaust Memorial Center. It happened at a meeting with Goldie, Joe Unger, Patricia, Rositta, and me.

With Abe rotating off as president, Joe is now taking over. He said he sees Patricia as the director of documentation and education and me as the director of community relations. I wasn't happy about that. Patricia then said that she felt if she was in charge of the department, I should answer to her. Joe and Goldie disagreed. I spoke up and said I thought I should head the education department because I am doing it anyway.

I was pleased when Rositta suggested giving Patricia the title of director of documentation and Holocaust studies and giving me the title of director of educational outreach. Everyone agreed. Patricia and I are now in parallel positions on the flowchart.

July 1, 1987

Goldie told me she was giving me a raise. I'll now be earning $14,000 a year—an improvement over what I was making, which was $9.00 an hour. I deserve more for what I accomplish, but it's a start.

September 10, 1987

Ramona just left a message on the answering machine about going to Boston for a few weeks. I guess she has decided to leave her job as secretary. So, I was left answering phones, typing letters for Goldie and Rositta, doing research on a grant, and trying to tend to the work in my department. Once again, I'm back to a secretarial position, along with everything else. Somehow, I get stuck with a lot of tedious and unchallenging jobs. I feel resentment crawling in.

I am often stifled at the Center. I certainly don't have the opportunity to blossom there as I have when I've been on my own. While I don't need center stage, I would like to be allowed to do more. Almost always, I am the behind-the-scenes person. I hope that will change soon, but it sure is slow going.

November 3, 1987

Goldie told me she'd like me to plan the lecture series, which will take place in February. She said it falls under education. Goldie wondered how I felt about doing that, and I told her I was thrilled, which I truly am. I like these kinds of projects. I would love to be the one chairing the series, but I doubt that will happen.

February 8, 1988

I was able to get the upcoming Student Awareness Days scheduled. They'll take place three days in a row, the week of April 26—28. That's what it was like last year—a real killer, but at least it's all set and finalized.

February 15, 1988

I went with Goldie to the Archdiocese of Miami for an interfaith meeting with Rabbi Sol Schiff from the Rabbinical Association in Miami, Monsignor Walsh, and others. Much of the discussion was about the Pope's upcoming visit to Miami. I'm not exactly sure why we were there, but it was interesting to learn more about our community.

On our way back to the office, I told Goldie I would like my salary to be between $17,000 and $18,000. She agreed I am earning way below what I deserve and will do her best to get me a raise. She told me when she retires, she hopes I'll be the assistant director. That surprised me, but honestly, it's not a position I would want. I'm happiest in education. Goldie said she recognizes what I have accomplished and that Patricia and Rositta respect my work. She also let me know that both Millie and Joe feel I am underpaid. She said this was not idle talk.

February 25, 1988

It pays to speak up! I got a raise today. I'm now making $17,000. I'm crawling up slowly, but it is happening. In July, I'll get a five percent raise.

March 16, 1988

At the executive committee meeting, Goldie spoke about the Miami Country Day School Student Awareness Day program. She said I staffed it (as I do all of them), "And I might add, she did a very fine job." That felt good. I wonder when I'll have the opportunity to chair a day.

I thanked Goldie for saying something nice about me at the meeting. She told me she likes to have the board know who does the work. I love that she gives credit to others and shares the glory. She realizes it only makes her look better when she does. That's the sign of a good administrator and what I always did when I was the one in charge.

March 28, 1988

The board just voted to change the name of our Center to the Holocaust Documentation and Education Center. That was a big decision and an important one. It best represents what we do.

April 26, 1988

Daryl left me a note and said that Patricia called tonight with good news on the book. I wonder what it is. While it enticed me to get involved in the Center, I haven't done anything on it. She hasn't mentioned it at all, so I'm not sure what she's doing with it either.

April 28, 1988

Today was the last of the Student Awareness Days this week. It was another full house.

I asked Magda Bader to sit with the teachers instead of spreading them out at tables with students as we usually do. When I arranged the teachers into a big circle, Goldie said she could see where I was once a camp director. I smiled.

As I walked around during the candle lighting, the students, facilitators, and survivors shared their feelings about the day. Some were so touching that I found myself becoming weepy. It is encouraging to see how teenagers can be so open with perfect strangers (especially their peers) after being with each other for less than six hours.

One girl began to cry as she talked of the prejudice she had experienced. She shared her fears and spoke from her heart. Sabina, the survivor at the table, told her how she is often afraid but keeps on going. At a few tables, I watched as the whole group joined hands. It was a beautiful picture of people coming together.

May 17, 1988

We had a meeting to discuss what we'll do with the four boys who desecrated Bet Shira. The judge has asked the Center to facilitate one of two educational programs they will be forced to participate in.

I suggested we keep a log of what we do with the boys. I also think they should read Anne Frank's diary.

It took a little convincing on my part, but Goldie finally agreed that since this is educational programming and since it falls under my department, I should be the one to oversee it. We will do the planning with Arthur Teitelbaum of the Anti-Defamation League (ADL), Rabbi Norman Lipson from the Central Agency of Jewish Education (CAJE), and I suggested we include Paul Hanson from Miami Dade Public Schools.

May 21, 1988

The sentence for the Bet Shira boys was mentioned in the *Miami Herald*. The four of them had drawn a swastika, wrote anti-Semitic slogans such as "Jesus Lives. You Can't Kill Him" and "Accept Hitler, Respect Christ" on Bet Shira, and smashed thirty of the synagogue's windows.

The church near Bet Shira put a Star of David on its lawn and donated $1,000 to repair the broken windows. Students from Miami Sunset High School painted over the slurs. The boys will have to pay $14,800 for repairs. They'll also have to serve two hundred community service hours. Coming to the Holocaust Center for programming falls under that.

June 16, 1988

I met with Patricia to tell her Goldie said I could work on the book and start writing some of the survivors' summaries. I spent the rest of the afternoon filing papers for her. She had two huge stacks, which I whittled down to one.

I began to log the HRS experience about the four teens. So far, it's all background, but it's my kind of thing, as anyone who knows me understands.

July 6, 1988

Today was a grueling day. We had our second session with the four teens who desecrated the synagogue.

Last week was mild in comparison to what this week was like. It may have been partly because the parents were with the boys last week, but they weren't here today. So, the boys said whatever they wanted, and much of it was brutal. For one, I don't think they comprehend certain issues. Many discussions dealt with semantics. For example, they did not understand why we refer to the Holocaust as a genocide when "You Jews are a religion and not a race."

The boys are doing a lot of scapegoating. They blame everyone for what happened to them. Their families all canceled their newspaper subscriptions because of what the *Miami Herald* wrote about the incident.

It is frightening to observe their attitudes. They're grossly prejudiced. They don't seem able to distinguish between certain groups like the ADL versus the KKK.

One of the boys said he was desperate and owed so much money that he thought of going to the KKK to get the cash. He also said that he was in deep "ca-ca" and that he contemplated suicide.

Another one acted like a total jerk today. He spoke with a British accent a few times and kept accusing Rabbi Lipson of putting words in his mouth. At one point, he coughed as if he were choking from them.

Our group today ended feeling less hopeful than we previously were. This experience is a tremendous battle, and I'm guessing it will be difficult moving forward.

I am keeping thorough notes on the entire process. In fact, at one point, one kid wanted to know if I had written down that he said, "If given a choice, I'd run over a little girl before a dog."

For sure, these boys are putting up screens and are not being honest with themselves. They use such awful, disrespectful language and think nothing of swearing in front of us.

Goldie brought up the symbols they used. She suggested that had they drawn circles and squares, the reaction may have been very different. Then, I mentioned the venue they chose. Next, Goldie asked if they would have desecrated a church, and all of them said no.

They told us they had been drunk. One boy said he thought mind-altering drugs and alcohol at their age should be legal. Rita asked him if he had had a drink since then, and he said, "Of course!"

This experience of working with the four boys is unique as well as challenging. I just hope we're going to make a difference with them. It's hard to know whether we are touching these kids in the slightest way. It sure didn't feel like it today.

July 8, 1988

The call from one of the mothers yesterday was tough. She expressed tremendous frustration at how her son and the others were treated in the newspapers instead of how other more serious crimes go unnoticed. It was hard to listen to some of what she said, since these boys deserve what they're getting. She told me one of the fathers had called the police after he overheard a conversation about what had happened and who was involved. She was not happy about that.

July 13, 1988

Today was our third session with the boys. Rita talked about her life before the Holocaust and what happened to her during those awful years from 1933 on. She spoke from her heart and shared what to most would be moving and hard to imagine. The boys showed no reaction and no empathy. It was tough to watch them sit there totally disinterested and unaffected. It's as if they've built walls around them that we don't seem to be penetrating.

July 19, 1988

Tonight, we met with most of the boys' parents. I wasn't surprised that one set of parents didn't show up. They are the ones who seem to be the most hard-core of all of them, and so is their son.

Our goal was for the parents to see who we were. I hope they felt reassured that we were doing the very best we could for their sons. We wanted them to understand that our hearts were in the right place. We hope the boys learn something to help them change their attitudes, which could not be worse.

July 20, 1988

Today's session was quite interesting. We discussed what happened, and the boys told us the assistant principal came in and took them out of class and brought them down to separate "cubby" holes with the police there. The school called their parents.

When asked if he desecrated the synagogue, one of the boys responded with a "no comment." Then he said after his mother freaked out, he confessed. Following that, there was a free-for-all with blaming one boy for an issue over who turned another one in.

One of the boys told us about his dream of being crucified. He was walking into the football stadium and saw three crosses lined up. He said crowds were gathering around to put them on the cross. Rositta asked why only three crosses, and he said because one of the guys goes to a different school.

Everyone has given up on one boy, and although I hate to admit it, I think I have too. I'm convinced his parents are filled with prejudice. Rita told us that when she looks at him, she sees an image of him wearing a Nazi helmet.

I am learning a great deal from these sessions. We have spent a lot of time talking about moral dilemmas. It has helped me see how important it is to teach others to be responsible for their actions.

July 26, 1988

This afternoon, I ended up in three meetings. One was to set up the three Student Awareness Days for Southwood Junior High School. The second was a lecture series meeting, and the third was with some guy who worked for a publisher and knew a lot about the field.

He was giving advice on *A Portrait of Survival*. He thinks the book Patricia is working on needs an entirely different format. She's not happy. I have had no time to work on it, so I have no idea what she's done or plans to do going forward.

July 27, 1988

Today's session began with Norm asking the reasons for "Why the Jews?" Patricia had felt it was important to ask that.

It turned out that some stereotypical, anti-Semitic feelings and answers came to the forefront. One boy said all Jews are wealthy, and sadly the other three agreed.

Another issue centered around the nursing home where they are doing community service hours. They all let us know they'd never want to be like "those" people. One of them said he would rather kill himself or his parents if they ever got to that point.

Sister Trinita's presence didn't change their behavior at all, although we had felt sure it would. However, it seemed that they responded better to her than to the rest of us. She asked them where they saw themselves in ten years and focused on their responsibility to others. It was somewhat positive, with their humanness surfacing to a small degree.

The one who has given us the most concern is obnoxious. His answers on the evaluation sheet reflected his awful attitude.

In the concluding minutes, we all spoke about the experience and what we had been trying to accomplish. I let the teens know we hoped something good would come from all of this and if we have changed their lives or their thinking in the slightest, we will have been successful in reaching some of our goals.

Before he left, one boy said we were kinder to them than anyone else has been. He told us he had learned a lot and thanked us. Another was kind, and of all of them, he's the one I feel most hopeful about. Two were completely silent. They never even said goodbye to us.

During our staff debriefing, there was much talk of despair. At that point, I spoke up and said I didn't feel that way but did feel we made a difference in these sessions. I can only hope that something good will come from all of this.

I also spoke up when they were talking about the program not accomplishing what we had hoped. At that point, I reviewed our objectives and how we achieved them:

- To impart knowledge about prejudice, the Holocaust, and its implications.
- To teach the boys they need to be responsible for their actions.

August 2, 1988

We had a staff meeting during which Goldie started by saying, "I have bad news—good news." She then told us she is resigning as of January 1st. We were all surprised and silently reacted to her announcement by thinking about how it personally affected us. In my case, I immediately thought about how I had told myself last year that when Goldie retires, I would move on. The truth is, though, I'm not ready to leave the work I'm doing.

August 11, 1988

Work was wild today. There were two calls which I took that I wish I hadn't. The first was a man who wanted to speak to Goldie, but he gladly talked to me when I said she was out of town. He wanted to know about our organization, and our conversation began rather friendly. Then, he asked what we were doing with the American Holocaust. I asked him what he was referring to, and he told me he meant the abortions and went on and on about that. After a long time when he began ranting, I hung up. I couldn't take it.

Later, another man called. He is a survivor who feels that no one wants to help him. He told me how he used to see Mengele at a store on Miami Beach, where he said Mengele worked. I knew right away this call would not be a good one!

He wanted us to help him sell his book. I told him we couldn't but that we would be interested in taking his testimony. He only wanted to know what he would get in return and see if we were prepared to hear the truth. After quite some time, I told him we couldn't help him. And so, our agency will go down on his list as another one that wasn't there for him.

August 17, 1988

My meeting with Goldie and Joe was fabulous. They told me they were going to keep me in my present position during the transition with the idea that they would like me to be the assistant director at some point and the director if Rositta were ever to leave. Meanwhile, there is no way I would want to do anything at the Center except to be the director of educational outreach. I told them that, and hopefully, they heard me.

Joe let me know I'm getting a raise. Once again, Goldie begged me not to accept any other job offers before going to them.

September 29, 1988

Yesterday, Rositta and I spent the day at the Marriott in Ft. Lauderdale along with Valerie Berman from ADL and Tom Dunthorn from the social studies department of the Florida Department of Education. We were reviewing social studies standards for Florida for grades three, five, eight, and eleven with the hopes of infusing Holocaust education into them. We accomplished our goals. Now, we have to hope the state approves what we suggest.

January 5, 1989

It is not the same without Goldie. While I know she had to retire, I am grateful to have had the opportunity to learn from and work with her. She taught me so much about organizing and, most importantly, about keeping cool during challenging moments. Goldie was a mentor unlike any I have ever had.

February 16, 1989

When I met with John Davies last week, he told me he feels that coming to a Student Awareness Day is by far the single best educational experience a student can have. That says a lot.

We had our meeting with Mark Freedman from the American Jewish Congress and Suzy Schneider from the Jewish Welcome Service from Vienna. They hoped we'd get involved in an exhibition on the Jews from Vienna before the war.

Mark made it clear he wanted me to work for him. I had to laugh because he was so obvious and talked about it right in front of Rositta. He started to joke around about how he'd give her $50,000, which would be for her giving me up, and then she'd also be able to hire a good executive secretary with the money. I'm not going anywhere.

March 24, 1989

I've been reading evaluations from the past two Student Awareness Days. Many students wrote they would take a stand when they see discrimination happening. It's a gratifying feeling to know we made teenagers aware of the importance of respecting one another and understanding that one person can make a difference.

Many students thanked us for the opportunity to come to the program. Most stated that the Student Awareness Day should stay just as it is. A few students suggested we serve better food, while another felt we should bring in a Nazi so that everyone could hear the other side. I don't think so!

I love watching how students and survivors interact. It doesn't take long before the students understand how these older men and women were once teenagers with the same hopes and dreams as they have. The survivors, who were strangers to the students at first, suddenly transform into their heroes. By the end of the day, they often give the survivors huge hugs.

I find it upsetting that someone at the Center seems to have forgotten how Student Awareness Days were first created. She came up to me and said she wanted to remind me that these days started well before I arrived at the Holocaust Center. While I didn't create them alone, I know for a fact that I brought the idea after what I had done at the Anne Frank symposium for students. All along, since our first one in May three years ago, I've been the one to implement these programs.

March 28, 1989

Patricia told me she knows how bad it is to do the work and have someone else get the credit. I told her that when I started working here, I quickly realized I would be in the background and would get little credit for so much of what I do.

I also let her know my work at the Center was important and meaningful and that I was not doing it to fulfill my ego. She seemed to understand.

April 13, 1989

Earlier at the Student Awareness Day, I overheard a survivor's enlightening conversation with the students at his table. One of them asked if he believed in God. The survivor answered by talking about his friend and himself.

His friend believed in God and felt the only way he survived the Holocaust was because of God. On the other hand, this survivor said that during and after the war, he wondered how there could be a God who would let the Holocaust happen and allow his entire family to die.

It made me think about Gene Greenzwieg, who recently addressed this topic. He claimed that the question to be asked when referring to the Holocaust is not *Where was God?* But instead, *Where was man?*

September 13, 1989

I am using the computer more often now. It's great to print out drafts in a matter of minutes. I wish I had a computer in my office, since I'm getting used to the convenience of it. I can accomplish so much more because I'm not handwriting second and third drafts as I used to do. It's a time-saver, and at this point, we need all the spare minutes we can get.

October 20, 1989

Yesterday I worked on the liberation chapter for the state curriculum on the Holocaust our Center is producing. Since, to our knowledge, no textbooks or Holocaust curricula have a chapter on the subject, it's been a challenge to write. Fortunately, I learned a little about the internet and have been using it for research.

While it is supposedly one of the more positive chapters in the Holocaust, it didn't end up being that way. Reading about the dead bodies piled like cordwood, the survivor guilt, and the way survivors found themselves alone with all their families gone, I began to think about liberation differently. Of course, to be free was a reason to celebrate, but it was not easy for those who lost everything. It seems there was nothing about the Holocaust that was positive.

March 1, 1990

Today, I had four volunteers working with me, collating papers for the programs ahead. I doubt anyone has any idea how much planning is involved in making these Student Awareness Days a success. Besides getting enough survivors and facilitators (one per every ten students with 250–600 students attending), the other items to have in place are the venue, speakers, lunches, schools with the correct number of students, handouts, buses, and miscellaneous details.

When we have cancelations at the last minute, it is maddening. The most important key to the success of the days is having a Holocaust survivor seated at every table. If they all show up, the day runs smoothly from the start. If not, I begin a juggling act to make it all work out.

March 7, 1990

The Student Awareness Day today was outstanding. Among the most meaningful moments of these programs is when the students stand up at the end of the day and tell us what the symposium meant to them. An eighth-grade African American boy came to the podium and said he had never heard about the Holocaust until his teacher told them they were going to the program. This student set the tone, and from there, a stream of kids came up to share their feelings. They admitted to prejudices they never even realized they had until today and talked about the responsibility to remember, take a stand, and make this a better world.

One girl shared how she has often thought her life was filled with problems and hard times. She went on to say how much she learned today and now realizes that she has nothing to complain about. "This day has helped me put my life in perspective."

On Wednesday, a Hispanic girl got up and said everything we'd ever want to hear about the day. She then ended by saying, "With Christ in our lives, everything will be fine." Everyone clapped, but inside, some of us cringed a little.

Another girl claimed she knows about prejudice because she is half African American and half Jewish. She cried as she spoke about how so much of her mother's family had to endure the horrors of the Holocaust.

Then, the real shocker was a girl who stood up and told us her mother was Jewish, her father was German, and her grandfather was a Nazi. The room grew immediately silent when she said that.

She admitted how ashamed she was to have that blood — that someone in her family was responsible for so much pain and suffering. As we were leaving, the same girl came out of the bathroom. About six survivors immediately surrounded her. They told her she was Jewish because her mother was. They also let her know they thought she was brave for getting up and sharing what she did. Each one hugged her and said they were proud of her. It was such a beautiful and touching scene. The survivors are often the ones who come forward and reassure students, wipe away their tears when they're upset, and show empathy in a way few others do.

The students learn some of the most valuable lessons in their lives from these programs. Some, who have always felt persecuted because of their skin color, sexual orientation, or religion, begin to understand they are not the only ones who have suffered. We have been responsible for changing attitudes, making students aware of the evils of prejudice, and helping them understand their responsibilities to society.

July 25, 1990

Today I helped Patricia catalog memorabilia. It's fascinating to see some of the items we have: a Hitler Youth armband, Nazi medals, a Nazi banner and badges, and pictures taken at liberation. Also, I came across a letter written by a young soldier who had liberated a camp. It was a fifteen-page account of what he had seen and felt. In addition, we have passports with a J for Jew stamped on them, some money issued in the ghettos, and documents stamped by the Nazi party.

I also saw two tiny photo albums with pictures of a mother and two children, much like those my parents have of Jerry and me. The only difference was that the little girl and boy had Jewish stars on their clothing and were later killed. Going through all the artifacts allows me to learn and also touch history.

October 6, 1990

As of this week, I have become the overseer of the entire state resource manual project. I now know exactly how much is completed on every chapter and what is yet to be done. Patricia, Rositta, Rita, and I are working hard to finish it. I've taken over organizing certain aspects to ensure we meet our deadlines. It has not been easy to pull off. Working with a procrastinator is frustrating for someone like me who doesn't put anything off.

We're finally beginning to receive approval from the letters I sent out to obtain permission to use copyright materials. My next job is to standardize and format the entire curriculum, which means vocabulary, headings, and so much more.

October 11, 1990

I got home from the office last night at 10:55. Patricia and Roberta were still there collating the curriculum, since we had no more wiggle room. It has to be completed by tomorrow before we go to Florida's west coast for the Florida social studies teachers' conference.

October 13, 1990

The presentation went well, thankfully. We experienced a great deal of enthusiasm in response to the curriculum. Patricia and Rositta did an excellent job giving a complete overview. It was a huge relief to be at that point where we were sharing our hard work with others hoping that Florida's teachers would take advantage of the grades 9–12 resource manual to teach the Holocaust to their students.

November 9, 1990

Yesterday at the luncheon, a beautiful plaque was given to Joseph and Mrs. Roslan, two Poles who had hidden three Jewish boys during the war. When he got up to accept, he began to talk and started to cry. Altruism was the subject of discussion throughout the day. Some of the questions that surfaced: Were these rescuers doing what someone should do, or were they going above and beyond one's responsibility? Are we our brother's keeper? What would you do if called upon to save someone at risk to yourself and your family?

January 1, 1991

Yesterday I mentioned to a few members of the Student Awareness Day committee that I'd like to deliver the prejudice portion for the Student Awareness Day. Their reaction was silence at first. The response I received was that they'd have to give it a lot of thought since they were considering several others. One said whoever it is will have to be savvy, confident in the subject matter, and be an experienced speaker. In other words, either she doesn't have confidence in me, or she just wants to keep me in the background and not at the podium. Another told me that I shouldn't take it personally—that it's no reflection on my capabilities but it's a rough subject, blah, blah, blah. I responded by saying I do take it personally and am not happy about it, but I thought we should just move on. I dropped it and changed the subject.

The truth is that I am furious about this. After all the speaking I did years ago for the Anne Frank exhibition, how could they think I am not qualified to talk on prejudice?

May 3, 1991

A woman came up to me to say thank you. Her daughter had attended our Student Awareness Day two years ago. She had come home moved and had spoken to her parents about it all night, asking lots of questions. She said her daughter shed many tears and still talks about the day and meeting a survivor. It's comments like that which make what I do incredibly meaningful.

January 24, 1992

I'm at Santaluces High School for our teacher seminar. We've had an excellent turnout of fifty-five teachers. The Holocaust coordinator from the Palm Beach Schools, Steve Byrne, is thrilled and said our reputation must precede us.

February 25, 1992

Today, Linda Lehrman, chairperson for the dinner honoring Sister Trinita, called every hour with questions and things for me to do. I attended a meeting for the aging conference, worked on organizing the next six Student Awareness Days, and prepared for a *Yom Hashoah* meeting tomorrow. It's a crazy time for me.

March 29, 1992

Today begins the First National Conference on Identification, Treatment, and Care of the Aging

Holocaust Survivor. For the next few days, I'll be making sure the logistics run smoothly. We have experts in the field who have come from all over the world to speak to medical and mental health care workers, survivors, and all others attending the conference. Rositta was busy last night and asked if I would take Dr. Leo Eitinger to dinner. I jumped at the chance. Daryl came with me, and we had an evening unlike any I've ever spent.

Dr. Eitinger is a world-renowned psychiatrist, author, and educator from Norway. He's a Holocaust survivor who studied the late-onset psychological trauma experienced by people who went through a separation and psychological pain in early life. He is devoted to researching concentration camp victims. Dr. Eitinger works on a committee to fight anti-Semitism and is involved in human rights organizations on various levels. With all he has accomplished and continues to do, we found him a humble, gentle man. To talk to Dr. Eitinger, one would never know he is as brilliant and sought after as he is.

During dinner, I learned that we share the same birthday—just many years apart, since he was born in 1912. At one point, I asked him if he had ever kept a journal, and he said he did after the war. He wrote in Norwegian. Later a friend, who wanted to read it, translated it into English. I asked if anyone else had read it, and he said, "Only Elie Wiesel."

Dr. Eitinger told me his wife keeps a journal, so Daryl told him I do too. He asked me lots of questions about my journaling and told me not to stop. He said he was especially interested in my discipline to be able to write daily.

By the time we said goodnight and dropped him off at the hotel, I felt like I had made a new friend. He told me he wanted to keep in touch with me through letters. I hope that'll happen.

April 20, 1993

We're on the plane to Washington, D.C. for the opening of the United States Holocaust Memorial Museum. It's the Center's first-ever mission, which Rositta and I have been working on steadily for a long time. We'll be on a tight schedule when we land.

Later. I'm standing in the Rotunda of the Capitol Building right next to a statue of George Washington. The United States Army Band has begun playing *America the Beautiful*. Members of Congress and the Senate are filing in. Outside, the cherry blossoms are in bloom on this beautiful spring day. Inside, I have goosebumps watching this ceremony unfold.

Later. Just listening to the band play Hebrew songs, hearing prayers in Hebrew, and looking up to see the history of our country encircling the dome all at once is awesome. The most incredible moment so far is watching the military from the various liberating troops march down the aisles with their flags. Survivors are reaching out into the aisles to touch, and in some cases, kiss the flags of the forces that saved their lives. I keep wondering how they must feel now to be in the U. S. Capitol, especially after where they've been and what they've endured in their lives.

April 21, 1993

We're now at the amphitheater of Arlington Cemetery. This time, the color guard and the liberating troops of the camps are marching with survivors. One of the survivors from our group, Ann Dean, cried out, "Bravo, bravo," when the United States flags came past her.

Leo Aspin, the Secretary of Defense, speaks about the lessons of compassion and courage overcoming evil. Now, John Eisenhower is reading the words of his father.

Later. In the National Children's Museum. On the wall:

> *For you are the new spring in the forest of the world.*
>
> — Gerda Weissmann Klein, Survivor

> *The first to perish were the children... The world's best.*
> *From these faces our new dawn might have risen.*
>
> — Yitzhak Katzenelson, Survivor of the Warsaw Ghetto

> *It may be too late for the victims but not for our children,*
> *not for mankind.*
>
> — Elie Wiesel, Survivor

Later. We took Ann Dean to the White House because she had told me that when she became a U.S. citizen, her friend failed the test. When I asked why, she explained that he answered pigeons instead of a flag when they asked him what flies over the White House. She said she needed to see the correct answer in person. While there, a Palestinian was protesting Israelis who had ousted the Arabs. Ann insisted we sing *Hatikvah*, so there we were — all eighteen of us singing the Israeli national anthem.

April 22, 1993

At the Dedication Ceremony. It's raining. I'm in row H up front, thanks to Rositta, who somehow got us into this section at the last minute. Ted Koppel, the master of ceremonies, is speaking. Skinheads are screaming out on the streets. Will it ever end? As I sit here, I know there is much I need to teach. We must educate the youth. My work has only just begun.

Elie Wiesel is talking about how President Clinton must turn the museum over to the young people of his generation. "For the dead and the living, we must bear witness.

"Why was there no public outcry? Why was there no help? How is it that man's silence was matched by God's?

"The only response is responsibility. How can one understand? We cannot remain indifferent. We must do something to stop what is going on in Yugoslavia."

Elie Wiesel just spoke about a woman who didn't understand why they were fighting in Warsaw. She was from the Carpathian Mountains, and the year was 1943. He went on to say how no one did anything to stop the war. He ended by telling us this woman was killed in Auschwitz. "Mr. President, that woman I talked about was my mother."

Chaim Herzog, president of Israel, is now speaking about how this nightmare has come alive for all of us.

I'm sitting next to Congressman Herb Klein from New Jersey, who has been quite friendly. He commented on how I was "taking notes" in my journal and told me he loved that I was doing so. Senator Ted Kennedy is three rows in front of me. I see Jesse Jackson just a few feet away, with Senator Howard Metzenbaum across the aisle. I'm pinching myself. How did I get here?

A Righteous Gentile is talking about how her parents told her not to show any preference between people—that we are all children of God. When she saw what was happening to the Jews, she knew she had to help them. I ask myself, why can't we all feel that way? Why does there have to be such hatred in our world?

Vice President Al Gore: "This museum will help us explore how the human race could let it happen. How else can we teach what humanity needs to know?" He is now introducing the president.

President Bill Clinton: "A head without a heart is not humanity. Far too little was done…There will come a time when the Holocaust will go from a shared reality to a memory…Despite our differences, we must not separate ourselves from our humanity…I hope those who survived have found their peace."

I had a perfect view of the Clintons and the Gores. The president was highly emotional as he lit the eternal flame. With him at the helm, I've got great hopes for our country.

Later. We went through the Hall of Remembrance in the museum. Someone explained that the six sides—three of which look out onto the Washington Memorial, the Lincoln Memorial, and the Jefferson Memorial—represent the ideals of America. Later, we marched with candles as the sun set over the city. What a beautiful way to end this powerful day.

Tonight before we went to our rooms, I asked Ann what the highlight of the day was for her. She told me it was when she saw them bring in the flag from the liberators of Dachau, where she had been liberated, and seeing John Eisenhower receive the medal for his father, who was responsible for her liberation.

April 23, 1993

Back at the United States Holocaust Memorial Museum. On the wall by the shoes is this quote:

> *We are the shoes. We are the last witnesses.*
> *We are shoes from grandchildren and grandfathers*
> *From Prague, Paris, and Amsterdam*
> *And because we are only made of fabric and leather*
> *And not of blood and flesh, each one of us avoided the hellfire.*

— Moses Schulstein 1911–1961

This museum tells the story of the Holocaust through artifacts, videos, graphics, and displays of all kinds. They have specific areas that are blocked with barriers so younger children cannot see the horrors.

The rail car, the boat, and the barracks help people understand what it was like. Of course, without the smells, sounds, and terror of the Nazis, it's not even close to what was. How could it be?

This trip will have a lasting effect on me. I have reaffirmed so much of what I already feel about my work as a Holocaust educator.

October 13, 1993

For a while now, Rositta has been talking about getting Holocaust education mandated in the state of Florida. Today she asked me to do research on the states that have succeeded in mandating the study of the Holocaust and what steps they took to get a bill passed.

She also asked me to start drafting wording, so I took out my legal pad and got to work. I drafted several versions. The one I submitted to her was: "The study of the Holocaust, which took place between 1933–1945, will lead to an examination of basic moral values, an investigation of human behavior, and an awareness for tolerance of diversity in a pluralistic society.

"This watershed, unprecedented genocide, in which millions perished, clearly illustrates the dangers of apathy, prejudice, scapegoating, indifference, and discrimination. The ramifications and implications serve as a living memorial to preserving the legacy of remembrance and safeguarding our future."

I'm sure it'll be changed many times over, but I attempted to put in words what we hope to accomplish.

October 20, 1993

Today Rositta submitted the final draft for the proposed language for required teaching of the Holocaust in Florida public schools. She tightened up my wording, and it reads beautifully now.

Our work is just beginning because, at some point, we'll need to find someone to sponsor the bill, gather the legislators to support it, and then get it passed. It is now our priority and something we're determined to make happen.

April 8, 1994

Sending Leo Shniderman to Tallahassee was probably the best move we made toward the passage of the mandate. His passionate remarks about his experiences in the Holocaust and his plea to the legislature led to a unanimous and favorable vote. We have every reason to celebrate. After a long and hard battle with a lot of persistence, we won! Students in Florida will now be required to learn about the Holocaust.

April 28, 1994

Today at the Holocaust Memorial on Miami Beach, Governor Lawton Chiles signed the bill making Holocaust education part of the Florida public school curriculum. He called the passage of this bill a "victory of education over tyranny."

We were supposed to have a considerably large bill signing, but it got scratched yesterday. I had arranged ten busloads of survivors and various school groups to come to the Holocaust Memorial on Miami Beach. We had it all organized when Norman Braman, who offered to fund all the buses, decided the event was getting too political and felt nothing that touches on politics should take place at the Memorial. Luckily, I had a paper trail of everyone I had made arrangements with, so I spent yesterday canceling it all. It was terribly disappointing to the survivors, who wanted to be there to witness this historical moment.

Instead, a small, hand-picked group gathered in the Miami Beach City Hall chambers for the signing. After all the hard work we did, it was gratifying to realize that Holocaust education in Florida is now a reality. It'll be interesting to see how it is implemented.

February 20, 1995

I finally have some time today to write about all that went on surrounding *A Reunion of a Special Family: 50 Years of Life after the Holocaust.*

The weekend of February 17–19, 1995 is one I will remember forever. It began many months before with the preparation of gathering 4,000 Holocaust survivors from all over the world. I have been knee-deep in lists for the past four weeks trying to seat everyone for the special dinner. That alone was an almost impossible task. Fortunately, Roberta and I worked on it together, locked in the library.

On Wednesday night, the staff stayed at the office until 9:30, just getting the tables matched to the seating charts. Then on Thursday, we finalized the tables and prepared the tickets. Among other jobs, I was in charge of twenty volunteers, who helped stuff folders and badges for each person.

That night, we never left the office. Unfortunately, we didn't get the lists we needed until late in the evening. It was a nightmare. We worked non-stop and only took a short break for dinner. I was frustrated, aggravated, and had no appetite. The pressure was over the top.

At 3:00 a.m., I sat down to eat cold fried chicken and chocolate cake. We finally finished everything at 7:00 a.m., when I eventually left for home to take a quick shower. I was at the Fontainebleau Hotel by 8:30.

Registration was to begin at noon. By 10:00 a.m., the survivors, who had been milling around since 9:00, started to form lines. They were doing their best to be patient, but survivors do not like standing in lines for obvious reasons.

Because I was in charge of all logistics for the weekend, I had to wait for the crew of volunteers coming from the Miami Beach Visitors and Convention Bureau. It was a disaster because people were frustrated. That was when I knew my role as a troubleshooter for the weekend was not going to be an easy one.

When twelve state troopers came marching in rows of three on Saturday morning, I immediately stopped them in the lobby and talked to them about the event. Survivors do not do well with men in uniforms marching like these guys were. They needed to understand what this event was about and who they would be working with for the next two days.

One of the most memorable parts of the weekend was the Survivors' Village in a huge room filled with signs of different European countries. Survivors gathered in the area representing their country of origin. Over the loudspeaker, someone would announce a specific town, ghetto, or camp and would ask anyone from that place to meet in a specified spot in the room. We also had a large message board where people could post notes asking for those they were hoping to find.

Throughout the weekend, we heard of many touching reunions. One, in particular, was when Branko Lustig, the producer of *Schindler's List,* was introduced to Henry Ehrlich, Rositta's father. When the two men met, they looked into each other's eyes, recognized one another, and began to cry. They had been together on the same transport from one camp to another over fifty years ago.

Reuniting was what the weekend was all about—not the behind-the-scenes aggravation of overbooking tables, people changing the table numbers so they could have a better seat, the sound system failing on one side of the room, frustrated people who couldn't get help fast enough, and on and on.

We had a program Saturday night with Eddie Fisher singing. The ladies were swooning as if they were teenagers watching their favorite movie star. Also, when the klezmer band played, the survivors got up in the aisles and danced the *hora* with every bit of life they had.

To me, seeing the resilient spirit of humans is one of the most beautiful and special feelings in the world.

Sunday night's dinner began with the U. S. Army Band playing Yiddish songs they learned for this occasion. Then soldiers, who represented all of the liberating Allied Forces, marched in with their flags while the announcer named the camp each particular division or unit liberated. I happened to be standing next to a survivor from Buchenwald and will never forget her gasp followed by tears and then clapping with joy when she heard the name of the division that liberated her.

When I went to talk to Arie, who was one of the organizers from the American Gathering in New York, I ended up standing next to Secretary of Defense William Perry, who told me he felt privileged to be there. Secret Service and our state troopers, who by then had become my new best friends, surrounded their table.

I also had the opportunity to speak to Elie Wiesel before he went up on stage. He addressed his remarks in Yiddish to his fellow survivors. Because of all those I was working with and met over the weekend, I thought about how people are people—regardless of their titles and fame, where they've been, and what they've accomplished. On the outside and inside, we are all just humans with strengths and weaknesses.

I stayed at the hotel on Saturday and Sunday nights. During the entire time I was there, and as much as I love the ocean, I only caught a glimpse of it for one minute on Saturday morning. That says it all.

February 26, 1997

Today's Student Awareness Day at St. Thomas University was a success because of the number of students who attended and all we accomplished. Someone from the school videotaped the entire day since it was the first of many prejudice-reduction programs Steven Spielberg is sponsoring for us on college and university campuses in South Florida.

The school's dean started the program by saying, "Can you imagine what it would have been like to sit at the feet of Jesus and listen and learn from him? Well, today we are indeed fortunate to sit at the feet of survivors of the Holocaust—people who experienced the worst tragedy in history."

March 13, 1997

Marcus Bickler, a ninth-grade boy, came to the Holocaust Center with his parents to deliver his contest entry. The theme this year is The Holocaust: Remember the Children. He drew a picture of Birkenau, the children, clouds—incredibly moving and graphic. I have it in my office next to my desk.

Mrs. Bickler told me it's spooky and probably sounds strange, but she thinks Marcus was there (pointing to the pen and ink drawing). She said he has been drawing since he was two—things he didn't even know about or was exposed to yet. I am astounded by his work.

May 6, 1997

I was the only woman at the meeting at the University of Miami, where I finally convinced the administrators to let us bring a Student Awareness Day to their campus. After I spoke for a while, they understood the philosophy behind the prejudice-reduction day and became enthusiastic about providing this experience for their students. Last week, I was at Nova Southeastern University, where the vice president also said yes to having a symposium. It's finally happening on the college campuses.

June 20, 1997

At the end of the teacher institute, we had the teachers share their feelings about the experience. I was in tears a lot and was not the only one who was. One teacher thanked us for allowing them to sit with different survivors each day and learn from them. Another talked about how she will take what she learned and pass it along to the hearts of her students.

When I got up to speak, I told them I'm a lucky lady because I have the privilege of working with and learning from the survivors and teachers. My heart is full after yet another wonderful week with educators.

September 23, 1997

Yesterday work was wild with finalizing plans for the tribute dinner and preparing for the board meeting. Joe Natoli, president of the *Miami Herald*, is chairing the dinner. He came to the Center yesterday so he could better understand all that we do. He's a young guy who has indeed climbed the ladder rapidly and seemed like such a *mensch*. My job is to draft his remarks.

September 26, 1997

I spoke to Joe Natoli in the morning. I was impressed that he answered his phone and was easily accessible without a huge ego. I needed to give him the names of three more VIPs for the dinner and go over their pronunciation.

Later. Before the event began, I went up to Joe and told him that one of the rabbi's names was pronounced differently from what I had first thought. He said, "I'm glad you're here to guide me. Tell me about this word "docents," which I think is a Jewish term." Sylvia Ziffer's introduction included docents when talking about the Jewish Museum of Florida. I explained what a docent is and then put my arm around his shoulder and said, "Joe, I suggest you don't let David Lawrence know you didn't know the word." We laughed.

October 21, 1997

Rositta is going to Washington tomorrow. Rita has decided not to come to Broward Community College Student Awareness Day, so I am chairing the day. This is a monumental first for me after all these years. Rositta said she could have asked many people but chose me because she knew I was *finally* ready. Eleven years later!

August 27, 1998

I was pleased when we met with the teachers who will write the elementary and middle school state resource manuals. It felt good to know this piece isn't going to be our complete responsibility as the others have been. That's a relief, although I know I'll be overseeing that part of the project in addition to revising the high school resource manual. We are working diligently to get this all done. It's a huge undertaking.

Rositta asked me to write a piece on journal writing with prompts for the various grade-level resource manuals. When I submitted it for approval, she remarked, "I wouldn't even begin to critique this. If anyone should know about journaling and what's appropriate, it's you."

September 16, 1998

We finished off everything on the state resource manuals except for the page numbering and a few of the messages. I'm super frustrated waiting for those. Nonetheless, I took it to FED-EX yesterday to meet our deadlines—a tremendous burden lifted. However, I still have a long way to go until it's complete.

September 24, 1998

The best news of the day was that the director of curriculum for the Florida Department of Education called and told me their department was impressed with the quantity and quality of the resource manual. What a relief!

October 6, 1998

Yesterday at work, I figured out the budget for the resource manual printings, which for me, was a challenge. I worked with Jean before I went to Rositta, so I had it all down pat by the time I met with her.

Then we worked on her message and the acknowledgments for the curriculum, which is the last thing to be done. She let me know she felt I was instrumental in overseeing the whole project, which I was. That felt good.

October 7, 1998

Dinorah came into my office to show me a copy of the finished text of the grades 9–12 curriculum, which is 941 pages. The thickness of the actual resource manual turned out to be 2½ inches high. Our binders, of which we have 2,500, are only 1½ inches. So right off the bat, we had a big problem. I suggested we use the 1½ inch binders for the grades K–8 manual, and luckily, we were able to order the right size binders for the grades 9–12 resource manual.

I got a call from John Weigman, chief of the curriculum, assessment, and instruction bureau for Florida's Department of Education. He let me know everything in the curriculum was approved. Roberta, Dinorah, and I stayed until 7:15 last night to get the manuals ready and done for today.

We had our Commissioner of Education's Task Force on Holocaust Education meeting, and although getting prepared for it was a bitch, it was worth it.

Commissioner of Education Frank Brogan came. He loved the piece we presented to him—a picture of the resource manual on a plaque with appropriate wording. Michael Olenick, the general counsel for the commissioner, told us he thought what we created was phenomenal—a "chilling" resource.

June 21, 1999

John Loftus, a former U. S. government prosecutor and author, is speaking. He just said Rositta and I are pioneers in Holocaust education.

June 24, 1999

When I think of all the students who will be touched by each teacher who has attended our institute, I know that as a result of this week, thousands of lives will change. These are some comments from the teachers:

"The sign of a good workshop is that this went by much too quickly."

"I intend to talk to and share this information with anyone who will listen to me."

"Because of the impact this has had on me, I can't imagine what this has done for you, the survivors."

"I will teach my students about the Holocaust and will teach them to teach others. We are your living witnesses."

"I have an empty desk in my room and have kept it there for all these years. I share with my students that this desk would have been for the grandchild or great-grandchild of someone who perished in the Holocaust."

September 22, 1999

I've just presented our resource manual at the Florida Association of Academic Non-Public Schools conference. I cut out a lot at the start of my talk when I realized the teachers in the private schools are not mandated to teach the Holocaust, since they don't answer to Florida state standards. So, instead, I just gave an overview, which was well received. Any time I can be with teachers, I am happy. I feel like I'm with like-minded people in many ways—those who understand the importance of educating our youth and devote their lives to doing so.

September 28, 1999

Work was insane yesterday. I never took a break because there was so much to do from so many angles—the grant I'm working on, reports for the board meeting, the task force, etc. Plus, Rositta has given me the entire ad journal to oversee. Today will probably be more of the same.

October 27, 1999

We had a meeting with people from the Grove Playhouse. They're going to be displaying our art contest winners during the play, *The Gathering*. From there, I had to go downtown to replace some pages with errors for one of the grants.

It seems that my job at the Center keeps changing and growing. I wish I didn't have to write grants, but I know the finances are always a concern—just like everywhere else I've been. Aside from that, I love what I do and am grateful to have all the varied experiences that I have had working there.

Reflections on Holocaust Documentation and Education Center Part One

I remember how I felt when I received the phone call from the Holocaust Center asking me if I would fill in and take the job as a secretary. It was quite a comedown from where I had been and where I hoped to be. Yet, I was grateful at that moment to be offered a job in an organization that was doing significant work.

What I didn't know was where it would take me. I had no idea what was possible, and especially since the Holocaust Center had already hired someone for the position which I desired. From this experience, I learned that sometimes we need to start at the bottom of the ladder and climb our way up gradually. I now see that being overqualified for a position doesn't mean we might not eventually get to a place where our skills are needed and appreciated and fit with what we are prepared or hoping to do.

I often felt frustrated that I wasn't allowed to chair programs, even as the director of the educational outreach department. Indeed, my work with the Anne Frank exhibit proved I could speak to crowds of people. It bothered me that I was held back, kept in the background for so long, and never allowed to fully maximize my potential. I found some of these old feelings surfacing once again as I read these excerpts.

An important lesson I learned early on working with Goldie has impacted the way I think many years later. Who could have guessed that that evening when she ended up speaking to those four people, when there were supposed to be fifty, would continue to influence my reactions to this day? Whenever I go out to speak or teach a new class, I have no expectations. It makes no difference to me how many people show up. Because of Goldie, I approach each experience knowing that if I touch one life, teach one person something, that's all that matters. Reading back to when that seed was planted fills me with gratitude.

I'll never forget the summer I devoted all my time to organizing both the memorabilia as well as the Holocaust Center's collection of photographs. I spent countless hours at my desk going through objects that brought back the evils that existed during the Holocaust. The photos were from prewar, during the Holocaust, the DP camps, and life after in the survivors' new countries. Some of the photographs left me with nightmares. I knew I was touching history—yet another incredible opportunity I had while working at the Holocaust Center.

When I reflect on what I wrote about the boys who desecrated the synagogue, I realize we did our very best to ensure they would wake up and understand that what they had done was hurtful and wrong. We met with such resistance from them, which was upsetting to all of us but especially to Rita, a survivor who had shared her painful experiences in the hopes of enlightening the boys.

With all that has gone on in our society lately, I can't help but wonder what has happened to those four individuals. When the white supremacists gathered in Charlottesville and cried out, "You will not replace us! Jews will not replace us!" and when the protesters gathered around the country and beyond after George Floyd was killed, my thoughts drifted to the boys. Where are they now? Did they learn anything and change their ways, or are they out there today shouting against anyone who isn't like them?

All of this unrest and anti-Semitism makes me think about the Holocaust survivors. I've spoken to many who are feeling frightened. Some of what they see is just too reminiscent of what they experienced leading up to the Holocaust. I can't even imagine what it must be like for them.

As I read the excerpts and recalled the many incredible experiences I had in the eighties and nineties, once again, I felt fortunate to have accomplished so much. The mission to the United States Holocaust Memorial Museum's opening, the gathering of Holocaust survivors on Miami Beach, and the conference on the aging Holocaust survivors were unique and wonderful. In retrospect, I realize that each was an important historical event that shaped my work at the Holocaust Documentation and Education Center.

Above all else, though, reading back led me to think about those years and the beginning of my career in Holocaust education. For me, the most meaningful and important piece was working with students and teachers and providing them with the opportunity to spend time with the Holocaust survivors. If I never accomplished anything else in my life, knowing that I helped to make this happen is enough for me.

Journal Prompts

- Have you ever taken a job you were overqualified for? Why did you take it? What was the outcome?

- Which is more important to you? Taking a job for money or one that coincides with your interests/passions but pays little? Why?

- What have titles in your career meant to you? In what way do you feel they define you?

- Do you think that an advanced degree in a subject is equivalent to years of experience in the area? Why or why not?

- How would you teach others to be responsible for their actions?

- Has there ever been a time when you did something and didn't take responsibility for it?

- Who has been a mentor for you, and in what way?

- Write about a unique or meaningful occasion in your life when you were moved to tears.

- What do you think about when you see the prejudice that exists in our country today?

March of the Living

*The old man sat on his stoop watching the teenagers in blue jackets
pass by as they marched from Auschwitz to Birkenau.
Where was he in 1941 when the trains brought people to that hell on earth?*

— Merle R. Saferstein

January 13, 1990

I'm going on the March of the Living! It's a once-in-a-lifetime opportunity and an experience that will enhance my role as a Holocaust educator. Plus, it will be a fantastic way to see Israel, which has been on my list of places to visit.

February 5, 1990

Yesterday was our first gathering of the teenagers and adults who are going on the trip. In the next few months, we'll get to know each other well. To have Gene Greenzeweig as our teacher leading these educational and preparatory sessions is a gift in itself. Not only is he inspiring, knowledgeable, and a true *mensch,* but he's also one of the founders of the International March of the Living.

February 9, 1990

Rabbi Stu Grant invited me to work with him and Patricia on planning the grief process groups. Since they are both psychologists, I'm honored he asked me. I'm not sure why he chose me, but I am glad he did.

February 10, 1990

The March of the Living is specifically for Jewish teenagers to visit concentration camps and inspire them to learn what prejudice and indifference did to six million Jewish people. Since bringing the Anne Frank exhibition to Miami and working at the Holocaust Center, I understand how important it is that the Holocaust be taught not solely as a Jewish issue.

While millions of Jews were killed, which is a tragedy, millions of others died as well. I wonder what I will learn and whether my more broad-based thinking will change in any way.

I feel a little nervous at the moment as I begin to absorb all of this. The trip will not be easy, yet I know it'll be important in many ways.

February 15, 1990

Last night, Stu, Patricia, and I met to discuss the group grief work we'll be doing. We talked about how we will handle the small break-out sessions. I suggested everyone in the circle first do some kind of an icebreaker before we begin to talk about our losses. Neither of them had thought about that, but it's important that the teenagers feel comfortable before talking about something so personal and painful.

February 18, 1990

After Stu did the initial session on grief, we broke up into groups. There were lots of tears. Since we gave them the option of talking about a loss they have experienced, a few in both sessions chose not to share. Hopefully, they will down the road. Stu told me that doing this grief work in advance of the trip will help prepare everyone to face the topic of death when we arrive at the camps.

I've learned that there isn't much we can say to console someone who is grieving. It's mainly our presence that brings comfort.

April 18, 1990

9:00 a.m. We have an hour until we arrive in Chicago. We left a little late because it took a while for everyone to settle in. The flight attendants appear frustrated as they climb over teenagers in the aisles.

About fifteen people on the plane aren't part of our group, so Stu explained to them what this trip was about. When it came to breakfast, the flight attendant announced that anyone who isn't having a kosher meal should turn on his light—a real switch from the norm. It feels strange to be in the majority when it comes to a religious issue.

5:00 p.m. We've just taken off. The flight will be seven hours long, and when we land in Warsaw, we'll spend the day touring before checking into our hotel.

The two hundred and ten of us from all over the United States are getting to know one another. It won't be long until there are no strangers among us.

April 19, 1990

6:00 a.m. About two hours ago, which was midnight Miami time, I looked out the window. Daylight was creeping onto the horizon—so much for this night.

The captain just announced we are descending into Warsaw. The reality is beginning to sink in.

5:30 p.m. I feel like these last twelve hours have been equivalent to a week. There's so much to process.

The first sight that confronted us when we landed in Warsaw was an El Al plane that flies here once a week. Somehow, seeing that Jewish star on the wing brought some comfort to my somewhat uneasy feelings.

As we approached the terminal, a soldier, clad in a drab olive-green uniform with a machine gun in his hand, stood at the door. From that moment on, aside from those on our trip, I haven't seen a single smile on anyone's face.

After we went through customs, we boarded our five buses, which will travel together through Poland and Israel. Lunches were placed on every seat, each containing two bottles of seltzer water, two radishes with the stems and leaves on them, two apples that look like they were on the ground of an orchard for a week, and a chocolate-covered wafer.

We were told to pack for cold weather, but it looks like we got lucky so far. The sun was shining all day with temperatures around 65°. Spring is in bloom, even in Poland. I must admit that I expected this country to be gray without any beauty. Instead, there were tulips, cherry blossoms, and lilacs everywhere I looked. Just as I found myself getting caught up in the glory of spring, I'd notice a train track and remember where I was.

Our first stop was a Jewish museum in what used to be the Warsaw Ghetto. Besides all the memorabilia, SS records and logs of people who survived were in the museum's archives. A few in our group found the names of their family members.

Outside the museum, my friend Gail and I struck up a conversation with a Holocaust survivor who lives in Australia and writes for the Jewish press. I'm not sure why he was here, but he let us know he's philosophically opposed to the March. Just as he began to explain why, we had to leave to move on to the next site.

Today was the 47th anniversary of the Warsaw Ghetto Uprising. I was fortunate to walk alongside Rita Hofrichter, a partisan who had fought in the uprising. She shared many of her reflections as we toured the streets where she once lived. She said much had changed, but everywhere she looked, memories were triggered.

At the Rappaport Memorial, a monument commemorating the Warsaw Ghetto fighters, two Polish guards stood at attention while others played a drum roll. Groups lined up in rows of four or five, and one at a time presented the guards with wreaths they placed on the monument's floor. Gail and I were a bit surprised to see the Australian survivor marching up to the soldier with a wreath in his hand.

In the crowd were hundreds of teenagers from all over the world—all participants of the March of the Living. It was the first time many of the groups came together. Also, among the observers were survivors, Polish mothers with their children, and an assortment of people of all ages enjoying the beautiful day.

We later went to see Mila 18, the headquarters bunker for the Jewish Combat Organizations, a Jewish resistance group. I only knew about it from reading the novel of the same name long ago. From there, we had lunch at a park near the monument for the Polish uprising.

At about 4:00 p.m., we finally checked into our hotel. We had dinner, met with all the adults to do some planning, and then all of us collapsed.

April 20, 1990

The wake-up call was at 5:30 a.m. today. No one promised this would be a relaxing trip, but I didn't realize we would have to exist on so little sleep.

We've already decided breakfast will be the best meal in Poland. The menu will probably be the same each day, but at least it's edible. We had hard-boiled eggs, dry cereal, cucumbers, radishes, prune butter, and bread. They served juice called *sok*, made from currant berries.

10:00 a.m. We're on the bus now on our way to Treblinka. A little earlier, Sandy explained it was one of the camps where people were sent to be exterminated. For the most part, when the Jews arrived there, their heads were shaved. In many cases, the Nazis then used the hair to make fabric and textile products. Over sixteen months, only sixty-seven Jews survived out of the approximate 900,000 who entered Treblinka. At the end of the war, the Nazis destroyed almost everything at the death camp, so nothing is left that indicates what happened there.

Just a few minutes ago, everyone on the bus was chatting with their neighbors. All of a sudden, we passed a train yard with rows and rows of tracks. Instantly, there was silence.

I keep wondering what the Jews thought when they traveled this same path. How could they breathe in those cattle cars? What did they know?

12:15 p.m. I'm sitting in the pine forest all by myself. Further into the woods are three Polish women who were pulling weeds when we arrived. When they saw our large group, they stopped their work and are now having a picnic lunch. The wind is stirring through the fir trees, sounding much like the ocean on a rough day at sea. As some of us were walking into the forest, a few thought the wind sounded like trains.

The spirits seem to linger here. I feel their presence in all that surrounds me. Birds are chirping; butterflies are flitting from one flower to the next; bees are gathering pollen from the dandelions; and unlike anything I have ever seen, thousands of ladybugs are crawling over the pine cones on the ground. Yet, we all know of the horrors that took place here. Were the birds singing long ago as people gasped for their last breath?

There's something eerie about this place. It looks like a lovely park that goes on and on for miles. The reality is that thousands of Jews are buried in mass graves in the ground we're walking on. Lives were wiped away in a moment, and for what?

Seventeen thousand stones of all sizes commemorate those victims who were killed here. Two hundred sixteen of them bear the names of towns and cities from where Jews were transported. It boggles my mind to comprehend what all this means. In my life, I mourn a single death with deep despair. Here vast numbers died, and for most, there was no one to mourn for them. I am unable to make sense of this horror.

3:00 p.m. Warsaw Cemetery. Before the Holocaust, Jews were buried here. During and after the Holocaust, no Polish Jews who died have marked graves. That is incomprehensible, but then so much of this is.

Although I usually do not like to be in cemeteries, I suddenly feel a serenity and peacefulness. At least, the people who rest here died a natural death—unlike those who lost their lives in Treblinka.

Occasionally, to process my thoughts and record what I'm experiencing, I need to go off alone and write in my journal. I'm now sitting on a log on a path that seems to go on forever. A white butterfly and a few birds are the only ones besides me in the area. Every place I look, I see tall oak trees, some with leaves and others with buds. There are graves everywhere but no one to care for them. A little later, we will be cleaning a small section of the cemetery. Many of the tombstones are covered with years of accumulated moss and weeds.

Today is Hitler's birthday. We are not allowed to go out onto the streets for security purposes, although we wouldn't want to anyway. I don't feel safe or welcomed here. We get strange looks from the Poles wherever we go.

11:25 p.m. We just met in our small group of ten for the first time. Hopefully, we'll be having these sessions often so we can get to know one another better. Tonight, we took the first step by sharing a bit of ourselves and how we're feeling after this difficult day. It amazes me how quickly people can become close under the right circumstances. All sense of time seems to have changed since we left home.

I am beginning to have new insights into what Judaism means to me. I am already identifying more closely with the traditions and have found comfort in being surrounded by an all-Jewish group.

The highlight of my day was when the B'nai B'rith buses pulled into Treblinka just a few minutes before we were about to leave. Two kids from our group ran up to me and asked if I had seen Michael yet.

There was something special about reuniting with him after what had felt like an eternity. The last time I saw him was the night before we left, when we were both running around the house with tremendous excitement over our forthcoming trip. Today, after I made sure he was okay, I asked him to show me how to set the alarm on my watch. I've tried unsuccessfully. He made it look so easy.

April 21, 1990

10:00 a.m. I just came back from services, which took place in the lobby where we're staying. I'm sure that has to be a first for the Forum Hotel in Warsaw. We continue to carry on with our praying, regardless of who is watching.

When I left services and approached the main lobby, I saw a young, blonde Polish soldier walk in. As I followed him, I took note of his green uniform, thick, heavy, black boots, and his goose step. Suddenly, I began to think about what it must have been like during the war when people were going about their business and were disrupted by militia telling them to leave or rounding them up in a matter of minutes.

11:30 p.m. After lunch today, our entire South Florida group went back to the old synagogue where we had gone when we first arrived in Warsaw. We participated in a service with the boys from our group leading the prayers. Since it is an Orthodox *shul*, the women and girls sat upstairs. We came downstairs after the service to kiss one of the *Torahs*, which dates back to before the war.

As we gathered to talk to one of the elders from the congregation, Leon began to sing a song with the man. Within minutes, everyone joined in and formed three concentric circles. We brought happiness as we sang and danced while celebrating life in a synagogue where there had been no joy for forty-five years. The looks on the men's faces made that clear to all of us.

As we walked through the streets on our way back to the hotel, we noticed signs of anti-Semitism. It still exists in Poland. There were post bills on buildings with the word *Juden* underlined. We also saw a swastika on one of the walls.

When we got back, we went into the dining room, where we were introduced to a Pole, known as a Righteous Gentile. Through an interpreter, we heard how this man, who was twenty years old, and his family saved Jews during the war. Courageous people like him who risked their lives for others signal hope to me.

After dinner, we went back to the Rappaport Memorial for a commemorative service in memory of those who had died in the Warsaw Ghetto. It was the first gathering of all March of the Living participants from all over the world.

April 22, 1990

11:00 a.m. Wake-up call was at 4:30 a.m. today since traveling to Oswiecim will take five-and-a-half hours. It's a gloomy morning with temperatures about 50°.

The countryside of Poland reminds me of Ohio. With spring everywhere, wildflowers dot the land. We have passed many dense woods along the way. I wonder if partisans hid in some of these forests during the war.

Joe spoke to us about the irony of Hitler. He remarked that if Hitler had concentrated on winning the war and not killing the Jews, the Nazis might have won.

5:30 p.m. As we approached Auschwitz, I saw a Polish family with three children walking out of the grounds licking ice cream cones. Something was drastically wrong with that picture.

The weather had warmed up, so we shed our extra layers of clothing before departing from the bus. Today we were finally allowed to wear our royal blue March jackets with a Jewish star on the back, which the Israeli artist Agam had designed. Everywhere I looked, I could see a sea of blue.

As we entered the outer gates of Auschwitz and got closer to the barbed wire fences, I felt nervous. My body stiffened as I came upon the ARBEIT MACHT FREI sign at the entrance to the camp. It wasn't because I, Merle, didn't want to go in. It was much more than that. I began to think about how the people must have felt when forced to enter all those years ago. At that point, my body froze, and I experienced a strong resistance. I did not want to take another step forward. It was strange because it seemed as if a force greater than myself was controlling me.

I eventually walked on through the camp and finally reached the United States contingency gathering spot. I noticed that the B'nai B'rith group was already lined up, so I looked up and down the rows for Michael. He was nowhere to be found. I asked one of his friends, and he told me that Mike would be back in a few minutes.

For a little while, I stood by and waited. However, within a short time, something strange happened, and I suddenly panicked and felt frantic. I began to desperately search the crowd looking for Michael. I examined every face hoping to find him.

At that point, all I could think about was how it must have felt to be a mother in Auschwitz searching for her child or a child looking for his mother. I had heard stories from survivors about being separated from their children when they entered the camp. How awful it must have been to have searched in vain, enlisting the help of everyone around them—never to find their daughter or son—knowing instead that they had burned in the flames of the crematorium.

I needed to calm myself down at that point, so I walked off between two barracks where it was quiet and where I could be alone. Like everywhere else I had been in Poland, I could hear the birds chirping. Even in Auschwitz, they sing and dandelions grow. I walked on until I came to the barbed wire fence with a sign that said, "Halt" and a guardhouse next to it. I quickly turned around and ran back to continue looking for Michael. Desperately, I again searched every face until after about twenty minutes, he finally appeared.

I explained to him what I had been feeling, and then we embraced, sobbed, and clung to each other. It was one of the most intimate moments we had ever shared as mother and son.

Now that several hours have passed since that experience, I can step away from it and realize I've opened a door a tiny crack to understand better how parents and children might have felt during those dreadful, horrific times when they were separated from one another. Of course, I will never presume to think I can even come close to knowing. There is no way any of us can.

The actual March of the Living began with the shofar blowing as 3,600 teenagers and adults from thirty-seven countries recreated an earlier march made by thousands of Jews as they were forced to go from Auschwitz to Birkenau. We walked in total silence as we made our way three kilometers from one camp to the next. Along the way, we passed Polish families, some of whom stared and laughed and even spat at us. Others just stood quietly and watched. The houses they lived in were old, which meant someone was living there during the Holocaust. When I hear that people claimed they didn't see anything, this is absolute proof that they did.

After about an hour of walking in the hot sun, we arrived at Crematorium Four, where the ceremony began. As soon as the first song was sung, the still air became cool and breezy. Once the candle lighting started, a strong wind blew in. Elie Wiesel then addressed those gathered, and as he talked, the skies darkened. At his first mention of the children who died in Auschwitz, rain fell from the heavens as if God, too, were crying. And when he finished speaking, the sun came out until we began to recite *El Moleh*, when, once again, it started to rain. As we concluded the ceremony by singing *Hatikvah*, which means the hope, the sun peeked out from the clouds.

We walked back to our buses in silence, with rain drizzling down on us. It is now a half-hour later, and it's been pouring out. Just minutes ago, a full, beautiful rainbow covered the eastern sky. In the back of the bus, Rabbi Berkson is explaining the biblical significance of rainbows — the covenant between God and all living creatures.

Rainbows have always represented hope and peace to me. Like all of nature's phenomenon, I see rainbows painted across the sky as a sign of God's work. However, after today's March with thousands of us going from Auschwitz to Birkenau, I overheard a few teens asking where God was when people were being forced to take that same path to their death? We need to have this conversation — maybe the rabbis can help us make sense of it all.

April 23, 1990

12:15 p.m. We're back in Auschwitz — this time for a detailed tour of the camp. We have been in various barracks that house displays behind glass of hair, dishes, brushes, suitcases, prosthetics, eyeglasses, and religious objects.

We've just left the gas chamber and crematorium. While we were inside, there was a group of German-speaking students. They watched us as we cried and not one of them came close to showing any expression of compassion. What are they thinking? How does it feel to be from Germany? Do they wonder if anyone in their family were Nazis? I have so many questions with no answers.

I wanted to light a candle for Shirley Lehman's family while I was in the crematorium, but somehow it didn't feel right. It was too confining and horrible in there. Instead, I lit it at the base of a tree on the edge of a newly-planted rose garden opposite the gas chamber.

1:00 p.m. I'm now in Block 27—the Jewish Museum. We have been to the killing wall and the barracks that were created for solitary confinement. We stood near the building where Mengele did his medical experiments, which is closed to the public. It's probably just as well. This whole place feels like hell to me. Sitting in this meditative room, which is lit by *yarzheit* candles, I've been able to find a little peace in my heart—yet I am angry and confused. How could all this have happened? What does it mean when man destroys others in such a sadistic and inhuman way?

5:20 p.m. We're on the bus again. I hated being in Auschwitz and couldn't wait to leave there. We went right from Auschwitz to Birkenau, where Erna Rubinstein, a survivor who had been in Birkenau, took us to the barracks where she had been interned. How could she walk back into that place? Yet, she did so with courage and strength and shared with all of us what life was like when she was there long ago.

The weather had drastically changed by 3:00 today. While I stood in some of the barracks sheltered from the fierce winds with four layers of clothes on in the middle of April, I couldn't help but wonder how anyone could have survived there during winter wearing one thin layer.

When we gathered for a ceremony at the bombed-out crematorium in Birkenau, it started to rain. We didn't even finish the service because the weather turned nasty.

11:45 p.m. I've just climbed into bed after a very long day. We met in our groups earlier when we arrived at our hotel in Cracow. Part of what we talked about was the strong support system we've created. Virtual strangers have been there for one another with a hug, a shoulder to cry on, or a hand to hold. Just watching everyone comfort each other has been a heartwarming sight.

Tonight, even though it wasn't my turn for bed check, I decided to say goodnight to the kids on my bus. It's been a rough few days, and a little tender loving and a hug hopefully will ease some of the pain everyone seems to be experiencing.

April 24, 1990

6:30 p.m. Today was a day of touring Cracow. Rita lived in this city and shared a good deal about what life was like back then. We went to Miodawa Synagogue, where she and her family belonged when she was a young child. While in the sanctuary, which Hitler had turned into a stable for his horses during the war, Rabbi Feldman talked to us about the importance of light in Judaism.

He told us that if we had one glass of water and shared it with everyone, we would each have very little. But if we were to share one candle, we would have a room full of light.

After we left the synagogue, a few of us snuck away and saw the school Rita had attended. While we were taking pictures of her standing in front of it, three Poles about twenty-five years old began to swear at her in Polish and asked her why the Jews were killing the Arabs. What an awful experience that was for Rita. We quickly whisked her away.

We had a service at Remah Synagogue. In the cemetery next to it, we met a Polish Jewish woman who told us about her present-day life in Cracow. She is retired but worked with one thousand non-Jews and existed by leading an assimilated life. She was thrilled to talk to Jews again.

Nick told us that while he was walking along, an old Jewish man came down the steps of his apartment. He saw the Jewish stars on our jackets and became excited. He told several of the teenagers that he hadn't seen a Jew in forty-two years and began to cry and hugged each of them.

In the afternoon, we had free time to wander up and down the central part of town. It was raining, so a few of us dodged into a restaurant and had Polish pancakes similar to strawberry crepes. It was the best food we've had since we left the United States.

We're back at our hotel now. Sophia and I just had a conversation about our prejudices. The teens are all talking about how much they hate the Poles. It's possible that today, many of them would probably like to see us dead and are not happy that we're in their country. Their stone faces frighten me. I admit to being as uncomfortable as the next around the Polish people — especially the older ones. I can't help but wonder what they were doing during the Holocaust.

Yet, I have grave concerns about the messages a few adult chaperones have passed along to the teenagers. If we allow them to leave Poland hating, we will be perpetuating prejudice. We must make them aware that not all Poles are bad. It's dangerous to generalize and lump everyone together. Indeed, we need to remember that today's generation of younger people is not responsible for what happened during the Holocaust. At least, fortunately, we have met one Righteous Gentile who saved Jewish lives and, of course, our wonderful Polish tour guides.

I won't rest well unless I discuss this issue with the kids. We must fight the evils of prejudice, hard as it might be. After all we've seen here, we have to change attitudes, which must begin with our own.

April 25, 1990

10:20 a.m. We're on our way to Majdanek. We stopped in the woods to pee and have lunch along the way. We've gotten quite adept at these bathroom breaks!

Sandy just repeated what Gene had told us last night about the camp. He said that Central Park is to New York as Majdanek is to Lublin. Also, in setting the tone for what we are soon to see, he said that in Treblinka, whatever devastation there had been could only be seen through our imagination. In Auschwitz, it was museum-like with displays behind glass. But in Majdanek, it's as close to reality as possible.

1:30 p.m. I'm on the steps of a stone monument overlooking a field of dandelions. Here, too, I hear the birds singing.

Even though we had been warned, it shocked me to see how Majdanek is truly right in the middle of the city of Lublin. We were driving down the main road where people constantly travel, and suddenly we took a right turn and were at the camp. I can see buildings a few hundred yards from the camp and some even closer from where I'm sitting.

The people in those buildings had to have seen everything. How could they have been so indifferent? What went wrong with our world? What can we do to prevent this from ever happening again? It amazes me that life goes on around this pit of hell. It makes no sense to me.

I've stayed back for a bit to absorb some of the feelings I have. Down below, I see the stream of blue jackets quietly walking along the path. As with the actual March on Sunday, all the youth together make quite a statement.

2:00 p.m. I've just walked out of the gas chamber. While I was in there, I felt claustrophobic. I couldn't help but wonder what my last minutes would have been like if I had been made to stand there forty-six years ago.

There are summer cottages whose gardens butt right up to the barbed wire. The edge of the gardens can't be more than twenty feet away from the barracks. Is it humanly possible that people were planting flowers and vegetables on one side of the fence while people were fighting for their lives just feet away? Scrounging for a blade of grass to eat?

2:30 p.m. Shoes and shoes—rows and rows of shoes—piles and piles of shoes—all sizes and shapes of shoes. Heels, ballet shoes, work shoes, shoes made of rubber, cloth, and leather. Shoes with no soles—shoes with holes in them. How many miles did each person walk in these shoes? Where did they go? Babies' shoes—some so tiny they may never have taken a step in them—never to have experienced life. Rooms full of shoes. I held one in my hand and wept.

The sun is no longer shining as it was when we arrived. Instead, it has begun to rain. The weather matches my mood.

4:00 p.m. I am sitting in a corner of the crematorium in Majdanek. I've been in here for forty-five minutes already. There's a violent thunderstorm outside. Those of us who came in earlier are stuck inside where thousands died. This has been the worst camp we've visited.

When we walked in, we immediately saw the table they had used for dissecting — pulling gold fillings out of teeth after the people were dead. In the next room is a display of human bones. Below that platform on which the bones rest is a Jewish star made out of *yahrzeit* candles. People have placed flowers everywhere.

The longer we stay in here, the harder it becomes. A little while ago, a man started chanting prayers in Hebrew. Although on some level it was comforting, in other ways, it brought many of us to tears. People have been sobbing, hugging, and clinging to one another as we all try to make sense of this cruel madness.

5:30 p.m. We're on the bus now and are heading for Warsaw, where we'll have dinner and then leave for the airport. This past week in Poland, I have witnessed sharing and caring like I've never experienced before. Generally, boys and men are reticent to cry, let alone hug one another. But here, all facades and barriers have been dropped. We leave no one alone to suffer.

We have had to deal with those teens who feel there's something wrong with them because they haven't cried. We've become sensitive enough to see that they need a friend when they are off alone, just standing there with no expression. The beauty of this experience is that we are all there for one another. Perfect strangers have become friends in this moment of need and place far from home. I've learned how some people, who may seem to have it all together on the outside because they're quiet or not crying, sometimes hurt more than one who is visibly upset.

When we finally got back to the bus, we learned that we had missed a memorial service. The truth is that we had our own while stuck in the crematorium. We have several hours until we get to the airport. Tel Aviv is our next stop. Everyone is anxious to get out of this country, which feels like a massive graveyard to me. Just thinking about a week in Israel is lifting our spirits. We are ready to celebrate life.

April 26, 1990

We arrived in Israel at 6:00 a.m. I loved seeing the sun rising over Israel as we landed. One of the first sights we saw was a group of Jewish refuseniks from Russia arriving at the airport. I immediately thought of all the life-saving and life-changing work Adele and Joel have done for Soviet Jews.

We went to Tel Aviv, where we picnicked and had our first decent meal of the trip, since the food in Poland was less than desirable. I can't believe I actually drank warm Pepsi all week. For someone who drinks only Diet Coke with lots of ice, it just shows how desperate I was for caffeine.

From there, we drove to the Museum of the Diaspora. There were some excellent displays, but since most of us hardly slept on the plane, we were too tired to fully appreciate them. I'm not great at staying in museums longer than two hours on my best day. Today was a wipe-out for me.

Once we left there, the buses took us to the *Kotel* in Jerusalem. I'd heard about the Western Wall forever, so to finally be standing there was incredible. The wish I placed in the *Kotel's* crevice was for peace for Israel and the rest of the world. After what we saw in Poland, I can think of nothing we need more than that.

It took us a while to check into our hotel. Fortunately, Sophia is my roommate once again. We all gathered for dinner, and after we ate, Larry Smith and I left and went to the Holyland Hotel to see Michael and Wendy. It was terrific to be with our kids again and to discuss our Poland experiences with them.

I love Jerusalem and am in awe of its beauty. It's a place I have always dreamed of seeing.

April 27, 1990

We were up at 6:30 a.m. to fit in everything planned for today. Ronit, our Israeli guide, explained to us about the government and was upset that Israel is currently in a state of confusion.

At Yad Vashem, we didn't tour the whole facility, which surprised me. It seems those in charge felt we had had our share of Holocaust immersion in Poland, but they did want us to see the children's memorial. There, by some act of genius, five candles are lit and with mirrors set in a certain way so that one and a half million lights shine — each one representing a child who died in the Holocaust. As we walked through that room, we heard the names of those children over a speaker. It was solemn and sobering.

The other thing we saw at Yad Vashem was the Avenue of the Righteous. Trees line the path — some first planted by the rescuers from different countries and their Israeli hosts, who were the Jews whose lives they had saved. We learned that when they first dedicated the Avenue of the Righteous, Goldie Meir declared, "The Jewish people remember not only the villains but also every small detail of the rescue attempts." She went on to compare the Righteous Among the Nations to drops of love in an ocean of poison and said, "They rescued not only the lives of Jews but had saved hope and the faith in the human spirit."

Later, in the Old City in Jerusalem, Ronit told us about the history of the area. I had a hard time keeping my mind on what she was saying. Besides being 95° and sunny, I never do well with too many facts and am much better with concepts. There were several in our group who were falling asleep wherever we stopped.

We went down to the *Kotel* once again. Then for lunch, we picnicked overlooking the city of Jerusalem. Earlier, Sandy stopped and bought us each a *falafel,* which was far superior to any I've had back home. Our services were outside tonight. Mike surprised me by joining us and then staying for dinner, which was a treat.

April 28, 1990

By 6:30 a.m. today, we were up and dressed. We had our choice of which services we wanted to attend. We all scattered in different directions. Joe and I walked to the Reform service, where two female cantors performed the majority of it.

The weirdest thing that happened was the older man from Australia, whom I had met in Warsaw and later saw at the Warsaw Ghetto Uprising commemoration, came and sat next to me. When I greeted him with *Shalom*, his comment to me was, "Yes, I remember you. We haven't completed our conversation." I was glad to talk to him after services for a bit, although we still didn't get into why he was opposed to the March. It's probably just as well.

When we got back, since it was Shabbat and we couldn't do much, we sat around and talked. I ended up going to my room for a much-needed two-hour nap.

After dinner, we all left to go to the *Yom Ha'Zikaron* ceremony with the March of the Living teens from all over the world. The holiday commemorates those who lost their lives in battle. The woman who wrote *Jerusalem of Gold* sang it. They chose one representative from each of the thirty-seven countries to go on stage and sing *Hatikvah*. That was an emotional moment for me.

Yom Ha'Zikaron is a sad day for everyone here. There probably isn't a family in Israel who hasn't experienced the death of someone while fighting for their country. Tomorrow we'll be in the throes of the magnitude of that loss.

April 29, 1990

Since it was *Yom Ha'Zikaron,* we spent the day touring various military battle sites and monuments. We stood on the top of a mountain with breathtaking views of the city while Ronit told us about the Israeli wars.

From there, we went to Latrun, where part of the 1948 War was fought. Lots of us climbed on the tankers that dotted the area. We attended a ceremony for David Marcus, an American Israeli commander who had volunteered to fight for Israel and was killed right before the battle ended.

For me, the most moving part of the day was the tree planting ceremony on the Judean hills. We planted our own March of the Living forest for Israel's fallen soldiers. Michael and I planted our trees together—mine in memory of Bonnie. While there, sirens blasted at 11:00 a.m. Along with the entire country of Israel, we stood in silence and solidarity.

After dinner, the mood drastically changed. We all went down to Ben Yehuda Street to join in the celebration of Israel's 42nd birthday. The streets were wild—rubber hammers hitting people over the head and tons of spray foam everywhere. After a few hours of the craziness, some of us left the partying and went to the King David Hotel and then to get *falafels.*

April 30, 1990

They finally let us sleep in today. However, everyone partied until so late last night that still no one got much sleep.

We headed to an air force base where many Israeli jets were on display. We saw a movie on the Israeli Air Force and the various battles they had fought. The prime minister of defense, Yitzhak Rabin, spoke to us about Israel and the importance of our support for their country. He emphasized that Israel is the homeland for all Jews.

They had set up souvenir stands and had dancers from various countries entertaining us. We wandered around and saw lots of friends from other buses.

At one point in the day, we had the chance to ride camels. I had never ridden one, so this was my opportunity. Rositta and I got onto a camel together and had lots of laughs.

Later in the day, the soldiers made a barbecue for all 3,600 of us from the March. Helicopters performing tricks flew overhead. Then after we ate, some entertainers sang, and we all joined in. They flashed a laser light show across the sky as well as a fabulous fireworks display. We ended the night by doing Israeli dancing on the air landing strip with Jews from all over the world.

May 1, 1990

Today was another 5:30 a.m. wake-up call. I'm not sure why we had to get up so early, but we've gotten used to no sleep. We left and drove up to the Golani Museum. I loved the beautiful rose garden most of all.

From there, we drove to the Golan Heights area. We saw the Jordan River and the Sea of Galilee. At one point, we stopped at a crucial area that had once been Syria, but Israel took it over in the 1967 War.

After that, we drove to Dahlia's grandparents' *kibbutz*, where she had lived for several years. The Jordan River ran through it, and mountains surrounded the area. We picked up three Israeli soldiers on our way back and brought them to Jerusalem. The girls had a good time talking to them. That night, several of us went shopping on Ben Yehuda Street.

Again, I went in to kiss all our kids good night even though it wasn't my turn. I am going to be sad to say goodbye to them.

May 2, 1990

It's hard to believe that today is our last day in Israel. Almost no one is ready to go home, but we know that the time has come. After dinner, we went to the Union of American Hebrew Congregations (UAHC) for closing ceremonies, which were moving.

May 3, 1990

On the way to the airport, many of the teens shared their feelings about the experience. It made me aware of how much we have yet to process.

We've said goodbye to our kids from Chicago and Toledo. Everyone was crying—not easy to leave them. We boarded the plane in Tel Aviv at 3:00 a.m.

In between the few hours of sleep, I've spent a good deal of time writing. It's hard to summarize a trip like this. It's been intense because we've lived together and have packed so much in such a short time. For me, some of the most special memories will be of bus 32—26—and all the adults and teenagers on it. Under normal circumstances, some who would never be friends have been there for one another and have formed deep relationships.

February 15, 1997

I am happy to be going on the 1998 March of the Living. How will this one be different? Who will I meet? For sure, I'll be more involved as an educator this time around.

Miles let me know that by facilitating journaling workshops for those going on the March all these years and encouraging everyone to write in their journals, I have made a significant contribution. I'll be leading another workshop, but this time since I'm going on this March, I will be part of the group, which will make the connection even more powerful.

July 29, 1997

Yesterday I learned that this March of the Living would be counted as my vacation time—not professional development as it was when we went the last time. I was surprised, disappointed, and pissed. Two weeks on a trip like this is anything but a vacation—especially when I am a Holocaust educator.

July 30, 1997

In my obligatory interview, I learned that Miles and Sandy both thought my training was in social work. Now, I understand why they had asked me to do the grief session in 1990. They discussed ways I could help them and get involved before the March. I'm excited to know that I'm on the team and will be in Israel for its fiftieth birthday.

December 6, 1997

At the March of the Living staff retreat. Gene: "Focus on the children over self. It's their March, not ours. The more you do, the more you will get from the experience."

Why have I chosen to go back to Poland to do this again? While I'm not exactly sure, this time, I will go as a more committed Jew and one who has a more profound sense of God.

January 11, 1998

Sandy is talking about prejudice: "Because it was us at one time, we have a moral responsibility to make sure it doesn't happen to others. It could happen to us again. As victims, we need to be the spokespersons—the consciousness of the world."

February 17, 1998

I made sure to tell the students to get to know the survivors and pay attention to them—especially when we visit the different sites. I talked about the resilience of the human spirit, since they need to understand some of what lies beneath the surface for the survivors. We want the students to realize how difficult it is for these individuals to go back to these awful places. They need to understand how the survivors have made good lives for themselves despite all they endured. Plus, they are the ones who experienced the horrors and can share their experiences with us as no one else can.

All of this is the part about being a teacher and a writer that I love. I can share information and touch lives, thus making a difference. I feel it's my gift to give, and in the end, it all comes back in some way.

April 16, 1998

As with the last March, we will be going to some of the darkest places and then the brightest spots in the life of the Jewish people. I wonder what will be the same and what will be different from the 1990 March.

Daryl asked me to describe in a paragraph what I was expecting from the trip. I chose four words: renewal, rejuvenation, spirituality, and connectedness.

April 18, 1998

Our El Al plane is pulling out from the gate. The flight attendant just said the travelers' prayer, first in Hebrew and then in English. It's pretty amazing to get on a plane and hear that.

The sign on the screen says: "Welcome aboard on this flight to Warsaw." Leaving for this trip was much less dramatic than when we departed from JFK. There wasn't even a sign at the gate when we left this time. Everyone is slowly getting acquainted. The teenagers have no clue what's in store for them. Home already feels millions of miles away.

April 19, 1998

11:00 p.m. in Warsaw: We're on bus 131 waiting to get our luggage. We have to keep our carry-ons with us, so it's particularly crowded, plus we have the camera crew on our bus. Each day, they'll be sending photos back home to our families.

Later. Sharing session. Greta, the survivor on our bus, said that the Warsaw Ghetto didn't look at all how she remembered it. When she was living there, it was overcrowded and compact. Today, it seems like a regular neighborhood.

Again, like last time, I see that the people here don't smile. Graffiti with swastikas and Jewish stars as we walk along show modern-day anti-Semitism. I feel hatred in the air.

Sandy: "Two wonderful things about Poland. The pillows invite us to sleep on them, and we will sleep well in Poland."

"The issue is to forgive. We cannot ever forget. If you forget, history will repeat itself."

April 20, 1998

On the way to Treblinka. I'm sitting with Piotr, the eighteen-year-old Polish Jewish boy who will be with us for the entire trip. The Lauder Foundation invited him to join us.

Last night I felt awful because Piotr was listening to the kids badmouth Poland. It concerned me, so I spoke to Sandy and told him we need to talk to Piotr about this. He gave me the go-ahead, and so I did. Fortunately, Piotr understood where everyone was coming from. I wanted him to know it wasn't anything personal. Like the last time, I need to talk to the teens about prejudice and their feelings about the Poles.

Later. We are a half hour from Treblinka. Sandy asked me to speak about the camp itself, so I gave a brief talk on the mechanics of Treblinka. Since I had only three hours of sleep last night, I drank a can of warm Pepsi to pep me up before I spoke.

Greta is talking about how her grandmother was sent to Treblinka. Before that, the poor woman had never left her home and spent her life taking care of her family.

We just crossed the first railroad tracks. It's always sobering. I can't help but think only of what it must have been like to be on a train and know where it was heading.

Treblinka. I'm in the forest. Dogs in the distance are barking. Surrounding me are birds calling to one another. Aside from those noises, this place is still. Drops from an earlier morning rain occasionally land on my jacket, making a plopping sound.

I sit here remembering the last time when ladybugs crawled at my feet. Where have they all gone? Are their spirits still gathered deep in this forest like those of the people who died in the flames of hell here?

Sandy offered us the option of running up the pathway which leads to the monument representing a chimney. I chose to run and arrived out of breath, wondering how those who were forced to run with German Shepherds barking at them felt as they went. It's hard to imagine what they thought as they approached their deaths.

In the distance, I see teenagers in blue jackets meandering among the stone monuments. I hear people talking, but I have chosen to find a quiet spot in the dense woods, far from civilization. The ground beneath me holds the ashes and bones of our people. Their lives were cut short because of ignorance, hatred, and prejudice.

A group is singing *Eli, Eli*—a song that always leads me to reflect on the Anne Frank exhibit opening and where my career in Holocaust education began.

Gene: "Everything you do for the rest of your lives will be in memory of those who are buried here."

This ceremony has been a moving one—loving words about all the children we lost and thoughts of those who could have built entire communities. What would our world have been like had they not perished? No one here today will ever be the same.

Sandy: "This is a place of imagination. It is sights without sounds—people without faces."

Tykocin. We're in a synagogue that was built in 1625 and remained untouched during the war. Someone renovated parts of it and, in doing so, discovered the writing and artwork on the walls.

There's a piano, so one at a time, some of the talented teens are sitting down to play. Music, a universal language, speaks to the souls of those of us listening.

Rabbi Mark Cohen: "An echo is God's way of responding. Sing louder. You are here to laugh in the face of it all."

Gene: "We're in a *shul* where no one *davens*. However, our being here brings this *shul* alive. Ultimately, what you do the rest of your life is what makes this place what it is."

...The line where we stopped to pee was long, and the bathrooms were disgusting. So, several of us went into the woods. It's faster and easier.

11:30 p.m. Sharing session: Yossi is reading an entry from his journal. "Thank God for what you have. Celebrate life. *L'chaim.*"

Risa: "Were they singing their songs when they were going on the train? What were they thinking? What were they feeling?

"'The entire world is a narrow bridge, but the main thing is not to fear.' A song we had sung many times was something we were actually doing as we went to Treblinka."

Nirah: "I thought the stones at Treblinka represented individuals. My heart sank when I heard they were representative of entire communities that were destroyed during the Holocaust."

Yoram: "The synagogue, an hour after we left, was back to an empty, hollow, neglected building. I felt sad that the dancing, singing, and praying didn't fill the hole for me."

Noreen: "The blue jackets looked like little threads of life weaving their way through the stones."

Daniel: "When I stood at one particular white rock, I felt like I honored my family who lost their lives in that community."

April 21, 1998

It's another cold, rainy day. It's fitting for Majdanek, where we'll be going. I hope to stay warm and protected because I know every raw nerve will be exposed within me.

In last night's session, one of the girls told us how she saw three men standing near the bus. One of the guys took his hand and motioned like he was slitting his throat. Anti-Semitism is alive in Poland.

Sandy: "The *yeshiva* in Lublin was like the MIT of *Talmud*. The requirements to be there were extremely difficult, and a cadre of scholars who knew everything by heart filled its rooms.

"Imagine a full library on your favorite subject. The Nazis burned the library. We are the people of the book. The greatest scholars of the world studied here.

"If you practice what's right for you, then you are a good Jew. We're going to the *yeshiva* to rekindle the flame. You'll find yourself on hallowed ground in holy territory. A building only has meaning because of the people there. Try to use your sixth sense and feel what was there."

Lublin *Yeshiva*. Rabbi Mark Cohen: "Every step we take in Poland is a step involving death. The Nazis were most afraid of this room because in here, there was the understanding of the morals and ethics of our people. This was to be a place where Jewish culture was created.

"The purpose to build a sanctuary is so God can dwell in it. According to this, it is to create a sanctuary in one's heart. Thus, we create a place for God to dwell.

"On the March, we have seen so much of what man can do to each other. We need to rise above that. The first step is to be a *mensch*. Be kind, considerate, sharing, caring, and then go out and do *mitzvot*. If you do that, you will do what Rev Shapiro built this building for."

Graffiti on the desk where I'm sitting: *Jude fahren nach Treblinka*. (Jews, go to Treblinka.)

Later. We've arrived in Majdanek. The huge monolith is designed to look like it could come crashing down just as the world came crashing down on the Jews.

Here I sit overlooking one of the most horrific places on earth. To my right is the city of Lublin. Apartments and buildings look down into this vast area where hundreds of thousands died. Blackbirds fly overhead. Dandelions blossom on the velvety green grass.

Fanny's group is leading the ceremony. How must this be for her as a survivor? I see the sadness in her face as those around her sing *My Zadie*. Tears stream down faces. Feelings are on the surface.

Just a half-hour ago, students on our bus were somewhat rowdy. They had no clue what was coming next. This sobering experience is another step toward the realization of what took place. Today more tears flow.

Gene: "We didn't bring you here to teach you to hate. We didn't bring you here to make monsters. We brought you here because you will be the witnesses. You must remember for those who were killed and teach your children and your grandchildren."

Broken dolls, smashed faces, crushed dreams, silent shofar, toothbrushes, hairbrushes, shaving brushes, perfume bottles, velvet hats, the smell of death everywhere.

Shuffling feet, bodies moving through. All came in. Few went out—a living nightmare.

Baby shoes, red shoes, sandals, shoes of men, women, and children, shoes, shoes, and more shoes.

Later. I'm looking down on seventeen tons of ashes. Sandy is talking about how impossible it is to understand why none of the ashes blow away. They don't go anywhere. Voices reverberate and echo here in a strange way. A plastic bag down below is sailing around the base of the ashes.

The only thing that led me to smile today was the bathroom—a marble room with six clean stalls. The irony of that alone blows my mind.

A survivor from another bus is talking about her experience. "Walk gently on the grass. Be very quiet so you can hear the anguished cries of those left behind. Listen to the heartbeats. Hope lies not in the divide but in the coming together."

An attitude of indifference existed among those who lived nearby during the Holocaust and continues to exist today. People drive by daily. To this day, the people of Lublin bury their dead in the cemetery on the corner of this property. How could they ignore what lies next to the graves? How can they look away from this hell hole?

Sandy: "The turtle only makes progress when he sticks his neck out. This was a sign on the desk of a Harvard president next to a statue of a turtle. The inmates made a statue of a turtle. Their message was, 'Go slowly. Don't work quickly.'"

April 22, 1998

I find the shock value is not nearly as overwhelming as the first time I came to Poland, but it seems as if, instead, all my feelings are going to a deeper place in my heart. I am absorbing everything in an altogether different way. I was moved to tears many times yesterday.

Gene told me after our closing ceremony at Majdanek, when he finished singing *Hatikvah*, he turned around and saw a blue and white striped flag with a yellow triangle upside down over a red one to make a Jewish star. It was the first time he had ever seen that.

We've talked a lot about how people were stripped of their humanity—forced to be less than human. Sandy said that for a person to wash his hands was resistance. Of course, there was almost no way to do that.

Later. On the train on our way to Cracow. There are eight of us in a small compartment. Everyone but me has gone to sleep. I'm watching the Polish countryside go by. It is hard not to think about the trains that took Jews to their death.

Crakow. Remah Synagogue. The cemetery behind this synagogue has gravestones from the sixteenth century. As I walked through the grassy area, I noticed snails crawling on the headstones.

We just learned that the law in Poland was that no synagogue could be built higher than a church.

Isaak Synagogue. All around us are prayers on the wall. One could look up and read instead of using a prayer book. Windows are always a high point in any synagogue because we should be looking up when we pray. There are twelve windows representing the twelve tribes of Israel.

On the way here, we saw an Orthodox *yeshiva* scholar with a big black hat and coat—a common sight sixty years ago but an infrequent one in Crakow these days.

Later. We're in the Crakow *mikvah*. It hasn't been opened since 1990, but an exception has been made for the girls and women in our group. During the Holocaust, ninety-three girls killed themselves because they were going to be taken by the Nazis. We performed a short service saying *Kaddish* for those who gave up their lives rather than let their oppressors rape them. The singing and praying of our girls gave me chills.

Later. We *davened mincha* in the parking lot with Rabbi Paley. It was quite a scene as we stood together in a circle. I was moved to tears when we sang *Shalom Rav* and looked up and saw birds in the sky overhead.

At one point, the bus in front of us let out black fumes right in our faces. It was kind of ironic, and for a few minutes, it reminded me of Poles gassing Jews. Then a small car came. One of the survivors refused to move out of the way. The car had to fit in between us, which was a bit harrowing. I looked over to the side and saw our Polish guide dancing to our singing in the midst of that.

Later. On our way to Birkenau. I just saw daffodils blooming. How do flowers grow here?

How crazy is it that we sit on this bus waiting for a train to pass as we head to a place where life was not sane and where train tracks led right to the concentration camp?

In the heart of Europe stands Auschwitz. It was the epitome of darkness among so much else and was placed here so trains from everywhere could easily access it.

9:50 p.m. Sharing session. Total exhaustion for everyone.

Dina: "Today, I stood at my great, great, great, great, great grandfather's grave in the Remah synagogue cemetery. The letters, candles, and blessings that sat at the base of his headstone were yet another sign of what a famous rabbi he had been."

Nirah: "My faith faltered yesterday for the first time ever. I wrote with intense emotions wanting to scream, to escape. I felt possessed in a way as I sat in the gas chamber. My only option was to pray."

Abe: "I feel like the Nazis didn't just kill six million Jews. They killed more because every day, other babies could have been born. The anticipation of death was probably worse than death itself."

April 23, 1998

We're on our way to Auschwitz. I just looked at a building along the road and saw two huge stacks with smoke billowing out—a reminder of how it was in the camps.

Auschwitz. This is a solemn moment, as so many have been this week. I'm standing in line to enter the gas chamber. Did the people who waited in line know they were about to be killed? Did any of them think they were going to be taking a shower? It is inconceivable to imagine how it was for them.

Later. We're in front of the barracks where Nazis brought the girls for their entertainment. Thinking about that turns my stomach. What brutal savages the Nazis were.

Trees line the path we have been walking on. Branches reach upward as if wishing they could get out of this God-forsaken place. As I write, I think about how the trees, birds, and butterflies might have brought the only comfort to anyone who was here.

We're in the room with cases of hair: brown, blonde, black, curls and braids, long and short. Sobs fill every corner of this space as girls and women identify.

Later. Downstairs in the prison. Yoram said he thinks it would be better to have been shot trying to escape than to have died in a gas chamber. I wonder where he would rate torture in solitary confinement.

Later. I've come to the back of barracks 11. The spirits surround me in this cemetery of anguish. Did those who were interned here ever see the blue sky or feel the presence of God?

Later. I'm now in the Jewish barracks in a room lit by glowing candles. The Israeli group is singing *Ani Maamim*. One of the comforting feelings in all of this is that a Jew is a Jew wherever he is. Something unspoken connects us and our spirits.

Hatikvah is now being sung softly, but the voices are slowly rising. It brings me to tears to hear the survivors, many of whom spent time here, sing the song which brings us all hope. Thankfully, we as Jews now have a land to call our own.

Sandy: "When one of them died, a piece of each of us died. As long as there is one person in the world who is a slave, none of us is free. We must respond and say *heneni* when the call comes.

"The worst part of the March is over. If you don't think I agonized over your tears, my children, I did. Why did I bring you here? Why did you come? Because this is what happens if you don't. You must say, 'I was here.' You must remember and witness.

"This ground is sacred. It is the ground that's drenched with the blood of your brother. Go out in the world and tell them you were here."

Later. The March started with the blowing of the shofar. I stood thinking about those souls in Auschwitz who might be stirred by its sound. Were the angels hovering around them? Did they know we were there marching for them — for those who are no longer alive to tell their story?

Later. I am meandering through the crowds. I see people I know wherever I go. I'm going to walk away from the ceremony and go over to the barracks.

Benjamin Netanyahu: "The pain will never go away. It refuses to leave. We know that if Israel had been established before the Holocaust, this would not have happened. Only the Jewish state can protect the Jewish people. You can make it stronger by joining us in the land of Israel."

I stopped walking along the path going out of Birkenau when a man began to sing *Eli, Eli*. Who would have ever thought this song would be sung in this place all these years later?

In front of me are rows of barracks with a guardhouse straight ahead. I'm sitting on the ground. An Israeli flag flaps over my head as someone carrying it passes by.

A butterfly flits around the growing flowers on the embankment near my feet. Dandelions grow everywhere. A survivor told me they would have eaten them if flowers were growing while they were there. He said there wasn't a blade of grass in Auschwitz — only mud.

On this earth where I sit, one and a half million people were killed. The spirits hover close by. They help me know my mission.

Later. I have to go back on the bus, but I don't want to. I hear someone singing *Ani Maamim*. I wonder how many people uttered those words when they were interned here.

Now *Hatikvah* — the final hope. We have survived. We have won — *Yerushalayim* — loud and clear.

April 24, 1998

We're on the bus heading to the Warsaw Cemetery. On our train ride, I sat with eight kids and had a great discussion on various topics: death, the Poles and the teens' reactions to them, the March, going home, bonding, the Polish experience.

At one point, I was going to leave to give them some alone time without an adult — especially since they started to talk to Piotr about drinking and drugs in Poland and the U.S. But they made it clear they wanted me to stay. I am grateful that, unlike some people, I love being with teenagers.

Warsaw Cemetery. I have gone off on my own. I wanted to be alone to experience the serenity of this place. The buds are in bloom, ready to burst forth from the trees. I feel like I'm in a park or woods up north in the U.S., but that is clearly not where I am.

One of the most meaningful experiences was when our group cleaned a section of the cemetery earlier. The tombstones were covered with moss, which we removed. We also weeded the area around the graves. By looking at the dates on these tombstones, no Jews have been buried here since before the Holocaust.

A group of Polish elementary school students has just come to the Janusz Korczak memorial. They're looking at the sculptures of the children as they learn about a Jew — an author and educator who devoted his life to Jewish orphans. Korczak was offered sanctuary but instead went with his children onto the train that took them to Treblinka. After hearing about him, these children laid down a bouquet of red roses at his feet.

Nozik Synagogue. We just had a dedication ceremony at the Lauder Resource School playground. There were fifteen three and four-year-old children. They sat on the steps and sang a few Hebrew songs for us. How surprised they were that we knew the words and joined them. Then some teens put the kids on their shoulders and danced around with them — what a joyous moment.

At the same time, a bird shit on me. The last time that happened was when I was on the 1990 March in Tel Aviv. Some say it's a sign of good luck, but it certainly does not feel that way.

The girls, including Fanny, are now dancing around the *bimah*. The boys are slowly joining the circle and are making a long chain around the synagogue. I would guess Gene is feeling fulfilled as once again his dream is realized.

Later. Today while we picnicked in the park, I stood by the street to prevent any of our teens from crossing. Some guy rode by, stuck out his middle finger at me, and yelled, *"Juden Raus."* That felt awful. Anti-Semitism still exists here and elsewhere around the world.

April 25, 1998

Vicki and I were in our room about to go downstairs when I heard someone yell, "Get out of my room. Have you been drinking?"

My first reaction was I didn't want to be the one to have to send someone home for drinking or deal with all that that entailed. But I understood my responsibility, so I ran out into the hall. I immediately saw Dina and her friend Estie. Dina was running with some guy. Estie told me she had fallen asleep in Dina's room. Dina had gone out and left the door open a crack because she didn't want to get locked out. When Estie awoke, there was a woman in her bra and pants sleeping next to her. The woman put on her clothes and ran out. Dina and one of the boys chased her. I chased them, and Vicki followed.

We ran to the bottom landing, where they prevented the woman from leaving. Vicki grabbed her back when she started to get out. I ran to get security. The guard I asked to help didn't speak much English, so I luckily found one of our Polish guides. He started to question the woman, who didn't give great answers.

She hardly spoke. So, then Zeus, the security guard from our bus whom the kids love, came. I felt better when he was with us. Two policemen and a man from the hotel's security questioned the woman.

Meanwhile, I went to see if anything was missing from Dina's room. As I ran up and down the steps, my adrenaline was flowing.

The guards wanted to know what our expectations were if she hadn't stolen anything. I knew it wasn't my place to decide, so I went to get Sandy and Gene. They chose to let her go. Sandy said, "It's *Shabbat.*"

He came with me and talked to the woman, with the guard and guide translating. He explained to her about Abraham and told her we Jews are compassionate people.

Everyone listened carefully. The woman turned to Sandy and Estie and apologized. Then Sandy told

Estie to remember the lesson and know that perhaps in doing what he did, there will be one more person who understands us Jews—a bridge will be crossed. It was a touching scene with many tears.

April 26, 1998

Warsaw airport. We have two hours to go before we leave. There's a group of teenagers jamming on guitars and flutes. They're hanging out, singing, dancing, playing, and letting loose.

And so, our time in Poland is drawing to a close. We have been to the pits and now are ready to go off to the land of milk and honey.

Later. We've landed in Israel. The kids are singing. The fun has begun.

The Wailing Wall. As I leaned against the Wall, I realized that Jerusalem stone feels cold even though it sits in the beating sun. The *Kotel* is considered God's mailbox. It is a place where God's presence is supposed to be stronger than anywhere else in Israel. They say that God answers all the prayers people put into the Wall. Miracles occur here.

5:30 p.m. We've had a full day. When we left the *Kotel,* they let us go to Ben Yehuda Street to have lunch. Patti, who knows Israel, chose a restaurant. We had pizza and cold diet Coke. What a difference from the food we ate in Poland and what a treat to finally have ice.

From there, we boarded the bus and drove north to the youth hostel in Galilee near the Lebanon border. When we arrived, we ate dinner, which was several courses—lots of typical Israeli food including salads, tahini, hummus, baba ganoush, and pita bread.

Now, we're sitting in a bomb shelter. The guide wanted us to experience this, although I'm sure it's different when one's life is threatened. It's scary to think Israelis live with the constant fear of being attacked. They often end up spending a lot of time here. It's their way of life. I wonder if they live with PTSD as a result.

What a difference a day makes. This is a trip in contrast: Poland versus Israel—dark versus light, death versus life, commemoration versus celebration, sadness versus joy, hate versus love.

April 27, 1998

I intend to pay close attention while in Israel this week. From our sharing last night, I can tell that many people experience something here that I don't yet have in my consciousness. While I love it and feel at home, I want to connect to this incredible country.

Last night, I told Patti that I would be happiest in Israel when I saw the ocean. As Vicki and I walked toward the cafeteria, I realized we were near the sea. I hadn't noticed until I looked out and saw white waves breaking.

Later. We're on our way. Red flowers line the road, and army bases guard the border from Lebanon.

Later. Rosh HaNikra Grotto. I'm in an area where the water is trapped. The sea rages. I closed my eyes and felt like I was in the middle of the most chaotic spot in the world. I thought about my life back home as waves rushed in and roared. Eventually, this will quiet down, and in reality, my life will as well.

Later. While the guard waited patiently for me, I was the last one to leave the grotto. Tears have been streaming down my cheeks. Maybe this is my awakening—spiritually and emotionally.

I have finally found my home here in Israel. The sea, which speaks to my soul, has been my heartbeat. My life is richer because of the ocean.

Later. We're on our way to a Druze village. The scenery changes from one minute to the next as I look out the window: agriculture, aqueducts built by the Romans, hills, dairy farms, banana groves, mountains, small communities, vast expanses, small parks, and roadside stands, people in fields.

Later. We're now in a Druze home sitting in a big room with chairs organized into groups of five and six. I see a woman outside the window sitting in front of a giant circular oven made of stone. She's wearing a scarf wrapped around her head, similar to a hijab. She takes round balls of dough, flattens them, and with her hands, spreads either a tomato sauce or some spices on top and puts them into the oven to bake. It only takes a few minutes to cook, then she piles them up.

They served us a vegetarian meal with stuffed zucchini, pizza-like food the woman made, olives, and Israeli salad. For dessert, I had a piece of baklava, which was extremely sweet and delicious.

Later. We've moved to another home in the Druze Village, which is comprised of eighty percent Druze, the rest Catholic, Muslim, and a few Jews. The Druze have been here for four centuries, and one hundred thousand Druze currently live in Israel.

According to their faith, there is no smoking, mixed marriages, drugs, drinking, or assimilation. They don't want to lose their culture. They believe in one God. They have free choice as to whether they want to be religious. They pray twice a week.

The Druze feel that all humans are connected. They don't believe in the resurrection—only that the spirit and *neshama* live on. When someone dies, they're put in a box with others buried on top of them. Past life deeds decide future lives. They try to create heaven on earth.

Atlit. We just finished touring the DP camp, where the Jews were sent when they first came here in 1948. The camp, which overlooks Carmel, is surrounded by barbed wire on all sides. I can't imagine how the Jews from Europe felt and what it did to their psyche to be locked in once again. Did they wonder why? Did they ever think they'd be free?

Yoram told me that once they were let out, the Israelis treated them poorly. They called them "soaps," accused them of surviving, and laid guilt because many from their families had been killed. It sounded like an awful experience for the Holocaust survivors interned there, waiting to live their lives in Israel. Didn't they suffer enough?

Later. The sun is setting on the Mediterranean Sea right by our youth hostel. At home, I see the sunrise on the Atlantic Ocean, but I rarely have the opportunity to see sunsets on the water.

Later. Tonight we went to the woods and participated in a simulation as if we were in the underground *Haganah*. It was an unbelievable night with thousands of stars in the sky—clear, beautiful, and special to be outside on this fabulous evening in Israel.

I walked through the woods with Risa. In the end, we went to the bridge and put our "dynamite" down. Then, someone set off a few fireworks. One of the Israeli men in charge of the experience talked to us about how fourteen *Palmach* blew up a bridge, but then they all died.

April 28, 1998

Acre Prison. We're on top of the prison overlooking the Mediterranean Sea. This place reminds me a little of Alcatraz in that it is surrounded by water on some sides. I feel entirely at peace because it's on the sea, even if it is a prison.

On the road. Flowers are everywhere I look. Roses in red, white, yellow, peach, and pink grow wild, as do hibiscus, violets, and pansies. I've pressed several flowers within the pages of this journal. Some day when I open it, along with my written words, they'll be a reminder of this moment in time.

We just saw an Arab village in the mountains. Cities pop up out of nowhere.

Safed. We're in an alleyway, which is said to be the narrowest alley in the Mideast. An old lady named Yohevet believes that the Messiah will come through right here. Therefore, she puts out tea and cookies for him every day.

Safed is the spiritual, mystical center of Israel. I hope to experience some quiet, special moments here. I want it to rub off in some way.

Joseph Caro Synagogue. The ark is on the southern wall because all arks face Jerusalem. In the United States, they face east.

Questions: What is our mission? Our aim? *Tikun Olam*? How does God fit in? What is creation all about?

Three sets of eternal lights hang in circles with different colored bases. Arched high ceilings are painted the same color as heaven. A menorah sits in the loft. In case the Messiah comes, it will light his way.

There are hundreds of old books of *halacha* from all over the world. "Better to kill a man than a book." John Milton said, "Kill a man, you kill a reasonable creature. You kill a book, you kill reason itself."

Safed Cemetery. This is the most beautiful of all the cemeteries I've ever been in. According to history, here in this cemetery are buried some of the wisest humans who walked this earth.

Just a few of us came here instead of shopping. We had our choice, and immediately, I knew I wanted to be here. And so, I sit in this town of mysticism by myself in a cemetery overlooking an exquisite field of red poppies, yellow and white daisies, all kinds of tiny purple and blue flowers, and Queen Anne's lace. Interspersed are graves with Hebrew engraved on them. I hear men praying in the distance. In front of me is a mountain range that reminds me of the mountains in Colorado. Hannah and her seven sons' graves are down below.

Out of nowhere, as I write in my journal, I hear a shofar blowing. How eerie this is. I wonder whether the spirits are awakening just as in Auschwitz when they blew the shofar at the start of the March.

Later. As I was leaving the cemetery, I saw a scorpion scurrying into a can. I also heard bees buzzing. It made me think of rabbis *davening*.

When we got on the bus, Nirah told me about her spiritual experience. She climbed up to a bridge and ended up meditating near where three men were praying. Startled, she opened her eyes when she heard the sound of the shofar. She thought she was having an out-of-body experience.

She said the men came over to her, blessed her, and kissed her forehead. Meanwhile, I had searched for the spot where the shofar was being blown and by whom. She never found him, but I did. I saw a man dressed in his black garb and big black hat standing way at the top of the cemetery's hill with his shofar in hand.

April 29, 1998

11:30 a.m *Yom Hazikaron.* A thin sliver of the moon hangs in the day sky. The sirens reverberate through the country. Silence reigns except for the piercing sound, much like a mother's cry at the news of her son's death while in battle.

Later. We stopped on the roadside, and everyone got out of the bus and listened to the sirens wail. We climbed up the embankment to watch what was happening down below. Aside from an ambulance and one truck, everyone stood still in respect for those soldiers who died fighting for Israel.

In this country, their day of remembrance holds significant meaning for everyone. Our Memorial Day in the United States doesn't seem nearly as solemn. In fact, for so many, sadly, it's just a day off work and an excuse to picnic.

Yoram just read a poem about an Israeli soldier who had been killed. He was named after his grandfather, who died in the Warsaw Ghetto. The grandfather had been named after his father, who was killed in a pogrom in Ukraine. The fear of death and persecution remains.

9:00 p.m. City lights are twinkling in the dark. They sparkle like our candles' flames which burn brightly. Just one week ago, we were in Poland for *Yom Hashoah*. This trip has flown by — except for certain moments in the camps, which seemed endless.

Yad Vashem. We went into the children's memorial. I stood there looking at the flames and thinking about my own two children and what they mean to me in my life. I also thought about last night's ceremony and how I stared at the flame. There is something about light that ignites my soul.

Har Herzl cemetery. Sandy: "This is a cemetery commemorating the holy people who gave their lives for their country. We remember these people and keep the connection with them and their memory alive, which in turn, keeps us alive."

Later. I'm sitting in a quiet place — a spot away from the crowds. This cemetery is unlike the neglected and deserted one in Warsaw, with graves of people long gone with no family to remember them. Instead, this cemetery is alive with bouquets because here, families visit regularly. Right near me is a family saying prayers and remembering their loved one. Young girls around sixteen to eighteen go from grave to grave *davening*.

Young soldiers pass by. They're simply kids who have been called for duty to serve their country. Gene says the ultimate challenge is that we have the opportunity to nurture, care for, and love the state of Israel.

Yom Ha'atzmaut. A completely wild scene on Ben Yehuda Street — boppers, crazy foam, spaghetti spray, Rolling Stones music, cappuccino, kids with telephones, bands, fireworks, snow foam everywhere, a wild celebration for Israel's fiftieth birthday.

April 30, 1998

We were leaving the Haas Promenade when we suddenly saw four planes flying above us, creating blue and white streamers. They circled the area doing a few dips.

Later. I planted two trees overlooking the Jerusalem zoo. One was in memory of Howie Robinson, Rebecca's friend who was killed in a car accident, and the other for life, growth, and the continuation of the state of Israel. This is a moment perpetuating all that Israel stands for and contributing to its future. Israel is a country of proud people who know what it means to have this land.

Later. Tonight was a celebration at Latrun—a most uplifting experience with *ruach* like I haven't experienced ever before. Seven thousand people sang Hebrew songs, danced, clapped, all feeling the spirit of Israel, fireworks, a brilliant red sunset, confetti, and horn blowers, a rainbow halo around the crescent moon, holding onto Ivy and singing, light show, excellent band, Israeli dancers, people from all over the world, yet a closeness shared with Patti and Vicki, Greta dancing through the aisle after it was all over, the Israeli music, and kids partying.

May 1, 1998

The Wailing Wall. A woman is screaming at someone. What a distressing experience. This is a place to pray for peace. What could be that awful that this person is so outraged? Can we ever have peace when there are angry people like her?

Sandy talked to us about the Sea of Galilee that receives and gives water. He then told us about the Dead Sea and how it only takes but doesn't give anything. Sandy compared how one is alive with things growing and the other is stagnant. He wanted to make sure the kids knew the difference between giving and taking.

May 2, 1998

We're soon on our way back to Miami. They've just said the prayer for our trip, and we're now taxiing. Saying goodbye to Israel was not easy. Will I ever have the chance to come back? I certainly hope so!

As far as the trip, there are some comparisons I can make to the 1990 March of the Living. One thing I liked much better this time was that we saw more of Israel and had a greater variety of outdoor activities. I appreciated nature in a wonderful way that I didn't have a chance to on the first trip. Plus, we visited fewer military bases this time around.

The rules were stricter on the first trip. The teens seemed to get away with much more this time. I also missed the constant open sharing on the bus that we did on the first March. But this experience had its memorable moments. Those of us on bus 131 felt connected and grateful to be together. We bonded even though there were cliques and subgroups.

After going through the concentration camps and seeing what happened to the Jewish people and experiencing a land filled with death and ashes, I am ready to go home with my renewed spirit. That began to happen for me in Israel. The beauty and creation that exists there moved me.

May 4, 1998

Someone asked me what the highlight of the trip was. One was the human connection, and, in that category, I would say that meeting and being with Piotr, my young Polish friend, was a tremendous gift.

Spiritual highlights were at Birkenau when I heard *Eli, Eli* and sat down and wrote, my time in the Safed cemetery, and in the grotto at *Rosh HaNikra*.

Good time highlights: The celebration at Latrun and the evening in the streets of Ben Yehuda for *Yom Ha'atzmaut*.

May 6, 1998

Tonight at a March meeting, we sat in a circle with everyone expressing how they've been feeling since returning home. A few of them have been keeping journals, which delights me knowing they realize the benefits of writing.

Sandy said, "You've gone through two weeks of acceleration. The rest of the world is on a different pace. They have no idea where we've been or what we've experienced. We need to be patient and kind and understand that they cannot imagine what our lives have been like."

Reflections on March of the Living

When I came home from the March of the Living both times, I knew I would never forget the weeks I had spent in Poland and Israel. But as with most memories, so much fades in time. Because I journaled my way through, I have a record of each day—the feelings, the sights, the varied and powerful experiences of the two trips.

As I read these excerpts, the stark details immediately flooded back to me—some that had long since vanished. There were moments when I could feel myself back in the camps, shedding tears at the horrors I was seeing and imagining.

It's almost impossible to describe what it was like to stand in a crematorium or a gas chamber, see the multitude of train tracks leading to Auschwitz-Birkenau, and feel the relief of leaving Poland. Yet, I have captured so much of this in my journals. Reading it was almost like going back in time to those trips—to being there surrounded by naïve teenagers whose worldview changed for them in a matter of a few short days. I saw how mine did too.

One thing that struck me from this perspective was how something like the March of the Living brought people together in a way that I've rarely seen elsewhere. Because we shared a common and difficult experience and were far from home, we relied on one another in different ways than usual. The teens bonded and were able to lean on each other. Someone was always there to wipe away a tear or give a much-needed hug.

When I went on my first March of the Living, I had been working at the Holocaust Center for four years and had come to understand that the Holocaust was a universal tragedy. Yes, six million Jews were killed, but five million others were as well. I was viewing the Holocaust from a broader base, understanding that this was a human issue. Prejudice, bullying, stereotyping, and all else that led to this horrific event in our history are not unique to only the Jewish people. Unfortunately, it continues to exist in our society today.

The March of the Living is a trip for Jewish teenagers from all over the world. Initially, I thought about what this trip might be like if it were open to teens of all races and religions. I wondered how it might differ if it were inclusive. Everyone benefits from learning about the Holocaust—how it started, what transpired, and how it impacted us in the future.

I didn't write that much about it, but at the time, I wondered how I would feel with the March of the Living being solely focused on the Jewish perspective. I hoped I would be open to why it was important to make this trip exclusive for Jewish youth only. In retrospect, I came to understand the significance of the March of the Living, which provided Jewish teens with the opportunity to witness what happened to their ancestors.

The trip helped the teenagers learn more about Jewish life before the Holocaust and their Jewish heritage. One of the March of the Living goals is to inspire students to live Jewish lives that reflect the values and traditions that existed prior to the war.

On a personal level, it helped me connect and identify with Judaism in ways I hadn't before. As I walked through Poland and thought about all those people whose lives were cut short because of anti-Semitism, I realized my role in keeping the traditions and beliefs of my religion alive.

When we arrived in Israel, I understood how Jews built lives from destruction to rebirth. The homeland of our people suddenly held an important meaning in my own life. As I reflect on these excerpts, I can feel the overwhelming contrast between how I felt in Poland versus Israel.

I now see how the trip impacted my life moving forward and how it enhanced my role as a Holocaust educator. I learned so much I was able to pass along to students and teachers alike. It also brought me closer to the Holocaust survivors in ways I couldn't have imagined at the time. I became a witness from having been there.

Journal Prompts

- Write about a surreal experience you've had—one that you couldn't have imagined unless you experienced it.

- Have you ever been a bystander in a situation? What were the circumstances? What might you have done to help instead of just watch or what did you do?

- Write about a time when you've thought the world had gone mad. What did you do to make sense of it?

- How do you react in painful and emotional situations?

- What do you do when you see that people are sad, confused, or having a difficult time?

- Write about a place you've always wanted to go to and then finally did.

- What smells, sounds, and sights trigger memories for you? What are the memories?

- When did you learn about the Holocaust, and what information has stayed with you since then?

- What feelings surfaced for you when you read these excerpts about the concentration camps?

In Search of Spirituality

You have to grow from the inside out. None can teach you, none can make you spiritual. There is no other teacher but your own soul.

— Swami Vivekananda

November 25, 1974

Tonight in the transactional analysis class, we chanted—something I've never done before. The vibrations of the voices and the warm, vibrant energy connected all of us, as in unison, we repeatedly sang "OM." The intensity left me with a feeling of peacefulness, unlike anything I have ever known.

December 2, 1974

As each person entered class tonight, I smiled and felt an immediate attachment knowing we had joined together last week in something indescribable and yet life-affirming. Ron pointed out that he had felt a tremendous amount of energy coming from our corner of the room. I wasn't the only one who knew that whatever happened in our last class carried over to tonight. There was closeness and a feeling of connection among us that hadn't been there before our chanting. For me, after being with two little ones all day, it was as if I entered into an alternate universe.

September 19, 1975

My religious beliefs are unclear at this point in my life. After being reasonably unobservant these last five years, I have found that nothing has "struck me down"—no consequences for not going to synagogue or following closely to how I was raised. I feel detached, and that's okay for now.

October 31, 1976

I sometimes find myself asking for strength to cope with whatever crosses my path, although I am unclear as to whom I'm praying. Other than that, I rarely think about anything related to religion.

September 28, 1978

Now that we are part of Temple Sinai, it feels welcoming and comfortable to be in synagogue—reminiscent of my life growing up. When Daryl is by my side, it adds an extra feeling of contentment, although his presence is solely for me since he has no interest in religion. During last night's services, I spent my time soul searching and examining areas in my life I need to improve.

November 28, 1978

Daryl and I were in the bedroom making love when Michael and Steve were outside with their bikes. Michael said they'd just stay out front. We weren't supervising them as we probably should have been. After a bit, when I went to call them inside, they were nowhere to be found. I panicked.

When describing the scene to Bev later, I said, "Until I found Michael, I felt as if God might be punishing me." Since I don't think of Judaism as a God-fearing religion, I wonder where those feelings came from.

November 14, 1981

Earlier today, Uncle John, the lifeguard, and I were walking toward each other to discuss the energy we were feeling here at the beach this morning. It's as if there was a presence, a spirit, but I can't describe it in words. It's one of those deep-in-my-soul feelings. Who would ever understand except someone who believes in something beyond what we know?

April 28, 1982

Last night in book club, we had a philosophical discussion on life and death and the purpose of our days on earth. Gerry talked about Jesus and her feelings on his teachings of love and caring. She believes there has to be life after death to give purpose to this short span on earth. She also has an absolute belief that God is always with her.

Almost everyone else felt the soul lives on. Rosemary said she hoped one day to be reunited with her mother, who died when she was born. Gerry felt the same way about her father, who died when she was a little girl.

October 12, 1982

The rabbi explained that prayer is for practice—that when one needs it, prayer can be comforting. He told me most people pray by rote, and for many, there's little touch with "God." He said the revelations usually come when one is searching within. Somehow hearing him discuss all of this made me realize just how normal my feelings are. I am rarely ever inspired by prayers. Yet, when I feel afraid or desperate, I find myself praying.

April 12, 1983

My favorite spots on earth are those untouched by humans. I feel angry when I see nature destroyed by greed and insensitivity to one's surroundings.

June 22, 1983

Tonight Cynthia and I got into a discussion about the Divine lover. She described how this love is purer and more universal than any other—the moment of meeting the true spiritual light. Since this is all new to me, the idea of ultimate love is one to explore.

June 26, 1983

I realize how fortunate I am to have a few people opening doors and holding my hand as they guide me into a world I know little about. I feel like I am on an adventure.

When I asked Tom if our relationship would have to change in any way as he steered me along the path to individuation, his answer was, "No, we're 'spiritual directors' for one another." I am on my way to learning about things I never knew existed.

August 14, 1983

My meditation experience with Cynthia at the beach took me away from my thoughts for a few moments. It was as if I was on a soft, white carpet of clouds while, in reality, I was on the sand staring out at the ocean.

September 2, 1983

Chrys talked to me about double numbers being master numbers. I've seen lots of 11:11 and 12:12 on the clock lately. She told me it usually follows a growth spurt in learning.

She read my tarot cards for me, and here's what came up: major balancing cards, getting back what I've given, finding success in what I do, meeting a younger man who gives to me, money coming to me. Purple and yellow (my two favorite colors) surround me. Number five, which stands for creativity, appeared. She told me to envelop myself in a white bubble to protect me from anyone sapping my energy and suggested I'm not alone but instead have guidance from other sources.

September 5, 1983

I decided to do the I Ching that Chrys had introduced me to earlier today. The message I got was to have goodwill toward man, set goals and follow them, and be comfortable going anyplace I want.

September 6, 1983

Today in Marianne's writing group, we joined hands in a circle and stared at a crystal—getting and giving vibrations to one another. I'm not exactly sure what it had to do with writing, but it was different than any experience I've ever had.

September 18, 1983

The man, who stopped by the palm tree where I was writing last week, came by again today. He's deeply spiritual and talked to me about the higher power.

He let me know when he broke his arm, he felt sure it was God's way of telling him to slow down. He believes we can't interfere with God's plan. He simply views the world as having an ultimate and supreme power that guides us and takes us along the path to where we need to be.

September 28, 1983

I stopped by the wooden shell shack in Hollywood that I've driven past many times. The owner is a spiritual soul, and much of what he said, I didn't understand. He compared man to a hot water boiler that can explode and a small mollusk that becomes unattached, its vacuum gone. I was with him for a reason today—for him to tell me something. I'm just not sure what it was.

October 5, 1983

After class at FIU, we talked about how inner strength suddenly appears when we need it. We also discussed psychic phenomena, which led to one woman telling us about Lilydale, New York—someplace connected to the Spiritualist movement. Supposedly, there were paintings done by spirits in a darkened room lit only with one candle. She explained how the paintings emerged. One was put under glass shortly after it was done, and then overnight, a red V appeared. It came right through the painting. No one knows how or why—just plain weird and spooky.

October 15, 1983

I'm at Biscayne College, attending an Edgar Cayce seminar. After reading about this workshop in the paper, my curiosity brought me here. Now, I'm wondering why on earth I ever came. I didn't think it would be religious, but I sure got that wrong.

So far, we've heard a lecture on the Essenes, the ascetic sect which lived around the time of Christ—something I'd never heard about before. The more the instructor talks about Jesus, I find myself expecting someone to come up to me and ask, "Hey, what's a nice Jewish girl like you doing in a place like this?" I am distracted by that thought and can't help but wonder what my mother would say if she knew I was here.

We also saw a movie on the last years of Jesus' life. In it, they told a story about the power of the sword which pierced Jesus. Supposedly, when in one's possession, that particular saber afforded total control to the person. For example, Hitler once overheard a guard say, "He who holds the spear, holds the destiny of the world for good or evil." Supposedly, Hitler eventually captured the sword, and then later in Germany, General Patton obtained it in a battle. At the exact time that Patton won the sword, Hitler killed himself. At least, that's what the movie claimed. It merits some follow-up research.

During the break, I talked to the lecturer, who asked if I have ever attended an Ira Progoff journal writing workshop—serendipitous that it has come up now, since I registered to participate in one next week.

She then told me Edgar Cayce often refers to Carl Jung in his works. Based on Tom's suggestion, I have just begun reading Jung's book *Memories, Dreams, Reflections.* Somehow everything's coming together in a synchronistic way.

After the break, the facilitator led us in guided imagery. He took us back to the time of the Essenes to a temple on a mountain. When I arrived on that sultry day, a long-bearded, elderly man greeted me by name.

In my meditation, I ended up sitting alone in the temple exploring the issue of how we live on after our physical being has died. At one point, my mind played tricks on me. My grandfather, who died when I was eighteen years old, told me there is more to come once we leave the physical world as we know it and enter into another realm.

Unfortunately, before he could tell me more, the instructor slowly brought us back to reality. I'm left with new feelings of wonderment.

The session ended after we formed a rotating, double circle and looked into one another's eyes — young, old, Hispanic, Anglo — and sang a mantra-like song about God and peace, over and over as we moved from one person to the next. At first, I had considered sitting this "dance" out but then decided to go with it. I'm glad because I experienced a most unusual and powerful connection with others by singing and staring into their eyes.

Now I'm home on my bed reflecting on the day. When I first came home and told Daryl about what took place, he called me a lost sheep looking for my flock, but that's not exactly true. I'm just curious to see how others interpret the world and how they think and feel. I also want to learn more about my inner self — my spirit, soul, and unconscious. For me, the best way to do this is by exposing myself to various people and experiences. In doing so, windows open for me to peer within.

October 19, 1983

I went with Cynthia, my one friend who's always ready for new adventures, to meet Bhek Sinha, the guru whom his followers refer to as Maharishi. The incense in his apartment reminded me of what it would be like in some faraway Indian mosque. The eclectic group of people who gathered greeted us with open arms.

I listened carefully the whole time he preached. He spoke of unity with God, the eternal, blissful one. He discussed love through moral, emotional, biological, psychological, and spiritual ways and the interdependency of it all. He feels our American traditions and customs are detrimental to finding God. He talked about reaffirming what we have daily, i.e., "My body is beautiful. My life is beautiful." Sinha said that life-affirmation comes before self-realization. He suggested we each choose to be a loving soul, and from that, we will reach Godly consciousness.

He spoke of the ten necessary moral values by which to live: non-violence, truthfulness, freedom from misappropriation (Don't take what doesn't belong to you.), devotion, non-attachment (individuality), purity, contentment, persistence in truth and beauty, self-study (study of the wisdom of God) and devotion (worship, prayers, and meditation of God).

Throughout the sermon, I kept wondering what I was doing at some guru's apartment on Miami Beach overlooking the ocean. While his messages were meaningful and positive, something within kept telling me I didn't belong there.

November 5, 1983

This morning in meditation class, the last thing we did was go into a guided reverie, sit under a tree, and follow where Jean, the facilitator, took us. When we finished, she asked us to come up with an affirmation to describe what we experienced. My affirmation was that I am a channel of power and love. It seems as if the primary purpose of this workshop was to help us reach a connection with God.

Service to God and man is supreme in this philosophy of meditation. The God Jean mentioned does not seem different from the one I learned about in Judaism. She said Christ a lot, but I can block him out and just get into the spiritual realm that fits for me.

Jean told me Jung was a religious man and Freud wasn't at all. She said it's what led to a split between them. According to her, believers often are envied by those who aren't — Freud looked at Jung as having something more.

November 10, 1983

Sonia and I talked about listening to our inner selves. She told me how she once took a different road than her intuition was telling her. Sonia found detours and roadblocks everywhere. From then on, she knew to listen more carefully to the voice in her head. I'm paying attention.

November 19, 1983

I was sitting on the bench at the bandshell, listening to a conversation with the "preacher" and a woman. She asked, "Why is God so good to me and not to others?"

He replied, "We can reason that God may help us find good if we properly accept the suffering we have. Instead of blaming, we must realize that this life is filled with some suffering. This will teach us to have patience and to love others." That didn't answer her question.

Then another woman sat down and said, "Do you mind if I listen? Jesus came into my life seven years ago." The conversation continued as the first woman talked about how she feels God is love. She was much broader in her thinking than the man and new woman. She claimed we each believe in God in our own way, that we are all equal, and that everyone on earth is the same.

The woman new to the conversation kept quoting Jesus. The other one debated whether one must believe in Jesus to go to heaven. In any case, I had to move on. It was more than enough for me today.

November 25, 1983

I found this in Chrys' numerology book on the number twelve, my number: "Thus, the vibrational force under the number belongs to the developed soul who has accumulated unusual inner strength through many and varied experiences.

"Foresight and acute perception make you a visionary. You are idealistic and feel compassion for all types of people, regardless of station in life. The desire to uplift others brings out the teacher in you. You can be a memorable teacher, speaker, preacher, or writer whose deep understanding of people's needs inspires them and opens new avenues of expression within them. Your talent for educating others cannot go unrecognized for long, and probably, you will become famous. You are the specialist who seeks accomplishment rather than glory but who always seems to gain recognition at the same time." I'll take it!

December 25, 1983

Tom told me a teacher in a theology class he took years ago declared, "The three major questions in theology are: Who am I? Where did I come from? Where am I going?" As he explained, this is the ultimate existential crisis.

Another question he suggests we might ask is: Is there someone greater than myself to live for?

February 17, 1984

Today is the last day for the missionaries at the beach before they head elsewhere. These people come, preach, and then move on.

They're talking about Jesus Christ and how we are all sinners. According to them, if we accept Jesus, he can change us. I don't get how people devote their lives to spreading the word—trying to convince others that their way is the right way—the only way.

April 15, 1984

Tom talked about how he was cloistered in the priesthood. I asked him what that was like. He explained it as "a focused life with no outside distractions. You focus inward, so you become contemplative, and you contemplate life at a prayerful level."

April 27, 1984

I just did I Ching, and this is what came up for me. Establish your goal and purpose, and the law of affinity will attract you to all those who will aid you in the fulfillment of your desire.

Salute the Divinity in everyone you meet. The past is dead. Nothing lives but this moment. Change your present thoughts and keep them that way, and you will affect your destiny.

I am on a spiritual journey. Sometimes, I lose track of that. Does everyone experience this searching? I wonder.

May 26, 1984

Chrys explained that she always asks for help from a higher source, which to her is God. She gets the messages through masters and spirit guides. Part of what she does is channel energy. She claims that while some of the Moral Majority people say that her work is the devil's work, they get in a circle and pray for others just as she does.

June 19, 1984

I'm at a transcendental meditation lecture. They are talking about meditation being the process of "falling awake—unbounded awareness." They claim a meditator's functioning level is better and more powerful. As one's mind settles down, it gets quiet and then becomes alert. One's body supposedly gets a good rest. They also said that with TM, people begin to act more in accordance with natural law.

August 26, 1984

Some woman just stopped by where I'm sitting under the palm tree and out of nowhere told me she used to put more investment in one's intelligence but realizes it's what's in the soul that counts. That's my food for thought for the day.

September 6, 1984

In the book *Why Bad Things Happen to Good People,* Rabbi Harold Kushner says God doesn't cause our misfortunes. Some of them are caused by bad luck, some by bad people, and some are simply an inevitable consequence of our being human and mortal—living in a world of inflexible laws. I never considered life's randomness, but maybe that's the only answer there is.

Rabbi Kushner believes we should pray to God for strength, hope, and courage. When they appear, we know God is there to answer our prayers. The rabbi believes tragedy is not part of God's plan and God is not responsible for it. Thus, we can turn to him when a tragedy occurs. Also, he views God as not in control but instead sees him as a source of comfort and faith. This way of thinking makes sense to me.

A good question to ask is, "Now that this has happened to me, what am I going to do about it?" The rabbi feels we shouldn't ask why it happened.

October 5, 1984

I was thinking about what my mom said about making sure to thank God for my dad's recovery.

Her messages are strong, but they don't fit for me. All I know is that I'm glad that my father is better. Maybe it's his doctor who deserves the thanks.

October 6, 1984

Today is Yom Kippur, and I'm not sure how I'm feeling. Yet, I couldn't help but pray all morning for something to smooth Carol and Bill's pain. Does praying matter? Does it bring comfort? Is there someone on the other end? At this point, nothing seems to help after Steve's untimely and tragic death.

I told Adele I felt more confused about all of this than ever before. I am having such trouble knowing who and what I'm praying to. I have so many unanswered questions.

October 7, 1984

Tom said God is different for every person and can never be summarized. That doesn't help me in my search.

The book I'm reading mentions that God is inside us and not an external force. Tom says God is not what we can picture in human terms, but something more. I'm beginning to understand on an intellectual level but not on an emotional one.

March 16, 1985

Esther explained that our faith must come in the belief that God is with us. She believes one never has to feel abandoned. I'm listening to anyone who can help me understand.

March 24, 1985

When we got home, Michael told us he was up later than usual because he was praying to God. He explained to God that Zane was too young to die and was a good kid.

March 28, 1985

"When the student is ready, the teacher will appear" is attributed to Buddha Siddhartha Guatama Shakyamuni and the Theosophists. So far, it has been true for me with Tom, who appeared when I was ready to open myself up to the spiritual world.

March 31, 1985

I took Chrys with me last night to the pipe ceremony. As soon as we walked in, she told me the auras of the people there were sending off negative energy. She later explained how she first spent time protecting us and then whispered that I didn't have to take in anything that didn't feel right.

The apprentice to Sun Bear, John Pele, brought sea glass, sage, and mullein to smoke. He passed around a shell with the mixture in it, a bird's wing to fan it, and a pipe. Whatever was in the pipe was no longer burning when it came to me, so I just went through the motions.

He spoke about his past life filled with drugs, alcohol, divorce, and mental institutions. He found this group of people and discovered his place among the medicine people. This Great White Brotherhood is way beyond me. Chrys said I'd find a gradual opening up as a result of this experience.

May 29, 1985

When I was walking on the Broadwalk today, Joseph, the old philosopher, stopped to talk. Out of nowhere, he told me he's grappling with the issue of God. When I asked him what God meant to him, Joseph replied that God is the creator. So, at least he's firm on that.

Then later, I was having a somewhat mundane conversation with my friend Gayle, who always walks along the sand carrying a heavy backpack. She abruptly changed the subject and told me she feels God is light, electricity, and energy. Interestingly, I didn't initiate the issue with either of them, but both just started talking about God. Am I sending out some vibe?

August 27, 1985

I've been reading *Tales from the Secret Annex,* Anne Frank's book of short stories. She possessed such a strong faith in God. Where did her feelings come from? Was she taught to believe at a young age? How is it that some people know God regardless of their religion, age, station in life?

September 10, 1985

Lois said she wishes she had more faith like Gerry Bell. We tried to figure out how one develops that faith. Does it come from being indoctrinated at an early age or needing it because one is lost and in search of something bigger than self?

October 24, 1985

We just got back from a lecture by Yosef Mendelevich, the Russian refusenik, who was tried in the Leningrad trial. He claims he survived by sheer faith and talked of how he prayed constantly. I am in awe of people who believe so strongly.

November 16, 1985

Mickie Carden told me God knows just how strong we are. She believes God never gives us more than we can handle. I am not so sure about that.

December 5, 1985

Rabbi Sufrin responded with "Please, God" to almost everything I said. I've never heard anyone else do that.

January 3, 1986

I'm at the bank. The teller has all kinds of Jesus messages around her station, like, "He has promised eternal life."

"I can do all things in Christ who strengthens me." Not my speed, but she believes. I'm not sure how she gets away with posting these thoughts in the bank.

January 11, 1986

After the Holocaust film, some woman asked me where God was through all of this. Fortunately, Sister Noël was standing nearby and answered by saying that God created us with free will. She made it clear that man was responsible.

February 22, 1987

There are never any guarantees. I do my best to live each moment as it comes. Some experiences are unexpected and completely out of my control but affect me, nonetheless. I appreciate the mystery of life and find the element of the unknown adventuresome and exciting. I haven't yet decided if I am a fatalist, feel I have control, or if something spiritual rules my destiny. I wonder if I'll have this figured out by the end of my life.

March 16, 1988

Gene Greenzweig's lecture at the Holocaust Center: *Where Was God? Where Was Man?*

"Not everything is within our realm of understanding. We must know that before we begin.

"As our culture has developed, there are no absolute values. The ultimate corruption was that society didn't place enough value on human beings. How do we react when we see evil? Man has the potential to reach the highest or go to the lowest depths. The real question is not where was God? The question is can I still believe in God?

"The first principle in Judaism besides God is that man has free will. He has choices as to whether he does good or evil. God has to stand back and let man practice that free will.

"Survivors differ in their thinking. Some lost their faith, while others grew to embrace it. Some had it, lost it, and regained it.

"The strongest form of resistance was that people fought to keep their value systems. By remaining firm in their faith, that was their answer to the evil they confronted.

"God stood aside and did not intervene, but he was a reaffirmation that gave people the faith to go on. Our responsibility is to continue it.

"Jews have lived by a standard. We can't have a relationship with God based on asking for favors.

"Man is put on earth to make this a better place to live. God may not answer us when we want him to, but he does answer us. He has been alive in our history.

"God should be our role model. Good and bad will happen, but we have to look to God as our teacher. The struggle is for us to change/repair the world—to make it a better place to live. The reaffirmation for the survivors was to have children and grandchildren."

March 21, 1988

This morning while I was meditating after my run, Ann Marie walked up the path. She asked if I was praying. I don't consider it praying—more that I am gathering my thoughts and resources.

April 10, 1988

In Rabbi Kingsley's remarks today, he explained that God's domain was the heavens. According to him, God made man to help him on earth since he can't do it alone.

April 29, 1988

I was walking onto the Broadwalk when I noticed a circular rainbow surrounding the sun. It felt like an omen that good things were coming. Of course, I made a wish. Are wishes prayers?

May 6, 1988

Frankie, from the Golden Sands, just asked me if I believe in God. He then asked what my religion is. When I said I was Jewish, he told me he had always heard that Jewish people don't believe in God. What a misconception! We need to educate one another, which, of course, I did.

September 18, 1988

I'm watching *The Last Temptation of Christ* and don't understand some of it. There is so much I don't know. I have lots of questions, which I'll ask Tom about.

Did Christ think he was the messiah? Did he disown his mother before leaving? Did he bring Lazarus back to life? Why does he say he is going to baptize everyone with fire? Did Jews have a baptism, and what did it mean? Why did Jesus get so angry? Did he believe he had to die on the cross? If so, why did he feel that way?

October 25, 1988

I'm almost done reading *Many Lives, Many Masters*. It deals with reincarnation and is probably one of the best books I've ever read on the subject. Do I believe in this? I'm not sure but am intrigued with the concept.

November 27, 1988

Over the weekend, I noticed a book in Chrys' bathroom—the kind to pick up when one has a question. By chance, I opened to the exact passage I needed to read.

My question had to do with my book, *A Slice of Life,* and the movie that George Zelma is planning to make from it. The answer was to have faith. Once I read that, I finally felt as though I could breathe again. I was beginning to give up hope, so I needed the reminder.

February 22, 1989

I brought to book club the tape Chrys made on past life regressions to share with everyone. As soon as we put it on, I was on my way. I first saw a cobblestone road, a village home, and a big, loving, caring peasant mother. It was just the two of us, and there were positive feelings along with good food.

The second scenario took me elsewhere. I began as a baby. Within a matter of minutes, Chrys said we were to meet up with our soul mate. At that point, I instantly grew up and found myself with Tom. I have no idea what it all means, but I am certainly open to the possibilities.

December 6, 1989

The woman across the aisle from me just took out her rosary. Maybe she'll pray for all of us on this turbulent flight. During stressful times, it seems people find comfort in their religious rituals.

February 1, 1990

When Sondra stopped by my chair, she asked what I liked about the ocean. I told her I like looking north, south, and east and seeing vastness with no end. I also said that although I'm unclear about my feelings about God, when I'm at the beach and look around me, I believe that some greater power created this.

September 27, 1990

We ate hurriedly and then went up to Lois and Shelly's to pay a *shiva* call. We were there in time for the *minyan*. I appreciate the traditions, community, and familiarity with the prayers in Judaism that bring solace. When a room full of people gathers to comfort a grieving friend, something meaningful happens.

February 26, 1993

Earlier today, I was talking to a man who is a journalist with the *New York Times*. He told me he believes that God writes our life story, and when he finishes, we are born to live it.

March 2, 1993

I grew up with a good amount of superstitions — like throwing salt over my shoulder to reverse bad luck or chewing on a piece of thread when my mother was sewing a button on a piece of clothing I was wearing, so she wouldn't sew my brains together. Tom recently told me not to worry about black cats walking crossing my path. He said it's all pagan beliefs, so it's one less thing to concern me. Of course, none of it makes sense, and to think I went along with it is even crazier.

April 6, 1993

Yesterday, when Jude was ranting at the office, she mentioned she had to put everything into God's hands. It reminded me it would be a good idea to call upon my faith (whatever that is at this point) to help us through the rough times. I must believe I don't have to do it all on my own as I sometimes think I do.

June 18, 1993

The woman in the card shop on Hollywood Circle told me she writes and talks to God all the time and feels God never sleeps, so her dreams are his work. I let her talk and did my best to listen and not judge or disagree. I just wanted to pick up a few cards and get out of there as fast as possible.

July 24, 1993

I now understand that being affiliated religiously is important—especially for younger boys and girls. Therefore, my job as youth director does have a purpose. Hopefully, their association with this Jewish youth group will create memories that will be enough to make them want to remain as Jews living a Jewish life. Why is it important? What does it all mean? Do the teens ask these questions? I don't think I ever did and, instead, took my religion for granted.

September 30, 1995

I just heard this quote by Pierre Teilhard de Chardin: "It's not about humans having spiritual experiences. Rather, it's spirits having human experiences."

October 11, 1995

Wayne Dyer talked a lot about God and his relationship with Him. Through meditation, he feels God's presence. He described the blissful state of mind he is left with after meditating. For sure, I don't experience that.

He believes the ultimate purpose in life is to find God. What happens to someone if they never find God or never even search for him? Does that mean their life has no purpose? I doubt that.

October 13, 1995

Adele believes there is a flame within each of us ignited by God. I told her I don't have any clear sense but continue to search for how God appears to me. When I'm in nature and at one in my surroundings, I believe there is a God, but I don't have the feeling that he sits on my shoulder, lives within me, or speaks to me.

November 19, 1995

The best part of the evening was talking to Norma's husband, a writer and an artist. He spoke about his spiritual search—how he feels that God is universal energy. He believes God is part of man, and man is part of God.

I am in deep search. I don't know what I'll find, but I keep looking. I wish I understood God—who, what, and how that energy and power fit in my life.

November 20, 1995

At Book Fair, a psychic talked about her mother, whose name was Rose. When her mother died, each time she saw a rose, she felt a deep connection to her mother—almost as if she felt her mother's essence. It helped me understand what's possible.

So, when I ran this morning, I decided to call upon some angels to take over and help me and us. It's probably the craziest thing, but yesterday when the psychic was talking, I decided it was worth being open to this. I have nothing to lose.

March 30, 1996

Stan believes that God is the natural energy that comes through us. He feels what we get from the ocean and how we feel when we're out here is what it's all about. I appreciated hearing his perspective because it makes sense to me.

April 20, 1996

I continue to listen, search, and wish for a specific sign to help me believe in God and turn my faith over to Him (or Her). The physical, natural evidence surrounding me helps a lot, but I'm still not 100% convinced. I'm not sure what it will take.

But more and more, I am telling myself I must have faith—that I need to turn my troubles over to a higher power. I wish I could believe in it enough to feel secure that it will work.

May 16, 1996

Sister Trinita Flood's funeral was at St. John Vianney Seminary, where she had been the dean after she retired as president of Barry University. The sanctuary was filled with priests, nuns, and other religious figures, and the mass had all the rites of the Catholic Church.

I had many questions as a result of being there today. After, when I met a brother from Barry University, I asked him why someone becomes a brother rather than a priest and what the difference is. He responded, "It is God's choice. A brother takes all the same vows as a priest but doesn't become ordained into the priesthood." He also told me that a vicar is a priest.

Later, when I discussed this with Tom, he also explained that the difference between a priest and a monk is that priests receive the sacraments and undertake the duties to celebrate them. Monks take on solemn vows of poverty, chastity, and obedience but practice monastic living alone or with other monks in a community. They choose a priestly life of meditation. Tom said he is a monk in many ways—not that I didn't already know that.

May 31, 1996

I was excited when Margaret invited me to be part of her group last night. Of course, I immediately thought about mine. Group for me is a place where I come together each month with my close friends and share about our lives in an intimate and meaningful way. I was excited to think I might be experiencing a conversation among Margaret's friends similar to my Group. Boy, was I surprised! I suppose my first clue should have been when she asked me if I wanted to wear a scarf that evening. Since the outfit I was wearing didn't need a scarf, I was perplexed.

About fifteen or twenty men and women around our age came over to Margaret's house and had a "meeting." They sat on the floor, which seemed strange. Then all of a sudden, they started praying to Allah. I was lost. The group, which I later learned were Sufis, appeared to be worshipping a guru, whose photograph Margaret had put on a low table in the front of her living room. In all probability, he was most likely their teacher — maybe equivalent to clergy, although I'm not sure.

The guru's mother, who was there, is a Jewish woman about ten years my senior. After the prayers, I asked her how it feels to have a son who is a guru. She told me he has always been like the Pied Piper and has had a following for most of his life. She described him as having been to another world and back.

Meanwhile, Larry sat in the kitchen eating lasagna. He wanted no part of what was going on in the living room. At some point, I joined him.

July 5, 1996

In the last month or so, I have begun to surrender to a higher power. I got to a point where the burden became overwhelming. I needed help. The moment during my jog — that rainy, dreary morning when I was feeling so desperate, I said aloud, "Okay, I can't do it alone." Right after that, I saw a beautiful rainbow and knew someone was listening — whatever that meant.

September 11, 1996

Last night before falling asleep, I could hear my mom praying. I'm guessing that after my father died yesterday, she found comfort in prayer.

For a few months now, I have seen how calling on my father-in-law to surround, protect, and care for Daryl has been helpful to me. Now, I will do the same with my dad. In real life, he was always there for me. I'm hoping it will be a source of comfort to think of him surrounding me in white light and helping me get through difficult days. Hopefully, his soul will envelop and protect me as he did throughout my life.

Jerry and I talked about how we can plan and feel in control, and then something happens that wipes it all away. It's a reminder that there must be a greater power.

September 18, 1996

Last night when I walked around the neighborhood, I saw a fabulous sunset. I've decided if there is a "committee in the sky" to color the sunrises and sunsets, my dad is the chairman. He will always be in my thoughts during those most glorious, wondrous moments.

October 27, 1996

I was listening to some testimony about God in which a woman talked about how she turned to God in times of trouble, prayed consistently, and found solace. A recent survey in the United States claimed that 89% of the people believe there is a God or a supreme being. I can't help but wonder how accurate that is.

November 9, 1996

I miss my father, but I am keeping his spirit close to my heart. Not five minutes after he died, I turned to my mother and said, "If there are angels, Daddy is up there with them."

January 9, 1997

At dinner, I talked to Daryl and Arnie about how I call on their father and mine to watch over us. They both told me they "speak" to their dad and wish he was here to give them advice. How unusual to talk to the Saferstein men about anything metaphysical.

February 26, 1997

I decided since it was 4:00, and I came home early because the Student Awareness Day finished on time, I would take a walk in Greynolds Park. On my way, I started to call on my angels, wishing I could find a way to deal with Allan. I also wanted these angels to encircle Daryl and help him handle the issues confronting him.

I was experiencing such anxiety that I felt like I was never going to get through another day. Daryl and I have been off the wall—a tough week and time in our lives. We had initially thought moving into the office and buying Allan's practice was a good move. However, now that HMOs have taken over, patients aren't paying what they used to. His office overhead is choking us. Because Allan was sick and out of the practice for a while before Daryl bought it, many of his patients had left and found podiatrists elsewhere. So, from the start, the numbers were not what Daryl had expected. What a mess this has been and a financial disaster for us that set us tumbling way down.

Anyway, I walked along the covered bridge path, someplace I never go alone. I just wanted silence and solitude. I sat for a few minutes on a bench looking out on the water, watching a duck sail across the lake and leaves swaying in the breeze.

After about an hour, I cut through one of the parking lots, thinking and plotting what we could do to salvage our financial state. And then, out of nowhere, a white Cadillac pulled up with Allan in it! He said, "I was looking for you." It's absurd to think that anyone would ever expect to find me at Greynolds Park on a Wednesday afternoon at 4:45. It just doesn't happen. Why would he even have said that?

In my head, I had been thinking about Allan, how Daryl could ever pay what he owes him, and what it would be like to face him. Any of those thoughts brought me fear and anxiety. And yet, the second I saw him, a calm came over me. I was confronting my fears.

Allan and I walked and talked for a long time. I left him one-and-a-half hours later as the sun was setting in the western sky—an unbelievably beautiful, colorful sunset. My dad gave me that gift.

I think I believe in miracles for the first time in my life. My meeting up with Allan this afternoon perfectly describes the Hebrew word *bashert*—meant to be. I have to believe this was Divine intervention. Of all things to have happened, this was the next step in my journey.

Once again, we have not crashed to the bottom. We are saved. I'm not sure how or why, but we have surrounded ourselves with good people who mean well.

February 27, 1997

After I saw Allan, I thought there would be no way I could have ever written a better script. Maybe *Celestine Prophecy,* which had seemed contrived, wasn't, after all. Perhaps that's the way it happens. I mean, how is it possible that this could have come to pass as it did, short of a miracle?

Later. Tom on angels: "Angels are an extension of ourselves. They're a spiritual reality—people we've known. Sometimes they intervene."

Yesterday felt like an angel moment I may remember forever. On Tuesday, I had picked up the little angel Dinorah had given me and told her I desperately needed help. That was undoubtedly the beginning of what feels like being blessed by the angels. After that, Daryl got in enough money to pay his bills except for the exorbitant rent. The landlord is letting him stay in the office until he finds a place to go.

I had prayed to Aunt Fay and my dad to spray angel dust on this journey of *A Necklace of Pearls.* It worked! Today, my agent, Arthur Fleming, sent me a letter to tell me what he has done to get the book to publishers.

March 2, 1997

Some woman in the airport is talking about how one day, when she needed help desperately, a man was right there for her. She then said, "It made me believe in guardian angels." My ears perked up. On a car's bumper today, I saw a sticker that said, "I believe in angels." I feel in sync with the universe.

March 11, 1997

Ron and I talked about him being a monk for eight years, leading to him discussing Jesus. I have a hard time attaching a quality of divineness to a human being. As a person, a teacher, and a master, I believe Jesus was special, but I'm not sure any person should be worshipped. Ron feels that something somewhere had to have been happening for an event as cataclysmic as the worship of Jesus to occur. What was going on around it?

March 25, 1997

There have been moments of despair when I have found myself surrendering and begging for help, courage, strength, and support. Rarely, though, have I lost sight of my blessings.

March 30, 1997

I stopped to watch an early sunrise service down by the turtle hatchery. Lots of nice-looking men dressed in white shirts and ties sat listening attentively. As I walked farther south, large groups of people were baptizing others in the water. A young guy just walked by dripping wet. I overheard him shouting, "I've been saved." And so it goes on this Easter Sunday at Hollywood Beach. What I don't see are women in bonnets like the old song I remember hearing.

July 25, 1997

John, the minister, just came by my chair at the shore to talk to me. He said he finds good comes to people who believe in God during tough times. Maybe it's true, but what about those who don't turn to God? What happens to them?

August 3, 1997

In the book *Rolling Thunder*, I loved the part about the sunrise. "When the sun starts to rise, we make our prayer, and when you see the bottom of the sun, that's when it ends."

October 31, 1997

In Gerry's letter, she wrote about her priest's sermon. He talked about how on a rainy day somewhere, the sun was shining elsewhere. He likened it to God being there even when we can't see or feel his presence.

November 14, 1997

Yesterday, whenever I felt a little shaky, I told myself, "The universe will provide." It was enough to keep me from making myself crazy. Do I believe it? I'm not sure, but I'm open to its possibilities.

Sometimes, I am afraid to have faith. This past year has been challenging. Stan repeatedly says, "Keep the faith," yet he is a non-believer.

What does that mean? I have faith in myself and my own power, but perhaps it's enhanced when turning it over to a higher power. Who is the God I believe in? I am not sure. I have no visual image. If anything, God is a spirit connected in some way to the angels who are watching over me.

November 15, 1997

Nancy and I discussed the higher power and how relying on it for guidance and support is such a help in times of need. She told me she has begun to pray and has received what she has needed, thus, experiencing the power of prayer. She explained that before she has necessary conversations with her husband, she asks for ways to say things so he will listen and hear.

I could relate and understand in a way I might never have before had I not experienced all that I have this year. Being in situations where I have desperately needed help, guidance, and support has brought me to this place.

November 16, 1997

As I walked and saw the neon pink and orange clouds of the sunrise, I thought of my father—his presence in my life and how much more spiritual I have become since his death. I do think of him as an angel working with God. And yet, I understand that life's mysteries are beyond explanation, despite my efforts to find meaning in my existence.

November 25, 1997

The more I read and listen to others, the more I tell myself it makes sense to accept the idea that there is a higher power—a creator of all of us—who awaits our acceptance, which brings creativity and possibility.

If nothing else, it brings comfort during anxious moments, and that sure helps. But also, I'm noticing signs along the way worth paying attention to.

I hear people say, "Just show up. Be present and stay in the moment. The rest will follow." More than ever, it's what I am doing lately.

December 6, 1997

Timing is important. I don't think there are coincidences, but more, events unfold in their own time as we move along the path. When I stay open, the experiences present themselves, and I grow as a result. That's how I am choosing to live.

December 8, 1997

Last night on my way home from dropping off my mother, I thought about ways to deal with some of the unsettled issues in my life. I contemplated turning it all over to God and believing whatever I am to experience is part of a bigger plan—one I may not have answers to now and may not ever understand.

Am I becoming such a believer I could do that? Is it possible for me to tell myself each time I get a questioning, uncertain pang that all I have to do is trust God has the answers, and I can count on it? If that's true, and I can avoid some anxious feelings, I could free myself in a new way.

To some extent, this means giving up control. If I turn it over and allow myself to believe there is a God, I might live a more peaceful existence.

And so, last night, I began to look for other paths to deal with some of this anxiety. When the bad feelings overwhelm me, I tell myself all I have to do is know God has a plan I must trust. I am hopeful this will continue to become more evident to me.

Maybe if God is too big to grasp at times, I can be satisfied with my angels. There is a sense of comfort in all of this.

December 15, 1997

There are people in my life who have a strong sense of belief. I admire their faith and maybe even envy it. After all, it is a gift to have a steadfast belief in something we can't touch, feel, or see.

I don't have to discuss it with anyone. I just have to experiment with it. I need to pay close attention to what comes my way, stay open, and show up all of which I have been doing.

February 6, 1998

I began reading Brian Weiss' book *Only Love is Real*. In it, he talks about how souls sometimes reconnect in different lifetimes what a comforting thought. While running today, I thought about how some people feel like soulmates and might have been in another one of my lifetimes. The good news is that we can choose to believe in reincarnation or not since no one knows for sure.

April 2, 1998

During difficult times, I am beginning to understand a more spiritual world. I'm finding myself:
- Exploring the possibilities.
- Paying attention.
- Looking for answers.
- Getting a clearer sense.
- Knowing I must keep at it.
- Being grateful for the anxiety passing.
- Wanting it all to go away.
- Finding that in time it does.
- Counting my many blessings.

April 16, 1998

It takes an awful lot for me to let it all go. But I also know that lately, I have constantly been praying. My group of angels is busy at work these days. I call on them all the time. I've got my father protecting us, keeping us healthy, cushioning us, and ensuring everything works out. I have Sylvia as project director in charge of seeing that the bankruptcy all turns out fine. I have Bonnie watching over Marcia, the court-appointed trustee, making sure she is good to us and knows that what we say is true. I have Grandpa Wolfe in charge of overseeing Joel, the lawyer. I have to believe this will work out and that we are on the back end of everything now.

April 22, 1998

Rabbi Cohen is talking about a rabbi who lived four hundred and fifty years ago and said, "I must keep God before my eyes always. Every righteous person walks before God. When any person stands or sits, he does so as an ordinary man bowing before a king. We, as Jews, only belong to God. Our souls belong to him."

I wonder if I am going to feel differently when I leave Poland. Hopefully, I can take some of these feelings back with me. I'm getting closer to God in this journey I'm on. Somehow, I am beginning to understand the side of life that can't necessarily be touched or seen but exists in a way I never knew before. I want to learn more. I want to open up to that world. I want to live my life as a person who can give and receive, teach, and learn.

April 28, 1998

During the *Yom Hazikaron* commemoration, I gazed at the glowing candle. Its burning flame made me think about life—how we each house our flame within and ignite one another's with our love, caring, thoughtfulness, and spirit.

My goal is to keep my flame lit and to kindle others'. I have a job to do. I must remember and follow my calling and my mission.

April 29, 1998

Rabbi Andrew Paley in services: "We say the same prayers every day so we can get beyond them. That allows us to go past the routine and get to more. The wisdom and beauty of the words are right at hand and let us stir our internal juices."

Rabbi Cohen is talking to us about what Orthodox, Conservative, and Reform Jews have in common. He began by saying how in Majdanek, he looked for the "Orthodox" shoes and couldn't see any differences. The boundaries we set in our lives separate us unnecessarily. The March of the Living leaders have decided to experiment and put us all together for prayer. The goal is to help us see the bigger picture, who we are collectively in the spirit of love.

May 1, 1998

I held onto the Wailing Wall and prayed to feel God's presence and be aware of the moments when He exists for me. I asked to be the best person I can be, maximizing my potential and touching lives in a way I haven't yet.

May 16, 1998

The sacred spirit of Israel sunk in this time around. I found myself aware of a special feeling deep in my heart. I closed my eyes when I heard the song *Jerusalem of Gold*, pictured the view from the promenade, and felt a peacefulness come over me. I am left with greater faith and a deeper connection and belonging to the Jewish people.

May 29, 1998

I was thinking about what Danny said about God closing one door and opening another. How heavy those doors sometimes feel and how much help I sometimes need to pry them open.

June 10, 1998

The birds are chirping as they fill our yard with their song. I read in a book recently where the author described birds singing as "God's music."

June 21, 1998

Earlier today, I was walking along the sand at sunrise when I came across a group of twenty or so people—two men, two children, and the rest women. They were singing gospel songs praising God. I sat on one of the lounge chairs, listened, and watched as they rolled their arms over their heads while singing of their joy in the Lord. I left just as some woman began preaching while many cried out, "Amen." What an uplifting moment in time to see all of them rejoicing with glee.

October 11, 1998

Rabbi Simon mentioned that when he hears people say they don't believe in God, what he hears is that they aren't sure who God is. He feels it's okay if one doesn't have irrevocable faith in God.

According to the rabbi, we cannot approach God face to face, yet He commands us to look at Him. God comes close to people who come close to Him. Traditionally, Jews believe that to understand what God is, we need to do *mitzvot* and there are many to choose from—613 to be exact!

December 5, 1998

In talking to Tom today, I'm aware of how I've evolved since our first conversations during our seminars by the sea in December '82 and January '83. I better understand what it means to have God in my life.

Tom read me a piece on grace. I never understood grace before, but I do now. He said it's the experience of the gates opening — being able to move past the roadblocks, crossroads, and impasses — when one has the go ahead to the next step.

December 10, 1998

Oprah talked about how she prays to God daily to come and sit in her heart. She lives in the moment and gives gifts when she feels the desire, not just at Christmas. She claims that her gift to herself and her friends is her encouragement that they too are their own best selves.

December 31, 1998

This year, I became more aware of all the people in my life who were there to support Daryl and me through our arduous journey. Somehow, whenever I needed someone, they were there. I began to develop faith and an understanding of God, which I never had before. No longer do I feel as if I have to do this by myself. Instead, I have a strong sense that a higher power is guiding me. It's mainly through people themselves that I have seen God. I have never felt alone in all of this.

April 26, 1999

Seeing the Dalai Lama in person was thrilling. Adele and I sensed tremendous joy emanating from him as he walked down the aisle at the auditorium at FIU.

He talked about the positive, constructive mental states — kindness, tolerance, goodness, compassion, caring, and forgiveness. He believes religions are meant to nourish the human spirit.

They provide an ethical framework. According to the Dalai Lama, "True spirituality is a mental attitude you can practice at any time."

June 2, 1999

I am starting to see how things come to me when I ask for them. The "Ask, and ye shall receive" has truth to it.

June 14, 1999

While I was making the bed today, a thought occurred to me. Am I experiencing what I am because I still have much I need to learn or deal with? Is it true that as we live, we are preparing for the next journey? Are we working through our karma now to avoid doing the tough stuff again in our next life? If so, what are the lessons I must learn?

Am I supposed to learn to do for the greater good and not for any recognition? Should I be giving glory to others while at the same time taking none for myself? Is one of the lessons for me to learn what it means for someone to be power-hungry — to need all the control? Must I just observe it all and accept someone who is consumed with self?

June 19, 1999

I told Maya how the Jehovah's Witnesses here at the beach bother me because they "peddle" their wares. She knew a few when she was young and felt they at least live close to their beliefs—their commitment to save others' eternal souls and pass along their "Word."

July 1, 1999

I needed time to process and absorb all that had gone on since Daryl's open-heart surgery. It took over our lives and played havoc with them. I asked Daryl what was different for him since his operation, and he said maybe he looks at life a little more philosophically.

What I know is that I feel more faith in God as a result. I used to worry about what would happen to us if Daryl got sick. Yet, although he did, we made it through and came out the other end, maybe even better than before since he has a healthier heart and quit smoking.

July 2, 1999

Gerry asked me today if I feel God put me on earth to accomplish my mission—to do His work. I told her I hadn't looked at it that way. But if I step back and think about it, we are all God's creations, so maybe I need to reconsider. Perhaps I am God's messenger that shines His presence on this earth. Regardless, I will continue to be there for others.

September 10, 1999

This week, the Baptists voted to concentrate their prayers these next ten days on converting Jews—getting us to believe in Jesus so we can be saved. An editorial in the *Miami Herald* said that Jews should pray that the Baptists can become more tolerant.

September 22, 1999

I well remember the days when we first moved to Miami. With our babies crawling around underfoot, Kate and I would sit and talk about our beliefs—trying to figure it all out. She eventually became a Mormon, and I stayed where I was with Judaism.

When I spoke to Vance today, I asked why they decided to leave the Mormon church. Kate left before he did. She went back to graduate school and started meeting other people. That's when Kate realized she had no desire to be involved with the church any longer. She was not interested in anyone telling her how to live and what to think.

Kate burned the undergarments the church made them wear. Vance had come home that day to a bonfire outside. She said they had given a whole chunk of their lives when they joined the church. She claimed that the positive of being a Mormon was that she had her five children.

Then one day, Vance opened up the church's magazine and saw a costly fixture they had imported to hang in the new church that was being built. At that point, he realized the church didn't need his money. Vance said the religion was confining and isolating and knew it was time to be out of there. Since he had been pretty high up in the hierarchy, I'm sure it has been a major life change for him.

November 14, 1999

Larry and I talked about God and how he became a believer. He said he first felt it when he was selling books in a low-income, unsafe neighborhood. He felt like God was watching over him. Secondly, one of his friends went to Israel and returned, having become more religious. They began to form a bible study group, and as they got to the second half of the *Torah,* he started to feel as if this couldn't have been written by man's inspiration alone.

February 25, 2000

Fern explained how, when she meditates and opens her mouth in a circle to breathe out, she feels like she's blowing into the universe—the connection to the universal consciousness is there.

This led to a discussion of putting things out into the universe. She feels incredibly connected to that world. Mostly, she just has to think something, verbalize it, and it happens. More and more, I understand that.

She talked about how when we empty our minds, we become clear and what comes in is what we might need to know and hear. She told me how sometimes a voice would talk to her—like on her car ride home when she listened to the voice repeatedly telling her she must write. She said it was so forceful that she had to yell, "All right already. I heard you."

March 6, 2000

The "Let go, let God" attitude makes sense because one worries a lot less and accomplishes more with faith. I'm working on this.

July 2, 2000

Carol has always felt God's presence with her and that she's never on her own to do anything alone. I asked how she developed this absolute faith. That's when I learned that Grandma Wolfe had told Carol this story. When Grandma was a little girl, she had been in a forest and was running scared when God's voice told her not to be afraid and that she would be okay. How lucky for Carol to have learned this from Grandma early on.

July 7, 2000

Lois' Kabbalah teacher explained that meditation helps connect us with our soul. She believes as long as we have God in our hearts, we will be protected in mind, body, and soul. God created the world for us to receive enlightenment.

Three ways to find your soul's purpose:

- Study
- Pray
- Do *mitzvot*

Lois and I stopped at a Messianic Jewish bookstore on our way home. Messianic Jews believe in Jesus as a Jew and call him Jehoshua. They feel he was the messiah of his time. They have lots of books on Judaism, so one could almost be fooled.

I quickly found myself rejecting almost all of it. Unlike Judaism, it doesn't feel legit. That's probably not right of me, since who am I to say what others should believe? Still, Jews for Jesus doesn't work for me.

August 6, 2000

The woman I spoke to today has studied Kabbalah for years and told me mysticism lies in numbers and letters and the meaning attached to them. She explained it's a lot like Buddhism in its belief that the soul lives on.

When I asked Abe Gittelson about it, he said the storefront kind of Kabbalah learning is not the true essence of it all. He believes one must first be a Jewish scholar for many years and understand the intricacies of the *Torah*. He said esoteric teachings explain the relationship between the eternal God and the mortal, finite universe. This is beyond me.

August 20, 2000

I had an interesting conversation about religion with Leonard the other day. When I mentioned other religions, he told me he feels there is only one truth—the Jewish religion. Others may have their beliefs, but he believes that Judaism is the only true way. He sounded like a fundamentalist, and it shocked me. I refuse to believe there's only one truth.

September 4, 2000

Before Howard broke the glass, the woman who officiated the ceremony shared the meaning of the tradition. She explained how in an interfaith marriage, the symbolism is about breaking the barriers and getting rid of what separates people. In a ceremony between two Jews who marry, breaking the glass reminds us there is still suffering in our world, even in the happiest times. Mostly, it reminds us that love, like glass, is fragile and must be protected.

July 5, 2001

The Wisdom of No Escape by Pema Chodron is about experiencing both the joy and the suffering, which occurs in every life. She explains how we must be fully alive, not wasting a moment of this transitory time we, as humans, have on earth. She feels we have the opportunity to experience, think, love, and make other people's lives better. The more I read about Buddhism, the more intrigued I am by it. One quote from the book that I loved is, "Meditation practice isn't about trying to throw ourselves away and become something better. It's about befriending who we are already."

July 8, 2001

I started reading *The Seat of the Soul* by Gary Zukav last night. So far, I understand that the soul is the part that sees the beauty surrounding us and connects with others. For me, one way of my being in touch with my soul is through journaling.

August 31, 2001

I'm working hard to be mindful in the moment:

- To be present in my experiences
- To understand the theory of abundance
- To know what it means to be human
- To feel the feelings as they surface
- To experience shame, truth, and understanding through dialogue
- To know that somehow the universe will provide
- To have a sense of faith
- To understand what it means to be at peace
- To pass along what I learn

I sometimes am in tune, and other times feel like I forget what I need to know. Yet, I am grateful to have gained knowledge, which I am incorporating into my life.

September 27, 2001

Being that today is Yom Kippur, it's a day of reflection. Do I believe God decides our fate today? I'm not sure. Do I think God knows and sees our every deed and every wrong? I can't be sure of that either. I don't see God as one who stands before us making those judgments and decisions.

I spend a lot of time thinking about self-improvement and looking at how I live each day. So, I don't feel like I come to Yom Kippur with a long list of wrongdoings. That's not how I function. If I have done something wrong, I do my best to rectify it as quickly as possible. I want to keep my slate clean, which is why I don't feel fearful that I am standing before God in judgment nor worrying if I will be included in the Book of Life.

If I were a rabbi giving a sermon today, I would talk about how to: live life so as not to fear, live life to its fullest, make each day count, do for others, ensure I am living my passion, and connect with others. This is much of what matters most to me.

October 23, 2001

Sue Rosenblum lost her son in the World Trade Center tragedy. Today, she told me she has found God in everyone who has shed a tear for her child whom they never knew or for those who have reached out to her. Michael Berenbaum agreed that this is where he finds God as well. He said he couldn't see September 11th as Divine punishment, and Sue said she definitely couldn't go there.

October 25, 2001

During these past two days in Tallahassee at the Commissioner of Education's Task Force on the Holocaust, I became more aware of what God is to others. Since that terrible day in September, people have been asking about God as they did during the Holocaust. The answer to where God was is most apparent in the face of those humans who have done good deeds, risked their lives, or were there for others. It helps me understand the divineness within each of us. In times of adversity, humanity surfaces.

Now, I want to live my life from the perspective of knowing, believing, understanding, and living with God in my heart. My work in Holocaust education helps because, as Elie Wiesel and some of the other survivors have told me, what I'm doing is God's work.

February 10, 2002

The other day, I heard a rabbi say there are no new souls. He believes they just keep being recycled.

February 19, 2003

When I think of how awful my mother's condition was last week and how seriously the doctors reacted, it is incredible that she has bounced back. She said it's because people said prayers for her in temple. I can't say one way or another, but I feel that it's nothing short of a miracle, since we didn't expect her to recover.

August 5, 2003

I was reflecting on my experiences having been the result of Divine intervention. I will never forget that time in Greynolds Park when I met up with Allan just when I was desperate to have a conversation with him. Another example was when I scooped up Sophia right before the halogen light exploded in the exact spot where she had been sitting. And then, more recently, when I stopped someone from touching my car right after a live electrical wire landed on it. With those examples from my own life, I believe there is more to our world than we can see or know.

February 7, 2004

At a *shiva* call for Wally's mother, the rabbi talked about prayer by saying we first need to count our blessings—to think about why we are grateful. Then, we need to thank God for these blessings, and after that, we can ask for what we need.

June 10, 2005

It's almost as if all core religions lead to the same path. In the end, it's not our skin color or religion that matters. It helps me better understand the concepts surrounding death, the soul, and the afterlife to know that people of different religious beliefs look at this part of human existence similarly—the universal truths.

June 27, 2005

According to the doctors, Alta's diagnosis is not good, with a slim chance of living. Yet, as I listened to her, I was taken with her strong belief in God. She mentioned how grateful she is, how people's prayers have elevated her, and how she has faith in God's plan. She is the epitome of the power of faith. Her rabbi let her know that her job now is to enjoy her life. He had told the congregation that no one is entitled to anything—that all things we have are God's gifts to us.

October 13, 2005

I'm pretty much thinking that "man-made" holidays are not necessarily where it's at in terms of connection to God. Instead, after my weekend in Colorado with Group, being out in nature and connecting to my dear friends in the way we did through deep conversations is where my spirituality resides.

September 26, 2007

We're in the car leaving Boulder heading to Estes Park. After lunch, Stephanie took us to a Methodist church where they have a Chartres labyrinth. There are the three Rs to walking a labyrinth. The first is walk in release. The second is receive when you stand in the middle, and the third is return when you step back out.

I became immersed in the meditative experience. One of the things that came up for me was to put my father on one shoulder, Cookie on the other, and Chuck guarding my heart.

December 27, 2012

I was putting my groceries in my trunk this morning when a sweet, young woman, who was proselytizing, approached me. Generally, I don't talk to people who try to "show me the way," but she asked me about spirituality. She was surprised that I disagreed when she said people are much less spiritual than they used to be.

We somehow started talking about reading, and I told her I had written a book. She was interested, so that led to a conversation about writing. She had been an English major but doesn't write, although she wants to. I gave her some tips, and she asked me if she could contact me about writing. I had to laugh. Who was converting who?

January 5, 2014

On Friday night, we went to Frank's wife's wake and service. The born-again minister, who preached in Spanish, had Frank's son-in-law translate into English after every few sentences. He tried to persuade everyone to embrace what he believed and kept calling for people to come up to the front to be saved. I found it an agonizing forty-five minutes of him talking about Jesus and eternal salvation. It shocked me that one would do that at a funeral.

January 18, 2014

Last night was Martin Luther King night at Temple Sinai with the New Birth Baptist Church. What an incredibly warm and wonderful evening of prayer with both our choirs singing together. Bishop Curry spoke and rocked the house. I was inspired and moved to tears by the experience of watching our congregants and theirs together. Sitting side by side in brotherhood made me wish this was the way life would always be.

May 27, 2014

Ellen told me she's been doing automatic writing for years. She explained how she protects herself from outside forces because when she didn't, the demons came in, and Ellen had a breakdown. She showed me the composition book where she writes everything down. It was fascinating to see how her writing drastically changes when it is spirits from beyond channeling through her and guiding what to write down.

June 10, 2014

I was with Lily, who was talking about how she left the Mormon church. She became disillusioned by its narrow-mindedness. She told me a little about what goes on in the inner sanctum. There are many rooms and chambers, and as they go further in, they become a more integral part of the religion.

Everyone brings white clothes like robes and hats and changes out of their street clothes before entering to pray. They have secret signals and handshakes. Lily said her parents, who are still active in the church, probably pray for her salvation.

November 3, 2015

Last night was the God Talks class with Rabbi Litwak. We each wrote about some of our issues with God, and then we talked about them.

One of the rabbi's practical ideas was to ask ourselves each night, where was God present in my life today? That might be a way to become more conscious of God. Another was, what question do you want to ask of God? My question was, how can I best serve you?

The rabbi said that watching everyone connect as we did helped him to see Buber's I-Thou come alive. I like that because I can honestly say I now understand that the essence of God is in us and is in our connection with each other. I've come a long way in my search, but I finally feel as if I've landed in a place that makes sense to me.

Reflections on
In Search of Spirituality

Recently, I was listening to the Good Life Project podcast with Jonathan Fields interviewing Agapi Stassinopolouos, the author of *Speaking with Spirit: 52 Prayers to Guide, Inspire and Uplift You*. She asked the listeners to think about the first time we thought about God. I can remember being in second grade sitting on our playground's asphalt and looking at seashells someone had brought home to Cleveland from Florida. I was in awe and wondered how they were created. How did the natural world evolve? Was it God's work? Perhaps that was my first truly spiritual moment.

Reading these excerpts and especially going back to 1974 allowed me to see the journey I've taken to get to where I am today. For so many years, I tried to fit what I thought God was into a neat box in my mind. It took me a long time to realize that it wasn't possible.

To this day, I can't say that I firmly believe in God the way my friend Gerry or my cousin Carol did. They never had doubts. In their minds, they just knew.

I can remember back to the mid-eighties when I had a conversation with Tom about God. I was filled with questions. He responded with something that helped me see that most people do not have a firm belief. He told me that even Mother Teresa questioned God at times. That helped. Since then, I've had various clergy from different religions tell me they, too, continue to search for answers.

Recently, when I read of the rescue workers in Surfside's Champlain Towers disaster or met the United Hatzalah's psychotrauma team from Israel, I reaffirmed my belief that God is within humans who are in service to others. I am comfortable with the image of God as the flame in people that ignites or touches one another in some meaningful way.

I've come to understand there is no one right way to believe. We are more alike than we are different. As I've learned about and observed other religions through the years, I've noticed their similarities. The basic principles most religions have in common are a belief in a supreme being to worship and the importance of treating one another with kindness, love, respect, and compassion.

What I continue to hold onto are the rituals and traditions I grew up with. When I was a young girl, we lived with my mother's parents. My grandfather was an Orthodox Jew who prayed daily.

Our home was filled with holiday gatherings where our family came together to honor the traditions passed down from one generation to the next. I treasure those memories and have done my best to carry them on with my family.

As the years have passed, I've come to understand the difference between religion and spirituality. If I were to describe myself, I would say that I am a spiritual being. I continue to be in awe of all that is not man-made. When I'm at the ocean meandering along the shore picking up shells, I feel all is right with the world. The sea is my sanctuary. I'm happiest when I'm outside in nature. Listening to the birds sing on my morning walks and seeing the colorful clouds at sunrise and sunset is what brings me joy. I love working in my garden, digging in the soil, and tending to my plants with butterflies flitting around me. Given my choice to visit a museum or hike, the latter is always my preference.

On July 10, 2017, I met with Rabbi Mark Phillipe, who led me in a past life regression. It was something I had been curious about for years, and in the end, it was one of the most spiritual experiences I've ever had.

Here, in part, are the journal excerpts I wrote when I came home.

We began with my conjuring up a childhood memory. I spoke of Grandpa Wolfe and how as a young child, I watched him pray. The rabbi had me describe the room and a few other details I remembered. Then he led me on a guided meditation and a quick body scan. After that, he counted backward from ten, and slowly, I was under.

He had me imagine myself on a train and told me to get off and describe a childhood memory. I talked about moving to Texas and having my father greet me at the train station. I described what I was wearing, how my father hugged me, and how I felt in his embrace. I was enveloped in that and became emotional. I sat in the car's front seat with my dad and was so happy to feel his love.

I got back on the train, which then moved backward. When it stopped, the rabbi had me get off and asked what I saw...It was the 1920s, and I was a woman in a *shtetl* in Poland with about fifty, one-room homes made of stone with thatched roofs...There was a little kitchen area, but we needed to pump our water from a well down the street. I had twins—a boy and girl, and they were about three or four years old...

The rabbi asked what we did for food. I told him we grew zucchini, cucumbers, and tomatoes and that our neighbors gave us wheat. "Did you have enough food?" "Mostly, yes," I replied, "but sometimes the children were hungry." "Did you have a house of worship in the town?" "No, but we gathered in a big barn to pray on Shabbat and the holidays."...

I was living a peaceful life, but I was sad because my husband had died...I was the teacher for the community's children. They all learned from me. Life was simple, and I was content...

I got back on the train. At first, it went slowly, but then it began to speed up as I went backward. When it stopped and I got out, the first thing I saw was a magnificent castle on a hill in the distance. I had on a maroon velvet dress with gloves and one of those pointed hats one would wear in Camelot. I remember saying that I was very sophisticated.

A fancy, horse-drawn buggy took me along a cobblestone street as we leisurely made our way up the big hill to the castle, where a servant greeted me. Once inside, my six children and fourteen grandchildren surrounded me. They all lived in the castle with me and my husband, who was quiet and reserved...

The country was Slovakia, and it was during the 1400s. I was also the community teacher and had a large room down in my basement where I would teach ten to fifteen students at a time—even the adults in our community. I learned from everyone and experienced a good life. I wanted for nothing...

The rabbi asked me if I wanted to go back to another life, and I said I did not need to do so. He told me to look down with the help of guides and talk about what I learned. I spoke about how I felt as a teacher—how my family was important to me—how connection mattered—how I was in control and felt positive, happy, and full of love.

...Then, he told me to look up to the spiritual world...He asked me about the cluster of souls I saw. None of them were in human form.

...He asked what I was doing there. I told him I was helping souls get acclimated to being in that realm. "Were you doing life review with them?" he questioned. "No, they did that before they got to me." "And so, you were again a teacher?" "Yes, I was."

He asked me if I wanted to experience more. I told him I didn't need to—what I needed to know was clear to me and satisfied my curiosity. I have been a teacher in my past lives—an evolved soul. Nothing surprised me. It all fits.

...When he brought me back, we talked about souls and why we return...He said at times, the more evolved souls come for a specific purpose. I immediately thought of the people in my life who I am helping and got choked up. I then understood they were part of the reason I was here. What I have done and am doing in their lives is meaningful. The rabbi told me he thinks I'm an advanced soul.

What happened in this past life regression confirmed what I know and feel about who I am. In that respect, the experience for me exceeded anything I dreamed it could have ever been.

Journal Prompts

·   What does God mean to you?

·   Describe any religious traditions you grew up with. What did they mean to you when you were young? Do you follow any of these traditions now as an adult?

·   How do you feel about organized religion?

·   In your opinion, what is the difference between spirituality and religion? Which resonates more for you? In what way?

·   Who do you turn to when you are experiencing a crisis? How does that feel?

·   Write about your spiritual journey. When did it begin for you?

·   When did you first begin to question the meaning of God?

·   What did this chapter lead you to think about?

Seawind Beach Retreat

One learns first of all in beach living the art of shedding;
how little one can get along with, not how much.

— Anne Morrow Lindbergh

April 25, 1994

When Adele and I walked tonight, she told me that for my fiftieth birthday, she would like to treat me to a week at the beach. What a gift! I am overwhelmed by the gesture and am also excited at the prospect. Since it's for my birthday, I suggested I wait until December, but she thinks I should go there this summer. I'll see what Jacky at Seawind Apartments says about availability before I make any decisions.

May 6, 1994

It's the middle of the night, and I've been up for an hour and am not falling back to sleep any time soon. My mind keeps looping back to what Jacky told me today — that I can have a room for one month this summer, and he'll only charge me $500. What a generous offer.

May 7, 1994

I saw Jacky on my walk this morning and had another conversation with him. Once again, he offered me the place, this time for three months. He said I could stay from mid-July through mid-October for $1,200. The longer we talked, the more I realized he was serious, and this was something I could possibly do. The only thing I can't have for that price is air conditioning, but with the ocean's breezes, I'll be fine.

Jacky was concerned about how Daryl will react. I am not worried.

The more I think about it, I must do this for myself. I plan to accept this gift for two reasons. First of all, I have dreamt about spending an extended period of time at the beach but never thought it could happen. Secondly, I have been working hard this year with two jobs and have been under a great deal of pressure, so it will be an excellent way to decompress. The timing couldn't be better.

The beach will be my haven and my studio. I can come and go whenever I want during those three months. I plan to read through some of my journals for the first time, take out meaningful excerpts according to various topics, and put them into a book—something I've wanted to do but have not had the space to begin.

Later. Just as I was writing under the palm tree opposite Seawind Apartments, Jacky came by and asked if I wanted to see the room—an efficiency apartment. I went upstairs and am pleased because there will be much more privacy than if I took one of the two rooms downstairs. I can sit on the balcony without seeing the Broadwalk if I don't want to, which means I can be as secluded as I like. So, that's decided, and I'm all set. Now, I need to present this to Daryl.

May 9, 1994

Daryl and I went to the beach for an Italian dinner at Angelo's tonight. After he enjoyed a big plate of spaghetti and was content, we sat on wooden lounge chairs down by the water.

I explained about the book I wanted to write from my journals, the prospect of my studio by the sea, and my thoughts about all of it. I let Daryl know my staying at the beach can serve as my Mother's Day, anniversary, and birthday presents all in one.

Since I am always coming up with something new, Daryl never knows what's next with me. He gradually got used to the idea and responded as I knew he would. He agreed to it but also wondered aloud what the guys in his card game would think. After all, it isn't exactly what most traditional wives would do.

I explained that he just has to tell them I'm writing a book. If I were an artist and had a studio where I would paint, maybe people would better understand. Few take my writing seriously, but hopefully, now they will.

Daryl hated the idea of my not having air conditioning and also of him having to schlep back and forth to see me. He wishes all he had to do was think of where to take me for my 50th birthday and just buy me some luggage. Sorry. Not happening.

By making this decision to rent a room at the beach, my life suddenly looks quite different. My needs have shifted. I had planned to spend a little money on what I thought were much-needed clothes, but that no longer seems important. I can certainly survive with what I have.

May 15, 1994

I told my parents about the beach apartment and my writing. They were excited for me, wanted to hear all about it, and were supportive of my dreams.

Honestly, I feared they might disapprove of my leaving home for such a long time and didn't expect they would understand. Instead, my mother surprised me and said they would give me money to make it happen. Never would I have imagined they would have reacted in this positive and generous way.

June 18, 1994

I dreamt last night about a computer and how to get one. I certainly can't afford to buy one. When running today, I decided I'd write the excerpts on legal pads and be okay with that. It will have to do. Besides, that way, I can work under my favorite palm tree or by the shore. Otherwise, I would have to be in the apartment plugged into electricity.

June 26, 1994

While I can't take time off from the Holocaust Center, I can at least spend my two-week vacation in solitude. I know for sure that I'll have to give up certain parts of my life if I truly intend to write this book.

Jacky told me a few men from South Carolina are repairing roofs down here and are staying in three of the rooms. That's good news because it'll be better not to be alone there. With only five efficiency apartments in all, it should be quiet enough to write.

I told Daryl last night he can come and go as he pleases. I hope to be at the beach much more often than at home   definitely on the weekends.

July 7, 1994

Before work, I went to Office Depot and bought legal pads, manila folders, scratch pads, a bottle of ink for my fountain pen, envelopes, and a new Rolodex. My list of preparations is slowly dwindling.

July 8, 1994

Next week at this time, I will be an official resident of Hollywood Beach. While it excites me, moments of doubt creep in. It's as if I'm ready to go, and then I wonder if it is unrealistic and crazy to be leaving home for three months.

July 9, 1994

Jacky just came by and told me I can move in as of right now. I can't believe it! I certainly didn't expect that. He said the room was vacant, clean, and ready for me. I'll probably move in mid-week.

July 10, 1994

Tom woke me early this morning to tell me he broke his leg sailing. He jumped in the water feet first and didn't realize it was shallow. Not good!

Since I was up, I decided to get ready and leave for Seawind Apartments today. I figured there was no reason to wait any longer. It made sense since Daryl is a zombie on Sundays after softball, and Mike and Sara are going away for the day.

I got dressed, took out my first stack of journals and money to pay Jacky, and began to pack up the car. I made spaghetti sauce for Daryl and Mike and then left.

I stopped at Publix and Eckerd's and shopped for what I needed. Then, I came here, paid Jacky $660, and now owe him $540. He told me where to park; my room is 108; and my parking spot is C. Having my own parking place at the beach is an extra bonus.

It took me about a little over an hour to settle in. I wanted everything to be well-organized, simple, and as uncluttered as possible. The space is perfect for me with just the necessities — a bed, couch, comfortable chair, tiny kitchen with a stove and refrigerator, small bathroom, table for two inside and one outside that seats four.

I would have been in a fishbowl downstairs. The umbrella on the table up here blocks the morning sun, so I can be out on the terrace in the shade starting early in the day. So, here I am on my first day of this great adventure. I don't need a whole lot else in my life if I have this. Slowly, I will shed layers.

I wonder how Daryl will do with me away for so long. Right now, he is being supportive and seems comfortable with my decision. I hope he'll come here often and will always feel welcome.

My ten journals are in the cupboard under the kitchen sink. I'm sure no one would ever take them. That feels like a secure spot.

On the balcony. I hear someone playing the saxophone at the Riptide to the north. Skaters are congregating down below on the corner of Nevada Street. Lifeguards are packing up and heading home. The beach with its spectacular view of the ocean in front of Seawind Apartments could be anywhere in the world.

I spent a few hours today reading the first journal I wrote in 1974. I'm probably copying more from it than I will use, but in entering what I've written under different subjects on my legal pad, I can see this will be a somewhat complicated process. Hopefully, it will flow once I get the hang of it.

What will this journey feel like as I walk back through my life over the past twenty years? Will I find jewels worthy of sharing with others? Will this help me decide how I want to spend the next fifty years?

Later. Pink clouds fill the skies over the sea, casting their rosy reflection upon the greenish-blue water. I am in awe of nature's magnificence and can hardly believe this is going to be my front yard for the next three months. To the west, the sun sets—an orange, purple, and pink sky signals the ending of this day—the first of my retreat at Hollywood Beach.

I read more from my journal when I got back inside. It's strange to go through my life in this way. My journal entries are sporadic, since I wasn't writing often at that point in my life.

In October '75, the recap is: Daryl had been practicing podiatry for three years; I was proud of him for how well he was doing; Rebecca was in pre-school; at two, Michael followed his sister around wherever she went; I craved more excitement in our lives and relished any free moment I had to myself, which was almost non-existent in those days.

I continually feel the need for space to write. With two jobs and life in general, my time is often not my own. Hopefully, being away these three months will be all I have dreamed it to be. I've always known that I couldn't start reading my journals unless I cleared the space and stepped away from my life as I usually lead it. I just never dreamed it would happen so soon.

Granted, I can't stop working—not an option. My job this summer at the Holocaust Center is to clean out all of the files. I have no programming to plan for the next few months, so that should be easy enough without pressure. Directing the youth group is on hold for the summer, which means I have nothing to think about there until after the High Holidays.

What will I cut out from my life this summer? For one, I will not be home much aside from probably once a week when I drop off my dirty clothes, pick up outfits for the week, put the journals I've read back in my safe, and take new ones to the beach. Being home that one night will be enough to catch up with whatever I need to do around the house, spend time with Daryl, Michael, and Sara, and maybe do some cooking for them.

Aside from that, I intend to curtail my interaction with people outside of work. I'll still walk with Marsha and Adele here at the beach, and Daryl will come a few nights a week, but other than that, I don't intend to see any of my friends—except for special occasions. I'm sure some won't understand, but I can't let that stand in my way. I must set clear boundaries.

I've only given my phone number to Daryl, the kids, my parents, and Tom, so I don't expect that I will receive many calls. That alone will be a welcome reprieve. If I want to talk to anyone else, since the phone in my room only accepts incoming calls, I will use the pay phone down on the corner of Nevada Street and the Broadwalk.

July 11, 1994
A fabulous, easterly breeze is blowing into my room this morning. I was up an hour or so during the night but fell back to sleep. By 6:15, I was wide awake and watched the sun rise over the ocean—

a glorious way to begin the day. I went out to run and saw several of the early morning regulars out exercising.

July 12, 1994

I've finally arrived back at the beach after a long day at the office. My legs are killing me from doing the steps here at the apartment. I walked up and down them way too many times on Sunday when I was moving in.

However, as much as they hurt, I smiled as I took off my jewelry and heels while making my way up the stairs. I walked in and immediately opened the sliding glass doors. Now, I'm out on the balcony, and it's like entering another world — transformed to a different place in time. The ocean is calmer than it has been. Hardly anyone is out on the sand. People are walking, skating, biking, and running on the Broadwalk.

I am so grateful to be here. There is nothing like coming home to the ocean — a perfect setting to write.

July 13, 1994

Daryl came here from his office, arriving when I did. We walked down to Nicky's for dinner. After we ate and meandered back to the apartment, the two of us sat out on the terrace. Daryl had full intentions of spending the night. However, because there were no ocean breezes, the room was too hot for him, even with the fans blowing air. He let me know there was no way he could stay. Was I disappointed? Not really. It means I won't have to listen to the television playing in the background, and it also gives me time to write in silence. So, I kissed him goodbye, and off he went.

I'm out on the balcony — the best seat in the house, for sure. The stars are ablaze on this beautiful evening at the beach.

July 14, 1994

After Daryl left last night, I read my journal and marked all the passages about the kids. Just when I was thinking how much I wanted to talk to Rebecca, she called me. I read her some of the parts I had written about her. We had some good laughs. I told her I wouldn't write her a personal will because it's all in my journals. She said she would excuse me. I probably will anyway.

When I hung up with her, Mike called, so I read him the passages I had written about him. He seemed to enjoy hearing them. I also spoke to Sara, and she caught me up on Camp Sinai's happenings, since she's working there as a counselor.

I read before I went to sleep. I had both fans on for a while and eventually turned one off. I was not that hot, but now I doubt Daryl will ever stay here if it's like this. He made that clear.

July 15, 1994

Adele met me at the beach last night, and we walked. She came upstairs after and talked about my book for a while. She told me she expects I'll probably be evaluating my writing and, as a result, may even change what I write in my journals from now on. We'll see. So far, I notice how I repeat myself, sometimes leave out details, and have not examined an issue as deeply as I wish I had.

Later. I went down to the beach, but there was a big, gray cloud out east. Just as I settled in, it began to drizzle, so I came upstairs. It's peaceful, windy, and quiet. Having a place to run to and not having to leave the beach and go home because of rain is a welcome treat.

Now, I don't have to go anywhere until Monday morning, so there is no reason for me to get in my car until then. I'll go home after work on Monday and stay there that night.

Later. Daryl, Sara, and Mike came here for dinner tonight. After the kids left, Daryl and I checked out a circle of people near the shore. They were playing drums and tambourines and were singing songs about Jesus. We didn't stick around.

Daryl asked me how I was coming along with the book. Since I want him to feel included, I read a few passages to him. Quite honestly, to me, they sounded ridiculous and uninteresting. I'll have to find my voice and figure out if this is going to work. I am filled with tremendous self-doubt tonight and am at a loss for how to describe it.

July 16, 1994

My walk with Marsha this morning gave me the chance to talk about what I've been feeling, which will be important to do periodically. I explained how this experience seems to have more ebbs and flows than I would have expected. Mostly, it's a matter of whether I have anything from my journals worth sharing. It's the question marks about all of this that leaves me unsettled. Last night, I was ready to pack it all in; however, I am determined to stick with this regardless of whatever happens.

Later. Sara and Mike came up to the apartment at lunchtime, and I made them tuna salad sandwiches. They like the idea of the beach apartment. What's not to like? I guess they might be around a bit more now, which works for me. I cherish my time with them.

Daryl came to the beach much earlier than I had expected. He first stopped and bought me ice cream—so thoughtful of him. We went in the water and talked and played in the waves for about an hour.

Then we came upstairs, showered, made love, and prepared dinner. We had roasted chicken, salad, and baked potatoes and ate out on the balcony.

When we finished, I read him an excerpt from my journal dated June 8, 1981, saying that someday I want to live on the ocean and write. I also said that perhaps I'd write the modern version of Anne Morrow Lindbergh's *Gift from the Sea*.

Daryl's watching a Marlins baseball game but is sitting on the terrace looking into the room. I told him he couldn't smoke inside, which upset him, but that's the way it has to be. He plans to leave when the game is over.

July 17, 1994

I woke up just in time to go out on my balcony and see the sky ablaze with color. I'm glad I didn't miss this sunrise. Every time I look up, there are changes as the oranges, pinks, purples, and yellows begin to move from the shoreline up into the dark, grayish clouds, which are suddenly turning neon pink and tinting the sea below.

At midnight last night, Tom called. The loud ring in the quiet of my sacred space scared me. He had fallen out of his wheelchair and was panicked. He's barely managing with his broken leg, and I am concerned about him. I didn't fall back to sleep. At that hour of the night, lots of people were on the Broadwalk with loud motorcycles and trucks in the alley—a Saturday night of partying.

Maria was in Daryl's office yesterday. I couldn't believe he had given her my number here. I let him know that was unacceptable. I had told Daryl early on not to pass out the number to anyone, but he didn't listen to me. The last thing I want is phone calls. To have this experience as a retreat, I need to narrow my world as best I can.

July 18, 1994

Last night, I saw several rainbows throughout the evening and made wishes on each one. There is nothing like looking out at the ocean and seeing a blaze of colors painted across the sky. The extra special treat was when one turned into a double rainbow—an awesome sight.

Today's pre-sunrise began with muted colors. It never became dramatic until seconds before the sun began to ascend over the horizon. At that time, the clouds turned sparkling pink. The radiant sun burst through and sent a golden glaze over the water. The glory of nature astounds me, especially here.

I'm going home tonight. I have a short list of things to do while there, plus Daryl is having two teeth pulled, so he'll need some TLC. I'm going to make cabbage soup for him, which he'll then have for several meals. In addition to him coming here a few times a week, I'll probably continue to head home on Mondays after work as a way to stay connected, which is essential to both of us.

July 19, 1994

I've got my legs up on the table on my terrace. The fabulous east breeze cools me down after walking into my sweltering apartment laden with bags. Daryl called me a bag lady when I left the house this morning and went off to work. There's no stopping me tonight. I am beginning to catch onto the process and am now on journal #5. I may be onto something as I experience a wide range of emotions going back in time and reading about my life.

July 20, 1994

At the office today, two people from Steven Spielberg's organization came to learn more about our oral history project and to get help in starting theirs. The Shoah project, the proposed name, hopes to interview 50,000 Holocaust survivors.

On my way back to the beach, all I could think about was what a sharp contrast these days are. Aside from the unusual excitement of today, little is happening at the office. My days there seem like a total blur. The hours pass slowly as I look to get back to my haven. Once here, I feel like a different person invigorated by the salt sea air.

When I drove up to Seawind Apartments, Al was sitting outside. He mentioned he notices I'm up in the morning even before he is. Today, I was coming back from my run when he took off for work. He asked what I was writing, and his reaction to hearing that it's eventually going to be a book was, "It's not about me, is it?" It amazes me how many men ask me if I'm writing about them.

July 21, 1994

I'm glad it's Thursday. When today is over, I will have my weekend again. They've always been special. However, now that I'm living at the beach, they're all the more so.

I love the simplicity of this place and the life I am leading here. I put out a picture of the kids and a few scenic pictures Lois sent me from her trip. I have no other decorations anywhere except shells. I am collecting those slowly and arranging them on the counter.

While I do the slightest amount of housework here, today I vacuumed because there was so much sand on the carpet. I've appreciated having a break from cleaning. I love knowing when I put something down, it will remain untouched by anyone else. Also, when I walk in, everything is as I had left it, which doesn't happen at home. I have no one here to clean up after but myself, and I pretty much take care of everything as I go. Plus, getting rid of any clutter or unnecessary items has brought me a sense of freedom. I am beginning to understand what the expression "less is more" means.

The phone just rang, but I'm not answering it since I'm writing. At times in this process, I get easily side-tracked. The interruptions send me off to another place and getting back to work becomes difficult. I am training myself not to reach for the phone just because it's ringing.

July 22, 1994

When I finished my run this morning, I walked along the shore lost in reverie and found some beautiful shells. I am pretty good at picking through those strewn along the surf's edge and uncovering ones with only a small portion showing. I long ago became a shell snob and only want the perfect shells without broken or ragged edges.

I've had a busy morning. I walked to the bank and then drove to the grocery store. I unpacked the groceries, swept down the steps, and got ready to head to the beach. I also bought an umbrella, since mine is bent and faded. With my errands done, I have the weekend free to do as I please. I came to sit under my palm tree and realized I had forgotten my journal. I went up to get it, came back down, and when I got ready to write, I didn't have my pen—so up again I went. Finally, I'm settled and ready to get to work.

Later. I've had a quiet day of journaling, excerpting, walking along the shore, napping, and feeling content. I've made a significant dent in journal #6. I also showered and took off my nail polish. I am living as simply as possible with the bare essentials only—a big change from my usual way of living.

July 23, 1994

After my run this morning, I saw Harmen, my neighbor next door. I apologized for our noise last night when Linda, Steve, Stacy, Laurie, Daryl, Mike, and Sara were here, but he was kind and blew it off. We had a brief but pleasant conversation about my writing and his work as a music therapist.

A storm has blown in from the west. Earlier today, all the winds were coming from the east, but they've shifted direction. Huge gray clouds are beginning to cover the baby blue skies. I feel sprinkles of rain and know what's coming my way. Everyone else has cleared off the beach, and I had better head upstairs before the raindrops blur my ink. It's moments like this when writing with a fountain pen becomes problematic.

July 24, 1994

An older man came and sat next to me on the bench at Garfield Street. He began talking about the weather and asked where I was from. He was born in Yugoslavia but came to the United States as a teenager. His entire family died in WWII. He enlisted in the Navy and became a pilot. He told me they saw Buchenwald early on and tried to tell the world, but no one listened.

In 1941, he was seriously injured and was in a coma for eight days. They brought him to Hollywood Beach Hotel, which he said was a naval hospital. He heard the doctors say he wouldn't make it until the next day, and although this man couldn't talk, he said to himself, "Not only will I live, but I will someday come back here." And here he is. I love the stories strangers on the beach share with me.

July 25, 1994

Yesterday I opened the cabinet below the sink, and a little mouse ran out. It scared the shit out of me. I'm fine as long as it disappears, and I don't see it again. Daryl thinks I should set a trap, but the thought of finding a mouse in a trap does not appeal to me.

July 26, 1994

I had a restless night's sleep. I got to bed later than usual and didn't need the fan until the middle of the night when I woke up in a sweat. I was out of bed before 6:20 and ran with a glorious, colorful sunrise. It was helpful to have that in the background as I struggled to run on the sand to Dania Pier and back.

This is the first time in my life I have ever lived alone. I went from my parent's home to Ohio State and then lived with them after I graduated until I got married six months later. So, being on my own like this is different from anything I have ever experienced. In these moments, when I am alone, thoughts and ideas float up from a place deep within.

I couldn't do this during most months of the year. In September, my life will dramatically change once I begin working with the youth group again. This current silence is precious because I know what's ahead. Daryl told me the vice president of education at temple called and left a message saying he wants to discuss programming for next year. I'm not ready for that. Soon, I'll be taking my two-week vacation, which will give me a total retreat.

August 4, 1994

The phones at the apartment are out of order and will be for the rest of the summer. The guys announced that the repairman from Southern Bell told them it's the equipment inside, and without Jacky here, they can't fix it.

Now no one can contact me unless they do it through Daryl or call me at my office. I will have more control over my time if the outside world can't reach me. That means I can sit here uninterrupted for hours at a time. The only downside is that if there is an emergency, I'm without that lifeline. At least, I'm only twenty minutes from home if Daryl needs me.

I went downstairs to call him from the pay phone and met up with Mark, who is staying here. Unlike me, he's freaked that we can't use our phones anymore.

At around 4:00, I went out and sat near Uncle John, one of my favorite lifeguards. We were chatting when a man stopped to talk to us. He has run thirty marathons—five in Catalina, seven at Pike's Peak, one in Athens, Greece, where the original marathon took place, and various other sites. He told us that he bicycled around the world for a total of five thousand miles last year.

He's a retired college professor of psychology. The three of us talked about nature, life, philosophy, and psychology. He's also a big fan of Leo Buscaglia, is fascinated with the work of Jacques Cousteau, and idolizes Mahatma Gandhi. As we were parting, he said, "I wonder if we met because it's reincarnation or because we read the same books."

Every once in a while, I meet someone here who stimulates my thinking and fascinates me. This man, John Scott, was one of those people.

August 7, 1994

Jacky would have a fit if he saw what was happening out front. There's a big party going on all weekend on the downstairs' patio and in the yard. One of the guys just brought two more twenty-four packs of beer. They've got WSHE blasting on the radio and are attracting a bunch of sleazy characters. It's like a free-for-all. I'm staying close to the shore now and am grateful that the crashing waves block out all the noise. Our quiet haven is currently as noisy as Hollywood Café.

When I took a walk to get away from the chaos downstairs, I saw Ed, who combs the shore for shells, holding his hands behind his back. I've been seeing him for years, but this was the first time we spoke. He asked all kinds of questions about my writing and talked about some of his favorite authors. Ed told me I need to be patient—that writing a book doesn't happen overnight.

I asked him what he used to do for a living, since he had told me he was retired. I learned he had been a diamond salesman as well as a stockbroker. Until then, our conversation had been interesting, but I immediately lost interest when he went on about the stock market. As soon as he asked me to go for coffee, I told him I had to get "home" and quickly headed back here.

August 8, 1994

I picked up May Sarton's journal to read, and something she had written prompted me to write. She described how her daily walk with her dog and cat cleared her head after work. It reminded me of my meditative walks on the shore after running in the morning or eating dinner in the evening. There is nothing like meandering along while humming *Eli Eli* with waves lapping onto the sand, sometimes bringing gifts from the sea. As Sarton described, "It airs my head and clears away the tensions of the morning work."

August 11, 1994

I generally don't spend time wondering what people think of me, but lately, it has crossed my mind, since Daryl says many people are asking him what's going on with us. No one I know would ever leave home like this and still be happily married. Yet, this is what I must do to live the life of a writer finally.

Tonight I decided to go to Nicky's for dinner and have a slice of their delicious Sicilian pizza. It was crowded, and Jack, my favorite waiter, was busy. He asked if I minded sharing my table. How could I refuse him since Jack always treats me like a queen and lets me sit and write for hours on end while he just keeps refilling my diet Coke? I knew Jack didn't want to turn anyone away.

And so, this motorcycle dude sat down. I smiled at him and continued writing. After a few minutes, he started a conversation by saying, "A book or a diary?" I answered him, and we ended up talking for a little while. At some point, I mustered the nerve to ask him about the mushroom tattoo on his arm. He laughed. "Remember those psychedelic mushrooms? Well, one morning, a friend and I were stepping through cow shit picking mushrooms. The next thing I knew, we were watching *All in the Family,* and I was having this put on my arm while drinking tequila and mushroom juice. Hardly hurt—like a pinprick or stepping on a sticker." I can't even imagine letting someone do that to my arm.

As soon as I finished my pizza, I left to come back here. While I enjoy the occasional conversations with strangers, I'm happiest when I am left alone to write.

August 12, 1994

Today begins my two-week vacation, and I don't have to leave Hollywood Beach. No one is counting on me for anything for the next sixteen days. My time will be mine to spend as I please—the ultimate in stepping away from my world.

Rain is moving north over the water. Way out at sea, there's a water spout that looks like it's dangling in mid-air, rapidly moving along while being dragged by a black, large, ominous cloud. I am holed up in my little cocoon.

Later. I'm out on my balcony, since it's only drizzling now. I love the briny smell of the air after a storm.

I just read in journal #15 how I was questioning why I was filling journals as I was. Even back then, in 1983, I had written that someday I would probably go back and pull material from them. How did I know that?

August 13, 1994

When I saw the neighborhood runners who were on the Broadwalk today, Harvey called out to me, "Ah, the missing wife." Later, on their way back, I ran with him and Ira, who immediately said he thinks what I'm doing is great. While it doesn't matter, it's lovely to know some people understand.

As I was sitting on a bench writing earlier, some guy walked by and declared, "Don't write me a letter. I'm here." What people come up with!

Then, a little later, another man sat down next to me. He didn't say a word, but I kept feeling him looking over at me. After a bit, he murmured, "Geez, it must be one hell of a diary you're writing." I just smiled, and he got up and left.

August 14, 1994

I decided to start writing in the oversized journal with at least two hundred thin-lined pages and a cover with an impressionistic painting of the gardens at Giverny by Monet. I doubt I'll finish it in these two weeks, but I sure as hell am not going to want to carry it with me when I go back to work. So, we'll see how I do.

Being down by the water is different from when I am on my balcony. I can smell the salt sea air, hear the birds calling as they fly above the water in search of their next meal, feel the mist from the waves slapping onto the shore, and see seashells as they wash up onto the sand. At this moment, I feel one with nature—communing with all that surrounds me.

I've completely lost track of time, which feels great. However, the tide creeping up close to my chair reminds me that many hours have passed.

August 15, 1994

Occasionally, my thoughts drift off to work—the Center and the youth group. Once I return to my life after my vacation, I will have to give both more attention. For now, I need to lie back and enjoy this well-earned time at the ocean. Knowing that Rositta won't be in the office while I'm away makes it easier for me. I have also thought about some friends' problems and realize I need to free my mind of everyone and enjoy the solitude. The less I see and talk to others, the clearer my head will be to do what I have set out to accomplish.

The beach is pretty deserted, with only five people for as far as I can see in either direction. Earlier, when I took a long stroll along the shore, a man walking by me looked at me and proclaimed, "This is heaven." He isn't far from wrong.

While I'm always looking for shells, my contemplative walks are more about taking a deep breath and digesting all I have been reading. Walking back in time requires me to reflect and then process all that lies before me on the pages of my journals.

Later. It's close to midnight, and I awoke a while ago. Since I couldn't go back to sleep, I decided to come out on the balcony to sit under the stars. The dim porch light is enough to write by. It's a crystal clear, gorgeous night, and not a soul can see me. It's a good thing since I only have underpants on.

August 17, 1994

Daryl will be here at some point, but I'm not sure when. My thoughts once again turn to May Sarton and how she wrote in *The House by the Sea* that having an appointment in the day changes things—shifts the point or focus of concentration. I wonder how long I have left to work until Daryl arrives, how much I can accomplish until then, and how my day will change when he's here. I'm distracted.

August 18, 1994

I continue to savor every moment of this beach life—reminding myself that I still have lots of time—more than I ever dreamed I'd have at the ocean. Yet, each second remains precious and meaningful.

Here I sit in the shade of my favorite palm tree, still in my bathing suit, feeling hungry but unwilling to stop writing and reading. The sun is about to set—a peaceful time of day, my most favorite after sunrise.

August 19, 1994

One way to kill a quiet day is to have a group of about twenty kids and adults settle near me. As soon as they arrived, I picked up and moved far away, but it didn't matter. One of the teenagers had a boom box about two feet long and played awful-sounding, loud music. He walked over to where I was and stood right in front of me with it blasting. I kindly asked him to move, but he didn't budge. Some people have no respect for others' space.

Later. As the group got ready to leave after a few hours here, one of the little girls began to clean up all the litter they had strewn on the sand. Everyone else just walked off toward the Broadwalk. I went up to her and let her know how I noticed that she cared about keeping our beach beautiful. She had such a big smile on her face when I told her that and continued picking up the mess the others had left.

Now, just a few minutes later, from where I'm sitting, I can see the last kid being stuffed into a crowded van. Quiet is about to return after their massive onslaught. I am so ready to embrace the peacefulness of the beach and am desperate to enjoy the rest of my vacation alone and uninterrupted by anyone.

Later. I just spoke to Daryl and am so pissed. He told me that Tom called and is coming here. How on earth is that happening?

He's fed up with New York and trying to get around with his broken leg. But why now while I am on my long-awaited vacation of seclusion? I don't want him or anyone else here. I crave absolute silence and solitude. How ironic that just a little while ago, I thought the group of families was an invasion. I have waited all year for the chance to have two solid weeks to myself. Regardless of what happens, Tom is ruining that for me. I feel angry and violated.

Everything will change with him here. It already has with just his phone call. I've been content wrapped in my little bubble, but now all I can think about is this is the ultimate disruption of my work, time, and space—my most treasured moments, which are rare in my life. His coming here feels like a test. I am not ready to share these days with anyone! I can't believe all I longed for has been taken away from me with one phone call.

Why? What am I supposed to be learning from all of this? And more importantly, how will I act when I see Tom? I feel fire coming out of my eyes—like my anger is burning through me.

A few days ago, I wrote about how one never knows what the next call will bring. I do not like having anything sprung on me at the last minute. I am someone who functions best when I can plan out my days, and while it isn't always possible, it's the way I am happiest. This is not what I had in mind.

Later. I'm back out on my balcony and finally alone. Daryl came, and I made dinner for us, which also wasn't in our plan. He was going to stay away this entire week and give me my space. Anyway, I vented to him and could tell Daryl felt awful for me. Together, we went to the airport and picked up Tom, who told us he had been a mess this morning and decided on a whim that he needed to get out of town. His broken leg and all that's transpired had put him over the edge.

He's staying at Howard Johnson's, although Daryl did offer to let him stay at our house. Tom made it clear he was here for himself. He told me he had no intention of ruining my vacation. I think it's too late for that. Can I blame the almost full moon on my reaction earlier?

I did whatever I could to be welcoming, although I'm not all that sure it came across that way. Hopefully, we will figure out how we can co-exist on the beach together as we always have in the past. For now, I guess I just need to let it go, which is a challenge for me.

August 20, 1994

I went over to see Tom this morning. We had a meaningful conversation during which we talked about how we felt yesterday. Tom told me he knew I would be angry, but he needed to come to the ocean to heal. I was grateful we could express our honest feelings with each other. Of course, that's how we have always been. It helped to clear the air, which was necessary to make this work.

Later. What a difference twenty-four hours makes. Earlier, Tom said something to me about my "killing" him, and I told him yesterday I wanted to. At least, we can joke about it now. Our time together will be different than it generally is since I am less apt to want to be with him as much as I normally would. Somehow, though, I feel sure we will find ways to make spending time together memorable. He is so glad to be here, and I understand that. Tonight, he told me about how much pain he has been in and how he already feels better just being at the ocean.

I have one more week left until I go back to work. The moment my thoughts drift to the office or my life away from here, I quickly lasso myself back. I don't suppose I could do what I'm doing forever (at least not yet), but I could for a whole lot longer.

August 22, 1994

Silence surrounds me. I have given a strong signal to everyone to keep away today. I plan to savor every moment because next Monday, I will be back in heels and in reality, but for now, I want nothing to interrupt my flow. I told Tom he needed to stay away, and he promised he would honor my wishes. Daryl already knew that today was a day to leave me alone.

By hardly talking to anyone and living alone, I rely on my thoughts without others' agendas to muddy the waters. I wouldn't understand this had I not stepped away from my daily life as I'm used to living it. Without outside influences, my mind is much clearer and free to access what's coming from within.

Plus, I can't seem to get enough of this writing, sitting on my balcony listening to the ocean, feeling the cool night air, and watching the electrical storm way out at sea. A full, orange moon is rising over the water.

August 23, 1994

On my run this morning, I thought about my life. The financial pressures remain my only albatross. At some point soon, I plan to jump into my take-charge mode and get the ball rolling. Daryl and I have some hard work ahead of us to get things straightened out. However, right now, that's all the thinking I want to do about this.

While jogging, some guy called to me and suggested I check out the turtle hatchery. Sure enough, when I got down there, baby turtles were crawling around. I watched as they slowly made their way to the ocean—another of nature's miracles.

I looked down a little while ago and noticed I had run about six miles with my t-shirt inside out. That's a clear sign of where my head is at.

In my journal, I just read about a man I had met at the beach in 1984 who imparted some great wisdom during our short conversation. One of the things he said is how we become prisoners of our possessions. The simpler we live life, the easier it is for us. I am glad to have shed so many layers during my time at the beach.

I doubt I ever would've been able to plunge into this project if not for this time here. I thought that at age sixty-five, I would retire and make room to begin, but I am glad I didn't have to wait until then. In response to the letter I wrote to Leo Buscaglia, he mentioned that he'd spend a year in seclusion to recharge after his promotional tour. While I am busy working on my book, that is exactly what I am doing.

I am learning more about the ocean and its ways. Each day differs with the atmosphere, the winds, and the sea constantly changing. For now, all I want is to live, sleep, breathe the ocean.

I just heard whistling, and down below was Tom walking along on the sand with his crutches. He called up to me and told me he was glad to be back with the human race. Tom asked me to stop by later, but I told him I probably won't. He waved and moved on. We have figured out our rhythm.

Later. I'm having a late, quiet dinner by myself. I have a mellow buzz from a glass of wine and marvel at this life I'm leading far removed from the way I usually do. Will I remember this solitude come January when I'm in the midst of some of my busiest moments at work?

August 25, 1994

Here comes the sun. It's so rare to see it rise right out of the horizon unencumbered by any clouds—just a large neon red ball rising from the depths of the sea surrounded by a colorful glow. Two birds are flying in front of the sun, looking like specks. The few white, fluffy clouds hang suspended in the sky. I soak it all in.

These are quiet days with few interruptions. Tonight, I told Daryl how different it is this week. Until now, I would sit by the water, and inevitably, someone would stop to chat, comment on my writing, or ask me a question. This week, it's almost as if I have a protective shield around me because hardly a soul has even said hello. I must be giving off vibes that say LEAVE ME ALONE!

Later. A few of the guys are home today, which is unusual for a Thursday with no rain. Al just went off fishing. Frank is playing mellow jazz music, which fits the day perfectly.

Living alone has helped me become resourceful and independent and not rely on anyone else. The fact that I fixed the screen door by myself says it all. I would never even attempt it if I were home.

Later. I'm the only woman staying here at Seawind Apartments. The men have been friendly and have treated me kindly, but for the most part, up until now, we have barely exchanged more than a few words. Tonight was an exception.

While I was under my palm tree earlier, I talked to Frank, who is staying in the downstairs corner apartment and hibernates all weekend until Sunday evening. Last week, I learned that Frank, a big, burly, African American man, has been nicknamed Bear by the others.

Then, Harmen and I had a serious conversation at the washing machines while we were doing laundry. We started by talking about existentialism, which shifted to prejudice, abuse, teaching, and then Viktor Frankl's *Man's Search for Meaning*. All of a sudden, we smelled fire, and he realized his dinner was burning. It was a quick ending to a meaningful and deep discussion.

The ocean is calm. On occasion, I hear a seagull signaling to his friends elsewhere.

Out at sea sits a ship ablaze with bright lights. Through my binoculars, it reminds me of a carousel. From here, it looks almost dreamlike. Having been on the other side and knowing it is one of those cruise ships that go out for a few hours and is filled with people gambling, stuffing themselves with mediocre food, and partying brings me back to reality. I much prefer where I am.

August 26, 1994

According to May Sarton, "Work needs space around it." That is something I have discovered here at sea in the summer of 1994. I've needed the solitude to let ideas float up—the quiet hours alone deep in thought, the meditative walks along the shore in search of shells, and the lulling of the ocean. This experience defies summarization. There is no box large enough to wrap all of this up and tie it with a bow.

To wake up, such as I have tonight at 3:00 a.m. and roll over to turn on a light and write is no simple task at home. Here, I can immediately pick up my pen and let my words spill out onto the page. While bits and pieces of my life appear in my dreams, most often at home, by the time I leave the room and begin to write about them, they have sailed off through the air like a feather in a current.

It's a blustery evening with strong winds coming from the northeast. The moon glistens and lightens a spot on the horizon, while most boats have headed home. The area looks desolate both off and on the sea. With its incoming and outgoing tides and white-capped waves rushing onto the shore, the ocean speaks to my soul.

At times like this, sleep evades me. Hours pass. I hear the winds playing havoc with the palm fronds outside my window. In the sanctity of my room, I lay sprawled on my bed, waiting for the first trace of color in the sky signaling the dawning of a new day.

A long night with no sleep like this one reminds me of the evening I spent at Tom's apartment in New York a while ago. Wrapped tightly in a fluffy, warm comforter with below zero temperatures just beyond the walls, I sat curled up on the couch, pen in hand, spending the wee hours writing — reminded of the time by the grandfather clock striking at every quarter of the hour.

August 27, 1994

While passing the paddleball courts near Garfield Street, I overheard some man telling a woman to check out a raft from Cuba, which had floated ashore near Howard Johnson's. So, I quickly made my way north to look for it. The raft had a styrofoam base and was carefully put together. There's a good chance the individual who charted the rough seas eventually made it to freedom.

As I stood among a crowd looking at the raft, some woman asked me if I had seen the one near Oceans II. That raft, which I saw later, was crude — made of wood, cardboard (at least it looked like that), and black rubber tubes. I doubt that the person who came in this raft had any chance of survival.

There was yet another one further north constructed with wood, rope, cloth, and some metal. We watched as the men from public works dragged it away. Supposedly, they're burning the rafts that land on Hollywood Beach. I saw a handmade wooden paddle that must have fallen off one of the rafts. No one wanted it, so I decided I would take it and use it to remind others about the price some pay for freedom.

Perhaps there is a museum I can donate it to, since it is now clearly part of Florida's history. It leans against my wall as an important reminder.

Later. It's 4:45 a.m. A City of Hollywood truck just rode by. I wonder if they're searching for more rafts floating onto these shores filled with people hoping for asylum.

August 28, 1994

I am on slow speed today. Earlier, I leisurely strolled along the shore. It's probably much better for me to mellow out and not come to a screeching halt at the end of my two-week vacation.

I saw another raft this morning — this one, even cruder but larger than the others, had an orange life vest attached to it. I wonder how many people were on it and if any of them made it ashore. Somehow, when I saw the workers drag away the raft, a sadness swept over me. It's such a reminder of the painful and dangerous risks people take to escape tyranny.

Later. I can't help but wonder how I will ever reenter my real world at 9:00 tomorrow morning. Fortunately, this isn't the end of my time here, just the conclusion of my vacation.

Without the responsibilities and obligations, I have experienced fewer people, demands, and layers. In all this time off from work, I have not worn any make-up or nail polish. I have become a bare-footed, sun-tanned beachcomber wearing only a bathing suit, my hat made from palm fronds, and shorts for two solid weeks. I have been unencumbered in every respect.

Life has become so much simpler. I've washed my clothes in gentle Ivory Snow and have hung them over my porch chairs. Within an hour or two, they are fresh and dry. I have simplified my life just as Anne Morrow Lindbergh did, except mine is for three months—not just two weeks like her stay was at the beach.

I have avoided listening to the news or reading a newspaper during these two weeks. I've chosen to be uninformed and out of touch. Plus, I haven't turned on the television since I've been here.

For both Daryl and me, this has been a new experience. In our own way, it's working because we are still giving each other what we need. I cook for him, call him, and love him, and he knows it. He is giving me the chance to be here with no guilt attached.

It is pouring out—a stormy afternoon at sea with nothing I have to do and nowhere to go. The door is opened barely a crack, yet the breezes blowing through here are strong and cool. A day like this is as close as it gets to heaven for the writer in me. I am in a cocoon in this apartment and am a free butterfly when I venture out. This is the day to absorb and inhale every last moment of my vacation. I have never been happier than I feel right now.

Tom was talking of the warm sand caressing his legs—the home of billions before us, the colors, the smells, the sea—our sanctuary by the sea. We have created us—whatever that is—right here at the ocean—this spot. He heads home soon, leaving all of this behind.

Since I've written about the beach throughout my journals, it'll be one of the main threads in the book. It will be woven in and out through the various topics I choose to include.

I'm known here as the writer and the woman who reads while she walks. People stop to tell me I'm an institution on Hollywood Beach. Now, since living here these past six weeks, I know a whole new group of regulars, who come at different times throughout the day, and other residents and shop owners along the way.

Besides the joy of creativity, one of the things I love about this experience is the fine-tuning. I am finding ways to sort out what I want in my world and am letting in only what feels right and belongs. It makes me thankful for every moment. I know exactly what matters to me—what I want around me and what I don't.

I wish I could bottle this moment—this most peaceful time in my life. Each precious second is a jewel to me. For the next six weeks, I will be in part two of my life away from home. I will still be staying here and appreciate this unique opportunity when I'm not out in the work world from 9:00 until 5:00.

Meanwhile, I am finishing the last lines of this oversized journal. I never expected I would write this much in these two weeks. I have now completed 191 journals since 1974. How is that possible?

August 29, 1994

Today was a challenge as I reentered my world at the Holocaust Center. Fortunately, there was little going on. I had almost no phone messages and nothing pressing that I had to do. I felt a bit removed all day with my eye on the clock, knowing all I wanted was to get back to the ocean.

Once I arrived here, it took no time at all to change out of my clothes, put on my bathing suit, and get downstairs. The minute I stepped onto the sand and walked along the shore, I knew I was where I belonged.

September 1, 1994

Frank greeted me when I pulled in from work and asked where I was. He said he's been peeking in on me and sometimes sees me out at 4:00 a.m. on the balcony writing. He's right about that.

When I was walking after dinner, some woman smiled at me and, as she passed, said, "Jesus loves you." I just looked at her. It was about the last thing I expected to hear from a passerby. I wanted to ask her how she knew but instead decided to keep on walking. Does saying that bring joy to someone? I can't help but wonder.

September 2, 1994

My week at work after my wonderful vacation felt like I was severing my arm from my body. Now that it's over, I am going to savor each moment of the weekend. The days and nights once again will belong to me.

I met a sea captain today when I was sitting on the bench near Seawind Apartments. I was fascinated with the romantic notion of his life. He didn't understand how I could love the ocean without traveling on it. After listening to him talk, I realized he needed to feel in control of the sea—as if that is possible.

When I told him about my fantasy of traveling around the world on a steamer, he agreed that it would be an incredible adventure. He said almost no one speaks English on those cargo ships, so my communication would be limited. I can handle that, since I want to write as I see the world from the sea.

September 4, 1994

I bought a newspaper and was reading it while sitting under my palm tree. Some woman passed by and asked if the world would end tomorrow (as predicted to happen in September by some quack). My reply was, "I certainly hope not." To which she answered, "Don't you believe in the third world coming?" I let her know I wasn't ready for this one to end yet.

Al was sitting on the steps when I was about to go upstairs, so we chatted for a bit. I told him the water was so clear he could reach down and grab a fish. I tease him all the time about the fish fry he keeps promising me, although he hasn't caught any fish yet. Before we all go back to our respective homes, we must have the party the guys have been talking about.

I like the rapport I've established with each of them. Frank noticed I was up early again today. No kidding! He also said, "I can't believe your husband would let a pretty lady like you out of his sight." He's sure I'm having an affair because he saw Tom here and Jeff, too, and is convinced that there's no way I am faithful to my husband. I assured him I was.

Later. Sometimes waking up in the middle of the night has its benefits. There's a crescent moon over the water casting its silvery light upon the sea. Stars dot the black velvet heavens. A delightful breeze blows from the south. The lulling waves and the flapping of palm fronds fill the air. Ah, the joy of being at the ocean and sitting on my balcony at 3:30 a.m. A couple walking hand in hand just passed down below.

September 6, 1994

I'm back at the beach. I have unpacked and settled in once again after a night at home and a day at work. My interlude away was pleasant, but I am glad to be here. While I was away, I had flashes of feeling this beach life is truly decadent. When I arrived back here, I realized I was not ready to give it up.

Mark greeted me and wondered where I had been. They had fish last night. Damn! I missed the party. We made a plan to cook together in two weeks, providing they catch more fish.

It's quiet here today, with few people around. Since Labor Day has come and gone, the vacationers are back up north. It's peaceful with calm, bright aqua water and flowing waves rippling onto the shore.

September 8, 1994

Last night, Daryl and I had a great steak dinner on the balcony. Then, we went down to the beach and sat in a lifeguard stand. We've made the most of our time together.

He was interested in my writing and asked me several questions. He's tuned in to me and can always tell when my eyes glaze over. That's when he realizes it's time for him to leave so I can get back to my journals. I'm grateful that he knows me so well and gives me the space I need.

Being at the beach provides me with much more opportunity to talk about my writing than anywhere else. People here see me with pen in hand, and many are curious enough to stop and ask what I'm working on. While there are times I'd rather not be disturbed, saying it all out loud helps me articulate what I'm experiencing.

September 9, 1994

I was wrong about the timing of high tide. Usually, I'm totally in sync, but I just got wiped away while I was napping.

There is a couple nearby that was kissing earlier and then stopped. Now, they're at it again. The woman is in silky bicycle pants and a halter top, and he's wearing what looks like boxer shorts. She's on top of him, slowly moving her body back and forth. They appear oblivious to anyone around them—lost in their own world. While it is inappropriate to be doing this in public, I enjoy watching them get more and more turned on. So, this is what voyeurism feels like. It looks like things are getting intense as they make love with clothes on.

September 11, 1994

What an unbelievable moment this is—turkey sandwich with lettuce on an egg roll, a tall glass of diet Coke with ice, blue skies with puffy clouds, and a seagull overhead. No one is directly in front of me or on either side. Again, for the thousandth time, I ask, "How did I get so lucky?"

Being isolated allows me to process all I'm experiencing. Reading through my journals continues to be a journey unlike any I've ever had. I will remember this as a time when I dropped out and went within to reflect, evaluate, understand, and create.

September 12, 1994

I hope I can fall asleep when I go inside. I have a full day ahead of me tomorrow—a late one at that and need the energy to make it through.

After I leave the beach and go home in October, I plan to enter my world in a different way from when I left it. I'll be busy, and my life will be full, but I intend to continue working on this book, which means I will be a lot less social than in the past. For now, I'm comfortable turning inward and want to stay that way for as long as I can. It's a magnificent night. I wonder how I'll be when I no longer have the ocean to soothe me on nights when sleep escapes me. The glory of this place spoils me.

September 13, 1994

I am finding people's reactions to my beach retreat most interesting. Some are astounded when I tell them where I've been all summer. A few have asked me if I'm getting divorced. I can only smile at their questions like, "Have you lost your mind? Can I move in? How did you manage this?"

September 16, 1994

At times, it is difficult to forget my world out there and transition back here. I have been thrown into another reality filled with people's expectations and work obligations. While I'd like nothing more than to be working on this book, I have demands at work, which are calling to me. A lot is going on this year, so soon I will have to shift gears and completely jump back in. We have a few special weddings to attend, the 50th anniversary of the end of WWII event, programming to plan at both jobs, my 50th birthday, and Daryl's too.

No one has a clue as to the contrast in the life I'm living right now. It would be so different if I just lived here. I will someday but not yet. In the meantime, I am grasping for sea air—embracing the ocean—making the most of every minute. It has been important to sit day after day, express myself through journaling, always in search of who I am and where I fit into the bigger picture.

September 18, 1994

A Santa Claus dressed in a yellow outfit just passed below. He has a huge gray beard, long hair, wears red shoes, and carries a colorful staff. In a deep voice in a language I don't understand, he calls out to people along the way. The guy is a character and has been coming to Hollywood Beach for years. I don't think I'm alone in wondering what his story is.

I just got into bed and finished *The House by the Sea*. Now I have begun *A Journal of Solitude*, also by May Sarton. On the first page, she writes, "I am here alone for the first time in weeks, to take up my 'real' life again at last."

It helps to read about May Sarton's life. When she describes how people affect her writing flow and what her writing is all about, I can relate to every word. She talks about how even her relationships aren't real unless she has time alone to explore what is happening or has happened. She notes that her life would be arid without the interruptions, both the nourishing and annoying ones. She explains how she tastes life best when she is alone. So much of what she writes resonates with me.

I just noticed that the date I'm reading in May Sarton's journal is September 18—yet another synchronistic moment in all of this. I am overwhelmed by the number of these occurrences which keep popping up during this time here at the beach.

I am slowly easing myself into Monday and the week in front of me as I work to get back into my life in the best and most positive way possible. I will take full advantage of being here at the beach, but I understand this to be the transition period. Who would have ever thought I would look at three weeks at the beach in that way?

When I spoke to Daryl, he told me Rabbi Rettig called and wanted me to know he met with the board, and they want the youth group to have a barbecue in the middle of October. I could have done without that on this perfect writing day.

I did my best to explain to Daryl how I didn't want to deal with this stuff on a Sunday. He'll probably never completely understand what this does to the writer in me. These interruptions take me to a different place in my mind that is far from working on my book.

When I walked up the stairs to my apartment, I heard a football game on. Mark was just coming out from the efficiency next to mine, so I told him it sounded just like home. I do not miss the droning of the television. My apartment is clean, and I am getting ready to make the shift from Sunday to Monday—beach bag to purse—bathing suit to slacks and a blouse—bare feet to stockings and heels.

I just thought about asking to have Group here on Tuesday. It makes sense to do that, so I won't have to leave the beach in the evening. Besides, I'd love to have my friends get a taste of what living on the beach has been like for me.

I am on the balcony writing by moonlight, which is bright when clouds don't hide the moon. It's hot in my room tonight. I may try to sleep out here since I can't fall back to sleep inside.

September 20, 1994

Group has left, and I'm out on my balcony. It rained on and off, so we were in and out, but it all worked out well.

Stephanie asked what was happening with my writing, so I shared with Group what I'd been doing. I never know what I'm going to say about it to anyone. In this case, I told them how big this project has become and how lucky I am not to have to wait fifteen extra years to begin. I also talked about how I have experienced the unpeeling of layers, turned the corner, noticed all the synchronicity, and decided on the format and packaging of my book. I'm hopeful they understood what this experience has meant, since it's important to me that they do.

In all, I was glad to share my sacred space with everyone tonight. Yet, I admit there were moments when I wished I was alone to write. It has become part of my daily routine. Today, between work and preparing for Group, I haven't had any time to do what I love most. That's why it's now after midnight, and I'm still up writing.

September 22, 1994

Bernice asked me today if I missed the possessions that generally surround me, and I told her I didn't at all. I could live with what I have right here for the rest of my life, and it would be enough for me. That says something about all the stuff I've accumulated.

Some men were here measuring the shoreline to check the beach erosion, since there has been a considerable amount of sand lost with the strong winds and wild seas. I had to laugh when I noticed the one of the guys with the telescope looking through it to watch the bikini-clad women. I suppose it's one of the perks.

A pelican formation just flew overhead with about twenty pelicans. Within the line of birds were two seagulls—something I had never seen before. I listened to the two seagulls squawking away and could only imagine that one might be saying to the other, "Hey, do you believe the pelicans let us in?"

September 25, 1994

There are times when I enjoy the parade of people passing along on the Broadwalk. Other times, I want no part of anything but my solitude. I feel depressed when I think of leaving.

Al is sitting downstairs. Some thin, beautiful woman just rollerbladed by singing to herself as if she didn't have a care in the world. I looked down as he checked her out, and at the same time, he caught my eye. I teased him, and we both had a good laugh.

Oh no! Two people on rollerblades just collided on the Broadwalk. It looks like they're both okay, but it can get dangerous if people aren't careful, which, unfortunately, so many aren't.

September 30, 1994

Luckily, I have the weekend to write and get my life in total perspective. It's an exceedingly quiet day here because it's virtually empty. There are only two people on the sand. I wouldn't mind some sun, but the overcast sky makes for excellent writing and thinking weather.

While I was downstairs, I saw Frank and a few of his cousins, all of whom seemed to be in a partying mood. Frank told me he loved the perfume I had on earlier and that he smelled it all the way to the Omni in downtown Miami, where he's working on the roof. He's too funny. He said Charlie never smelled better. I actually can hear the guys talking about me now. One just said I'm hot, and the others agreed. Al thought I was thirty-five. Frank was sure I was forty-four, and Mark said that I look to be twenty-eight from afar. Well, that's certainly an ego booster! They are sweet and harmless and have been great company when I've wanted it. I love how they have respected my space.

So, here I am on my second to the last Friday. Next week at this time, I'll just be coming back from the youth group activity. Somehow, I will be that much closer to home.

October 1, 1994

This weekend is turning out to be the best one yet. I have no one to answer to. Daryl is away in the Keys with his card buddies. Every conversation I have is my own choice. Everything I think and do belongs only to me.

I am holding on to every hour for dear life and am embracing my solitude before completely reentering my other world. I cannot imagine when I'll be alone again, and most likely, it'll never be like this has been. I'm sure the writer in me will crave it. At those times, I will have to remind myself how fortunate I was to have had this time away.

As I face going home, I'm thinking about how I plan to do some serious "spring" cleaning. I want to get rid of all the books I'll never read again, clothes I'll never wear, and knick-knacks I've collected that I no longer want to clutter my surroundings. I've learned how little I need to make myself happy.

In a way, part of me feels like I am sharing this time and space with May Sarton, since her journals have come alive for me in a surreal way. Her words paint pictures that live on in my dreams.

Even though I still have nine days here, I feel myself closing in on the end. I have accomplished more than I ever dreamed I would. My life at the beach has been productive and positive. The six journals, counting this one I've filled since I arrived, will forever remain a record of this rare and wonderful experience.

Some people who have only seen me here at the beach would be shocked to see me out in the real world and probably vice versa. Few have a clue about who I am or what I do. I am different here without all the frills and responsibilities. Those here see me as a beachcomber and a writer. In my life as I usually lead it, I doubt that anyone would think of me as laid back and casual. It's as if my two worlds never collide.

October 2, 1994

It's about as quiet as my life ever gets here with none of the guys at home today. No one is out exercising or sunbathing because of the rain.

I am absorbing and learning about myself in all of this. As I prepare to leave the beach, I realize I am different from when I walked in on July 10th. Within the two-and-a-half miles of Hollywood Beach, I have rediscovered myself. The writer in me has flourished here at the ocean. With all these endless hours, I have written, read, studied, and learned. My countless walks along the shore have cleared my mind. I have nurtured and nourished my soul. I have gotten in touch with a part of me that has been yearning to emerge. Finally, like a genie, I have been set free.

Later. I'm back out on the balcony. I'm going to miss being outdoors constantly. I have spent so much time outside. Once I get home, I'll have to contend with the mosquitoes in my backyard.

Out of nowhere, the wind picked up, turned the balcony's umbrella's spokes inside out, and bent and broke them. Then the rains came. In the pouring rain, I had a hell of a time getting the umbrella out of the hole in the table where it sits. I guess I'm lucky it didn't break sooner.

Later. It's hard to settle in on a day like today when it keeps raining off and on. Each move from one place to the other changes my mood and breaks my train of thought. And then there are times when the journal I'm reading is intense, and I need to get up and do something else — usually, it's a walk on the beach.

Last night, I came across this question I had written in my journal ten years ago. Where will I be someday when I am reading this journal? Who would have ever thought then that I would be writing a book in my efficiency apartment on Hollywood Beach?

Never in my wildest dreams did I foresee an experience like this happening. Maybe it will teach me sometimes an early birthday present is a good thing. Always, I have liked to wait to open gifts and cards on my birthday just like my dad did. Now, I understand there are times we must seize the moment and not put it off.

Later. When I went down to the beach, Frank and his son were getting in their truck. I noticed a coin fell onto the ground. As he went to pick it up, I saw tar on it. So, I said, "Be careful. It's covered with tar." To which he replied, "Hello? We're roofers and work with tar all day long." He got me on that one.

Frank told me he figured out why I use the pay phone so much. He's sure I'm making calls to all my boyfriends. Frank is trying so hard to "break the code," as he says. He can't believe I am for real — that I am happily married and all. We've had fun together, and I want it to stay that way.

One of the things I have loved about living alone is that I only have to clean up for myself. Also, I like waking up at any hour and turning on a light without getting out of bed. Besides that, I like to do what I want — no television and no smoke from cigarettes, with everything staying neat and clean. These are the pluses, but on the flip side, I miss the fun, the companionship, the foot and neck rubs, the sex and play, the love. I wouldn't trade my life for anyone else's. I am a lucky lady and know it.

This week, I must start making a consolidated reentry list and get organized. I am not going to allow myself to be depressed. Instead, I am determined to flow back into my life and be content to live as I always have.

The ocean is deep within my soul. It teaches me and gives me something that nothing else does. I will be bringing it home with me. Slowly, as I go back into that life, I will do my best to keep a few grains of sand between my toes. I can never leave the ocean entirely behind me.

As for leaving here, I will have to walk out the door, turn the key, and be grateful for the experience. So much is about to change as my schedule picks up. I feel myself starting to cross over the line.

Someday when I read my journals from this beach stay, I'll see a blossoming that generally comes in the spring of one's life. I have a hell of a lot I want to do in these next fifty years. Coming here was an important beginning. Step by step, I will accomplish my goals as I always do.

I have been writing so much this weekend and during these three months. I have put my entire life into perspective.

I think I'll be able to leave the solitude easier than I can the ocean. Its rhythm has become mine. At moments like this, I just have to keep repeating over and over, "I'll be back!" Once Jacky comes home, it will be a whole different ballgame. That will also help me to separate from here.

For now, I have to do my nails and then pack up for work tomorrow. My Sunday night ritual always saddens me a bit. However, I must face my reality. Slowly, my forthcoming reentry is beginning to sink in. Still, I have six more days here to cherish.

October 3, 1994

It's a brutally hot day even at 6:00 p.m. I may need to go in the water soon to cool off.

A woman just stopped for a moment and imparted her wisdom, "Make every day count." We smiled at each other, and then she moved on. I'm doing my best to follow her advice!

As I sit here, I contemplate what I will take home with me: the start of a book, six recently completed journals, a beautiful collection of shells, marvelous memories, and an understanding of who I am and what brings joy into my life.

Later. I'm out on the balcony, and it's 2:45 a.m. The winds of the past week are but a memory. This night is still. Stars dot the sky. A ruffle of waves rolls onto the shore. There is not a soul in sight. Near Dania's pier, I see several boats lining the horizon.

Sitting out here like this in the middle of the night will soon be over. Instead, I'll be wandering around my house in the wee hours, looking for the perfect place to sit and record my thoughts.

October 5, 1994

Once again, I realize life can change in one moment. Daryl showed up at the beach out of nowhere to tell me that Uncle Rubie had died. All of a sudden, everything shifted for me. I immediately knew my time at the beach was over. I needed to pack up, head home, and make arrangements to fly to Cleveland for the funeral.

Hardest besides leaving the ocean was saying goodbye to the guys. I never did see Harmen, so I left him a note. Frank got home just as I was going, and he seemed sad. He told me that when the guys told him I was leaving, he couldn't believe it and hurried back to see me. He let me know they were all counting on my being there for five more days.

In a way, maybe it is better that I didn't spend the rest of the days saying goodbye to the beach as I would have. On the other hand, my abrupt departure was difficult at best.

Daryl was a great help taking all my stuff downstairs and then bringing it into the house. I did a hurried job both unpacking and packing for the trip. As I look around, I see that every corner of the house needs attention when I get back from Cleveland.

October 6, 1994

I don't know what time it was last night, but I woke up in shock because I saw a man in my room. I was disoriented. It took me a while to realize it was Daryl, and by then, my heart was rapidly pounding.

Once I was up, I decided to write. Daryl was too funny when he started to tell me I should go back to sleep instead of leaving the room. He asked why I was going to write at that hour, but he quickly caught himself.

I guess there will be adjustments on both our parts until we settle in and get back into our groove. Of course, I'm now on my way to Ohio, so that will probably disrupt our flow in even more ways.

I am quickly getting back to my old self. I put two rings, earrings, a bracelet, and my watch on today—something I haven't done in months. The layers are gradually beginning to pile back on.

July 10, 1995

Last year today, I was moving into Seawind Apartments to begin my adventure. Here I am one year later. What have I learned? What have I accomplished?

The experience at the ocean provided me with a foundation and the space to figure out what I want to share with others from my journals. Slowly, I found those pearls buried within the pages of thirty-seven journals and wove them together into *A Necklace of Pearls*.

In retrospect, my time at Seawind Apartments allowed me to look at my life through both a telescope and a magnifying glass. I reveled in celebration whenever I discovered where I had first planted a seed which later led to an accomplishment or an awareness. I continually experienced serendipity and synchronicity. I cried and laughed. I plunged to the bottom of the pit and climbed mountains.

Now, sitting under my favorite palm tree looking at Seawind Apartments, I feel nostalgic. Part of me wishes I could be staying there again, but this isn't the right time.

I just finished reading *An Unknown Woman* and identified with the author as she closed up the place by the sea where she had lived for three months. It reminded me of my final days here. My time of soul searching and coming together came to an end for me in much the same way it did for the author.

Throughout my time at the beach, I gained a better understanding of why I kept journals and embraced my passion. That alone was life-changing.

Reflections on Seawind Beach Retreat

As with all memories, some are easier to look back on than others. In this case, reflecting on this time of my life filled me with joy. I suppose to anyone reading these excerpts, it is evident how exceptional this experience was in my life.

In the seventies, when I first read *A Gift from the Sea* by Anne Morrow Lindbergh, I wanted to go off to the beach just as she did. I had read it several times before I left for the ocean in the summer of 1994. The book planted a seed in me—one which eventually blossomed.

For years, I wrote about my journals and what I thought I might someday do with them. I also knew I needed time and space to work on any writing project. So, by the time I checked into Seawind Apartments, I was clear on what I wanted to accomplish.

During the time I was at the beach, I read through approximately sixty of my earliest journals. I wrote *A Necklace of Pearls,* which consisted of excerpts based on various topics from thirty-seven volumes. I hadn't separated them as I've done with these—but more about that in volume two.

I was excited to get an agent, whom I found in *The Writer's Market,* and was thrilled that he believed *A Necklace of Pearls* had a good chance of getting out in the world. At that point, I didn't have a computer of my own, and the internet was still foreign to me. So, I had no way of checking him out. Meanwhile, the book never did get published. To this day, it sits in a drawer along with a few other of my unpublished manuscripts. Many years later, out of curiosity, I decided to look up the agent. It turns out he was listed as one of the twenty worst agents in the country. I could only laugh about that.

The first time I had gone back and read any of my journals was in the summer of 1994. That experience alone was fascinating to me. Yet, I realized that so much of what I'd written was simply a record of my life. I noticed that I didn't dig deep and explore any of the subjects as I did in later journals. Still, I was excited to walk back in time.

Being at the beach allowed me to know myself better. Living alone afforded me the chance to step back and take stock. Above all else, I stripped myself of my outer world and climbed into my inner one.

When I read these excerpts, I was immediately transported to that time and space when I felt I was living my life as a writer. I was right back at the ocean, remembering those nights when I sat on my balcony under the stars with the waves rolling onto the shore, when I settled under my palm tree opposite Seawind Apartments for hours writing, and when I had a sense of freedom I had never felt before or after.

I had almost forgotten that Tom came to the beach during my time there. It wasn't until I came upon those excerpts that I immediately was back in that moment when I first found out he was on his way down to Florida. It took me right back to my anger and upset. Reading further made me feel much better because of how we had worked through that. Of course, in retrospect, I knew the outcome, but still, it was a relief to read and see how the two of us had communicated and made that time together work.

As I think about what others said about my going off to the beach alone for three months, now, in retrospect, I am intrigued by all the rumors that spread around the community. I only heard a few "through the grapevine," but I know many people had much to say about me and Daryl and what they thought was going on in our marriage. We were solid and knew we could do this. It was never an issue for us, but it certainly was gossip material for others. Today, I ask myself why people create stories when they have no idea what's happening in someone else's life.

Above all else, when I think about the summer of 1994 all these years later, I realize I was fortunate to have had this experience. It remains a highlight in my life and the beginning of my journey through my journals.

Journal Prompts

- What have you ever dreamed about doing, didn't think it could happen, and then it did?

- What is your greatest fantasy? How can you make it come true?

- Write about a time when you felt free to be who you are unencumbered by others.

- Have you ever had an opportunity to do something, but you didn't because you sabotaged it?

- Write about a time when you had a perfect plan to do something, and someone came and interrupted it for you. How did you feel?

- Have you ever had a rumor spread about you? What was it? How did you feel? Why do you think it happened?

- Write about a time in your life that brings back wonderful memories.

Afterword

Twenty years ago in January 2002, I began working on my legacy journal project. I well remember the sense of accomplishment I felt in October 2016 when I finally finished culling excerpts from the three hundred and fifty-nine journals I had completed at that time. As I prepared to tackle the thousands of pages of excerpts, I faced the herculean task of deciding what to include in this book and the one that follows. It took me six years to whittle down the excerpts in order to create two reasonably-sized books.

In July 2021, my friend Reizel asked me if she could interview me about the project. As a journalist but someone who had never journaled, she was fascinated with what I was creating. Our initial conversation has turned into an ongoing Tuesday afternoon discussion about the process, experience, and creation of both volumes of *Living and Leaving My Legacy*—all of which have helped me explore my thoughts and feelings about this journey.

During the six months prior to completion, more than ever, self-doubt surfaced. I asked myself questions like: Why would anyone want to read about my life? Who will care? Is putting this book out into the world self-indulgent? Am I fooling myself to think I have something worthy to share?

Then, as if that weren't enough, I grappled with just how much of my personal life and feelings I was willing to include. Periodically, I heard my beloved late mother's voice saying, "Never air your dirty laundry in public." I felt vulnerable talking about issues that most would never consider sharing with anyone.

My friend Maya encouraged me to include the more painful aspects of living. While initially I felt reluctant, one of my goals was for others to read about my life in order to discover what resonated in theirs. Thus, even though I hesitated, I understood why it was important to share some of those extremely difficult experiences. Vulnerability continued to surface over and over again throughout the entire process.

What I found most interesting was that a few of the early readers wanted more details for certain incidents. For example, one asked me why I hadn't explained what happened for me to write, "Spare me! Sometimes I wonder if I'm fit to be a mother." Or another questioned why I didn't share the root of our financial problems. The simple reason was that I wasn't always comfortable including all the particulars. As it was, I felt exposed sharing what I had.

I grappled with which of the twenty-two subjects to include in this book and which in volume two. Whenever possible, I considered the chronological order of what took place—with one topic naturally succeeding the other. In the end, this volume includes more of my earlier experiences, and the second volume reflects the latter part of my life.

Looking ahead to what follows, I am excited about the next book, which begins with a chapter about my legacy journal project. Because my career has morphed and I have become a legacy educator, the last topic in *Living and Leaving My Legacy, Vol. 2* focuses on legacy. Following that, I include a step-by-step guide to writing an ethical will as well as a listing of legacy projects for anyone who might be inspired to do some legacy work.

As I reflect on writing *Living and Leaving My Legacy, Vol. 1,* I once again celebrate having given myself the gift of journaling. What struck me during the process was how extraordinary it was to walk back through forty-two years and have all my memories come alive for me. Granted there were moments that were not easy to relive. But for the most part, I rejoiced at what I had committed to paper.

Reading back in my journals allowed me to see how present I have been as a result of journaling. By recording all that I did, I have preserved my life in a way few ever do. I have shared it with you, the reader, in the hopes that it will help you understand that how we live our lives becomes our legacy.

If you care to share any feedback, reactions, or thoughts as a result of reading the book or if you would like to book a speaking engagement, please contact me at **www.merlersaferstein.com** or at **info@merlersaferstein.com.**

Book Club Discussion Questions for
Living and Leaving My Legacy, Vol. 1

The author claimed that her life without her journal writing would be like a snail without its shell. Is there anything in your life that is so important to you that you would feel like this? If so, what is it? What are you passionate about?

If you journal, what have you found the benefits to be? Would you recommend journaling to others, and if yes, why?

If you don't already journal, did reading the book encourage you to start?

Which chapter most spoke to you and why? Which chapter was your favorite? Which chapter did you learn the most from?

Was there anything in the book that stuck out for you—that you thought about after reading it or talked about to others?

If you wrote on any of the prompts, which ones were they and why did you choose them?

What emotions were evoked while reading the book? What led you to feel this way?

What resonated most for you and made you think about your own life?

Before reading the book, did you think about your legacy? Since reading it, what are your thoughts about your legacy?

After reading the manuscript, would you do anything different in your life?

What has been your greatest accomplishment?

What has been the biggest challenge in your life that you have overcome?

What will you do to ensure that you will be remembered in the way that you want to be?

Acknowledgements

I am indeed fortunate to have many people in my life for whom I am grateful. As I made my way through this legacy journal project, sharing with them has helped keep me afloat.

Thank you to Eva Cutler and Millie Nitzberg, my two loving nonagenarians, for being interested in my journal writing from the day I met each of you at the Holocaust Documentation and Education Center. As two of the earliest readers and then again as you both read a later draft, your reactions and sharing what resonated for you has been meaningful and priceless.

A special thank you to Lois Sklar, my dear friend of fifty-four years. You've not only sat at my side as I've journaled, but from the start you have been engaged in listening to me talk about this journey. I thank you for your guidance, edits, advice, delight in my success, and love.

My sincere gratitude to Tom Osborne, who is laced through the pages of my life. As the first writer I connected with in 1982, your unending support, special friendship, and confidence in me has helped me reach this moment of finally sharing my journals with the world.

Sprinkled through this book is mention of Group. We first came together in 1994, and since then, each of you has enriched my life in ways impossible to describe. Several years ago while in the midst of this journal project, I asked if you would be willing to finish putting it together should I die before I completed it. That alone says everything about who you are to me. In order of when I met you, I give thanks.

To Adele Sandberg, you have been a mirror for me. Your encouragement, generosity, help in maximizing my potential, continuous support, and belief in me as a writer has meant the world to me. You are a cornerstone in my life, and your family is my chosen family.

To Marsha Levine, as a cherished friend and an integral part of this book from its earliest stages, your invaluable feedback has been a true gift in my life. You've been a steadfast sounding board, cheerleader, reader of many drafts, and someone who shares in my joy.

To Stephanie Layton, you have listened for hours on end about this book. I have appreciated your encouragement each step of the way as well as how you've shown an interest in my writing ability. Thank you for all of that.

To Maya Bat-Ami, thanks for listening as I endlessly expressed my deepest feelings and thoughts related to the writing of this book. I am grateful to you for encouraging me to include the shadow side and all that comes with it. Your friendship has made a difference in my life.

413

My thanks to Reizel Larrea-Alvarez for our weekly Tuesday conversations which began with an interview ten months ago. I've appreciated your difficult questions which have led me to think about this book in new ways. Thanks for your enthusiasm, feedback, curiosity, and deep insight.

I am grateful to Rochelle B. Weinstein for always understanding those moments when being a writer is less than glamorous as well as those when I'm soaring. Your generosity in guiding me through the author world has been unsurpassed. I treasure our friendship.

To Jaes Seis of Great Mother Press, thank you for making this entire publishing experience one of complete joy. You have helped me bring my journals from the darkness of my safe out into the light of the world. I am filled with gratitude for both you and Jenny Menzel, artist extraordinaire and graphic designer of the book's cover and its interior, for listening carefully and ensuring that *Living and Leaving My Legacy* is exactly as I dreamed it to be.

Thank you to Kathleen "Kay" Adams for agreeing to write the foreword for this book. As a master teacher and leader in the world of journaling, you have been a visionary and a mentor to me and countless others. To have you on board with this project has meant so much to me.

I am especially grateful for my expert team of editors who spent hours on end and provided me with meticulous editing and proof-reading, constructive criticism, and keen insights. You have each helped make this book the best it could be. My heartfelt gratitude to Carolyn Kottler, Dara Levan, Carolyn Lodish, and Margery Sanford.

A special thank you to those who generously gave me the gift of their time reading drafts of this book and offering invaluable feedback. Sincere thanks to Sarah Deane, Laura Grushcow, Susan Hurwitz, Josse Lee, Mike Lewis, Maxine Mirowitz, Jan Reek, Michelle Rothenberg, Joel Sandberg, Sheryl Sandberg, Linda Schlein, Dori Solomon, Rosemary Tann, Aemi Tucker, and Sally Voorheis.

Thank you to the talented writers in Gilda's Club's Women's Writing Connection, who have encouraged me and, through your writing, have shared from your hearts: Tatiana Acero, Sharon Bacon, Morgen Chesonis-Gonzalez, Kim Lykins and all those in the past, including Marie Ireland and Kathy Weinberg of beloved memory, who were part of our group during their cancer journey. A special thanks to Julie Klein who has lovingly been by my side on this writing journey for many years.

I've been speaking and teaching about legacy for nine years and have worked with hundreds of individuals. In my more recent classes, I have talked about my book with the following women and am thankful to them for their zeal for this project. Thank you to Jayne Clarin, Vicki Einhorn, Avis Feldstein, Phyllis Koss, Pamela Lear, Joan Rozansky, Amanda Rivera, Loretta Trepedino and all those who have studied with me on this legacy journey. Much gratitude to Amy Atkins who suggested I ask questions at the end of each chapter. Those questions morphed into the journal prompts which completely changed the trajectory of this book.

Thank you to Beth Jacobs, the one person above everyone I know, who truly understood my journey because she too, was reading her journals while I was reading mine. Sharing that meaningful experience with you, Beth, has been incomparable.

In the later stages of this journey, I have had the good fortune of working with three special women who are helping me navigate the world of marketing. Thanks to Ann-Marie Nieves, Michelle Glogovac, and Pamela Sheppard.

Thank you to Dorte Abrams, Margaret Ballanoff, Carol Berman, Barbara Bostic, Dave Christison, Tammi Leader Fuller, Amy Gelb, Carol Goldman, Priscilla Jones, Geoff Lee, Jeff Levine, Betti Lidsky, Leslie Peiken, Elysha Pomerantz, Jodi Rozental, Michael Rothenberg, Steve Rothenberg, Bella Saferstein, Sara Saferstein, Sophia Saferstein, Alyson Salzedo-Benison, David Sandberg, Michelle Sandberg, Amy Schefler, Stephen Schlein, Lyn Smith, Halle Tucker, Jake Tucker, Steve Tucker, Lynn Weisman, Donna White, and Aileen Zarin who have cheered me on and have shown your enthusiasm during the twenty years of my writing this book.

I am also grateful to Sherilyn Adler, Sam Applebaum, Dalia Berlin, Lonnie Cantor, Arlyne Frankel, Enid Garber, Ellen Hanson, Sue Klau, Kathy Miller, Rose Schreiber, Sammi Siegel, Ellen Suppa, Ellen Turko, Ella Windheim, and Ilsebill Wolfe. Thanks for showing up to Sunday morning journaling circle and listening to me talk about this book since we began writing together in April 2020.

A special thanks to my son Michael for your determination in making sure I see myself for who I am and what I have accomplished. Sharing some of our wonderful memories from within this book with laughter and loving, warm feelings has been the best.

To my daughter Rebecca, I have been deeply touched by your interest in every aspect of my legacy journal project. You've been by my side throughout the journey, and for that and so much else, I am filled with gratitude. I'm still laughing over when you called and said, "Mom, here's a list of things a daughter should never have to read about her parents."

And most importantly, thank you to my husband Daryl, who has been with me since well before I began journaling. As the first reader, you've listened carefully, given me space to write and work on *Living and Leaving My Legacy* for years on end, encouraged me, and bestowed upon me your generous blessings to share certain parts of our lives even when I'm sure you'd rather I didn't. Your unparalleled support has meant everything to me. I love you.

While my parents are no longer alive to see this legacy project come to fruition, I am filled with gratitude to them for being the loving, caring parents who raised me to look for the positives in life, appreciate my connections with others, and live with integrity and love in my heart.

Made in the USA
Las Vegas, NV
25 January 2023